MERCANTILE LAW

RANKING, SPICER & PEGLER'S

MERCANTILE LAW

incorporating

PARTNERSHIP LAW and THE LAW OF
ARBITRATION & AWARDS

Thirteenth Edition

by

R. E. G. PERRINS, F.C.A.

and

P. R. O. STUART, B.A. (OXON),
Solicitor

HFL (PUBLISHERS) LTD
9 BOW STREET, COVENT GARDEN,
LONDON WC2E 7AL

First Published *1911*

Thirteenth Edition .. *1972*

This Edition © HFL (PUBLISHERS) LTD

1972

ISBN 0 372 01609 X

Printed in Great Britain by

THE STELLAR PRESS HATFIELD HERTS

PREFACE TO THE THIRTEENTH EDITION

In this new edition of *Mercantile Law* we have incorporated the changes in the law since the appearance of the last edition. These include the Misrepresentation Act, 1967, the Companies Act, 1967, the Trade Descriptions Act, 1968 and the Banking and Financial Dealings Act, 1971 as well as such important decisions as the Suisse Atlantique case, *Saunders* v. *Anglia Building Society* and *Lewis* v. *Averay*. The facts of the last-named case were similar to those in *Ingram* v. *Little*, but the Court of Appeal decided to follow *Phillips* v. *Brooks* rather than *Ingram* v. *Little*. Consequently we have excluded *Ingram* v. *Little* from this edition since it appears that the case is now unlikely to be followed.

We should like to thank Mr A. Jeffreys, Barrister-at-Law, for his help in preparing this edition.

R. E. G. PERRINS
P. R. O. STUART

London,
May, 1972

TABLE OF CONTENTS

CHAPTER I
CONTRACTS

CHAPTER I (*continued*)

CHAPTER II

AGENCY

CHAPTER III

SALE OF GOODS AND HIRE-PURCHASE

CHAPTER IV

NEGOTIABLE INSTRUMENTS

CHAPTER IV (*continued*)

CHAPTER V

BAILMENTS AND SECURITIES

CHAPTER VIII

PARTNERSHIP

TABLE OF STATUTES

TABLE OF CASES

ABBREVIATIONS USED IN REFERENCES
TO CASES CITED

Abbreviation		Reports		Date	Court
A. & E.	..	Adolphus & Ellis ..	..	1834—1841	Queen's Bench
A.C.	..	House of Lords and Privy Council Appeal Cases		1891—	House of Lords
All E.R.	..	All England Reports	..	1936—	All
App. Cas.		House of Lords and Privy Council Appeal Cases		1875—1890	House of Lords
Atk.	..	Atkyns	..	1736—1754	Chancery
B. & Ad.	..	Barnwall & Adolphus	..	1830—1834	King's Bench
B. & Ald.	..	Barnwall & Alderson	..	1817—1822	King's Bench
B. & C.	..	Barnwall & Cresswell	..	1822—1830	King's Bench
B. & S.	..	Best & Smith	..	1861—1870	Queen's Bench
Beav.	..	Beavan	..	1838—1866	Rolls Court
Bing.	..	Bingham ..	..	1822—1834	Common Pleas
Bing. N.C.		Bingham's New Cases	..	1834—1840	Common Pleas
Bos. & P.N.R.		Bosanquet and Puller's New Reports		1804—1807	Common Pleas
C.A.	..	Court of Appeal			
C. & P.	..	Carrington & Payne	..	1823—1841	*Nisi Prius*
C.B.	..	Common Bench ..	..	1845—1856	Common Pleas
C.B.N.S.	..	Common Bench New Series		1856—1865	Common Pleas
C.P.D.		Common Pleas Division	..	1875—1880	Common Pleas
C. Rob.	..	Chr. Robinson	..	1798—1808	Admiralty
Camp.	..	Campbell	..	1807—1816	*Nisi Prius*
Carth.	..	Carthew	..	1687—1700	King's Bench
Ch.	..	Chancery	..	1891—	Chancery
Ch. App.	..	Chancery Appeals	..	1865—1875	Chancery (Appeals)
Ch. D.	..	Chancery Division	..	1875—1890	Chancery
Cl. & F.	..	Clark & Finnelly ..	..	1831—1846	House of Lords
Co. Rep.	..	Coke's Reports	..	1572—1616	King's Bench
Com. Cas	..	Commercial Cases	..	1895—1941	All
Cowp.	..	Cowper	..	1774—1778	King's Bench
Cox	..	Cox	..	1783—1796	Chancery
D. M. & G.		De Gex, Macnaghten and Gordon		1851—1857	Chancery
De G. & J.		De Gex & Jones ..	..	1857—1859	Chancery (Appeals)
Dow	..	Dow	..	1812—1818	House of Lords
Dowl.	..	Dowling	..	1830—1841	Bail Court
Drew.	..	Drewry	..	1852—1859	Vice-Chancellor's Court
E. & B.	..	Ellis & Blackburn	..	1852—1858	Queen's Bench
East	..	East	..	1800—1812	King's Bench
Esp.	..	Espinàsse	..	1793—1807	*Nisi Prius*
Ex. Exch.	}	Exchequer	..	1847—1856	Exchequer

Abbreviation	Reports	Date	Court
Ex. D.	Exchequer Division	1875—1880	Exchequer
Giff.	Giffard	1857—1865	Vice-Chancellor's Court
H. & C.	Hurlstone & Coltman	1862—1866	Exchequer
H. & N.	Hurlstone & Norman	1856—1862	Exchequer
H. Bl.	Blackstone, H.	1788—1796	Common Pleas
H.L.	House of Lords		
H.L. Cas.	House of Lords Cases	1847—1866	House of Lords
Hobart	Hobart	1603—1625	King's Bench
Ir. L.R. Q.B.D.	Irish Law Reports, Queen's Bench Division	1867—1900	Queen's Bench, Ireland
Ir. Rep.	Irish Reports	1838—	All
Johns.	Johnson	1858—1860	Vice-Chancellor's Court
Jur.	Jurist Reports	1837—1854	All
K.B.	King's Bench	1901—1952	King's Bench
L.J. C.P.	Law Journal, Common Pleas	1822—1876	Common Pleas
L.J. Ch.	Law Journal, Chancery	1822—1949	Chancery
L.J. Ex.	Law Journal, Exchequer	1822—1876	Exchequer
L.J. K.B.	Law Journal, King's Bench	{1822—1837} {1900—1949}	King's Bench
L.J. Q.B.	Law Journal, Queen's Bench	1837—1900	Queen's Bench
L.R.—C.P.	Common Pleas	1865—1875	Common Pleas
L.R.—Ch.	Chancery	1865—1875	Chancery
L.R.—Ch. App.	Chancery Appeals	1865—1875	Chancery (Appeals)
L.R.—Eq.	Equity	1865—1875	Chancery
L.R.—Ex.	Exchequer	1865—1875	Exchequer
L.R.—H.L.	House of Lords	1865—1875	House of Lords
L.R.—Ir.	Irish	1865—1875	Irish Courts
L.R.—P.C.	Privy Council	1865—1875	Privy Council
L.R.—Q.B.	Queen's Bench	1865—1875	Queen's Bench
L.T.	Law Times	1843—1947	All
Ld. Raym.	Lord Raymond	1694—1732	King's Bench
Lev.	Levinz	1660—1696	King's Bench
Ll. L.R.	Lloyd's List Reports	1919—1950	All
Lloyd's Rep.	Lloyd's Reports	1951—	All
M. & G.	Manning & Granger	1840—1844	Common Pleas
M. & W.	Meeson & Welsby	1836—1847	Exchequer
Macq.	Macqueen	1849—1865	House of Lords
Mer.	Merivale	1815—1817	Chancery
Mod.	Modern Reports (Leach's)	1669—1755	All
Mont. & Ch.	Montagu & Chitty	1838—1840	Bankruptcy
Morrel	Morrel	1884—1893	Bankruptcy
P.	Probate	1891—1971	Probate, Divorce and Admiralty
P.C.	Privy Council		
P.D.	Probate Division	1875—1890	Probate, Divorce and Admiralty
Ph.	Phillips	1841—1849	Chancery

Abbreviation		Reports				Date	Court
Price	..	Price	..	..	..	1814—1824	Exchequer
Q.B.	..	Queen's Bench	..		..	1841—1852 1891—1900 1952—	Queen's Bench
Q.B.D.	..	Queen's Bench Division	..			1875—1890	Queen's Bench
R.R.	..	Revised Reports	..		..	1785—1866	All
S.J.	..	Solicitors' Journal			..	1857—	All
Salk.	..	Salkeld	..	..	..	1689—1712	King's Bench
Sim.	..	Simons	..	..	..	1826—1852	Chancery
Stark.	..	Starkie	..	..	..	1814—1823	*Nisi Prius*
Swan.	..	Swanston	..	..	..	1818—1821	Chancery
T.L.R.	..	Times Law Reports		..		1884—1952	All
T.R.	..	Taxation Reports	..		..	1939—	All
Taunt.	..	Taunton	..	..	..	1807—1819	Common Pleas
Term Rep.		Term Reports (Durnford & East)				1785—1800	King's Bench
Ves.	..	Vesey, Junior	..		..	1789—1817	Chancery
W.L.R.	..	Weekly Law Reports		..		1953—	All
Y. & J.	..	Younge & Jervis	..		..	1826—1830	Exchequer

INTRODUCTION

Mercantile law is the term used to denote that part of the general law of England which is concerned with such matters as are usually the subject of what may be called business transactions. It is now only a branch of the general law of contract, which for the sake of convenience is considered in textbooks under various headings, such as agency, sale of goods, insurance, and so on. Each of these special types of contract is subject to its own particular rules, but it is also subject to the general law of contract, in so far as the special rules do not replace these principles.

Many of these special rules, however, differ in origin from the broader principles relating to contracts generally, which evolved as part of the *common law* of England. The common law is the basis of English law. It is of considerable antiquity, and is derived from the customary law which, prior to the centralisation of justice after the Norman Conquest, was applied by local courts, each district having its own customs. These customs were gathered together by the judges of the King's courts during the reign of Henry II and his successors and applied throughout the country, thus becoming a body of law common to the whole of England.

The law merchant, or *lex mercatoria*, on the other hand, evolved from the general custom of merchants, and is one of the few branches of English law to have been influenced by continental legal methods. Because of the continual movement of merchants from place to place during the Middle Ages, and the need to attract trade from abroad, the rather cumbersome procedures of the English common law were not the most satisfactory method of dealing with disputes between merchants. Instead, every market and fair had its own court, at which disputes could be dealt with in a summary manner by the Clerk of the Market or some similar official. Special courts also existed at the main trading centres and ports. In these courts the custom of merchants, with which continental merchants were familiar, could be applied. These customs, though regarded as binding between the merchants themselves, were not initially recognised by the common law courts. Even when in the course of time the customs of merchants became recognised by the courts, the existence of such customs had to be proved as fact in cases of doubt.

As the common law courts became stronger and more effective, they gradually absorbed the work of the mercantile courts, a process which was completed in the 17th and 18th centuries under the influence of Lord Holt and Lord Mansfield.

The law merchant, then, is

... neither more nor less than the usages of merchants and traders in the different departments of trade, ratified by the decisions of the courts of law, which, upon such usages being proved before them, have adopted them as settled law ... By this process, what before was usage only, unsanctioned by legal decision, has become engrafted upon, or incorporated into, the common law, and may thus be said to form part of it' (*Goodwin* v. *Robarts* (1875) L.R. 10 Ex. 337 at p. 346).

From the 14th century onwards the main defects of the common law had been remedied by a separate branch of law known as *equity*. If a person could not obtain satisfaction for a grievance at common law, he could petition the King for relief, such petitions being referred by the King to his Chancellor. In the 15th century a special court, called the Court of Chancery, was set up under the direction of the Lord Chancellor to deal with these petitions. At first the Chancellor decided these cases according to his own ideas of 'equity,' but gradually a body of principles were evolved which would be applied in each case, and these became known as the rules of equity. Many of the principles of the law of contract are equitable in origin, as well as the remedies of specific performance and injunction. The legal rules applying to trusts, partnerships and mortgages also had their origin in the Court of Chancery.

The rules of both common law and equity are now based entirely upon existing judicial decisions, and judges are generally bound to apply the rules laid down by their predecessors under 'the doctrine of judicial precedent.'

Since 1873 equity and common law have been administered side by side in the same courts. The Judicature Acts, 1873–1875, reorganised the structure of the courts and created a new Supreme Court of Judicature, consisting of the High Court of Justice and the Court of Appeal. The High Court is divided into three divisions, the Queen's Bench Division, the Chancery Division, and the Family Division. Most cases involving questions of mercantile law come before the Queen's Bench Division, which has taken over the work of the old common law courts. The Chancery Division, which has taken over the work of the former Court of Chancery, hears mercantile cases in which the equitable remedies are sought, and also administers those branches of mercantile law, for example, bankruptcy and company law, which have been expressly given to it by statute. Admiralty jurisdiction, relating to maritime matters, particularly in respect of collisions at sea and salvage has since 1971 been exercised by the Queens Bench Division. Appeal from any of these Divisions is to the Court of Appeal, and thence, with leave, to the House of Lords.

Where the amount in dispute is relatively small, disputes can be heard more quickly and more cheaply in county courts, of which there are a considerable number throughout the country. In questions arising out of contracts, the county courts can hear actions where the sum in dispute does not exceed £750, unless both parties agree to submit to its jurisdiction, in which case the amount is unlimited.

In the Queen's Bench Division a special court, known as the Commercial Court, sits for the purpose of dealing with cases arising out of the transactions of merchants and traders. The procedure in this court is somewhat more summary than in the other Queen's Bench Courts, so that cases can be dealt with more quickly. In spite of this facility, many businessmen prefer to have their disputes settled by arbitration (see Chap. IX) rather than by a court of law.

In 1956 a new court, the Restrictive Practices Court, which is of the same standing as the High Court, was set up under the Restrictive Trade Practices Act for the judicial investigation of certain trading agreements. Its jurisdiction has subsequently been extended by the Resale Prices Act, 1964.

Since 1971 the judges of the Queen's Bench Division have sat outside London to hear civil cases both in the High Court and in the Crown Court. In the latter (which has replaced the Assizes) the judges hear cases of serious crime (less serious criminal cases being tried in magistrates' courts). The main difference between civil and criminal actions lies in the purpose of the action, which in the former case is to compensate the person injured, and in the latter to punish the offender, usually by a fine or imprisonment. Many wrongful acts are, in fact, both crimes and torts (*i.e.*, civil wrongs which do not arise out of any contractual or other special relationship between the parties, but out of the breach of a legal duty which is owed to persons generally).

From time to time the common law has been modified by statute, particularly to provide for new situations for which the common law has no remedy, and to alter the existing law where changed circumstances have made it inadequate. This process has become increasingly important over the past century, and additionally during this period statute law has been used to bring together the existing rules of common law and equity on a particular topic into a single statute, thereby making the law much more manageable. Examples of such 'codification' in the field of mercantile law are the Sale of Goods Act, 1893, the Bills of Exchange Act, 1882, the Partnership Act, 1890, and the Marine Insurance Act, 1906.

It will be noted that, throughout the text, a statement of law is frequently followed by a reference to a case in which that law was declared or illustrated. These cases are contained in 'reports' to which reference is made by the recognised abbreviations. (A list of these abbreviations and the reports to which they refer is set out on pp. xxxvi-xxxviii, *ante*.) At the present time the semi-official Law Reports consist of 'Appeal Cases,' which contain cases decided by the House of Lords and the Judicial Committee of the Privy Council (the appellate court from certain of the dominions and colonies); and reports for each division of the High Court, and the decisions of the Court of Appeal on appeals therefrom. The only other series of general law reports now in publication are the 'Weekly Law Reports,' and the 'All England Reports.' Certain special series of reports are still published, such as 'Lloyd's Reports' and 'Tax Cases.'

CONTRACTS

§ 1. *Definition of a Contract*

A contract may be defined as an agreement between two or more persons, which may be legally enforced if the law is properly invoked. In every contract some right is acquired by one party and a correlative obligation or liability is undertaken by the other. In most contracts both rights and obligations attach to *each* party. It is extremely important to know what agreements constitute contracts in law, since, in respect of an agreement which is not a contract, there is no redress if either party fails to carry it out; while the breach of a contract normally gives rise to a legal remedy.

Contracts are divisible into three classes:
(a) contracts of record;
(b) specialty contracts;
(c) simple or parol contracts.

(a) Contracts of Record

A contract of record is the obligation which is imposed by the entry of the proceedings in the records of a superior court. The principal classes of contracts of record which are now found are (1) judgments, and (2) recognisances.

(1) *Judgments*

A judgment is an obligation imposed by a court upon one or more parties in favour of another or others. It depends for its binding force, not upon the consent of the parties, but upon the authority of the judicial representative of the Sovereign delivering the judgment. A judgment is therefore an order of the court, and since it is an obligation imposed upon a party, it is not strictly a contract which rests upon agreement.

(2) *Recognisances*

A recognisance is a contract made with the Sovereign through her judicial representative. It is generally in the nature of a promise to do some particular act, or to answer to a penalty stated in the recognisance, such as an undertaking by a person tried upon a criminal charge to come up for judgment if called upon, or a promise to pay a specified sum of money if an accused person, out on bail, does not appear at the trial.

The terms of a contract of record admit of no dispute, but are conclusively proved by the record itself.

(b) Specialty Contracts

A specialty contract, or deed, is one which is not only reduced to writing, but is also executed under seal, and delivered. Both sealing and signature are essential for the proper execution of a deed (Law of Property Act, 1925, s. 73).

The delivery may be actual or constructive; as a general rule it is made simultaneously with execution. The modern method is to affix a paper wafer, forming a facsimile of a seal, which the party executing will touch with his finger, saying 'I deliver this as my act and deed.' The characteristics of specialty contracts are dealt with in § 4 (a), *post*.

(c) Simple Contracts

A simple contract is one which is created either by an oral promise, by writing not under seal, or by implication. A parol contract is, strictly, a contract entered into by word of mouth; but the term is frequently used to denote all simple contracts. Most contracts entered into in ordinary commercial transactions fall within this classification.

A contract arises by implication where either there is no express contract in existence but some right and correlative obligation are inferred by reason of the circumstances, or the parties are already in contractual relationship upon some matter and collateral terms are to be inferred therefrom. As an illustration of the former class, a surety who has been called upon to pay a debt which the debtor has failed to discharge can claim contribution from a co-surety; or an agent of necessity (*q.v.*) can claim reimbursement from the person in whose interests he has acted. The right of an agent to remuneration where the contract had made no specific provision affords an example of the latter class; the law often assumes a promise to pay a reasonable or customary amount for the services rendered. Contracts may also be implied where a party indicates his intention by a mere act, *e.g.*, boarding an omnibus.

In certain cases the law imposes an obligation, analogous to a contractual obligation, on a person who has not agreed, expressly or implicitly, to be bound thereby. An example is the obligation which rests on a person to repay money which has been paid to him for a consideration which has wholly failed. Such obligations are said to be *quasi-contractual* (see *post*, § 14).

§ 2. *The Essentials of a Contract*

The essentials of a valid contract are:

(1) Offer and acceptance, *i.e.*, a distinct communication by the parties to one another of their intention.

(2) Consideration, except where the agreement is under seal.

(3) Compliance with any particular requirements as to form.

(4) Intention to create legal relations.

(5) Capacity of the parties to make a valid contract.

(6) Genuineness of the consent expressed in the offer and acceptance.

(7) Absence of any element rendering the contract void or illegal by statute or common law.

(8) Possibility of performance at the time the contract is entered into.

If any of these essentials is lacking, the contract will be either void, voidable, or unenforceable.

A *void* contract is one that is destitute of legal effect, and is therefore, in reality, no contract at all. Examples are gaming or wagering contracts or contracts induced by an operative mistake of fact. From the usually accepted definition, it might be inferred that a void contract is illegal, but while it is true that an illegal contract, *i.e.*, one which contravenes the law, is void, the latter term is much wider in its application and a contract may be void though not illegal (see *post*, § 9).

A *voidable* contract is one which is capable of affirmation or repudiation at the option of one of the parties without reference to the other party, such as a contract entered into by an infant which confers rights of a continuous nature on him, *e.g.*, the purchase of shares in a limited company.

An *unenforceable* contract is one that cannot be enforced by legal action because of some technical defect, *e.g.*, where the necessary memorandum required by statute has not been brought into existence, or where the remedy has been barred by lapse of time. The contract itself may be perfectly valid, and may be properly carried out by the parties concerned; but in the event of breach or repudiation, the legal remedies to secure performance or obtain damages are not available to the injured party.

§ 3. *Offer and Acceptance*

(a) General Nature of Offer

An offer may be made in one of four ways:

(1) In the offer of a promise, followed by simple assent; this, in English law, is only applicable to contracts under seal, since a promise not under seal is binding only where valuable consideration is given for it.

(2) In the offer of an act for a promise; as in the common case of an omnibus plying for hire, whereby the proprietors of the omnibus impliedly offer to carry a passenger to his destination in consideration of the passenger's implied promise to pay the fare.

(3) In the offer of a promise for an act; as where a reward is offered for the recovery of lost property.

(4) In the offer of a promise for a promise, as where A promises to pay B a certain sum on a future day, if B will promise to perform certain services for him.

The offer or acceptance, or both, may be made either by words or by conduct. If A sends goods to B's house, and B accepts or uses the goods, B will be liable on an implied contract to pay what the goods are worth; the offer is made by sending the goods, the acceptance by their use or consumption. An offer may be made to a particular person, or to persons generally, or to a particular class of persons. (4) above is an example of the first case, (2) and (3) are examples of general offers.

If the contract is completed by one of the parties, it is said to be an *executed* contract; but if something has still to be done by both parties, it is said to be an *executory* contract.

An offer must be distinguished from a declaration of intention, as where an auctioneer advertises his intention to sell by auction specific goods on a certain day (*Harris v. Nickerson* (1873) L.R. 8 Q.B. 286). It must also be distinguished from an invitation to make an offer; for instance, a trader who exhibits goods for sale does not thereby make an offer even though he employs a 'self-service' system in his shop (*Pharmaceutical Society of Great Britain* v. *Boots Cash Chemists* [1952] 2 Q.B. 795). The same principle without doubt applies to a normal advertisement of goods for sale. In each case there is no contract until an offer to buy is made by a customer and is accepted by the trader.

An offer, to be capable of acceptance, must be definite in its terms, not leaving matters to be agreed in the future. Thus, a purported acceptance of an offer to buy a lorry 'on hire-purchase terms' does not constitute a contract if the hire-purchase terms are never agreed (*Scammell* v. *Ouston* [1941] A.C. 251). But if the contract provides the means for ascertaining the terms, *e.g.*, by a submission to arbitration if the parties cannot agree, there is a binding contract (*Foley* v. *Classique Coaches, Ltd.* [1934] 2 K.B. 1). The offer and acceptance may, however, operate retrospectively, so that where the parties have carried out transactions with each other before the contract was agreed, and on the assumption that it would ultimately be agreed, those prior transactions are governed by the terms of the contract (*Trollope & Colls, Ltd.* v. *Atomic Power Constructions, Ltd.* [1962] 3 All E.R. 1035; see *post*, p. 26).

(b) Communication of Offer

An offer must be communicated to a person before it is capable of acceptance. If, for instance, a reward is offered for information leading to the conviction of a criminal and someone supplies the information without knowing of the reward he cannot thereafter lay claim to it (see the American case of *Fitch* v. *Snedaker* (1868) 38 N.Y. 248).

If A does work for B without the request or knowledge of B he cannot sue for the value of his work (*Taylor v. Laird* (1856) 25 L.J. Ex. 329); an acceptance of services may, however, be sufficient to show an implied contract to pay for them, if at the time the defendant had power to refuse or accept the services; but the opportunity of accepting or rejecting must be given.

(c) Termination of Offer

An offer may be terminated by (1) lapse, (2) revocation, or (3) rejection.

(1) *Lapse*

An offer may lapse:

(i) By failure to accept within the time prescribed for acceptance.

(ii) By failure to accept within a reasonable time, if no time is prescribed.

In *Ramsgate Hotel Co.* v. *Montefiore* (1866) L.R. 1 Ex. 109, an offer to take up shares in a company on 8th June was held to have lapsed before 23rd November of the same year when the letter of acceptance was received.

(iii) By the death of one of the parties before acceptance. The offer ceases to be effective if the *offeree* dies before acceptance, as it then becomes incapable of being accepted by the person to whom it was made (*per* Warrington, L.J., in *Reynolds* v. *Atherton* (1921) 125 L.T. 690, at p. 695). The death of the *offeror* will clearly terminate the offer if the subject-matter of the proposed contract is personal to the offeror, e.g., the performance of services by him; otherwise, if the offeree accepts the offer without knowledge of the offeror's death, it seems that the offeror's estate will be bound by the contract (*Bradbury* v. *Morgan* (1862) 1 H. & C. 249).

(2) *Revocation*

An offer may be revoked, *i.e.*, withdrawn by the offeror, at any time *before acceptance*, but cannot be revoked thereafter.

In *Great Northern Railway Co.* v. *Witham* (1873) L.R. 9 C.P. 16, a company advertised for tenders for the supply of certain goods, and the defendant's tender was accepted; this offer was expressed as follows: 'I undertake to supply the company for twelve months with such quantities of [stores of specified types] as the company may order from time to time.' Various orders were in fact executed, but subsequently the defendant refused to fulfil an order for goods within the terms of the offer.

Held: The defendant was liable for breach of contract. His tender was a standing offer, and each order given by the company constituted an acceptance to the extent indicated; though his revocation was effective as regards future orders, it could not relieve him of liability upon an order given before his withdrawal.

An exception to this rule is made by s. 50 (5) of the Companies Act, 1948, whereby an application for shares in or debentures of a company which is made in pursuance of a prospectus issued generally is irrevocable until after the expiration of the third day after the time of the opening of the subscription lists.

A further exception arises under s. 11 of the Hire-Purchase Act, 1965, which gives a hirer or buyer under a hire-purchase, credit-sale or conditional sale agreement a right to cancel the agreement in certain circumstances although his offer has been accepted by the owner or seller of the goods (see Chap. III, § 3 (b) (3)).

Revocation of an offer, in order to be operative, must be communicated and brought to the knowledge of the offeree.

In *Byrne* v. *Van Tienhoven* (1880) 5 C.P.D. 344, the defendant made an offer to the plaintiff on 1st October, asking for a reply by cable. The offer was received on 11th October, and immediately accepted in the method indicated. The defendant had posted a letter revoking his offer on 8th October, but the letter did not reach the plaintiff until 20th October. It was held that the revocation, not having been brought to the knowledge of the offeree before the acceptance, was inoperative.

It is not necessary for the offeror himself to communicate the fact of revocation to the offeree. It is sufficient for the offeree to receive notice of it from a third party whom he believes to be reliable, even if the latter was not authorised by the offeror to make the communication (*Dickinson* v. *Dodds* (1876) 2 Ch. D. 463).

Revocation may be express or may be implied from the conduct of the offeror in putting himself in a position where he is no longer able to carry out the proposed contract, *e.g.*, if A offers to sell his house to B, and then sells it to C before B has accepted the offer (*ibid.*).

An offeror who, without consideration, gives the offeree a specific time in which to accept or reject the offer, is not bound to wait until the time expires, but may withdraw the offer at any time before acceptance, as the promise to keep the offer open is not legally binding (*Cooke* v. *Oxley* (1790) 3 T.R. 653). For such a promise to be enforceable, it must either be supported by consideration or be given under seal.

(3) *Rejection*

If the offeree rejects the offer or makes a counter-offer, the original offer is terminated (see *infra*).

(d) Acceptance must Agree with Offer

The acceptance of an offer must agree entirely with the terms of the offer, and must not be conditional. If acceptance is made, but on terms other than those originally proposed, it amounts to a rejection of the original offer and the making of a counter-offer, its effect being, in the eyes of the law, to destroy the original offer altogether.

In *Hyde* v. *Wrench* (1840) 3 Beav. 334, A offered to sell his farm to B for £1,000. B offered to buy it for £950, which A refused. B then purported to accept A's offer to sell for £1,000.

Held: The counter-offer by B to buy for a lower price amounted to a rejection of A's offer to sell for £1,000, which thereupon became incapable of acceptance.

But a counter-offer must be distinguished from a mere inquiry whether the offeror is prepared to modify his terms, which will not destroy the original offer.

In *Stevenson* v. *McLean* (1880) 5 Q.B.D. 346, a vendor offered to sell iron for immediate delivery. The offeree telegraphed to inquire whether the offeror would be prepared to deliver over a period of two months, thus postponing dates of payment. The offeror did not reply, but sold the iron elsewhere. The offeree then purported to accept the offer as it had been made.

Held: The telegram was not a counter-offer, but was a mere inquiry, and a contract was validly concluded by the offeree's acceptance.

Where there is a communicated offer, and an unconditional acceptance of the offer, the court will not go into the question of the motive which induced the acceptance (*Williams* v. *Carwardine* (1833) 4 B. & Ad. 621). In this case, a woman gave certain information for which a reward had been offered, not to obtain the reward, but to ease her conscience. She was nevertheless able to claim the reward.

(e) Offer or Acceptance 'Subject to Contract'

When an offer or acceptance is made 'subject to contract' or by the use of like words, it is a question of construction whether the parties do or do not intend to be bound before a formal contract is signed.

Sometimes the intention is that the parties shall be bound by the informal agreement, which is afterwards to be put into more precise and formal language.

In *Branca* v. *Cobarro* [1947] K.B. 854, an agreement contained the words 'This is a provisional agreement until a fully legalised agreement drawn up by a solicitor and embodying all the conditions herewith stated is signed.'

Held: This language, particularly the word 'until,' implied that the agreement was intended to be immediately binding and to remain so unless and until superseded by a subsequent formal agreement.

On the other hand, the words 'subject to contract' frequently imply that the matter remains in negotiation until a formal contract is settled and the formal contracts are exchanged. In such cases there is no contract until the formal agreement has been signed.

In *Spottiswoode, Ballantyne & Co., Ltd.* v. *Doreen Appliances, Ltd.* [1942] 2 K.B. 32, an agreement contained the words 'subject in the usual way to your references being satisfactory, and to the terms of a formal agreement to be prepared by our solicitors.'

Held: The intention of the parties was that no contract should exist unless and until a formal agreement had been entered into.

The point of time at which such agreements become binding is usually when physical exchange of contracts takes place.

In *Eccles* v. *Bryant* [1948] 1 Ch. 93, vendors agreed to sell freehold property to a purchaser 'subject to contract.' On 11th June the vendors' solicitors wrote to the purchaser's solicitors stating that the vendors had signed their part of the contract and that they were ready to exchange. The purchaser signed the duplicate contract and his solicitors posted it to the vendors' solicitors on 18th June. The vendors changed their minds and did not send their part in exchange.

Held: There was no contract, since the parties did not intend to be bound until exchange of parts had taken place.

(f) Communication of Acceptance

The acceptance must be communicated by the acceptor in the manner prescribed or indicated by the offeror. What will amount to communication of acceptance where the acceptance invited is the doing of an act will often depend on whether the offer is a general one, made to the world at large, in which case the doing of the act is generally sufficient communication of acceptance, or whether it is the offer of a promise for an act, made to a specified individual, when actual communication of the acceptance would usually be required by the terms of the offer, express or implied.

In *Carlill* v. *Carbolic Smoke Ball Co.* [1893] 1 Q.B. 256, the company offered, by advertisement, to pay £100 to anyone who contracted influenza after using their smoke ball. After Mrs Carlill had used the smoke ball she caught influenza, and sued the company for the promised reward. The company was held liable. It was urged that a notification of acceptance should have been made to the company; but the court held that this was one of the class of cases in which, as in the case of reward offered for information, or for the recovery of lost property, there need be no acceptance of the offer other than the performance of the condition.

In either case, however, there must be a clear, external manifestation of consent: silence cannot constitute acceptance.

In *Felthouse* v. *Bindley* (1862) 11 C.B. N.S. 869, F offered by letter to buy his nephew's horse for £30, adding 'If I hear no more about him, I consider the horse mine at that price.' The nephew did not reply, but informed the defendant, an auctioneer, who was going to sell his stock, that the horse was to be kept out of the sale. The defendant inadvertently sold the horse to a third party.

Held: F had no claim to the horse, as his offer had not been accepted.

The general rule is that communication of acceptance is not complete until it is received by the offeror. An important exception is made, however, where communication is by letter, telegram or similar means which involve a time lag between dispatch of the acceptance and its receipt by the offeror.

In *Henthorn* v. *Fraser* [1892] 2 Ch. 27, Lord Herschell said:

'Where the circumstances are such that, according to the ordinary usages of mankind, the post might be used as a means of communicating the acceptance of an offer, the acceptance is complete *as soon as it is posted*.'

If an offer is made by post, it must be taken, in the absence of any request to the contrary, to invite a reply through the post. If the offer is revoked, it still remains open during the whole time the letter of revocation is in transit; but the acceptance is complete the moment the letter of acceptance is posted, even though the letter never reaches the offeror (*Household Fire Insurance Co.* v. *Grant* (1879) 4 Ex. D. 216). Accordingly, if the letter of acceptance is posted by the offeree before he receives the letter of revocation, there is a binding contract. Even if the acceptance were immediately revoked by telegram, such revocation would be inoperative. Delivery of the letter to a postman not duly authorised to receive letters for posting is not equivalent to posting (*Re London and Northern Bank* [1900] 1 Ch. 220).

The contract is made at the place where the acceptance is completed. This may often be of importance in determining the law governing the validity of a contract, *e.g.*, where the offeror is resident in one country and the offeree in another.

In *Entores* v. *Miles Far East Corporation* [1955] 2 Q.B. 327, an offer was sent from England to Holland by the Telex system, under which a message typed in one country is at once recorded in another. The offer was accepted by the same means. A question of jurisdiction having arisen, it was held that the acceptance was not complete until it was received by the offeror, and the contract was accordingly made in England.

§ 4. *Form and Consideration*

Either form or consideration is necessary in a valid contract as evidence of the intention of the parties to create a legally binding obligation.

(a) Form

By 'form' is meant some solemnity attaching to the expression of agreement, as in the execution of a deed. It is sometimes stated that a deed imports consideration, which means that the form is sufficient of itself to give effect to the contract.

The characteristics of a deed are:

(1) Estoppel operates, unless the deed was obtained by fraud or duress, or is tainted with illegality.

Estoppel is a rule of evidence by which, if a man has by words or conduct induced others to believe in the existence of certain facts, knowing that they might act on this belief, he is prevented from denying the existence of such facts. It is of three kinds, *viz.:*

(i) Estoppel by record, indisputable against all parties.

(ii) Estoppel by deed, indisputable against the parties to the deed.

(iii) Estoppel by conduct, *e.g.*, 'holding out' in partnership (*q.v.*).

(2) It merges into itself any simple contract dealing with the same matter.

(3) Any right of action is barred at the expiration of twelve years from the time the cause of action first accrued, instead of six years as is the case with a simple contract; but a right of action to recover rent or mortgage interest, even though payable under a deed, is barred after six years (Limitation Act, 1939).

(4) It requires no consideration to support it.

As regards the last rule, the absence of consideration cannot be pleaded as a defence since the execution of a document under seal is looked upon as a solemn act whereby the parties are precluded from denying what they have stated in the instrument, *i.e.*, the doctrine of estoppel operates against them. It must not be inferred that consideration is absent in the case of all contracts entered into by deed; far from it. This form is often adopted to prevent denial of other matters dealt with therein, *e.g.*, it is essential that a vendor of an interest in land should not be able to deny his title. But when there is no consideration intended, as in the case of a gratuitous promise, a deed must be executed to render performance enforceable against the promisor. Nevertheless, the courts will refuse the remedy of specific performance, or indeed any other *equitable* remedy, in respect of a gratuitous promise even though under seal.

A 'BOND' is a promise under seal to pay a sum of money as a penalty for the non-performance of some condition which is the real object of the bond. At common law the entire sum named as a penalty was held to be payable on breach of the condition, but in equity no more could be recovered than the amount of the damage actually sustained by breach of the condition, and this is all that can now be recovered.

An 'ESCROW' is a deed *delivered subject to a condition*; as soon as the condition is fulfilled it becomes operative, and acquires the character of a deed. If a document is delivered as an escrow, it cannot be recalled before the condition on which it depends is fulfilled (*Beesly* v. *Hallwood Estates, Ltd.* [1961] Ch. 105).

An 'INDENTURE' was at one time a deed with the edges of the paper or parchment indented, whereas a 'DEED POLL' had the edges cut straight. In the former case, there being two parties, the two copies of the deed were written on the same parchment, and then divided with an indented cutting, so that the two documents could be subsequently fitted into one another. There is now no such distinction, but an indenture is executed by two or more parties, and there are two or more copies; whereas a deed poll is a unilateral deed, such as a deed of gift, executed by one party only.

(b) Consideration

All simple contracts, whether in writing or made by word of

mouth, require consideration to support them. By consideration the law means *valuable consideration*, which must consist of something capable of being estimated in money. In *Currie v. Misa* (1875) L.R. 10 Ex. 162, valuable consideration was defined as:

'Some right, interest, profit or benefit accruing to one party, or some forbearance, detriment, loss or responsibility given, suffered or undertaken by the other.'

It should be added that the benefit is given or the detriment incurred 'in return for a promise.'

The more modern approach is to regard consideration as the 'price' paid for the other party's promise:

'An act or forbearance of one party, or the promise thereof, is the price for which the promise of the other is bought, and the promise thus given for value is enforceable' (*Dunlop Pneumatic Tyre Co., Ltd. v. Selfridge & Co., Ltd.* [1915] A.C. 847, at p. 855).

The consideration for one person's promise may be a promise made to him by the other and the consideration is then said to be *executory*. On the other hand, where one party promises something in return for the other party doing something, then until it is done there is no consideration; but when it is done, the consideration is *executed*, and the first party's promise becomes a binding contract. Thus, where a reward is offered for a lost dog, the return of it to the owner by the finder, with knowledge of the offer, will be an act constituting consideration; and the consideration being executed, it only remains for the offeror to fulfil his promise of the reward.

Consideration does not necessarily confer a benefit *on the person making the promise*. For instance, X may promise to pay Y the sum of £1 if Y will forbear from suing Z, or in consideration of Y lending money to Z. If the forbearance or lending, as the case may be, is carried out, there is consideration for the promise made by X although he obtains no material advantage therefrom. Both these kinds of transaction are illustrated by a contract of guarantee (see Chap. V, § 4).

Although an agreement not supported by consideration is not enforceable, yet a bare promise is not necessarily entirely devoid of legal effect. Where a promise given without consideration is intended to create legal relations and to be acted upon by the promisee and is in fact acted upon, with the result that the promisee's position is altered, the promisor cannot bring an action against the promisee which involves the repudiation of his promise or is inconsistent with it (*per* Asquith, L.J., in *Combe v. Combe* 1951 [2] K.B. 215, at p. 225).

In *Central London Property Trust, Ltd. v. High Trees House, Ltd.* [1947] K.B. 130, the plaintiffs, landlords of a block of flats leased to the defendants, agreed to accept a reduced rent because of war conditions. At the end of the war the plaintiffs claimed the full rent both retrospectively and for the future.

Held: The plaintiffs were entitled to the full rent from the end of the war when their agreement ceased to operate, but they were bound by their agreement during the war years, as the defendants had acted upon it.

The reason for this rule is that it would be contrary to the principles of equity that a person should be allowed to enforce rights which he has promised to relinquish, where the promisee has relied on that promise and thereby altered his position. This equitable doctrine is akin to the common law rule of estoppel, and is sometimes referred to as 'promissory' or 'quasi' estoppel.

This equitable principle does not, however, extend to allowing a promisee to sue on a bare promise. For example, if a landlord, instead of agreeing to reduce a tenant's rent, agreed without consideration to pay him back part of the rent which had already been paid, the tenant would be unable to sue for that payment, for in order to succeed he would have to show that consideration had been given for the promise. The principle is to be used as a shield and not as a sword; and it will only apply where the facts of a case satisfy the conditions laid down by the Court of Appeal in *Combe* v. *Combe* (*Tool Metal Manufacturing Co., Ltd.* v. *Tungsten Electric Co., Ltd.* [1955] 2 All E.R. 657, H.L.). Furthermore, the promisor may withdraw his promise on giving reasonable notice; the promise only becomes final and irrevocable if the promisee cannot resume his former position (*Ajayi* v. *R. T. Briscoe (Nigeria), Ltd.* [1964] 3 All E.R. 556).

The rules relating to the giving of consideration are:

(1) *Consideration is always required to enforce a simple contract*

This rule has already been considered.

(2) *The consideration must be of some value in law*

So long as the consideration is of value it is not necessary that it should be adequate; this is a matter for the parties themselves when entering into the contract. Everyone is free to make whatever bargain he pleases and, unless there is some attendant factor which would enable rescission to be obtained, the courts will not interfere. If fraud is alleged, however, the courts will consider whether inadequacy of the consideration is evidence thereof. Moreover, in any case where an equitable remedy is sought, for instance, where specific performance of a contract is desired, the court may inquire into the adequacy of the consideration, as the granting of an equitable remedy is in the discretion of the court. And where it is sought to uphold a contract in restraint of trade the presence and adequacy of consideration may be material in considering the question of reasonableness.

This requirement excludes consideration which consists only of natural love and affection, or which rests upon a moral as distinct from a legal obligation (*Beaumont* v. *Reeve* (1846) 8 Q.B. 483). This is sometimes known as 'good consideration' to distinguish it from 'valuable consideration' which alone will support a contract.

An illustration of the principle that consideration must have some legal value is afforded by the rule that payment, or a promise of payment, of a lesser sum than one which is already due cannot be consideration for an agreement to treat the whole debt as discharged (*Foakes* v. *Beer* (1884) 9 App. Cas. 605). If £20 is due, the debtor cannot hold the creditor to a promise to take £10 in full satisfaction, for payment of £10 cannot be consideration for the discharge of a debt of £20. If, however, some variation is made in the terms of payment, this may amount to consideration for the discharge, e.g., if a cheque is given for the lesser sum (*Sibree* v. *Tripp* (1846) 15 M. & W. 23), or payment is made on a day earlier than that on which it is due (*Pinnel's Case* (1602) 5 Co. Rep. 117a). It would seem that the doctrine of 'promissory estoppel' could now be invoked by the debtor in such a case, if he could show that all the conditions laid down in *Combe* v. *Combe* (*supra*) were satisfied.

The above rule is part of a wider principle that if a party to a contract makes a fresh promise to the other party to do what he is already legally bound to do, he cannot rely on that fresh promise as consideration to support a promise by the other party.

In *Vanbergen* v. *St. Edmund's Properties, Ltd.* [1933] 2 K.B. 223, V was indebted to a company in the sum of £208. He agreed with the company to pay the money into a particular bank by a certain date in consideration of the company not serving a bankruptcy notice which had been issued. He paid the money as agreed, but owing to a misunderstanding the company served the bankruptcy notice. V sued the company for damages for breach of contract, alleging the harm caused to his reputation by service of the bankruptcy notice.

Held: His promise to pay the money was no consideration for the company's promise not to serve the bankruptcy notice, as he was already bound to pay the money.

This case also shows that the fresh promise does not constitute consideration merely because it varies the conditions of the original obligation (here the condition as to place of payment) if variation is made for the convenience of the party who is bound.

The position is similar when a person who is under a public duty to do a particular thing specifically promises another person, being a member of the public entitled to the performance of that duty, that he will carry it out. The promise does not constitute consideration.

In *Collins* v. *Godefroy* (1831) 1 B. & Ad. 950, a person who had been summoned by *subpoena* to give evidence in a lawsuit was promised by one of the litigants a payment of £6 6s. for his trouble. It was held that the witness could not recover the amount, as he had given no consideration for the promise, being already bound as a public duty to give evidence.

But if one who is under a public duty promises to do more than that duty requires of him, that promise will constitute consideration to support a contract.

In *Glasbrook Brothers* v. *Glamorgan County Council* [1925] A.C. 270, the county council promised that the police would give a colliery company a greater degree of protection against the action of strikers than the authorities considered necessary, in consideration of the colliery company's agreement to pay £2,200. It was held that the payment promised was recoverable.

The position is different if a party to a contract makes a promise to a *third party* to carry out his obligations under the contract. Here it seems that the promise to the third party constitutes consideration sufficient to render enforceable any promise which that third party made, because the third party obtains the right to insist on performance of the original contract, and the promisor suffers a detriment by incurring an additional liability on that contract, *viz.*, towards the third party.

In *Shadwell* v. *Shadwell* (1860) 9 C.B. N.S. 159, A had made a contract with B to marry her, and A's uncle agreed to make him an allowance of £150 a year, in consideration of his marrying her. It was held that the uncle's promise was enforceable.

In the case of an arrangement with creditors, the consideration to each creditor for his promise to accept the composition is the promise of the other creditors to assent thereto and be bound by the scheme (*Good* v. *Cheeseman* (1831) 2 B. & Ad. 328). Consideration therefore exists as between the creditors themselves; as between the debtor and any particular creditor, the bar to an action by the creditor for the full amount owing has been explained on the grounds that it would be a fraud on the other parties to go behind the composition agreement, but can now be regarded as coming within the doctrine of promissory estoppel.

(3) *Consideration must move from the promisee*

A person who seeks to enforce a simple contract must show that he or his agent has furnished some consideration to the promisor or to some other person at his request. This is usually expressed by saying that the consideration must move from the promisee. This rule is closely connected with the doctrine of privity of contract (see *post*, § 11(a)), which precludes a person from suing on a contract unless he is a party to it; but the two principles must be carefully distinguished, since consideration is not necessarily given by every party to a contract. If, for example, X promises Y and Z that he will pay Y £50 if Z supplies him with certain goods, and the payment is not made although the goods are supplied, Z can sue X, but Y cannot, since, although he is a party to the contract, he gave no consideration for X's promise.

(4) *The consideration must be legal*

The consideration must not be illegal or of an immoral nature, or contrary to public policy, on the principle *ex turpi causa non oritur actio* (an action does not arise from a base cause). This is more fully dealt with in § 9, *post*.

(5) *The consideration must be possible*

This is considered in § 10, *post*.

(6) *The consideration must not be past*

A past consideration is one which is not induced by the promise of the other party, but is completed before the promise is made, and is, in effect, no consideration at all.

In *Re McArdle* [1951] Ch. 669, the testator had left his house to his wife for life and then to his children. The wife made various improvements to the house, and the children later signed a document addressed to her in which they promised to repay her the amount she had spent on the improvements.
Held: As the work had been completed when the promise was made, the consideration was past, and the promise could not be enforced.

A past consideration will not support a subsequent promise unless the two are so interlocked that the promise subsequently given consists merely in qualifying the consideration which it had already been agreed, expressly or implicitly, should be given.

In *Lampleigh* v. *Brathwait* (1616) Hobart 105, B committed a murder and asked L to use his influence to secure a pardon. This necessitated expense on L's part, and B some time after the pardon had been secured promised to pay him £100, but did not fulfil the promise. L was held to be entitled to payment since B had requested him to perform the service he had rendered, which could therefore not be regarded as a purely voluntary act on L's part. (If L had *offered* to attempt to secure the pardon, the decision would doubtless have been different.)
In *Re Casey's Patents* [1892] 1 Ch. 104, the owners of certain patent rights told C that, in consideration of his having acted as manager in working the patents, they would give him a one-third share of the patents. They subsequently claimed that the promise related to past services, so that they were not bound by it.
Held: The past service raised an implication that it was to be paid for, and the subsequent promise was binding as an admission of this fact, which fixed the precise amount payable.

From these cases it seems that where a request is made which is substantially an offer of a promise upon terms to be afterwards determined, and services are given in pursuance of that request, a promise to pay what the service is worth may be inferred, and any subsequent promise amounts to fixing the worth of the service.

A person may revive a debt barred by the Limitation Act, 1939, by means of a subsequent promise in writing to pay it. Strictly, this is not an exception to the general doctrine of past consideration, since an action to recover the debt is based on the *original* contract and not on the subsequent acknowledgment. It is true the acknowledgment enables an action for enforcement (which had lapsed) to be brought, but such acknowledgment is really given without consideration at all.

A past consideration is sufficient to support a cheque or other bill of exchange (Bills of Exchange Act, 1882, s. 27 (1); see Chap. IV).

(c) Contracts which must be entered into by Deed

The following contracts are not binding unless made by deed:

(1) A gratuitous promise (*Rann* v. *Hughes* (1778) 7 T.R. 350).

(2) A transfer of shares in statutory companies (Companies Clauses Act, 1845, s. 14).

(3) A transfer of a British ship or any share therein (Merchant Shipping Act, 1894, s. 24).

(4) A conditional bill of sale (Bills of Sale Act, 1882, s. 9; see Chap. V, § 6).

(5) A legal mortgage of an interest in land (Law of Property Act, 1925, ss. 85, 86).

(6) A lease of lands, tenements, or hereditaments for more than three years, with certain exceptions (*ibid.*, ss. 52, 54).

The former rule that contracts must be under seal if entered into by corporations other than companies formed under the Companies Acts was abolished by the Corporate Bodies Contracts Act, 1960. All corporations may now contract in the same way as ordinary persons.

(d) Contracts which must be in Writing

The following contracts are required by statute to be in writing:

(1) Bills of exchange and promissory notes (Bills of Exchange Act, 1882, ss. 3, 83).

(2) Assignments of copyright (Copyright Act, 1956, s. 36).

(3) Contracts of marine insurance (Marine Insurance Act, 1906, s. 22).

(4) A transfer of shares in a company registered under the Companies Acts (Companies Act, 1948, s. 75).

(5) An acknowledgment of a debt barred by the Limitation Act, 1939, although this is not strictly a contract. It is rather a means of enforcing a remedy under an existing contract.

The above contracts have no validity at all unless they are in writing.

(6) Hire-purchase, credit-sale and conditional sale agreements under the Hire-Purchase Act, 1965.

The absence of writing in this case does not make the contract completely void, but renders it unenforceable against either the hirer or the guarantor, and the owner cannot recover the goods from the hirer, unless the court sees fit to order otherwise (see Chap. III, § 3 (b)).

(c) Contracts which must be Evidenced in Writing

Certain contracts, although perfectly valid subsisting contracts, are unenforceable by action unless evidenced in writing.

(1) *Contracts of Guarantee*

By s. 4 of the Statute of Frauds, 1677, no action can be brought on a promise to answer for the debt, default or miscarriage of another (*i.e.*, a guarantee) unless the agreement, or some memorandum or note thereof, is in writing, and signed by the party to be charged or some other person lawfully authorised by him (see Chap. V, § 4).

(2) *Contracts for the Sale or other Disposition of Land*

Section 40 of the Law of Property Act, 1925, lays down a similar rule with regard to contracts for the sale or other disposition of land or any interest in land.

Non-compliance with the requirements of these statutes does not invalidate a contract, but no action can be brought upon it until the omission is made good. The note in writing may be made at any time between the formation of the contract and the commencement of an action, but not after the action has commenced.

The rule requiring writing is a rule of evidence, and it will therefore prevail in any action brought in the English courts, even if the proper law of the contract is foreign (*Leroux* v. *Brown* (1852) 12 C.B. 501; see *post*, § 15).

The memorandum must contain the names of the parties, and describe the subject-matter of the contract. Where one of the parties is described but not named, parol evidence will be allowed to identify him (*Sale* v. *Lambert* (1874) L.R. 18 Eq. 1).

The consideration must also be shown where the contract is governed by the Law of Property Act (*Wain* v. *Warlters* (1804) 5 East 10); but this is not required in the case of contracts of guarantee (Mercantile Law Amendment Act, 1856, s. 3).

The memorandum may consist of various documents, so long as they are connected; an envelope and the letter enclosed in it are sufficiently connected together for this purpose (*Pearce* v. *Gardner* [1897] 1 Q.B. 688).

In *Timmins* v. *Moreland Street Property Co.* [1958] Ch. 110, a plaintiff brought an action for damages for repudiation of an oral agreement for the sale of freehold property as evidenced in writing by a stopped cheque signed by the purchaser and a receipt for a deposit on the purchase signed by the vendor. It was held that the two documents did not together constitute a sufficient memorandum, because it was not possible to link the cheque which contained the signature of the party charged with the receipt which did not. The agreement was consequently one on which no action could be brought.

Where documents refer to other documents, they may be connected by parol evidence (*Cave* v. *Hastings* (1881) 7 Q.B.D. 125). All the terms of the contract must, however, appear in the writing, and parol evidence cannot be admitted of terms not appearing in the writing (*Greaves* v. *Ashlin* (1813) 3 Camp. 426).

The memorandum must be signed by the party to be charged, or his agent. It is not necessary to have the signature of both parties to make a contract enforceable (*Reuss* v. *Picksley* (1866) L.R. 1 Ex. 342). The signature need not be written in ink; it may be in pencil, or may be printed or stamped, or it may consist of a mark; but the intention of the person giving it must be to regard it as a signature recognising the whole contract (*Baker* v. *Dening* (1838) 8 A. & E. 94). The signature must be so placed upon the document that it governs the whole of it; but it need not necessarily be placed at the end of it (*Caton* v. *Caton* (1867) L.R. 2 H.L. 127).

An auctioneer, before sale, is an agent for the vendor only; but upon completion of the sale, *i.e.*, after the fall of the hammer, he becomes also agent for the purchaser, and can sign any document necessary to satisfy the statute. His authority to do so cannot be revoked after the hammer has fallen (*Van Praagh* v. *Everidge* [1902] 2 Ch. 266).

The Equitable Doctrine of Part Performance

The absence of a written memorandum will not necessarily be fatal to the enforcement of the contract if the contract is of such a nature that the court could have decreed specific performance if it had been in writing. In such a case – in practice this only applies to contracts concerning an interest in land – an oral contract may be enforced in equity if there has been a *part performance* under the contract, and with a view to it, by the party seeking to enforce it, to the knowledge, and with the consent of, the other. There must be proper evidence of a concluded oral contract, and the act relied on as part performance must be referable to some contract such as is alleged, and to no other kind of transaction. The payment of money is generally not an act within this principle, since it may be referable to other transactions than the one alleged, but entry into possession of land, for example, usually would be.

In *McManus* v. *Cooke* (1887) 35 Ch. D. 697, A verbally agreed to purchase a plot of land from B, and B agreed to build a house on the land to certain specifications. While the house was being built A inspected it on various occasions and made suggestions which were carried out by B. A finally refused to carry out his contract, claiming that there was no written memorandum referring to the contract. It was held that this was a case where the court could have decreed specific performance, there had been part performance by B to the knowledge and with the consent of A, and therefore the contract could be enforced.

If these requirements are satisfied the court may order specific performance of the contract; the common law remedy of damages is not available in such a case.

(3) Moneylending Contracts

By s. 6 of the Moneylenders Act, 1927, no contract for the repayment of money borrowed from a moneylender or interest thereon, and no security given in respect thereof, is enforceable unless a note or memorandum in writing is made and signed personally by the borrower, and a copy thereof delivered to or sent to the borrower within seven days of the making of the contract. If it is proved that the note or memorandum was not signed by the borrower before the money was lent or the security was given, the contract cannot be enforced. The note or memorandum must contain all the terms of the contract, and in particular:

(i) The date on which the loan was made. If an incorrect date is inserted the contract is unenforceable even though no one is deceived, and a surety would be discharged from his liability (*Gaskell, Ltd.* v. *Askwith* (1929) 167 L.T. 376).

(ii) The amount of the principal.

(iii) Either the rate per cent. per annum of interest charged, or the rate per cent. per annum represented by the interest charged as calculated in accordance with the provisions of the First Schedule of the Act.

If a contract is unenforceable through failure to comply with these provisions, a borrower may be entitled to delivery up of securities without having to repay the money owing (*Cohen* v. *J. Lester, Ltd.* [1939] 1 K.B. 504; see *post*, § 9 (a) (3)).

§ 5. *Intention to Create Legal Relations*

Whether or not an agreement is to create legal obligations is primarily a matter for the parties themselves. If they clearly deny such intention the courts will respect their wishes and not enforce the agreement.

Thus, in *Rose and Frank Co.* v. *Crompton Bros., Ltd.* [1925] A.C. 445, an agreement contained a clause to the effect that the contract was to be 'binding in honour only.' It was held by the House of Lords that the court must give effect to the clause and that consequently an action could not be sustained on the agreement.

In *Jones* v. *Vernon's Pools, Ltd.* [1938] 2 All E.R. 626, an entrant in a football pool signed a form stating that the sending in or acceptance thereof should not be attended by legal consequences. It was held that no legally enforceable contract had been created.

An express exclusion of the intention to create legal relations must be clear and unequivocal. The use of the words '*ex gratia*' will not suffice, as this shows only that the promisor does not admit any pre-existing liability, not that he intends to avoid legal liability once his promise is accepted (*Edwards* v. *Skyways, Ltd.* [1964] 1 All E.R. 494).

Where there is no express indication of intention, certain presumptions will apply depending on the nature of the contract.

(1) *Commercial Agreements*

In the case of commercial agreements it will be presumed that the parties intend to create legal relations. The presumption can be rebutted by evidence to the contrary, but the onus of establishing that it was not intended to create legal relations is a heavy one (*Edwards* v. *Skyways, Ltd., supra*).

The extravagant claims and promises often made in advertisements are not normally regarded as being intended to be legally binding. In *Carlill's* case (*ante*, p. 8) the advertisers had stated that they had deposited £1,000 with their bankers to show their sincerity. The court implied from this that it was intended to make a legally binding contract, but had this statement not been made, the plaintiff may well not have succeeded in her claim.

(2) *Domestic Arrangements*

In the case of arrangements or agreements between husband and wife or between other members of a family, it is presumed that these are *not* intended to be legally enforceable.

In *Balfour* v. *Balfour* [1919] 2 K.B. 571, a husband promised to pay his wife an allowance of £30 a month while he was abroad. After some time he ceased to pay the allowance and the wife sued him for breach of contract. It was held that no legal relationship had been contemplated and therefore the wife's action failed.

But the mere fact of a domestic relationship does not preclude the possibility of an intention to make a contract.

In *Simpkins* v. *Pays* [1955] 1 W.L.R. 975, the three members of a household took part in a newspaper competition, the entries being made in the defendant's name. The entry was successful and the defendant received a prize of £750. She refused to share this with the others claiming that there was no intention to create a legal relationship.
Held: The agreement was in the nature of a joint enterprise, and legal relations were contemplated. The plaintiff was therefore entitled to one-third of the prize money.

§ 6. *The Terms of the Contract*

Once the offer has been accepted no new terms can be added to the contract by either party, or the existing terms varied, except by a new agreement (see *post*, § 12 (a)). In order to determine the precise obligations undertaken by each party it is therefore necessary to examine the statements made by them during the negotiations preceding the completion of acceptance. The question may arise whether a particular statement was intended to be a term of the contract or a mere representation inducing the contract. In the case of a contract which has been reduced to writing, it may be alleged that the written document does not represent the full agreement. In addition to the terms expressly agreed by the parties, certain further terms may have to be implied by custom, by statute or by the court. Furthermore, not all the terms may be of equal importance, so that the contract will have to be examined to determine what is the consequence of a breach of a particular term.

(a) Construction of the Contract

In the event of a dispute, the terms of a purely oral contract must be proved by the evidence of the parties and of witnesses. If the contract has been reduced to writing, then *prima facie* the writing represents the whole of the terms of the contract, so that no difficulty will normally be found in deciding what its terms are, though questions as to the meaning of these terms may arise.

In considering the meaning of such terms, the principal rules of interpretation to be applied are:

(1) The language must be construed to carry out the intention of the parties as shown by the terms of the agreement.

(2) Words must be presumed to have their literal meaning.

(3) If there are two possible interpretations, one legal and the other illegal, the legal construction must be adopted.

(4) Words are to be construed most strongly against the party who drew up the contract.

As a general rule oral evidence cannot be admitted to add to, vary or contradict a written document. There are, however, certain exceptions to this rule, the most important of which are:

(1) Oral evidence is admissible to prove a custom or trade usage.

(2) Oral evidence may be given to show that the contract was made subject to a condition precedent (see (d) (1), *infra*).

(3) Where the *whole* contract was not reduced to writing, oral evidence can be given of the additional terms.

(4) Oral evidence can be given to explain a *latent*, but not a *patent*, ambiguity. A patent ambiguity is one which is apparent on the face of the document, *e.g.*, where two terms are clearly inconsistent. A latent ambiguity is one which is not apparent. In the latter

case oral evidence may be adduced to identify persons or things mentioned in a contract, or to show that words apparently unambiguous were used in a special sense by the contracting parties, provided that such evidence merely explains and does not contradict the terms of the contract. This rule is frequently applied in mercantile contracts, where evidence is adduced to show that by the custom of merchants certain words are used in a technical sense other than their usual meaning.

(b) Terms and Representations

As will be seen later (*post*, § 8 (b)), the remedy for a misrepresentation inducing a person to enter into a contract is rescission of the contract, subject to certain limits, sometimes with a right to damages. A breach of a term of the contract, on the other hand, will always give rise to an action for damages, and may also entitle the innocent party to repudiate the contract. It thus becomes important to determine whether a statement made by one party to the other was intended to be a term of the contract or not. If the statement is made for the very purpose of inducing the other party to act on it by entering into a contract, and in reliance upon the statement he enters into the contract, that is *prima facie* ground for inferring that the statement was intended to be a term of the contract; but the person making the statement can rebut this inference by showing that he was innocent of any fault in making it, and that it would not be reasonable for him to be bound by it (*per* Lord Denning, M.R., in *Dick Bentley Productions, Ltd.* v. *Harold Smith (Motors), Ltd.* [1965] 2 All E.R. 65, at p. 67).

In this case the plaintiff purchased a Bentley car from the defendants in reliance upon their statement that the car had been fitted with a new engine and gear box and had done only twenty thousand miles since then. The representation as to mileage was untrue, but not fraudulent.

Held: The statement amounted *prima facie* to a term of the contract, and the inference had not been rebutted, as the defendants were in a position to find out the true mileage: accordingly, the plaintiff was entitled to damages.

The inference may be rebutted if the person making the statement had no special knowledge as compared with the other party, and believed on reasonable grounds that the statement was true.

In *Oscar Chess, Ltd.* v. *Williams* [1957] 1 All E.R. 325, the plaintiffs were car dealers who were selling a new car to the defendant and taking his own car in part exchange. Relying on the registration book, the defendant informed the plaintiffs in good faith that the car was a 1948 model, and this was accepted by the plaintiffs. In fact the car was a 1939 model, the registration book having been altered by a previous owner. In consequence, the defendant was allowed more than the true value of the car. The plaintiffs' action for damages failed, on the grounds that the defendant's statement was a mere representation.

(c) Collateral Contracts

A person who is induced to enter into a contract by an innocent misrepresentation made by the other contracting party or by a third party may be able to recover damages, despite the fact that the representation was not a term of the contract, if he can show that there was created a separate and *collateral* contract with the person making the representation, under which he agreed to enter into the main contract in consideration for the promise contained in that representation.

In *Andrews* v. *Hopkinson* [1957] 1 Q.B. 229, the plaintiff was considering the purchase of a second-hand car. The defendant, a car dealer, told him 'It's a good little bus; I would stake my life on it.' The plaintiff, relying on this statement, entered into a contract for the hire-purchase of the car with a finance company. The car proved to be seriously defective, and the plaintiff, who was precluded from suing the finance company by a term in the hire-purchase contract, sued the dealer on the collateral agreement. The plaintiff was held to be entitled to damages against the dealer for breach of his undertaking before the hire-purchase contract was made.

In *Wells (Merstham), Ltd.* v. *Buckland Sand & Silica Co., Ltd.* [1964] 1 All E.R. 41, the defendants warranted that their 'B.W.' sand was suitable for the purpose for which the plaintiffs required it. To save carriage costs, the plaintiffs placed their orders for the sand with a third party who then bought the sand from the defendants without telling the defendants that the sand was for resale to the plaintiffs. The sand delivered did not conform to the warranty, and the plaintiffs suffered loss.

Held: The defendants were liable in damages for breach of the collateral contract.

In the particular case of a contract to which the Hire-Purchase Act, 1965, applies, any representations in respect of the goods to which the agreement relates made by a third party in the course of antecedent negotiations are now deemed to have been made by him as agent of the owner, *i.e.*, usually the finance company, and thus the owner is personally liable as principal in respect of such representations.

A misrepresentation made negligently, although not fraudulently, by a third party may now also be actionable in tort, as a result of the decision of the House of Lords in *Hedley Byrne & Co., Ltd.* v. *Heller & Partners, Ltd.* [1964] A.C. 465, in which the established principle that a person is not liable in negligence for a mis-statement which results in financial loss was effectively overruled (see *post*, p. 44).

(d) Express Terms

The terms of the contract may be classified into two categories: conditions and warranties. A *condition* is a term which goes to the root of the contract, the breach of which gives the injured party the right to treat the contract as discharged and also to claim damages. A *warranty* is a term which does not go to the root of the contract, but is merely subsidiary to the main agreement, the breach of which entitles the injured party to sue for damages, but does not discharge him from performance of his own obligations under the contract. In deciding whether a term of a contract is a condition or a warranty, the court must in each case try to determine the intention of the parties as expressed in the agreement in the light of the surrounding circumstances. The fact that the parties have used one or other of these terms is not conclusive.

In *Behn* v. *Burness* (1863) 32 L.J. Q.B. 204, a charter-party was made in relation to a ship described as being then 'In the port of Amsterdam.' It was held that this statement was intended to be a substantive part of the contract, since it is well known that charterers rely on such statements as the basis of calculations on which important arrangements depend, and therefore the contract could be repudiated if it were not true.

In *Hong Kong Fir Shipping Co., Ltd.* v. *Kawasaki Kisen Kaisha, Ltd.* [1962] 2 Q.B. 26, shipowners who had agreed to let a vessel to charterers for two years delivered the vessel with an inadequate and incompetent crew, largely due to whose inefficiency the engines, which were very old, were damaged on the first voyage under the charter, involving a delay for repairs of some five months. A new and efficient crew was provided, but before the ship was made seaworthy the charterers claimed to repudiate the charter. The owners admitted breach of the term in the contract that the ship would be seaworthy, but claimed that the charterers were not entitled to repudiate.

Held: The breach of the contract was not so fundamental as to entitle the hirers to repudiate but only gave them the right to claim damages. The charterers were thus themselves liable for breach of contract for wrongful repudiation.

In the latter case it was pointed out that certain terms, such as a 'seaworthiness' clause, do not create a single obligation only, but consist of a collection of obligations of varying importance, some of which may justify repudiation, while others will give the right only to damages. It follows that such terms may be treated as both conditions and warranties, depending upon the nature of the breach. The position is further complicated by the development of the doctrine of the 'fundamental obligation' (see (g), *infra*). In spite of these difficulties, however, the traditional terminology of conditions and warranties is still retained by the courts.

The word 'condition' is also used to describe extraneous facts upon which the existence of the contract depends. In this sense two types of condition may arise:

(1) *Condition Precedent*

A condition precedent is a condition, express or implied, that the contract shall not bind one or more of the parties unless and until some stated event has happened.

In *Pym* v. *Campbell* (1856) 6 E. & B. 370, the defendants agreed to buy from the plaintiff a share in an invention, but it was agreed between them that the contract should not be binding unless approval of the invention was obtained from a third party. This approval was not obtained, and it was held that the defendant was not therefore bound by the agreement.

(2) *Condition Subsequent*

A condition subsequent is one under which the contract shall cease to be binding at the option of one or other of the parties on the happening of some future event. An illustration may be found in the 'excepted risks' of a charter-party, where the occurrence of such an excepted risk releases the shipowner from the strict performance of the contract and, if it should take place while the contract is wholly executory, the parties are altogether discharged (*Geipel* v. *Smith* (1872) L.R. 7 Q.B. 404).

(e) Implied Terms

In addition to those terms expressly incorporated into the contract by the parties themselves, the contract may arise in a context which requires certain further terms to be introduced by implication, although no reference has been made thereto by the parties. Such 'implied terms' may, like express terms, be in the nature of conditions or warranties.

(1) *Terms implied by Custom*

Any custom attaching to the particular trade or to the locality to which the contract applies may be implied into the contract, if it is sufficiently established to justify the fact that its terms are not incorporated in the contract, the parties being presumed to be aware of its existence. To be enforceable it must not be inconsistent with the terms of the contract nor contrary to law; it must be certain, reasonable and consistent, and must be generally accepted by the mercantile community.

(2) *Terms implied by Statute*

Under certain statutes, *e.g.*, the Marine Insurance Act, 1906, the Sale of Goods Act, 1893, and the Hire-Purchase Act, 1965, certain terms are implied into all contracts governed by those statutes. These are set out in the chapters dealing with these particular types of contracts.

(3) *Terms implied by the Courts*

In certain cases the courts have shown themselves willing to imply terms similar to those which are implied by statute. Thus terms will be implied into a contract for work and materials analogous to those implied under the Sale of Goods Act (*Samuels* v. *Davis* [1943] K.B. 526), and in hire-purchase contracts which do not fall within the statutory limits, terms are implied similar to those applicable to contracts within the Hire-Purchase Act (*Karsales* (*Harrow*), *Ltd.* v.

Wallis [1956] 2 All E.R. 866; *Yeoman Credit, Ltd.* v. *Apps* [1962] 2 Q.B. 508). (See Chap. III.)

Apart from these particular cases, the courts are generally reluctant to intervene by adding terms to those which the parties have expressly agreed, and will only do so where a further term is essential to give 'business efficacy' to the contract (*The Moorcock* (1889) 14 P.D. 64). Such an implied term is based on the presumed intention of the parties.

In *Trollope & Colls, Ltd.* v. *Atomic Power Constructions, Ltd.* [1962] 3 All E.R. 1035, the parties had conducted transactions with each other for many months before the contract between them was finally agreed. The court held that, since the parties must have assumed that a contract would in due course be made, and had carried out work on this assumption, a term must be implied into the contract that the contract should apply retrospectively to all that had been done in anticipation of it.

(f) Terms Excluding or Limiting Liability

It frequently happens that in the course of making a contract one person delivers to another a document which purports to set out the terms of the contract or refers to other documents in which the terms are set out, and which limits or excludes the liability of the party delivering it. Typical examples arise where a person takes clothing to be cleaned or leaves a suitcase at a cloakroom. If the other party has agreed to the terms, he is naturally bound by them. The problem which arises in connection with these 'ticket' cases, as they have come to be known, is whether he is bound by the terms if he has *not* read them. For the person issuing the ticket to be able to rely on an exemption clause, he must show:

(1) That the document was an essential element in the making of the contract, *i.e.*, a contractual document, and not merely an acknowledgment of payment.

In *Chapelton* v. *Barry Urban District Council* [1940] 1 K.B. 532, the plaintiff wished to hire deck-chairs from the defendant corporation. Beside a stack of deck-chairs was a notice stating: 'Hire of Chairs 2d per Session.' The plaintiff took two chairs and received two tickets, which he put into his pocket without being aware that they contained any conditions. On the back of the tickets were the words 'The Council will not be liable for any accident or damage arising from hire of chair.' When the plaintiff sat down the chair gave way and he was injured. He claimed damages from the corporation.

Held: The plaintiff was not bound by the conditions and could recover damages. He was entitled to assume that the ticket was merely a receipt for the money he had paid, and that the only conditions were those printed on the notice displayed near the chairs, which constituted the offer he had accepted by taking the chairs.

(2) If the document is an integral part of the contract, that the defendant did what was reasonably necessary to give the plaintiff notice of the conditions. If there is a reference to the conditions on the face of the document, this is normally sufficient notice of them.

In *Richardson* v. *Rowntree* [1894] A.C. 217, the plaintiff claimed damages from the defendants for personal injuries sustained on board the defendants' ship on which she was a passenger. The defendants relied on a condition in the ticket which limited their liability to 100 dollars. When the plaintiff received the ticket it was folded so that no writing was visible unless and until she opened it.

Held: The plaintiff had not been given notice of the conditions, and was therefore entitled to the full amount of damages she claimed.

Similarly, in *Sugar* v. *London, Midland and Scottish Railway Co.* [1941] 1 All E.R. 172, the date stamp on a railway ticket obliterated the words 'For conditions, see back.' It was held that the passenger was not bound by the conditions, of which he had no actual knowledge, on the grounds that no steps reasonably sufficient to bring them to his notice had been taken.

In *Thompson* v. *London, Midland and Scottish Railway Co.* [1930] 1 K.B. 41, the plaintiff, who could not read, had an excursion ticket taken for her by her niece on the face of which were printed the words 'Excursion. For conditions see back.' On the back was a notice that the ticket was issued subject to the conditions in the company's time-tables and excursion bills, which excluded liability for any injury, however caused. The plaintiff was injured in the course of the journey and claimed damages.

Held: The fact that the plaintiff could not read did not alter the legal position. She was bound by the special contract made on the excursion ticket on the acceptance of the ticket, the indication of the special conditions by reference to the time-tables being sufficient notice of their existence and content.

(Although the general principles laid down in the above cases still apply, the Transport Act, 1962, now makes void any provisions in a contract for carriage by rail which purport to exclude or limit the carrier's liability for injury to, or death of, a passenger; see Chap. VII, § 2).

If the plaintiff has actually signed the document, he is bound by the conditions contained therein, provided that he is aware of the general nature of the document, unless he was induced to sign by some fraud or other misrepresentation on the part of the defendant.

In *L'Estrange* v. *Graucob* [1934] 2 K.B. 394, the plaintiff bought an automatic machine from the defendants on terms contained in a 'sales agreement' which included a number of clauses in small print. She signed the document without reading it. It was held that she was bound by the terms of the document, and that no question of notice arose in such a case.

In *Curtis* v. *Chemical Cleaning and Dyeing Co.* [1951] 1 K.B. 805, the plaintiff took a dress to the defendants' shop to be cleaned, and was given a document headed 'receipt' which she was asked by the shop assistant to sign. On asking for what purpose her signature was required she was told that the document exempted the defendants from certain risks, particularly the risk of damage to the beads and sequins on the dress. In fact, the receipt contained a condition that the defendants accepted no liability for any damage, however arising. When the dress was returned to the plaintiff it was found to be stained, and when sued by the plaintiff the defendants relied on the exclusion clause. The Court of Appeal held that the defence must fail, because the assistant by an innocent misrepresentation had created a false impression in the mind of the plaintiff as to the effect of the document which she had been induced to sign.

Written conditions may be incorporated into an oral contract, provided that this is done at the time the contract is made.

In *Olley* v. *Marlborough Court, Ltd.* [1949] 1 K.B. 532, a man and his wife, on arrival at a hotel as guests, in accordance with the custom of the hotel paid for a week's board and residence in advance. They then went to their room in which there was a notice stating: 'The proprietors will not hold themselves responsible for articles lost or stolen, unless handed to the manageress for safe custody in a sealed package and a receipt obtained.' The wife later closed the self-locking door of the room, went downstairs and hung the key on the board in the reception office. In her absence the key was wrongfully taken by a third party who entered the room and stole her furs.

Held: The contract was completed before the guests went to their room and no subsequent notice could affect their rights.

In the case of an oral contract, nothing less than actual knowledge of the exemption clause will suffice.

In *McCutcheon* v. *David MacBrayne, Ltd.* [1964] 1 All E.R. 430, M, as agent for the appellant, arranged for the appellant's car to be shipped in the respondents' vessel. The car was lost when the vessel sank, due to the respondents' negligent navigation. The respondents resisted a claim for damages, relying on a clause excluding liability for negligence in their conditions of carriage, which were displayed in the office at which the contract had been made and on board the ship. M had been given a receipted invoice, which he did not read, on which it was stated that goods were carried subject to the conditions specified on the respondents' sailing bills and notices. The respondents usually required a risk note to be signed by which the consignor agreed to be bound by the conditions of carriage, but, due to an oversight, M had not signed such a note. He had, however, done so on previous occasions in respect of similar arrangements, although he had never read the contents of the notes or the conditions displayed in the office and on the ship. The respondents contended that the conditions were imported into the contract by reason of the previous dealings.

Held: The contract was purely oral, and, in the absence of any contractual document, the principle of the 'ticket cases' had no application. The appellant and his agent had no knowledge of the conditions, and accordingly the respondents' liability was not excluded. Previous dealings were only relevant if they proved actual knowledge of the terms, and assent to them, which was not the case here.

The Misrepresentation Act, 1967 has now affected the position in respect of misrepresentations made before a contract. If any agreement contains a provision which would exclude or restrict either the liability to which a party would be subject by reason of any misrepresentation made by him before the making of the contract or any remedy available to another party to the contract by reason of such misrepresentation the provision will have no effect except so far as a court or arbitrator may allow it as being fair and reasonable in the circumstances of the case (s. 3).

(g) The Doctrine of Fundamental Obligation

Attempts have been made by the courts to restrict the effect of exemption clauses by means of the rule of interpretation that a written contract will be construed strongly against the person who drew it up, and by strict application of the doctrine of privity of contract (see, for example, *Midland Silicones, Ltd.* v. *Scruttons, Ltd.*, *post*, p. 58). A third, and more effective, method is by the doctrine of the *fundamental obligation*. A person can only rely upon an exemption clause if he has carried out the basic obligations imposed by the contract. If the breach is such that he has failed to satisfy the fundamental purpose for which the contract was entered into, so that, in effect, he has not performed the contract at all, he cannot seek the protection of such a term.

This has for many years been the principle underlying the rule in the case of carriage of goods by sea that deviation from an appointed course will terminate the liability of the marine insurer or cargo owner. In recent years this principle has been applied much more widely.

In *Karsales (Harrow), Ltd.* v. *Wallis* [1956] 2 All E.R. 866, the defendant agreed to buy a Buick car on hire-purchase, having inspected it and found it to be in good condition. The defendant entered into a contract which contained a term that 'No condition or warranty that the vehicle is roadworthy or as to its age, condition or fitness for any purpose is given by the owner or implied herein.' The vendor left the car outside the defendant's premises, but on inspection it proved to have several parts missing or broken and to be completely incapable of self-propulsion. The defendant refused to accept it or to pay the hire-purchase installments.

Held: The defendant was entitled to refuse to accept what was in effect, not a car at all. The plaintiffs, to whom the rights under the contract had been assigned, were not entitled to rely on the exemption clause to avoid performing the fundamental obligation imposed by the contract.

In *Charterhouse Credit Co., Ltd.* v. *Tolly* [1963] 2 All E.R. 432, the defendant obtained on hire-purchase a car which proved to have a seriously defective back axle. He decided to have the car repaired, but before he was able to do so he became ill, and was unable to pay the instalments. The owners re-possessed the car and sued for damages. The defendant counterclaimed on the grounds that the car was unroadworthy, and the plaintiffs pleaded an exemption clause.

Held: The defect in the back axle made the car completely unroadworthy so that it constituted a breach of the fundamental obligation imposed by the contract. The fact that the defendant had chosen not to repudiate but to affirm the contract did not entitle the plaintiffs to rely on the exemption clause, as they had lost their right to do so by their breach of the fundamental obligation.

The doctrine will not normally apply where the breach is not deliberate.

In *Hollins* v. *J. Davy, Ltd.* [1963] 1 Q.B. 844, the plaintiff garaged his car on the defendants' premises. The defendants handed over the car to a fraudulent person who told them he was authorised by the plaintiff to collect it. The defendants relied on a term of the contract excluding liability for loss or misdelivery of any vehicle in their hands. It was held that they were entitled to rely on this clause as the misdelivery was merely a negligent performance of the contract and not a breach of a fundamental obligation.

But a *deliberate* misdelivery may constitute such a breach.

In *Sze Hai Tong Bank, Ltd.* v. *Rambler Cycle Co., Ltd.* [1959] A.C. 576, shipowners contracted to carry the defendants' goods to Singapore, undertaking to deliver the goods only on the production of the bill of lading and only to the persons entitled under it. They delivered the goods to a person who was not entitled to receive them, without production of the bill of lading, and relied on a comprehensive exemption clause to avoid liability. It was held that their conduct had constituted a deliberate disregard of one of the fundamental obligations of the contract, so that the exemption clause did not protect them from liability.

And the House of Lords has decided that it is a question of construction of the contract whether an exemption clause can excuse a fundamental breach.

In *Swisse Atlantique Societe d'Armement Maritime S.A.* v. *N.V. Rotterdamsche Kolen Centrale* [1966] 2 All E.R. 61, the respondents agreed, by a charter party made in December 1956, to charter a vessel from the appellants for a voyage from the U.S.A. to a port in Europe and succeeding voyages for two years. The ship had to be loaded and unloaded at a specified rate and if delay was caused which was not due to reasons beyond the control of the respondents demurrage was payable at the rate of $1,000 per day. In September 1957 the appellants regarded themselves as entitled to treat the charter party as at an end owing to the respondents delays in loading and discharging the ship. This was not accepted by the respondents but in October 1957 the parties agreed that without prejudice to their dispute they would continue to carry out the charter party. The appellants claimed that if the delays were such as to put an end to the charter party the demurrage provisions did not apply and they were entitled to recover the full loss they had suffered owing to the ship not having made as many voyages as she might have done.

Held: Since the appellants had elected in October 1957 to affirm the charter party they were bound by the demurrage provisions which were for payment of agreed damages. The principle that if there is a breach of a fundamental obligation an injured party can ignore an excluding term, is a rule of construction and not a rule of law. It is, therefore, subject to the intention of the parties.

§ 7. *Capacity to Contract*

Certain persons are by law incapable, wholly or in part, of binding themselves by a promise, or enforcing a promise made to them. The main classes of persons so affected are as follows:

(a) Aliens

An alien has full contractual capacity, except that he cannot acquire property in a British ship (Merchant Shipping Act, 1894, s. 1). On the outbreak of war, however, contracts already made with an alien enemy are suspended during the continuance of hostilities. The rights under them are not annulled, but revive and can be enforced upon the conclusion of peace. This rule of law is subject to the exception that if the continuance of the contract is contrary to public policy, the contract is dissolved *in toto* – an exception so important that the majority of cases fall within the ambit of the exception rather than within that of the rule itself.

The test of a person being an alien enemy is not his nationality, but the place in which he resides or carries on business (*Porter* v. *Freuden-*

berg [1915] 1 K.B. 857), and a person voluntarily resident or carrying on business in an enemy country, or in enemy-occupied territory, is an alien enemy, even if he is a neutral or a British subject.

During hostilities contracts cannot be entered into with alien enemies without a licence from the Crown (*The Hoop* (1799) 1 C. Rob. 196). An alien enemy in this country may not, unless here by licence or under crown protection, enter into contracts and has no power to sue for or exercise any property right during the subsistence of his enemy status, but he is not precluded from defending an action brought against him or in connection therewith.

Foreign states and sovereigns are not subject to the jurisdiction of the courts of this country, unless they choose to submit themselves to it (*Mighel* v. *Sultan of Johore* [1894] 1 Q.B. 149). They can enforce contracts but contracts cannot be enforced against them, unless they waive their immunity. Members of the diplomatic staff of foreign missions have a similar immunity in respect of contracts entered into by them, unless these arise out of professional or business activities outside their official functions; and members of the administrative, technical and service staff enjoy immunity for official acts, but are liable on contracts entered into outside the course of their duties (Diplomatic Privileges Act, 1964). Certain international organisations and the officers thereof are also protected.

(b) Infants

An infant is a person who has not yet attained the age of eighteen. The effect of contracts made by him during infancy varies according to whether the contract is:

(1) a contract for necessaries;

(2) a beneficial contract service;

(3) a continuous, or voidable, contract;

(4) a contract declared void by the Infants Relief Act, 1874;

(5) a contract not falling within any of the above categories.

(1) *Contracts for Necessaries*

These are absolutely binding on an infant, and it is essential, therefore, to consider what contracts fall within the description. In *Peters* v. *Fleming* (1840) 9 L.J. Ex. 81, Parke, B., said:

'The true rule I take to be this, that all such articles as are purely ornamental are not necessary, and are to be rejected, because they cannot be requisite for anyone; and for such matters, therefore, an infant cannot be made responsible. But if they are not strictly of this description, then the question arises whether they were bought for the necessary use of the party *in order to support himself properly in the degree, state and station of life in which he moved*; if they were, for such articles the infant may be responsible.'

By s. 2 of the Sale of Goods Act, 1893, 'necessaries' are defined as such goods as are *suitable to the infant's condition in life*, and to his *actual requirements at the time of sale and delivery*. Although most of the decided cases have related to a sale of goods, the term 'necessaries' is not restricted to such transactions, but covers work done and services rendered.

The court will consider in the first place whether the goods or services may be regarded as necessaries in any circumstances; if it decides in the affirmative, it is then a question of fact whether the goods or services constitute necessaries in the particular case, for it is the station in life of the infant that has to be considered, and what would be necessaries in one case, would not be in another. In any event, if an infant *is* held liable he is not bound to pay the *contractual* price of the goods or services if the court decides that it is an unreasonable one. He is only required to pay a reasonable price (Sale of Goods Act, 1893, s. 2).

The following have been held to be necessaries in the particular circumstances of each case:

A racing bicycle (*Clyde Cycle Co.* v. *Hargreaves* (1898) 78 L.T. 296).
A servant's livery (*Hands* v. *Slaney* (1799) 8 T.R. 578).
Horse exercises, when ordered by a doctor (*Hart* v. *Prater* (1837) 1 Jur. 623).

On the other hand, the following have been held not to be necessaries:

A silver-gilt goblet (*Ryder* v. *Wombwell* (1868) 38 L.J. Ex. 8).
Eleven fancy waistcoats (*Nash* v. *Inman* [1908] 2 K.B. 1).
Flying lessons for a solicitor's articled clerk (*Hamilton* v. *Bennett* (1930) 74 S.J. 122).

Contracts for an infant's education come within the category of necessaries (*Roberts* v. *Gray* [1913] 1 K.B. 520).

(2) *Beneficial Contracts of Service*

An infant is bound by a contract of apprenticeship or service provided that, on the whole, it is for his benefit (*De Francesco* v. *Barnum* (1890) 45 Ch. D. 430). If the contract is substantially for the infant's benefit, but contains onerous stipulations, *e.g.*, provisions involving undue restraint of trade, the court may grant relief from these provisions and permit the remainder of the contract to stand (*Bromley* v. *Smith* [1909] 2 K.B. 235).

If an infant carries on a trade, he cannot be sued on contracts made by him during his minority. In *Mercantile Union Guarantee Corporation, Ltd.* v. *Ball* [1937] 2 K.B. 498, for example, an infant haulage contractor was held not to be liable on a hire-purchase contract for a lorry acquired for use in his business.

An infant can be made bankrupt in respect of an enforceable

debt (*Re a Debtor (No. 564 of 1949)* [1950] Ch. 282); but if he is adjudicated bankrupt on an unenforceable debt, because the fact of infancy is not disclosed, the court has a discretion to set the order aside, which it will normally exercise in the infant's favour, unless there are also other legally enforceable debts on which an order could have been made (*Re Davenport* [1963] 2 All E.R. 850).

(3) *Continuous, or Voidable, Contracts*

Under this head are classed certain contracts which are binding on an infant unless and until he repudiates them, either during infancy or within a reasonable time of attaining full age. In the latter case, repudiation must take place within a reasonable time, and he will be deemed to have affirmed the contract if he does any act in relation thereto after coming of age; rescission is not then possible.

Continuous contracts, that is to say, contracts which confer some rights of a continuous nature, include relationships arising out of:

(i) membership of a limited company;

(ii) membership of a firm;

(iii) tenancy agreements.

There is nothing illegal in an infant holding shares in a company (*Lumsden's Case* (1868) L.R. 4 Ch. 31), but if the shares are not fully paid up the infant will be able to avoid liability for calls made on him by repudiating his membership either during his minority or within a reasonable time of reaching full age. Although the contract can be rescinded, the money paid to the company by the infant cannot be recovered unless there has been a total failure of consideration, *i.e.*, the shares were valueless during the time they were held. The fact that no dividends were paid will not be sufficient proof of absence of value (*Steinberg* v. *Scala (Leeds), Ltd.* [1923] 2 Ch. 452).

An infant may also be a partner in a firm and, while he cannot during his minority be sued for the firm's debts, he is bound by the partnership accounts as between himself and his co-partners. If he repudiates his membership upon coming of age, he is only entitled to his share of the partnership fund as then ascertained. In the absence of rescission, he will be regarded as a partner in the ordinary way and will be liable for debts accruing after attaining his majority (*Goode* v. *Harrison* (1821) 5 B. & Ald. 159).

Although at common law a lease granted to an infant was voidable at his option, s. 1 (6) of the Law of Property Act, 1925, now provides that an infant is not capable of acquiring or holding any legal interest in land. A lease to an infant will operate as an equitable interest which he has the power to avoid in the same way as other continuous contracts, but he will be liable for rent accrued during his occupation, and similarly for rent accrued after he has attained his majority, if he does not repudiate the contract within a reasonable time of coming of age (*Davies* v. *Beynon-Harris* (1931) 47 T.L.R. 424).

(4) *Contracts declared Void by the Infants Relief Act, 1874*

Section 1 of the Infants Relief Act, 1874, provides that all contracts, whether by specialty or by simple contract, entered into by infants–

  (i) for the repayment of money lent or to be lent, or

 (ii) for goods supplied or to be supplied (other than contracts for necessaries), and

(iii) all accounts stated with infants,

shall be *absolutely void*.

Notwithstanding the fact that the Act declares these contracts to be 'absolutely void,' the other party is bound by such a contract and the infant may sue him. Further, although as a rule property received under a void contract may not be retained, in an infant's contract which is void property may be recovered only if there has been a total failure of consideration; so that, where a contract with an infant has been wholly or partly performed, and he has paid any money in regard thereto, he will be precluded from bringing an action for the recovery of the amount paid.

In *Valentini* v. *Canali* (1889) 24 Q.B.D. 166, an infant had rented a house and had purchased certain furniture already in it, for which he had partly paid. He entered into occupation, but subsequently repudiated the contract. It was held that although he was entitled to rescind, he could not recover the amount paid for the furniture in view of his use and enjoyment of the goods during his occupation of the premises.

In *Pearce* v. *Brain* [1929] 2 K.B. 310, an infant exchanged a motor-cycle for a motor car but, owing to defects in the car, brought an action to have the transaction set aside as being void under the Infants Relief Act, 1874. The court decided that, as the infant had used the car and enjoyed the benefit of the contract, the transaction could not be set aside, and the motor-cycle could not be restored to him.

(5) *Other Contracts*

Any contract not falling within any of the above categories, *e.g.*, a contract to marry, is unenforceable against an infant at any time, even when he has become an adult.

At common law, although a non-continuous contract, other than a contract for necessaries, was not binding upon an infant, he could bind himself on coming of age by expressly ratifying the contract. The Infants Relief Act, 1874, s. 2, now provides:

No action shall be brought wherewith to charge any person upon any promise made after full age to pay any debt contracted during infancy, or upon any ratification made after full age of any promise or contract made during infancy, whether there shall or shall not be any new consideration for such promise or ratification after full age.

Ratification of a non-continuous contract is ineffective even if made for a fresh consideration. Thus, if an infant had borrowed money, and on coming of age promised to repay it in consideration of a further advance being made to him, the promise would be ineffective; and similarly where, having while an infant promised to marry, he affirmed the promise on coming of age. But if on coming of age he makes a new contract, and not merely an affirmation of the old one, for a fresh consideration, the new contract will be binding; so that where, for example, an infant had promised to marry without agreeing a date and after coming of age the date were to be agreed, this might amount to a new promise, namely to marry on a particular day, and if so would be enforceable (*Ditcham* v. *Worrall* (1880) 5 C.P.D. 410).

An infant is not liable on a negotiable instrument, *e.g.*, a cheque, even if it has been given in payment for necessaries (*Williams* v. *Harrison* (1691) Carth. 160). Nor can the guarantor of a loan to an infant be made liable on the guarantee where the fact of the infancy is known to all parties, since there is no debt in law due from the infant as the principal debtor (*Coutts & Co.* v. *Browne-Lecky* [1947] K.B. 104).

(6) *Betting and Loans (Infants) Act, 1892*

Under this Act, it is a punishable offence to invite an infant to borrow money or to enter into betting transactions. Should any circular relating to transactions coming within the provisions of the Act be sent to any person at any university, college, school or other place of education, presumption of the infancy of such person attaches unless the sender proves that he had reasonable ground for a contrary belief.

(7) *Torts*

An infant is generally liable for his torts, unless the tort is directly connected with a contract, so that the action is, in effect, an indirect way of enforcing the contract (*Jennings* v. *Rundall* (1799) 8 T.R. 335). But if it can be shown that, although connected with a contract, the plaintiff's claim is *in substance* a claim *ex delicto* (*i.e.*, arising out of tort), the action is maintainable.

In *Fawcett* v. *Smethurst* (1914) 84 L.J. K.B. 473, an infant hired a car to fetch his luggage from the railway station. He then decided to drive further and damaged the car in an accident.
Held: He was not liable to the owner in tort for the accident, as he had done no more than drive the car, which was the action contemplated by the contract.
In *Ballett* v. *Mingay* [1943] K.B. 281, an infant borrowed an amplifier and microphone, and failed to return them on demand, having lent them to a third party. The infant was held to be liable in tort, as his action in parting with the possession of the articles was outside the terms of the contract.

If a contract is void under the Infants Relief Act, 1874, an infant is not estopped from relying on the statute by the fact that he has falsely represented himself to be of full age, and no action will lie for the tort of deceit (*Leslie* v. *Sheill* [1914] 3 K.B. 607). But if an infant fraudulently obtains goods, and they are still in his possession, he may be compelled to restore them under the equitable doctrine of restitution (*Lemprière* v. *Lange* (1879) 12 Ch. D. 675). The doctrine only applies, however, where fraud is proved (*Cowern* v. *Nield* [1912] 2 K.B. 419), and does not extend to cases where the infant has parted with possession of the goods, or where he has obtained money, unless the actual notes or coins can be identified (*Leslie* v. *Sheill, supra*).

(c) Persons of Unsound Mind and Drunken Persons

The contracts of persons of unsound mind are voidable, but not void. If the other party was unaware of the insanity the contract will hold good. A defendant who seeks to avoid a contract on the ground of his insanity must plead and prove not merely his incapacity, but also the plaintiff's knowledge of that fact (*Imperial Loan Co.* v. *Stone* [1892] 1 Q.B. 599).

A contract is capable of being made or ratified by a person of unsound mind during a lucid interval.

Any contract made by a person while he is completely intoxicated, so as to be incapable of appreciating the effect of an agreement, may be avoided by him provided the other person knew of his condition (*Gore* v. *Gibson* (1845) 13 M. & W. 623). If he does not avoid it the contract will remain good (*Matthews* v. *Baxter* (1873) L.R. 8 Ex. 132).

Where necessaries are sold and delivered to a person who by reason of mental incapacity or drunkenness is incompetent to contract, he must pay a reasonable price therefor (Sale of Goods Act, 1893, s. 2).

(d) Corporations

A corporation is *a legal person*, albeit an artificial one, with a legal existence distinct from the people who are members of it. As such it can both sue and be sued and it may be prosecuted and punished for those criminal offences which it is capable of committing.

Corporations may be created:

(1) by charter granted by the Crown, *e.g.*, the Hudson's Bay Company;

(2) by special Act of Parliament, *e.g.*, water companies and nationalised undertakings such as the National Coal Board;

(3) by registration under the Companies Act, 1948, and its predecessors; or

(4) by registration under certain other statutes, *e.g.*, the Industrial and Provident Societies Act, 1965, and the Building Societies Act, 1962

The contractual capacity of a corporation is governed by the method of its creation. A chartered company has all the contractual powers of an ordinary individual (*Baroness Wenlock* v. *River Dee Co.* (1887) 36 Ch. D. 674), although the Crown may forfeit the charter if it exceeds the powers set out therein. A statutory corporation, on the other hand, can only enter into such contracts as it is expressly, or by necessary implication, empowered to make by the statute creating it (*Attorney-General* v. *Great Eastern Railway Co.* (1880) 5 A.C. 473); while a company incorporated under the Companies Acts can only contract within the limits expressly or impliedly laid down by its memorandum of association (*Ashbury Railway Carriage and Iron Co.* v. *Riche* (1875) L.R. 7 H.L. 653).

Any contract purporting to be made by a corporation which is not within its powers or reasonably incidental to them is *ultra vires* (*i.e.*, beyond its powers) and void.

(e) Married Women

Although formerly subject to certain legal disabilities, a married woman may now contract and incur liabilities in exactly the same way as other persons.

§ 8. *Genuineness of Consent*

It may happen that in an apparent contract, valid in all other essentials, the consent to the agreement may have been so given or obtained that it did not express the true intention of the consenting party.

This may arise from mistake, misrepresentation, fraud, duress, or undue influence.

(a) Mistake

Mistake may be either a mistake of fact or a mistake of law.

(1) *Mistake of Fact*

For a mistake of fact to have any effect upon the contract it must be so fundamental to the contract that the parties are not in true agreement. Where such a mistake exists it nullifies or negatives the apparent consent and makes the contract absolutely void and of no legal consequence whatever. A mistake of this kind may be made by one party or by both. A mistake which is not so fundamental as to negative the consent does not affect the validity of the contract (*Bell* v. *Lever Bros., Ltd.* [1932] A.C. 161).

A mistake of fact invalidates the contract in the following cases:

(i) *Mistake as to identity of parties*

Where there is a mistake in the mind of one party as to the identity of the person with whom he is contracting, the contract is void if the identity of the other party is material to the contract and the mistake is known to, or induced by the fraud of, that other person.

In *Boulton* v. *Jones* (1857) 2 H. & N. 564, Jones ordered goods from Brocklehurst, and Boulton, who had taken over the business of Brocklehurst, supplied them without giving notice that the business had changed hands. Jones had a set-off against Brocklehurst, and upon learning that the goods had not come from him, he refused to pay for them.

Held: Boulton was unable to recover, as he could not show that there was a contract with himself.

In *Cundy* v. *Lindsay* (1878) 3 App. Cas. 459, Blenkarn offered by letter to buy goods from the plaintiffs, signing the letter in such a way that the name appeared to be 'Blenkiron & Co.,' a reputable firm carrying on business in the same street as that from which Blenkarn wrote. The plaintiffs, believing they were contracting with Blenkiron & Co., supplied the goods to Blenkarn on credit, and Blenkarn immediately resold them to the defendant. The plaintiffs sought to recover the goods from the defendant.

Held: The plaintiffs were entitled to recover the goods, as the original contract was void for mistake, and therefore no title could pass to the defendant.

The assumption of a false name may have the effect of so misleading a person as to induce him to contract with a person with whom he would not otherwise have contracted.

In *Sowler* v. *Potter* [1940] 1 K.B. 271, the defendant, who had been convicted of committing disorderly conduct in a café, changed her name by deed poll and obtained a lease of premises for use as a restaurant from the plaintiff who was unaware of her true identity. It was held that the contract was void.

Where, however, the seller is prepared to contract with anyone, so that the identity of the purchaser is immaterial, a mistake as to the purchaser's identity, although fraudulently induced, will not make the contract completely void.

In *Phillips* v. *Brooks* [1919] 2 K.B. 243, a jeweller sold a ring to a purchaser and accepted his cheque in payment upon the false representation that he was Sir George Bullough, in whose name the cheque was signed. The ring was pawned to the defendant, and the jeweller sued for its recovery, the cheque having been dishonoured.

Held: As the jeweller would have been willing to sell the ring to any other person, the mistake did not render the contract void *ab initio*. Although the contract was voidable for fraudulent misrepresentation, the purchaser was able to pass a good title to the defendant, as the contract had not by that time been avoided, and so the plaintiff was not entitled to recover the ring.

In *Lewis* v. *Averay* [1971] 3 All E.R. 907, the plaintiff advertised his car for sale. A rogue presented himself as Richard Greene, the well-known film actor, and offered a cheque. The plaintiff asked for proof of identity and the rogue produced a pass to Pinewood studios with a photograph of himself and an official seal. The plaintiff then let him have the car but the cheque was subsequently dishonoured.

Before this occurred the rogue had resold the car to the defendant who bought it in good faith.

Held: the contract between the plaintiff and the rogue was voidable for misrepresentation but had not been avoided at the time when the defendant bought and so he had a good title to the car and was entitled to keep it.

The contract was voidable and not void because there was a presumption that the seller was dealing with the person physically present before him even though the purchaser assumed the identity of another person.

(ii) *Mistake as to identity or existence of subject matter*

Where a mistake is made by one party as to the quality or quantity of the subject-matter of the contract, the maxim *caveat emptor* (let the buyer take care) applies, and the remedy (if any) of the injured party will be an action for misrepresentation or for breach of any condition or warranty that may have been broken. Similarly, where a common mistake is made by both parties as to an attribute which merely affects the value of the subject-matter, this does not invalidate the contract.

In *Leaf* v. *International Galleries* [1950] 2 K.B. 86, the plaintiff bought from the defendants a picture which they both mistakenly believed to have been painted by Constable. As a result of this mistake the plaintiff paid a price much in excess of the true value of the picture.

Held: The contract was voidable for misrepresentation, but the mistake as to the value of the picture did not make the contract void *ab initio.*

But where a mistake, common to both parties, is made as to the very *existence* of some state of facts which forms the whole basis of the contract, the contract is void.

In *Cooper* v. *Phibbs* (1867) L.R. 2 H.L. 149, one party purported to grant a lease of property to a person to whom in fact it already belonged, although both believed that it belonged to the lessor. This was a state of fact which formed the whole foundation of the contract, which was accordingly held to be void.

This rule has received statutory recognition where the mistake relates to the existence of specific goods. By s. 6 of the Sale of Goods Act, 1893, where there is a contract for the sale of specific goods, and the goods without the knowledge of the seller have perished at the time when the contract was made, the contract is void.

Similarly, where there is a genuine mistake by both parties as to the *identity* of the subject-matter of the contract, that is, where one party intends to contract with regard to one thing and the other party intends to do so with regard to some other thing, there is no contract.

In *Raffles* v. *Wichelhaus* (1864) 2 H. & C. 906, the defendant agreed to buy goods of the plaintiff to arrive '*ex Peerless* from Bombay.' There were two ships of this name sailing from Bombay, but the defendant meant that which arrived in October, and the plaintiff meant that which arrived in December.

Held: There was no valid contract between the parties.

(iii) *Mistake as to a term of the contract*

A mistake as to a term of the contract does not generally affect the validity of the contract.

'Where there has been no misrepresentation, and where there is no ambiguity in the terms of the contract, the defendant cannot be allowed to evade the performance of it by the simple statement that he has made a mistake. Were such to

be the law, the performance of a contract could seldom be enforced upon an unwilling party who was also unscrupulous' (*per* Baggalay, L. J., in *Tamplin* v. *James*
(1880) 15 Ch. D. 215).

Where, however, the fact that one party is mistaken as to a term of
the contract is *known* to the other party, and the latter does not
correct it, the court will not enforce the contract.

In *Hartog* v. *Colin and Shields* [1939] 3 All E.R. 566, an offer was accepted to
sell hare skins at a certain price per pound. The preliminary negotiations had been
carried out on the understanding that the skins would be sold at a fixed price per
piece, and it was a trade custom to fix the price by reference to a piece.
Held: The purchaser must have known the mistake made by the sellers, and
accordingly could not enforce the contract against the sellers.
In *Webster* v. *Cecil* (1861) 30 Beav. 62, C wrote to W offering to sell property
for £1,250. W knew that this was an error and that C meant to offer it for £2,250.
W accepted the offer but the court refused to grant a decree of specific performance.

A mistake as to a term of the contract must be distinguished from a
mistake as to some factor influencing the making of the contract, but
not forming an actual term thereof (see *ante*, § 6 (b)). In the latter
case the mistake, even if known to the other party, does not invalidate
the contract.

In *Smith* v. *Hughes* (1871) L.R. 6 Q.B. 597, a purchaser agreed to buy oats,
believing that they were old oats, when in fact they were new oats. His mistake
was known to the vendor, who kept silent. It was held that although the mistake
induced the contract, it was not a mistake as to a term of the contract, and therefore did not invalidate the contract. Had the purchaser thought that the oats were
being sold to him *as* old oats, and had the vendor realised this mistake but kept
silent, the contract would have been void.

(iv) *Mistake as to the nature of a written document*
When a person is induced to sign a contract in the mistaken belief
that it is a document of an entirely different kind from that which it in
fact is, he can claim that his mind did not go with his pen (*non est
factum*) and he is not bound by the contract.

The scope of the plea of *non est factum* was defined by the House
of Lords in *Saunders* v. *Anglia Building Society* (also reported under
the name of *Gallie* v. *Lee*) [1970] 3 All E.R. 961).

In *Saunders* v. *Anglia Building Society* a widow aged 78 signed a document
which she understood to be a deed of gift conveying her house to her nephew.
In fact the document was in form a conveyance of the house to L for £3,000
(which the widow did not receive). She signed the document without reading it,
her spectacles being broken at the time.
L mortgaged the house to a building society (producing the conveyance for
this purpose), but did not keep up the payments. The widow claimed *non est
factum* as against the building society (which claimed the house under the
mortgage).
Held: the widow's plea failed. A person claiming *non est factum* must prove
that he was not negligent and, generally, that he found out the general effect of
the document signed.

For the plea to succeed there must be a fundamental difference between the document signed and what the signer thought it to be but the old distinction between the character of the document and its contents was no longer valid.

The earlier cases of *Carlisle and Cumberland Banking Co.* v. *Bragg and Howatson* v. *Webb* were overruled by this decision.

(v) *Mistake in expressing contract*

Where, owing to a *common* mistake, a written contract does not properly express the real intentions of the parties to it, the contract is not enforceable because it does not embody their real agreement; but equity may allow *rectification* of the instrument so as to express their real intention and enforce it as rectified. This will only be done, however, where:

(*a*) the parties were completely agreed on the terms of the contract;

(*b*) the parties intended that the exact terms of the contract should be reduced to writing, and this intention continued unchanged up to the time it was reduced to writing;

(*c*) the mistake is a purely literal one made in expressing the agreement in writing;

(*d*) there is clear evidence of the real intention of the parties, and of a mistake common to both parties.

A *unilateral* mistake may also enable the party who has made the mistake to have the contract rectified, if he proves beyond reasonable doubt that he believed a particular term to be included in the contract and that the other party, with knowledge of this belief, had omitted or varied the term in reducing the contract to writing.

In *A. Roberts & Co., Ltd.* v. *Leicestershire County Council* [1961] Ch. 555, a contractor tendered for a contract for the building of a school, completion to be in eighteen months. The council accepted the tender, but when the contract was drawn up the period stipulated for completion was thirty months. The contractor executed the contract without noticing the alteration, and the council, who knew he was unaware of the alteration, did nothing to disillusion him The contractor would have stipulated for a higher price in the case of a tender based on a thirty months' period.

Held: The contractor was entitled to have the contract rectified by the substitution of eighteen months for the thirty months' period.

(2) *Mistake of Law*

A mistake of law will not affect the validity of a contract at all, by virtue of the rule *ignorantia juris neminem excusat* (ignorance of the law excuses no-one).

(3) *Money Paid under Mistake*

Although, on the above principle, money paid under a mistake of *law* cannot as a rule be recovered, it may be recovered where it would be inequitable that the party receiving the money should retain it; for instance:

(i) If the payee or his agent knew of or induced the payer's mistake of law, and took advantage of it, the payer may recover. Where an insurance agent said that a policy 'would be all right' when he knew that the proposer had no insurable interest in the life concerned, the company had to return the premiums (*British Workmen's Assurance Co.* v. *Cunliffe* (1902) 18 T.L.R. 425); but not where the insurance agent misrepresented the law, both he and the proposer being equally ignorant of the mistake (*Harse* v. *Pearl Life Assurance Co.* [1904] 1 K.B. 558).

(ii) Money paid under a mistake of law to an officer of the court, such as a trustee in bankruptcy, may be recovered in equity (*Re Condon, ex parte James* (1874) 9 Ch. App. 609). This is known as the 'high-minded principle.'

(iii) Money paid under protest to avoid a threat of seizure of goods may be recovered if it transpires that there was no right to seize the goods (*Maskell* v. *Horner* [1915] 3 K.B. 112).

(iv) Money paid under mistake to a person who is in a fiduciary relationship with the payer may be recovered.

Misapprehension as to the effect of a contract is a mistake of law (*Ord* v. *Ord* [1923] 2 K.B. 432), but a mistake as to a particular right such as a person's title to land is a mistake of fact (*Cooper* v. *Phibbs*, *ante*, p. 38).

Money paid under a fundamental mistake of *fact* may be recovered if the payer believed he was legally liable to pay.

In *Kelly* v. *Solari* (1841) 9 M. & W. 54, the defendant's husband had been insured with the plaintiff, but had not paid the last premium, and the insurance had therefore lapsed. On her husband's death, the defendant claimed the insurance money, and the plaintiff, forgetting the lapse, paid it to her. It was held that the plaintiff could recover the money.

In *Morgan* v. *Ashcroft* [1938] 1 K.B. 49, a bookmaker through a mistake on the part of his clerk overpaid a client the amount due to him for betting winnings. On discovering the mistake the bookmaker sought to recover the amount overpaid as money paid under a mistake of fact. It was held that since there would have been no legal liability to make the payment, even had the true facts been as believed, the bookmaker was not entitled to recover.

The latter decision may, however, be explained on the grounds that the mistake was not fundamental. It seems that money paid under a mistake of fact may be recovered if the court considers the mistake to be sufficiently serious, and if its effect was to impose upon the payer a *moral*, although not a legal, obligation to pay.

In *Larner* v. *London County Council* [1949] 2 K.B. 683, an employer voluntarily made up the Army pay of an employee to an amount equal to his civil salary but overpaid him owing to his ignorance of increases in the employee's service pay. Had the facts been as supposed, the employer would have been only morally, not legally, bound to make the payment, but the mistake was held to be sufficient to enable the employer to recover the amount of the overpayment.

A mistake of fact need not be mutual; and there need not be fraud or misrepresentation on the part of the person receiving the money.

On the other hand there are situations where money paid under a mistake of fact cannot be recovered. Thus, money paid to an agent who has actually paid it over to his principal cannot be reclaimed; or otherwise on the grounds of estoppel or breach of duty.

(b) Misrepresentation

The importance of distinguishing between a representation and a term of a contract has already been noted (*ante*, § 6 (b)). A representation is a statement of fact made by one person in order to induce another person to enter into a contract. If the statement is untrue, but the person making it believes it to be true, it is known as an *innocent misrepresentation*; if it is untrue to the knowledge of the person making it, it is a *fraudulent misrepresentation*.

(1) *Essentials of Misrepresentation*

A person who wishes to show that he was induced to enter into a contract by a misrepresentation, whether innocent or fraudulent, must prove:

(i) that the representation was a statement of a material fact, not, *e.g.*, a statement of law or an expression of opinion;

(ii) that it was made before or at the time the contract was entered into;

(iii) that it was made to induce the other party to enter into the contract;

(iv) that it did, in fact, induce him to enter into the contract, though it need not have been the only factor which influenced him;

(v) that the statement was untrue.

(2) *Disclosure of Material Facts*

Generally speaking, if one party knows of certain facts which, if disclosed to the other party, might influence him in deciding whether or not to enter into the contract, he is under no obligation to make these known to the other party.

There are, however, certain cases where such disclosure is required, and a failure to disclose material facts in such a case will constitute misrepresentation. This will be the case where an omission results in the statements which are made being rendered untrue or misleading (*Peek* v. *Gurney* (1873) L.R. 6 H.L. 377). Furthermore, if a statement which was true at the time it was made subsequently becomes false before the contract is concluded, there is a duty to correct it, otherwise it will be treated as a misrepresentation.

Complete disclosure is also required in respect of those contracts which are said to be *uberrimae fidei* (of the utmost good faith). The most important of these are:

(i) contracts of insurance (*Seaton* v. *Heath* [1899] 1 Q.B. 782);

(ii) contracts to subscribe for shares in companies (this is now governed by the Companies Act, 1948);

(iii) contracts of family arrangement for the settlement of property (*Gordon* v. *Gordon* (1821) 3 Swan. 400);

(iv) contracts for the sale of land, in which case the vendor is under a duty to disclose any defect in his title.

Contracts of guarantee and partnership are also sometimes described as being contracts *uberrimae fidei*, as there is a duty of disclosure after the contract has been made. They cannot strictly be placed in the same category as those referred to above, however, as there is no duty of disclosure before the contract is entered into.

(3) *Remedies for Misrepresentation*

A person who has been induced to enter into a contract by an innocent misrepresentation made by the other contracting party is entitled to rescind the contract, or, under the Misrepresentation Act, 1967, he may obtain damages unless the other party can show that he believed, up to the time of making the contract, that his representations were true and he had reasonable grounds for believing so. The Court, or an arbitrator, can award damages as an alternative to rescission in a case of innocent misrepresentation where it would be equitable to do so. (S. 2 (2) Misrepresentation Act, 1967). Damages are also recoverable against the person making the representation in the following cases:

(i) Where an agent innocently misrepresents his authority (see Chap. II).

(ii) For omissions from or misrepresentations in a prospectus (Companies Act, 1948, ss. 38, 43).

(iii) If the representation has been incorporated into the contract as a condition or a warranty, or forms the basis of a 'collateral' contract (see *ante*, § 6).

(iv) In the case of a *negligent* misrepresentation, where the relationship between the parties is such as to impose a legal duty to take care in making such statements. Such a duty arises where there is a confidential relationship between the parties, as in the case of solicitor and client and banker and customer (*Woods* v. *Martins Bank, Ltd.* [1959] 1 Q.B. 55), and in other cases where in the ordinary course of business one person seeks information or advice from another in such circumstances that a reasonable man would know that his skill or judgment was being relied on, and the person so asked does not qualify his answer so as to show that he does not accept legal responsibility (*Hedley Byrne & Co., Ltd.* v. *Heller & Partners, Ltd., ante,* p. 23). Thus, a banker who is asked for a reference concerning a customer by a third party must give an honest answer based on the information available to him from his own dealings with the customer, and failure to do so will render him liable in damages to the third party if he gives an inaccurate reference and the third party acts on it to his detriment (*ibid.*).

Rescission of the contract involves the restoration of both parties to the contract to their former positions. The right to rescind is lost:

(*a*) If the party seeking to rescind expressly or impliedly affirms the contract with knowledge of the misrepresentation, *e.g.*, by attempting to sell property received under the contract to a third party.

(*b*) If the parties cannot be restored to their former positions, *e.g.*, where property transferred under the contract has been consumed or substantially altered.

(*c*) If the plaintiff does not act promptly on discovering that the representation was false. Lapse of time is strong evidence of affirmation of the contract, and may preclude the right to rescind even where the plaintiff has acted promptly on discovering that the representation was untrue (*Leaf* v. *International Galleries, ante,* p. 38).

(*d*) If innocent third parties have acquired rights in the subject-matter of the contract for value.

These limits to the right of rescission demonstrate the importance of the distinction between void and voidable contracts. As has been seen, void contracts are completely ineffective, whereas a voidable contract is binding upon both parties once the right of rescission has been lost. This distinction is well illustrated by the cases on mistaken identity (*ante,* pp. 37, 38).

The party seeking to rescind must be willing and able to give up all benefits received under the contract, but is entitled to be indemnified by the defendant in respect of obligations which have been necessarily assumed under the contract (*Whittington* v. *Seale-Hayne* (1900) 82 L.T. 49).

(4) *Fraudulent Misrepresentation*

Fraudulent misrepresentation entitles the injured party not only to rescission but also to damages if he has in fact suffered loss as a result of the misrepresentation. A representation is fraudulent where it is made knowingly or without belief in its truth, or recklessly, careless whether it is true or false. The whole difference between innocent and fraudulent misrepresentation thus lies in the intention with which the mis-statement was made.

In *Derry* v. *Peek* (1889) 14 App. Cas. 337, a company had statutory powers to operate trams by steam power, provided the consent of the Board of Trade was obtained. The directors, believing that such consent was a mere formality, issued a prospectus stating that the company had the right to use steam power. The plaintiff purchased shares in the company relying on this statement. The Board of Trade refused its consent and the company was wound up.

Held: The statement was not fraudulent, as the directors honestly believed it to be true.

The remedies open to a person who has been induced to enter into a contract by a fraudulent misrepresentation are:

(i) to affirm the contract and sue for damages for the tort of deceit;

(ii) to avoid the contract, with or without suing for damages in tort;

(iii) to sue for damages in tort, if he has, by negligence or otherwise, lost his right to rescind.

Where a statement is made as to the character, conduct, credit, ability, trade, or dealings of any person with the intent or purpose of enabling such person to obtain credit, money, or goods, no action can be brought for fraudulent misrepresentation unless the statement is in writing signed by the party to be charged (Statute of Frauds Amendment Act, 1828, s. 6). The signature of an agent is not sufficient (*Banbury* v. *Bank of Montreal* [1918] A.C. 626).

(c) Duress and Undue Influence

Duress and undue influence render a contract voidable at the option of the party injured.

(1) *Duress*

Duress consists in actual or threatened violence, or imprisonment, or threat of criminal proceedings, against the contracting party, his wife, parent, or child. It must be inflicted or threatened by the other party to the contract, or else by one acting with his knowledge and for his advantage.

(2) *Undue Influence*

Undue influence is moral pressure. If certain relations, parental or confidential, exist between the parties, the court will presume that such influence has been exercised, unless it can be shown that the donor or promisor has been placed in such a position as would have enabled him to form an entirely free and unfettered judgment, independent altogether of any sort of control, as where independent legal advice has been obtained with full knowledge of all material facts (*Allcard* v. *Skinner* (1887) 36 Ch. D. 145).

Undue influence is presumed in the case of transactions between parent and child, solicitor and client, guardian and ward, and trustee and beneficiary, for example, but not as between husband and wife (*Howes* v. *Bishop* [1909] 2 K.B. 390), or between an engaged couple (*Zamet* v. *Hyman* [1961] 1 W.L.R. 1442). Where there is no such presumption, undue influence may nevertheless be *proved* to exist and the contract thereby rendered voidable.

§ 9. *Void and Illegal Contracts*

Certain types of contract are expressly declared by statute or common law to be either void or illegal. Although, in either case, the contract is of no legal effect as between the parties, yet the distinction is important in its effect upon collateral transactions. An illegal contract vitiates collateral transactions as well, but a contract which is merely void but not illegal does not.

(a) Contracts Rendered Void or Illegal by Statute

(1) *Gaming and Wagering Contracts*

(i) *Wagering contracts*

Wagering is the staking of something of value upon the ascertainment of the truth concerning some past or future event (*Carlill* v. *Carbolic Smoke Ball Co.* [1893] 1 Q.B. 256). Each party must stand either to win or lose upon the determination of the event. It is not a wagering contract if one party may win but cannot lose, or may lose but cannot win, or if he can neither win nor lose (*Ellesmere* v. *Wallace* [1929] 2 Ch. 1). The stake must be the only interest of the parties in the contract. Therefore, a contract of insurance is not a wagering contract so long as the assured has an insurable interest in the subject-matter of the insurance.

The question whether the parties are interested in something more than the winning or losing of a stake depends upon the substance of the agreement and not its form (*Brogden* v. *Marriott* (1836) 3 Bing. N.C. 88). Contracts made on the Stock Exchange are an example of this. If there is a real intention to take or deliver the stocks dealt in, the contract will be good, but if the agreement relates to differences only, it is in the nature of a wager (*Universal Stock Exchange* v. *Strachan* [1896] A.C. 166).

By s. 18 of the Gaming Act, 1845, all wagers are *void* and no suit may be brought at law or in equity to recover any money or valuable thing alleged to be won upon any wager. Although void, wagering contracts are not illegal, so that collateral transactions are not affected. Moreover, although the loser cannot be sued on the contract, nevertheless, if he chooses to pay the winner, he is not entitled to recover the money, although the payment has been made without consideration, as he is deemed to waive the benefit of the statute by making the payment.

If the loser makes a further promise to pay for a fresh consideration, this promise is also caught by the section, and cannot be enforced.

> In *Hill* v. *Hill* (*William*) (*Park Lane*), *Ltd.* [1949] A.C. 530, the respondent bookmakers, to whom the appellant owed £3,635 12s. 6d. in betting debts, obtained an order from the committee of Tattersalls that the appellant should pay £635 12s. 6d. within fourteen days and the balance by monthly instalments of £100. The appellant failed to comply with the order, but subsequently gave the respondents a post-dated cheque and promised to begin the monthly payments in consideration of the respondents' agreeing to refrain from enforcing the order – which would have involved his being posted as a defaulter and being warned off Newmarket Heath. The cheque was dishonoured, and the instalments were not paid.
>
> *Held:* The payments which the appellant had agreed to make were payments of 'a sum of money alleged to be won upon a wager' within the second limb of s. 18. of the Gaming Act, 1845, and accordingly were not recoverable.

The section further provides that no action can be brought to recover money which has been placed in the hands of a stakeholder to abide the result of a wager. This precludes the winner from recovering the money deposited by the loser, but does not prevent either party from recovering his own stake before it has been paid over by the stakeholder (*Burge* v. *Ashley & Smith, Ltd.* [1900] 1 Q.B. 744).

By the Gaming Act, 1892, any promise, express or implied, to pay a person a sum of money paid by him under or in respect of a wagering contract is null and void, and no action can be brought to recover the money. Thus, if an agent pays bets for his principal, he cannot recover the amount from his employer, although normally an agent has a right of indemnity in respect of money paid by him. But this provision does not prevent a principal from successfully bringing an action against an agent who has placed bets on his behalf and received winnings which he refuses to hand over, as money had and received by him to the use of the principal (*De Mattos* v. *Benjamin* (1894) 63 L.J.Q.B. 248; see *post*, § 14 (e)).

(ii) *Gaming contracts*

A gaming contract is a wager upon the result of a game of chance. Formerly, as well as being void under the above rules, many forms of gaming were also illegal. Under the Gaming Act, 1968 all gaming is now lawful, provided it satisfies the conditions prescribed by the Act. Gaming contracts are, however, still *void* under the Gaming Acts, 1845 and 1892.

Furthermore, by the Gaming Act, 1835, all *securities* given for money lost upon a gaming contract or in repayment of money lent for gaming are deemed to have been given for an *illegal consideration*. This provision, which does not apply to other wagering contracts, is important as regards collateral transactions. If a bill of exchange or promissory note is given in respect of a gaming contract, under the Act of 1835 such security is deemed to have been given for an illegal consideration, and the holder can be called upon to show that value has been given and that he did not know of the illegality. If, however, the wager is not on a game, although the transaction is still void, it is not tainted with illegality, and a bill or note given in payment is not given for an illegal consideration but for no consideration at all; to a holder in due course it is immaterial whether or not he knew the circumstances under which it was given.

(iii) *Loans for purpose of wagering*

Where one person lends money to another for wagering purposes, he may in certain circumstances be able to recover the loan. Where a loan is made to enable the borrower to discharge betting debts already incurred, the loan is recoverable, unless there is a definite agreement that the money will be used only for the purpose of paying off the debts (*Re O'Shea* [1911] 2 K.B. 981). If, however, there is such an agreement, or if the third party himself pays the winner, whether voluntarily or at the request of the loser, the payment falls within the provisions of the Gaming Act, 1892, so that the third party is not entitled to recover the amount paid from the loser (*Tatam* v. *Reeve* [1893] 1 Q.B. 44; *Woolf* v. *Freeman* [1937] 1 All E.R. 178).

If money is lent for the purpose of gaming, it is not recoverable if the gaming is illegal (*M'Kinnell* v. *Robinson* (1838) 3 M. & W. 434). As has been seen, no form of gaming is now illegal *per se*, but if the gaming is to be conducted illegally, the right of recovery will be excluded under this rule.

If the gaming is lawful the position is somewhat uncertain. Money lent for gaming abroad in a country where gaming is lawful is recoverable by an action in this country (*Saxby* v. *Fulton* [1909] 2 K.B. 208). If the lender is paid by cheque payable in England, he is not entitled to sue on the cheque, which would be an illegal security under the Gaming Act, 1835, but he would be able to sue on the loan (*Société Anonyme des Grands Etablissements du Touquet Paris-Plage* v. *Baumgart* (1927) 43 T.L.R. 278). It should follow from these decisions that a loan made for lawful gaming in this country is recoverable, but it was held in *Carlton Hall Club* v. *Laurence* [1929] 2 K.B. 153 that such a loan was void. The correctness of this decision was, however, doubted by the Court of Appeal in *C.H.T., Ltd.* v. *Ward* [1963] 3 All E.R. 835.

In this case the proprietors of a club issued chips on credit to the defendant to be used for the purpose of lawful gaming. The defendant's account was debited with the face value of the chips and sent to her weekly for settlement. If she won she could have the amount credited or be paid cash in exchange for the chips she still had when she finished playing. The proprietors sued to recover money debited to her, alleging that the issue of chips was equivalent to a loan for lawful gaming.

Held: The issuing of chips was not equivalent to the lending of money; the nature of the transaction was that by giving credit the club paid the gambling debts and the defendant promised to repay that sum to the club, so that the defendant's undertaking was unenforceable under the Gaming Act, 1892.

The Court, having considered the cases referred to above, expressed the view that, had the transaction been a loan for the purpose of lawful gaming, the plaintiffs would have been entitled to succeed, and it is likely that this view will will be preferred in the future.

The Gaming Act, 1968 provided that the licensee of premises where lawful gaming takes place may not make a loan or allow credit to enable a person to take part in the game or in respect of losses incurred in the gaming (s. 16). In certain circumstances the licensee may give cash or tokens in exchange for a cheque drawn to enable a person to take part in gaming on licensed premises. Under the 1968 Act such a cheque is enforceable if:

(*a*) it is not post dated;

(*b*) it is exchanged for the equivalent amount of cash or tokens;

(*c*) it is delivered to a bank for payment or collection within two banking days (s. 16).

(2) *Leeman's Act, 1867*

Under this Act, any sale of shares in a joint stock banking company is void, unless the numbers of the shares, as shown in the register of the company, are stated in the contract. The custom of the London Stock Exchange is to ignore this provision, but this custom cannot be upheld, and if the principal was not aware of it he cannot be made liable on a contract not complying with the Act should he repudiate the contract (*Perry* v. *Barnett* (1885) 15 Q.B.D. 388). But if the principal was aware of the custom, then, even though he repudiates the contract, he must indemnify his broker, who takes up the shares to avoid being declared a defaulter (*Seymour* v. *Bridge* (1885) 14 Q.B.D. 460).

(3) *Moneylenders Acts, 1900 and 1927*

Every person whose business is that of moneylending, or who advertises or announces himself as carrying on that business, is a moneylender within the meaning of the Moneylenders Acts, with the following exceptions:

(i) pawnbrokers in respect of business carried on under the Pawnbrokers Acts;

(ii) friendly societies, building societies, and certain other societies and bodies corporate lending money in accordance with special Acts of Parliament;

(iii) banks and insurance companies;

(iv) persons carrying on business not having for its primary object the lending of money;

(v) bodies corporate exempted by the Board of Trade.

A moneylender must not carry on business as such in any name other than his authorised name, or at any place other than his authorised address. He is required to hold a moneylender's certificate and to take out an annual excise licence. If, in entering into any transaction, a moneylender contravenes any of these provisions, the transaction is illegal and void. The moneylender cannot maintain any action to recover the money lent or enforce any security taken by him in the course of such a transaction.

Since, however, the transaction is made illegal for the protection of borrowers, the illegality will not prevent the borrower from obtaining a declaration that the security is void, and the return of his security. Such a declaration may be made subject to equitable terms, *e.g.*, that the plaintiff repays the amount owing to the moneylender (*Lodge* v. *National Union Investment Co., Ltd* [1907] 1 Ch. 300); although it seems now that such terms will only be imposed in exceptional circumstances (*Kasumu* v. *Baba-Egbe* [1956] A.C. 539).

It is illegal to charge compound interest, or to provide for an increase in the rate or amount of interest by reason of the borrower's default, but the moneylender may charge simple interest at a rate not exceeding that chargeable under the contract in respect of any payment in arrear.

Where proceedings are taken by the moneylender for the recovery of money lent or the enforcement of any agreement or security made or taken, the court has power to re-open the transaction where it is satisfied that the transaction is harsh and unconscionable or that the rate of interest charged is excessive. The court will then assess the rate of interest which it considers reasonable in the circumstances, or may vary any agreement made (Moneylenders Act, 1900, s. 1). Should the rate of interest charged by the moneylender exceed 48 per cent. per annum, the court, in the absence of evidence to the contrary, will presume that the rate so charged is excessive, and that the transaction is harsh and unconscionable (*ibid.*, s. 10 (1)).

As to the *form* of moneylenders' contracts, see *ante*, p. 19.

(4) *Restrictive Trade Practices Act, 1956*

(5) *Resale Prices Act, 1964*

The provisions of these Acts are considered in Chap. III, § 2.

(b) Contracts Void or Illegal at Common Law

At common law the following contracts are declared to be either illegal or void as being contrary to public policy.

(1) *Illegal Contracts*

(i) *Agreements to commit an indictable offence or civil wrong*, *e.g.*, to commit an assault (*Allen* v. *Rescous* (1687) 2 Lev. 174). A person cannot take a benefit under a contract or otherwise where that benefit would be secured by the performance of a criminal act. Thus, a murderer (or his estate) cannot participate in the distribution of the estate of his victim. This principle formerly applied to a claim made under a life assurance policy where the assured had committed suicide while sane (*Beresford* v. *Royal Insurance Co.* [1938] 2 All E.R. 602). Suicide ceased to be a criminal offence under the Suicide Act, 1961, but such a claim might still be invalid as being contrary to public policy. It is otherwise where a man commits suicide during temporary insanity (*Horn* v. *Anglo-Australian Co.* (1861) 30 L.J. Ch. 511), subject to the terms of the policy in question.

(ii) *Agreements injurious to the State in its international relations*, *e.g.*, a contract with an alien enemy (*Esposito* v. *Bowden* (1857) 7 E. & B. 763), or a contract to be performed in a foreign country, and illegal by the law of that country, other than a penal or revenue law (*Regazzoni* v. *Sethia* [1958] A.C. 301).

(iii) *Agreements injurious to the public service*, *e.g.*, the assignment of the salary of a public servant (*Wells* v. *Foster* (1841) 8 M. & W. 149), or an agreement that a person should for valuable consideration use his influence with the Government to procure a benefit (*Parkinson* v. *College of Ambulance, Ltd.* [1925] 2 K.B. 1).

(iv) *Agreements to defraud the Revenue* (*Napier* v. *National Business Agency, Ltd.* [1951] 2 All E.R. 264).

(v) *Agreements to pervert the course of justice*, *e.g.*, to compound a felony for a consideration (*Williams* v. *Bayley* (1866) L.R. 1 H.L. 200).

(vi) *Agreements involving maintenance or champerty*. Maintenance is assisting either party to a lawsuit with money or otherwise when the party giving the assistance has not sufficient legal or moral interest in the lawsuit. Champerty is maintenance given upon an agreement to share in the money or property recovered.

(vii) *Agreements of an immoral character*, *i.e.*, agreements for an immoral consideration, or to further an immoral purpose (*Pearce* v. *Brooks* (1866) L.R. 1 Ex. 213).

(2) *Void Contracts*

The following contracts are void, but not illegal:

(i) *Agreements prejudicial to the status of marriage*

A promise by a spouse to marry a third party as and when he (or she) may be in a position to do so is void, but not where the promise has been made after a decree *nisi* for divorce has been pronounced against the promisor, the decree not yet having been made absolute (*Fender* v. *Mildmay* [1937] 3 All E.R. 402). Marriage brokage contracts, whether to procure marriage with a particular person or generally, are void (*Hermann* v. *Charlesworth* [1905] 2 K.B. 123).

(ii) *Agreements to oust the jurisdiction of the courts*

The parties to a contract may agree to have disputes of fact between themselves decided conclusively by a private tribunal, but an agreement to make such a tribunal the final arbiter on questions of law is void (*Lee* v. *Showmen's Guild of Great Britain* [1952] 2 Q.B. 329). An arbitration agreement does not normally constitute an ouster of the court's jurisdiction (see Chap. IX, § 3 (c)).

(iii) *Agreements in restraint of trade*

A contract in restraint of trade is one which restricts, wholly or partially, the right of a person to carry on his trade or profession. Such an agreement is *prima facie* void as being contrary to the public interest. Nevertheless such a contract may be enforced if it can be proved that (1) the restraint is reasonably necessary to protect the interests of the person in whose favour it is imposed, (2) it is not unreasonable as against the person restrained, and (3) it is not contrary to the public interest.

Such agreements are of three main kinds:

(*a*) agreements between the vendor and purchaser of the goodwill of a business;

(*b*) agreements between employer and employee;

(*c*) agreements between manufacturers or traders.

(*a*) A purchaser of a business is entitled to impose such restraints as will reasonably protect him against the vendor's future competition. Such agreements will normally be enforced as the parties are usually 'at arm's length,' and the purchaser is in a position to protect his own interests.

In *Nordenfelt* v. *Maxim-Nordenfelt Gun Co.* [1894] A.C. 535, Nordenfelt, who was a maker of guns and ammunition, sold his business, which was world-wide, to the respondents for a large sum of money, and agreed to cease to carry on the manufacture of guns and ammunition, or any business liable to compete with the business of the company, for a period of twenty-five years. After some years Nordenfelt broke the agreement, and the company sought an injunction to restrain him.

Held: The restraint against trading in guns and ammunition was reasonable and enforceable, but the restraint from carrying on *any* business in competition with the company was wider than was reasonably necessary to protect the proprietary interest of the company, and that part of the agreement was therefore void.

Thus, a general restraint against competing in *any* trade or business will be void, but a contract not to compete in a particular trade or business, even if the restriction is unlimited as to time and space, will be upheld if it is not injurious to the public interest, and if the restraint imposed is necessary to protect the proprietary interest of the purchaser.

In *British Concrete Co., Ltd.* v. *Schelff* [1921] 2 Ch. 563, the plaintiffs carried on business throughout the country as manufacturers of 'B.R.C.' road reinforcements. The defendant carried on a small business selling 'Loop' road reinforcements. The plaintiffs bought the defendant's business, and the defendant covenanted not to compete with them in the manufacture or sale of road reinforcements within ten miles of any of their branches.

Held: The covenant was void, since (1) the plaintiffs were only entitled to protection in the sale of 'Loop' reinforcements, not of road reinforcements generally; and (2) the company was only entitled to protection in relation to the business it had bought, and not to that which it was already carrying on.

(b) The test of reasonableness as applied to restraints imposed by an employer upon his employee is much more stringent than that between vendor and purchaser as, more often than not, the employer is able to dictate his own terms to the employee. An employer will never be entitled to protection from the mere competitive use of personal skill by an ex-employee (*Morris* v. *Saxelby* [1916] 1 A.C. 688). But a covenant will be held reasonable which is no wider in its limits of space and time than is necessary to protect what may be called the property of the employer, *e.g.*, the trade connection, trade secrets or confidential information of the employer, having regard to the nature of the business and the employee's position in it, even if it has the effect of preventing to some extent the future competition of the employee.

Thus, a restraint on a solicitor's clerk that he would not, after leaving the service of the solicitor, act professionally for any person who was or had been within the previous five years a client of the firm was held not to be wider than was reasonably necessary for the protection of the firm's practice (*Lewis* v. *Durnford* (1908) 24 T.L.R. 64). A similar restraint upon a solicitor's clerk that he would not practice as a solicitor within seven miles of the office, without limit of time, has also been held to be valid (*Fitch* v. *Dewes* [1921] 2 A.C. 158).

On the other hand, where a salesman in the credit drapery trade covenanted not to canvass, during the five years following the termination of his employment, any customer who was on his employer's books during the three years up to termination, the Court of Appeal, having considered the salesman's status, held the covenant to be too wide and therefore void (*M. and S. Drapers* v. *Reynolds* [1956] 3 All E.R. 814). But a covenant entered into by a salesman dealing in agricultural products, that he would not for two years after the end of his employment canvass those who were the employer's customers during his employment, was held not to be unenforceable merely because it was unlimited in area and not limited to customers of whom the employee had knowledge or with whom he had contact during his employment, the restraint being reasonably necessary to protect the employer's business (*G.W. Plowman & Son, Ltd.* v. *Ash* [1964] 2 All E.R. 10). In this case the court held that, although the covenant did not mention the type of goods to which it applied, it was nevertheless limited, on its true construction, to goods in which the employer dealt. If an employer carries on more than one business, he cannot enforce a restraint as regards any business other than that in which the employee was actually employed (*Leetham* v. *Johnstone White* [1907] 1 Ch. 322).

The same principles are to be applied where there is a contract between two employers that neither will employ the former employees of the other.

In *Kores Manufacturing Co., Ltd.* v. *Kolok Manufacturing Co., Ltd.* [1959] Ch. 108, two companies carrying on the same type of manufacturing business each agreed to refrain from employing any person who had been employed by the other during the previous five years.

Held: The restraint, which was in any event unreasonable in extent of time, was void as being an attempt to prevent the employees from using their personal skill and knowledge in the service of another employer and not to protect a proprietary interest of the contracting parties.

The court may examine the validity of such contracts between employers at the instance of an employee, although he himself is not a party to the contract (*Eastham* v. *Newcastle United Football Club, Ltd.* [1963] 3 All E.R. 139).

A servant who is wrongfully dismissed from his employment without proper notice, so that he can elect to treat the contract of service entirely at an end, is no longer bound by any covenant in the contract restraining his activities after the termination of his employment (*General Billposting Co.* v. *Atkinson* [1909] A.C. 118).

Quite apart from any express restraint, where an employee acquires information of a confidential nature in the course of his employment, it is an implied term of the contract that he will not disclose such information to third parties or use the information for his own personal benefit, even after the termination of his employment (*Robb* v. *Green* [1895] 2 Q.B. 315, see *post*, p. 96).

(*c*) Most restrictive trading agreements between manufacturers and traders are regulated by the Restrictive Trade Practices Act, 1956, and the Resale Prices Act, 1964 (see Chap. III, § 2). In consequence, the common law rules relating to such agreements are now rarely invoked. But these rules remain of practical importance for two reasons. In the first place, the Acts are concerned only with the interests of the public generally; an agreement approved by the Restrictive Practices Court might still be challenged at common law as being unreasonable in the interests of the parties. Secondly, the Acts do not apply to all such agreements; in particular, agreements appointing a person sole distributor of goods and those whereby a dealer agrees to purchase all his supplies from a single supplier are outside the 1956 Act, although a provision therein for resale price maintenance would be void under the Act of 1964.

At common law the courts have shown themselves unwilling to declare a collective agreement voluntarily entered into by traders to protect their commercial interests to be unreasonable as between the parties themselves, although they will do so where the terms of the agreement are particularly onerous.

In *McEllistrim* v. *Ballymacelligott Co-operative, &c., Society* [1919] A.C. 548, the society manufactured butter and cheese from milk supplied by its members. Members were precluded from selling milk to any other person, and no member could withdraw from the society without cancelling or transferring his shares, for which the consent of the society was required. The arrangement was held to be unreasonable between the parties, as its effect was to impose a life-long embargo upon the freedom of the members to trade.

The enforceability of 'sole supplier' agreements between a petrol company and a garage owner was considered by the House of Lords in *Esso Petroleum Co. Ltd.* v. *Harpers Garage (Stourport) Ltd.* [1967] 1 All E.R. 699. One agreement was for four years five months and this was held to be reasonable and so enforceable. The other agreement was for twenty-one years, and was held to be unenforceable as being too long.

Contracts in restraint of trade require consideration to support them, whether they are under seal or not (*Hitchcock* v. *Coker* (1837) 6 A. & E. 438); in fact, this is a class of contract where the court will require to be satisfied of the adequacy (or at any rate, the reasonableness) of the consideration, particularly as between a vendor and a purchaser. If a person acquires the goodwill of a business, and, to reap the benefit of his bargain, requires the vendor to enter into a covenant not to carry on a similar business within a specified time or area, such protection should only be afforded where an adequate price has been paid for the goodwill.

(c) The Effect of Illegality

The effect of illegality upon contracts is as follows:

(1) If the object of the contract is to perform an illegal act, the contract is void, though the parties to it may not have known that the act was illegal (*Waugh* v. *Morris* (1873) L.R. 8 Q.B. 202).

If the parties are *in pari delicto* (equally at fault) neither can bring an action on the contract (*Parkinson* v. *College of Ambulance, Ltd., ante*, p. 52). In three cases, however, money paid or property transferred under such a contract can be recovered:

(i) Where the parties are not *in pari delicto*, the innocent party can recover anything he has paid or transferred under the contract. This is the case where one party has been induced to enter into the contract by fraud, duress or oppression (*Hughes* v. *Liverpool Victoria Legal Friendly Society* [1916] 2 K.B. 482).

(ii) While the contract is still executory, either party may recover money or property handed over if he renounces the contract and makes his claim before the illegal purpose has been substantially performed (*Kearley* v. *Thomson* (1890) 24 Q.B.D. 742); but this *locus poenitentiae* (opportunity for repentance) is lost when the contract has been substantially performed (*Taylor* v. *Bowers* (1876) 1 Q.B.D. 291), or when the contract is frustrated by circumstances outside the control of the parties (*Bigos* v. *Bousted* [1951] 1 All E.R. 92).

(iii) Property can be recovered if the action does not require disclosure of the illegality. Thus, if property is hired for an illegal purpose, the rental cannot be claimed nor can the property be recovered during the period of hire. But once this period has terminated, the owner can recover the property by virtue of his right of ownership.

(2) Where the contract is lawful in its inception, but one of the parties, unknown to the other, has an illegal intent, *e.g.*, where a lease is taken of premises, the lessee intending to use them for immoral purposes, the rights of the innocent party are unaffected by the illegality, and he is entitled to recover under the contract. If he discovers the illegal intent before the contract is completed, he may avoid it (*Cowan* v. *Milbourn* (1867) L.R. 2 Ex. 230); but if, having discovered the illegal purpose, he allows the contract to be performed, he cannot recover under it. A principal is deemed to have knowledge if his agent knows of the illegality (*Apthorpe* v. *Neville* (1907) 23 T.L.R. 575).

(3) As has already been seen, all contracts founded on an illegal contract are themselves entirely devoid of effect.

Where a contract is void at common law, but not illegal, money paid under the contract is apparently recoverable (*Hermann* v. *Charlesworth, ante*, p. 52). Furthermore, if the contract is divisible, that part of the contract which is bad may be rejected and the rest of the contract enforced as a valid agreement (see the *Nordenfelt* case, *ante*, p. 53). An illegal contract cannot be so divided (*Bennett* v. *Bennett* [1952] 1 K.B. 249). Collateral contracts based on the void contract are not themselves affected.

§ 10. *Possibility of Performance*

A contract is void if performance is impossible at the date when it is entered into; but the impossibility must be complete, and not merely in relation to the capacity of the promisor, for what one person cannot do, another may be able to do (*Thornborow* v. *Whitacre* (1705) 2 Ld. Raym. 1164).

For the position where the impossibility arises subsequent to the formation of the contract, see *post*, § 12 (c).

§ 11. *Transfer of Rights and Duties under the Contract*

(a) The Doctrine of Privity of Contract

A contract cannot confer rights or impose liabilities on any persons other than the parties to it, and consequently no one may seek to enforce a contract to which he is not a party (*Price* v. *Easton* (1833) 4 B. & Ad. 433).

In *Dunlop Pneumatic Tyre Co., Ltd.* v. *Selfridge & Co., Ltd.* [1915] A.C. 847, the plaintiffs were manufacturers of motor tyres. They sold them to agents, Dew & Co., under a price maintenance agreement whereby the agents undertook not to resell at a price less than the retail price listed by Dunlops. Dew & Co. sold tyres to Selfridges who undertook with Dew & Co. that they would not sell at less than the list price. In breach of this undertaking Selfridges sold to customers at less than the list price, and Dunlops brought an action against them. It was held that Dunlops could not sue on a contract to which they were not a party; and even if Dunlops could be regarded as undisclosed principals, so that the promise by Selfridges could be regarded as made to Dunlops, there was no consideration moving from them to support the promise. (This case would now fall within the exception created by the Restrictive Trade Practices Act, 1956, *infra*.)

In *Midland Silicones, Ltd.* v. *Scruttons, Ltd.* [1962] A.C. 446, the bill of lading of a consignment of goods included a clause limiting the liability of the shipowners for loss or damage to the goods. The goods were damaged while being unloaded by stevedores employed by the shipowners. The consignees sued the stevedores for the full amount of the damage, and the stevedores sought to rely on the limitation clause.

Held: The stevedores were not parties to the contract of carriage and were therefore not protected by the limitation clause.

The doctrine of privity of contract is subject to a number of exceptions, the most important of which are:

(1) Where a promise amounts to the creation of a trust, it will be enforced at the instance of the beneficiaries who, although not parties to the contract, are deemed to have an equitable interest therein (*Royal Exchange Assurance* v. *Hope* [1928] Ch. 179).

(2) Under s. 25 of the Restrictive Trade Practices Act, 1956, a person who has supplied goods subject to a condition as to the minimum price at which the goods may be resold may enforce the condition against any person who subsequently acquires the goods for

resale with notice of the condition. The scope of this exception is now considerably limited by the Resale Prices Act, 1964 (see Chap. III, § 2 (d)).

(3) Under s. 207 of the Road Traffic Act, 1960, a third party may in certain circumstances enforce a motor insurance policy directly against the insurer (see Chap. VI, § 5).

(4) The doctrine of the undisclosed principal in agency (see Chap. II, § 9 (c)).

Apart from these limited exceptions, rights under an existing contract may in certain circumstances pass to third parties by assignment or by negotiation, and both rights and duties may pass by novation, operation of law, or, in the case of a lease by privity of estate.

An example of rights passing by operation of law is given by *Beswick* v. *Beswick* [1967] 2 All E.R. 1197, where a coal merchant agreed in writing to assign his business to his nephew in consideration for which the nephew agreed to pay £6·50 a week to the uncle for the remainder of the uncle's life and after his death £5 weekly to the uncle's widow. The coal merchant died intestate 20 months later and after his death the nephew made only one weekly payment to the widow.

Held: The widow, although not a party to the contract could, as administratrix of the estate of her husband (a contracting party), enforce the agreement by way of an order for specific performance. She was not entitled, under s. 56, Law of Property Act, 1925, to sue in her personal capacity on a contract to which she was not a party.

(b) Assignment

Assignment means the transfer of rights by act of the assignor in such a way that the assignee obtains a title to those rights, enforceable by him against the person liable even without his consent. Thus, if A owes money to B, B is said to assign his right to the debt to C if he transfers the rights in such a way that C can recover direct from A.

Liabilities or duties under a contract cannot be assigned, for the person liable cannot escape his obligations by purporting to throw them on the shoulders of someone else. But in the case of contracts where the personal skill or qualification of a party is not required, there is no reason why he should not arrange for a third party to perform on his behalf, though the original party to the contract remains liable to the other party for due performance. For example, in the case of a building contract, the builder may sub-contract various parts of the work, though he would remain liable to the owner for faulty work by the sub-contractors. The architect, however, would be unable to arrange for performance of his work by some other person, because the building owner would rely on his personal skill.

Although rights under a contract are in general assignable, yet if rights are conferred on a party for reasons which are personal to him, he will be unable to assign (*Kemp* v. *Baerselman* [1906] 2 K.B. 604). For example, A might agree to supply goods to B and to allow him extended credit as a result of a long business association; B would not be entitled to assign his right to receive the goods on such extended terms of credit (notwithstanding that B would remain liable for payment), because those terms were intended to be personal to him. Or again, a publisher could not assign his right to publish an author's book to another publisher, because an author relies on the reputation of the particular publisher with whom he has contracted (*Griffith* v. *Tower Publishing Co., Ltd.* [1897] 1 Ch. 21).

Thus, where an employee has contracted to work for a particular employer, he cannot be compelled without his consent to work for anyone else, nor could he substitute another to perform his work for him (*Nokes* v. *Doncaster Amalgamated Colleries, Ltd.* [1940] A.C. 1014). This is a point of great importance when a sale of a business is contemplated.

A bare right to litigate and recover unliquidated damages (see *post*, § 13 (b)) is not capable of assignment for it savours of maintenance; but a right of action which is incidental to property may be assigned with that property.

Assignments of rights under contracts may be either legal or equitable.

(1) *Equitable Assignments*

The common law has never recognised assignments, upon the principle that if a contract has been entered into between A and B, and A desires to transfer his rights under that contract to C, he should first obtain B's consent. Such an arrangement would then take the form of a release by B of A from the contract and an acceptance of C in his stead, *i.e.*, there would be a substituted contract.

Equity afforded relief from the rigidity of this rule by permitting assignments without the consent of the other party to the contract first having been obtained. The motive underlying the recognition in equity of such assignments seems to be that since the other party to the contract was under an obligation to perform a duty, it was immaterial to him who benefited from the fulfilment of the contract so long as he was completely discharged upon performance.

As indicated below, statutory provision now exists for making legal assignments, *i.e.*, assignments which are effective apart from the principles of equity. But an assignment may still take effect in equity if it fails to constitute a legal assignment through non-compliance with the statutory requirements, provided a clear intention to assign is shown.

The disadvantage of an assignment taking effect in equity only is that if the right assigned is a legal right – that is, a right which is recognised at common law, *e.g.*, the right to payment of a contract debt – the assignee is obliged to sue in the name of the assignor, joining him as defendant if he declines to come in as plaintiff. But if equitable rights are assigned – that is, rights only recognised in equity, *e.g.*, an interest under a trust – the assignee can sue in his own name.

The assignee takes subject to equities, that is, subject to all defences that might have prevailed against the assignor. This is a necessary rule, as the other party to the contract cannot, without his consent, be deprived of any defences which he could have pleaded had an assignment not been made.

Consideration is not necessary to support an equitable assignment, whether of a legal or an equitable right, provided that the assignment is complete and unconditional. Thus, a creditor under a contract can effectively pass his rights by way of gift by means of an equitable assignment. But an assignment on a condition to be fulfilled in the future, or an assignment of a debt which is to arise in the future, ranks merely as a contract to assign, and consideration is necessary to make it effective unless it is under seal.

An equitable assignment is valid as between assignor and assignee without notice being given to the debtor. Nevertheless, notice of assignment should be given, as payment to the assignor before notice will release the debtor from his obligation. After the debtor has received notice, he cannot safely pay the money to anyone but the assignee, nor can he plead any right of set off which arose after he had notice. Furthermore, successive assignees rank, not according to the date of the assignment, but according to the dates at which notice of the successive assignments were given to the debtor.

(2) *Legal Assignments*

By the Law of Property Act, 1925, s. 136 (re-enacting the Judicature Act, 1873, s. 25), the assignee of any debt or other legal chose in action acquires the legal right to the debt or other chose in action, and all remedies, legal and equitable, in respect thereof, if the following conditions are satisfied:

 (i) the assignment must be absolute;

 (ii) it must be in writing, signed by the assignor; and

 (iii) express notice in writing must be given to the party to be charged. The notice takes effect at the date when it is received by the debtor or person liable (*Holt* v. *Hetherfield Trust, Ltd.* [1942] 2 K.B. 1).

The phrase 'debt or other legal chose in action' means 'debt or right which the common law looks on as not assignable by reason of its being a chose in action, but which a court of equity deals with as being assignable' (*Torkington* v. *Magee* [1902] 2 K.B. 427). Thus, any assignable right, whether legal or equitable, can be the subject of a legal assignment.

Since the assignee has legal as well as equitable remedies, he can sue in his own name; but he takes subject to any equities existing between the debtor and the assignor.

Where possible, assignments will now comply with the statutory requirements. If not, *e.g.*, if the assignment is not absolute, or it is made orally, or notice of assignment is given orally, it may still be enforceable in equity, subject to the rules stated in (1) above. Thus, although part only of a debt can be assigned, the assignment, not being of the whole debt, is not absolute, and so can only be an equitable assignment (*Williams* v. *Atlantic Assurance Co.* [1933] 1 K.B. 81).

The Act says nothing about consideration having to be given by the assignee, and the debtor, when sued, cannot set up as a defence the want of consideration between assignor and assignee.

(3) *Assignment of Leases*

The assignment of leases differs from the assignment of other rights, inasmuch as both rights and liabilities can be assigned with the property, provided they 'touch and concern' the property, and are not personal to the original parties to the lease. Liability on the covenants in a lease may arise by privity of contract – between the original parties – and by privity of estate – where an assignee takes the *whole* estate created by the lease. By privity of contract the lessee remains liable to the lessor during the whole of the term of the lease. Upon assignment, the assignee becomes responsible for the performance of the covenants by privity of estate, but should he default, recourse can be had against the lessee. The assignee indemnifies the lessee against this potential liability. Should a further assignment be effected, the second assignee assumes responsibility.

A sub-lease of *part only* of the unexpired term of the lease does not create any privity of estate between lessor and sub-lessee, the lessor's rights being solely against the original lessee, who will have rights under the sub-lease against the sub-lessee.

(4) *Other Assignments*

Special rules apply to the assignment of moneylenders' debts (Moneylenders Act, 1927, ss. 16, 17), policies of life assurance (Policies of Assurance Act, 1867, s. 1) and marine insurance (Marine Insurance Act, 1906, s. 50), and certain other choses in action.

(c) Negotiability

Certain written instruments have the characteristic of negotiability which enables the rights created by the instrument to pass from one person to another without notice to the person liable in respect of it.

A negotiable instrument gives a right of action to the holder of the document for the time being, in his own name; the holder is, with certain exceptions, not prejudiced by defects in the title of his transferor, and does not hold subject to such defences as would be good against his transferor (*i.e.*, he takes the instrument 'free from equities').

Negotiable instruments are dealt with in Chap. IV.

(d) Novation

Both rights and liabilities may be transferred by the substitution of a new contract in place of the one already made, with the consent of all parties affected. The new contract may be made between the original parties or, more usually, there is substituted some new person, in place of the original debtor or creditor, who takes over the rights and liabilities of the person whom he displaces. A change in the members of a partnership is a common example of a novation where, expressly or by implication, the old and new partners and the firm's creditors agree that the latter shall look to the new partner (and to the remaining ones), in place of the partner retiring, for the discharge of their debts.

(e) Operation of Law

The rights and liabilities under a contract may also pass from one person to another by operation of law. This occurs on bankruptcy by the vesting of a bankrupt's property, including his rights of action, in the trustee, and on transfer of a deceased person's contracts, other than those for personal services, to his personal representative.

A distinction must be drawn between such cases and assignments which are effected by the parties themselves. In the former case, the transfer takes effect automatically without any specific assignment.

§ 12. *Discharge of the Contract*

Contracts may be discharged by agreement, performance, subsequent impossibility, or breach.

(a) Discharge by Agreement

Discharge by agreement may take place by waiver, by accord and satisfaction, or under an express term of the contract.

(1) *Waiver*

Waiver is an agreement between the parties that they shall no longer be bound by the contract. Such an agreement may be made at any time while the contract remains executory, *i.e.*, something remains to be done by both parties, and may take one of three forms:

(i) Complete dissolution of the original contract, the parties being completely released from any obligation towards each other.

(ii) Dissolution of the original contract and substitution of an entirely new agreement in its place, *e.g.*, by novation (*ante*, § 11 (d)).

(iii) Partial dissolution, by modification or variation of the terms of the original contract, without altering it in substance.

An agreement to waive a contract, like any other agreement, must normally be supported by consideration or be under seal in order to be effective. Nevertheless a partial waiver purely for the benefit of one party, if intended to be acted upon, and if relied on by him in altering his position, prevents the other party from afterwards requiring performance of the contract (*Combe* v. *Combe, ante* p. 11). Where the waiver constitutes a complete dissolution of the contract, each party will have given up some benefit which he is entitled to receive from the other, and this will constitute the consideration for the agreement.

The waiver of a right of action on a bill of exchange does not require consideration; but the waiver must be *in writing*, or the bill must be delivered up to the acceptor (Bills of Exchange Act, 1882, s. 62).

The agreement to waive the contract, whether completely or partially, may be made orally, even where the original contract is under seal or in writing (*Berry* v. *Berry* [1929] 2 K.B. 316). If, however, the original contract is one which is required to be evidenced in writing (see *ante*, § 4 (e)), a variation of the original contract by partial dissolution will not be effective unless the variation itself is evidenced in writing (*Goss* v. *Nugent* (1833) 5 B. & Ad. 58). The reason for this is that there must be written evidence of the *whole* agreement, and here the subsequent variation is not so evidenced. Accordingly the original contract stands and can be enforced without the variation. If, on the other hand, the waiver constitutes a complete cancellation of the original contract, and the substitution of another contract in its place, the original contract is determined even if the cancellation is by word of mouth only, for there is nothing in law to prevent the cancellation, as distinct from variation, of such a contract by oral agreement (*Morris* v. *Baron* [1918] A.C.1). In this case the original contract is completely discharged, even though the new contract may be unenforceable if that, too, is made orally.

(2) *Accord and Satisfaction*

Where one party has completely performed his obligations under the contract (and, usually, when the other party is in breach of the contract) he may agree to release the other party from his obligations, and may effectively do so either by a release under seal, or by receiving some fresh consideration in return for the release. Where the agreement is supported by a fresh consideration, it is called accord (or agreement) and satisfaction.

The satisfaction can be constituted merely by a fresh promise to do something different, in which case the original rights are extinguished, and, if the fresh promise is not performed, action lies only on that fresh promise and not on the original contract. On the other hand the satisfaction required may be the actual carrying out of the fresh promise, in which case the original cause of action is not extinguished until the later promise is actually performed (*British Russian Gazette, Ltd.* v. *Associated Newspapers, Ltd.* [1933] 2 K.B. 616). Whether the satisfaction consists in the mere promise, or only in the actual carrying out of the promise, is a question of fact depending on the intention of the parties when they made the accord. For instance, suppose that A agrees to sell B a new Austin motor car, and that B is at all times ready and willing to pay. A, however, is unable to effect delivery, and offers B a new Morris car instead. B agrees, but he receives neither motor car. He sues for damages for non-delivery. Does he claim for non-delivery of the Austin car or for non-delivery of the Morris car? The answer depends on whether B agreed to accept the promise to deliver the Morris as satisfaction of his original rights, in which case he claims damages for non-delivery of the Morris, or whether he agreed to cancellation of his original rights only on actual delivery of the Morris.

The commonest example of the application of the principle of accord and satisfaction is the allowance of a cash discount. The creditor receives his money at an earlier date than that on which he could otherwise demand payment (having regard to the customary or agreed term of credit), and the risk, however small, of a bad debt is eliminated. Other examples are (i) where there is a dispute as to the amount, and a compromise is effected; (ii) a settlement of un-liquidated damages; and (iii) compromises under deeds of arrangement and in bankruptcy.

(3) *Discharge by Express Term of Contract*

The contract may itself provide for discharge in certain circumstances, *e.g.*, on the expiration of a specified period of time, at the option of one or other of the parties, on the non-fulfilment of a condition precedent, or on the happening of a condition subsequent (see *ante*, § 6 (d)).

(b) Discharge by Performance
(1) *Actual Performance*

A contract is normally discharged by both parties performing their obligations under it. A contracting party is only discharged from his obligations in this way when he has completely and precisely performed the exact obligation that he has undertaken. Anything less than complete performance will normally not release him, and will not enable him to enforce the contract against the other party, though in certain circumstances he may sue on a *quantum meruit* (see *post*, § 13 (c)).

(2) *Time for Performance*

Where the parties do not prescribe any particular time within which the contract is to be performed, the contract must be completed within a reasonable time. Where the time for performance is fixed in the contract, the question arises whether time is of the essence of the contract, in which case the contract must be performed within that time. This will be the case if the parties expressly provide that time shall be of the essence, or where the nature of the contract makes it imperative that the prescribed time should be precisely observed, or where one party gives reasonable notice to the other that the contract must be performed within a specified time (*Rickards (Charles), Ltd.* v. *Oppenheim* [1950] 1 K.B. 616). If time is not of the essence, a failure to perform within the time specified will not in itself constitute a breach of contract.

In mercantile contracts a stipulation as to the time of *payment* is not normally of the essence of the contract (Sale of Goods Act, 1893, s. 10), but stipulations as to time other than that of payment, *e.g.*, of delivery, will normally be of the essence (*Reuter* v. *Sala* (1879) 4 C.P.D. 239).

(3) *Tender of Performance*

Where the performance of his obligations by one party requires the concurrence of the other, a tender of performance in accordance with the terms of the contract is equivalent to actual performance. In the case of a tender of goods which is refused by the buyer, the seller is completely discharged from further liability, and may recover damages from the buyer for breach of contract. On the other hand, in the case of a tender of money, although the debtor is not obliged to make a further tender, his obligation to pay the debt remains, and if he is sued for payment he must pay into court the sum tendered, whereupon he will be entitled to the costs of the action. A valid tender of payment also has the effect of stopping interest running, and generally extinguishes a right of lien.

To constitute a legal tender of payment, there must be:

(i) An offer of payment in legal currency to the creditor or his authorised agent. By the Coinage Act, 1870, and the Currency and Bank Notes Act, 1928, legal tender consists of:

Gold coins issued by the Mint, to any amount.
Bronze, not exceeding 20p.
Silver coins (of not more than 10p each) not exceeding £5.
50p coins not exceeding £10.
Bank of England notes, to any amount.

(ii) Actual production of the money, unless production is dispensed with by the creditor (*Finch* v. *Brook* (1834) 1 Bing. N.C. 253).

(iii) A total absence of any condition attached to the tender.

(iv) An offer of the *exact* amount of the debt. It cannot be made a condition of the tender that change should be given (*Robinson* v. *Cook* (1816) 6 Taunt. 336), but the debtor can tender a sum larger than the amount of the debt in satisfaction if he has not the exact amount (*Dean* v. *James* (1833) 4 B. & Ad. 546). Moreover, it will be a good tender if, although change was demanded, it was for some other reason that the creditor refused the tender (*Bevans* v. *Rees* (1839) 5 M. & W. 306).

(4) Payment

A contract may be discharged by payment where the liability of one party to the other consists in the payment of a sum of money. A debtor is bound to seek out his creditor and pay him (*Walton* v. *Mascall* (1844) 13 M. & W. 451), and payment should, primarily, be made in money, but may, *with the consent of the creditor*, be made by cheque or other negotiable instrument. In this case the payment is *conditional* on the instrument being honoured, and, if dishonoured, a double right of action arises, one on the original consideration and one on the dishonoured instrument. If, however, the creditor has been offered cash, and requests a bill or cheque instead, then the payment is *absolute*, and the right of action on the original contract is lost, the only remedy being to sue on the dishonoured instrument (*Sard* v. *Rhodes* (1836) 1 M. & W. 153).

Payment by a third party does not discharge the debt, unless the debtor assents to the payment, or subsequently ratifies it (*Smith* v. *Cox* [1940] 2 K.B. 558).

If the creditor expressly or by implication requests a remittance through the post, the payment will be deemed to have been duly made should the letter containing the remittance be lost in transit. The fact that remittances have been made by post over a period of years does not raise the implication that the creditor has agreed to the practice merely because he has raised no objection (*Pennington* v. *Crossely* (1897) 77 L.T. 43). Moreover, the debtor is not protected if he remits to his creditor in an unauthorised manner, even where he has taken reasonable precaution against loss.

Thus, in *Mitchell-Henry* v. *Norwich Union Life Insurance Society* [1918] 2 K.B. 67, there was no payment where a sum of £48 was sent in Treasury notes and cash by registered packet, and the money was stolen after delivery upon the creditor's premises. Even though the creditor intended payment through the post, this did not authorise the debtor to send so large a sum as £48 in notes and cash.

(5) *Appropriation of Payments*

When a debtor who owes several debts to the same creditor makes a payment which is insufficient to discharge the whole of his indebtedness to that creditor, it is essential that an understood basis of appropriation should exist. Suppose that A owes two debts to B, and one is statute-barred and the other is not. A makes a payment which is insufficient to cover both debts. If B is at liberty to appropriate the payment to the statute-barred debt, he will thereby have succeeded in getting paid where he had no right of action. Or if one debt is guaranteed or secured and the other is not, B will be interested to appropriate the payment to the unsecured debt, as he can enforce his guarantee or security to obtain payment of the other.

The rules relating to appropriation of payments are:

 (i) The debtor may appropriate the payment to a particular debt or debts at the time of payment.

 (ii) If the debtor does not do so, the creditor may appropriate it as he chooses, at any time.

 (iii) If there is a current account, it is presumed that payments are appropriated to the debts in order of date (*Clayton's Case* (1816) 1 Mer. 529).

If the debtor appropriates at the time of payment, and the creditor does not agree with such appropriation, his only remedy is to refuse payment, and stand upon his legal rights (*Croft* v. *Lumley* (1858) 5 E. & B. 648). If the debtor does not appropriate, but pays the exact amount of a particular debt, it is presumed that the payment is in discharge of that debt (*Marryatts* v. *White* (1817) 2 Stark. 101).

The creditor may only appropriate where the debtor does not do so, and until he has informed the debtor of his appropriation he may alter it (*Simpson* v. *Ingham* (1823) 2 B. & C. 65). He may if he chooses apply the payment to a statute-barred debt (*Mills* v. *Fowkes* (1839) 5 Bing. N.C. 455), but not to an illegal debt (*Wright* v. *Laing* (1824) 3 B. & C. 165).

Where a hirer or buyer is liable to the same owner or seller under two or more hire-purchase or conditional sale agreements to which the Hire-Purchase Act, 1965, applies, he is entitled to appropriate payments in respect of those agreements in any way he sees fit, notwithstanding any agreement to the contrary; and if he fails to make any such appropriation, the payments are to be appropriated to the respective debts in the proportions that those debts bear to one another (Hire-Purchase Act, 1965, s. 51). In this case the creditor has no right to appropriate in any event.

Should a customer pay trust moneys into his banking account and subsequently withdraw money for his private use, the rule in *Clayton's Case* will not apply, and the amounts so withdrawn will be set off against the customer's own funds, irrespective of the dates upon which the deposits of the trust money had been made (*Re Hallett's Estate* (1880) 13 Ch. D. 696). But if there are two or more beneficiaries under separate trust funds and the amount ultimately standing to the credit of the account is insufficient to meet all the trust obligations, the rule in *Clayton's Case* will be followed in order to ascertain to what portion of the balance the beneficiaries are respectively entitled (*Re Stenning* [1895] 2 Ch. 433).

(6) *Receipts*

A debtor is not entitled at common law to insist upon a receipt when paying a debt. The Stamp Act, 1891, ss. 101-103, provided that it was the duty of a creditor to give a receipt on request by the debtor if the amount paid was £2 or upwards but these sections were repealed by the Finance Act, 1970. A receipt is not *conclusive* evidence that the money stated to have been paid was in fact paid, but it affords very strong evidence of that fact.

As to the position where payment has been made by cheque, see Chap. IV, § 3 (e) (1).

(7) *Interest on Debts*

The law does not, as a rule, in the absence of agreement, imply a promise to pay interest on a debt; but in the following cases simple interest will be allowed in addition to the amount of the debt:

(i) where there is an express agreement to pay interest;

(ii) where it is chargeable in accordance with a trade custom (*Re Anglesey* [1901] 2 Ch. 548);

(iii) on bills of exchange, generally 5 per cent. (Bills of Exchange Act, 1882, s. 57);

(iv) to a surety who has paid the debt, generally 4 per cent. (*Petre* v.1 *Duncombe* (1851) 20 L.J. Q.B. 242); or on money due under a contract of indemnity (*Omnium Insurance Corporation, Ltd.* v. *United London and Scottish Insurance Co.* (1920) 36 T.L.R. 386);

(v) on a judgment, 4 per cent. (Judgments Act, 1838, s. 17);

(vi) on an arbitrator's award, at the same rate as a judgment debt (Arbitration Act, 1950, s. 20);

(vii) in proceedings for the recovery of any debt or damages, the court may order the inclusion of interest in the sum for which judgment

is given at such rate as it thinks fit for the whole or any part of
the period between the date when the cause of action arose and
the date of the judgment (Law Reform (Miscellaneous Provisions) Act, 1934, s. 3).

(c) Discharge by Subsequent Impossibility

Impossibility of performance arising after a contract has been
entered into does not *prima facie* excuse a party from his obligations
under the contract; if he cannot perform what he has promised he
must pay damages, even though the impossibility has arisen through
no fault of his own. If he wished to guard against any particular risk,
he should have inserted a clause to that effect in the contract, such as
the 'strikes or bad weather' clause frequently found in building
contracts.

In *Budgett* v. *Binnington* [1891] 1 Q.B. 35, the unloading of a ship was delayed
beyond the date agreed with the shipowners owing to a strike of dock labourers.
The shipowners were held to be entitled to damages, the impossibility of performance being no excuse.

(1) *The Doctrine of 'Frustration'*

Where, however, the impossibility is of such a kind as to amount to
'frustration' in the legal sense of the word, both parties are excused
from further performance.

'Frustration may be defined as the premature determination of an agreement
between parties, lawfully entered into and in course of operation at the time of its
premature determination, *owing to the occurrence of an intervening event or change
of circumstances so fundamental as to be regarded by the law both as striking at the
root of the agreement, and as entirely beyond what was contemplated by the parties
when they entered into the agreement.* If, therefore, the intervening circumstance is
one which the law would not regard as so fundamental as to destroy the basis of
the agreement, there is no frustration. Equally, if the terms of the agreement show
that the parties contemplated the possibility of such an intervening circumstance
arising, frustration does not occur. Neither, of course, does it arise where one of
the parties has deliberately brought about the supervening event by his own choice.
But, where it does arise, it operates to bring the agreement to an end as regards
both parties forthwith and quite apart from their own volition' (*per* Viscount
Simon, L.C., in *Cricklewood Property and Investment Trust, Ltd.* v. *Leighton's Investment Trust, Ltd.* [1945] A.C. 221).

Supervening events which are of such a fundamental character as
to bring about frustration and to release both parties from further
performance of the contract may be classified as follows:

  (i) Where a contract is made on the basis of the continued existence
     of a specific thing, or the continuance of some existing state of
     affairs, or the happening of some future event, further per-
     formance will be excused if the specific thing ceases to exist, or
     the state of affairs ceases to continue, or the event fails to take
     place.

In *Taylor* v. *Caldwell* (1863) 3 B. & S. 826, a contract was made for the use of the Surrey Gardens and Music Hall on four days in the summer for the purpose of giving concerts and fêtes. Before the date arrived, the hall was destroyed by fire.

Held: Further performance of the contract was excused, because it had been made on the basis that the hall should continue to exist.

In *Krell* v. *Henry* [1903] 2 K.B. 740, a contract was made to hire a room, the object being to view the coronation procession of King Edward VII. Owing to the King's illness the procession was abandoned.

Held: The contract had ceased to bind the parties, as the taking place of the procession was the basis of the contract.

(ii) Death of either party will excuse further performance of a contract of personal service. Illness or other incapacity will similarly excuse, if the disability is of such a nature as to make performance practically impossible.

In *Robinson* v. *Davison* (1871) L.R. 6 Ex. 269, a pianist was prevented by illness from playing the piano in accordance with his contract at a concert to be given on a specified day.

Held: The pianist was not liable in damages for his failure, since the whole contract between the parties was based upon the assumption by both that the performer would continue in sufficient health to play on the day named.

This rule only applies to contracts which require personal performance; in other cases illness is no excuse, and in the case of death the personal representatives of the deceased will be liable for the performance of the contract.

(iii) A change in the law rendering further performance illegal discharges a contract. Examples of frustration of this nature arise in connection with contracts which cannot be performed on the outbreak of war because they would involve trading with the enemy, and contracts for the sale of goods which cannot be performed owing to the subsequent imposition of a rationing system.

The doctrine of frustration applies only when there has been such a fundamental change of circumstances that the contract no longer applies to the situation. A mere 'uncontemplated turn of events,' such as an abnormal rise or fall in prices, a sudden depreciation of currency, an unexpected obstacle to execution, is not sufficient to enable the court to declare a contract to be at an end.

In *Tsakiroglou & Co., Ltd.* v. *Noblee Thorl G.m.b.H.* [1962] A.C. 93, sellers agreed to ship groundnuts from Port Sudan c.i.f. Hamburg. The usual route for such shipment was via the Suez Canal, which was blocked due to military operations. The sellers did not ship the groundnuts, claiming that the contract had been frustrated.

Held: The shipment could have been made via the Cape of Good Hope, and, since the customary route was closed, the sellers should have used the alternative route. The fact that they might thereby be put to greater expense did not fundamentally alter the contract, which was thus not frustrated.

(2) *Law Reform* (*Frustrated Contracts*) *Act, 1943*

Where a contract has become frustrated, and the parties thereto have for that reason been discharged from the further performance of the contract, the Law Reform (Frustrated Contracts) Act, 1943, provides that:

(*a*) all sums paid to any party in pursuance of the contract before the time of discharge are recoverable, and all sums payable to any party before the time of discharge cease to be payable (subject to (*b*) below);

(*b*) a party who has before the time of discharge incurred expenses in connection with the performance of the contract, may, if the court so allows, retain or recover all or part of such expenses out of the money so paid or payable to him;

(*c*) a party who has obtained a valuable benefit before the time of discharge by reason of something done by another party in connection with the contract must pay to that other party such sum, not exceeding the value of the benefit, as the court thinks just having regard to all the circumstances of the case.

In estimating the amount of expenses incurred, overhead expenses and personal services are taken into account, but not insurance money payable by reason of the frustration unless the contract or any enactment imposed an obligation to insure.

The Act does not apply:

(i) If, although the contract has become frustrated, the circumstances are not such as to excuse further performance. In such a case, damages for breach of contract may be payable by the party in default in the normal way.

(ii) To contracts containing express provision as to frustration, so far as such provision is inconsistent with the Act.

(iii) To any part of a frustrated contract which is severable from the rest and which has been wholly performed at the time of discharge.

(iv) To a contract for the carriage of goods by sea or a charter-party.

(v) To a contract of insurance.

(vi) To a contract for the sale of specific goods which perish before the risk has passed to the buyer (in this case s. 7 of the Sale of Goods Act, 1893, will apply), or to any other contract for the sale of specific goods, where the contract is frustrated by reason of the fact that the goods have perished.

(d) Discharge by Breach

Breach of contract may take place in three ways. A party under a contract may repudiate his liabilities under it; he may by his own act make it impossible to fulfil them; or he may totally or partially fail to perform what he has promised.

(1) *Repudiation (Anticipatory Breach)*

If one of the parties to a contract expressly or by implication repudiates his liabilities before the time for performance has come, the other party is discharged, if he so pleases, and may immediately sue for the breach (*Hochster v. De la Tour* (1853) 2 E. & B. 678); but the repudiation must be of the whole contract.

In *Mersey Steel and Iron Co. v. Naylor* (1884) 9 A.C. 434, the company had agreed to sell to N a quantity of steel to be delivered in specified monthly instalments. Two instalments had been delivered when the company went into liquidation. N refused to pay for the steel delivered, unless under an order of the court, being under the erroneous impression that there was no-one to whom payment could safely be made.

Held: The company was not entitled to repudiate the contract and refuse to deliver the other instalments, as N's refusal to pay in the circumstances did not amount to a repudiation of the contract.

Alternatively, the person entitled to performance may refuse to accept the repudiation and treat the contract as still existing, in which case the legal position of the parties is unaffected by the repudiation. The promisee may then hold the other party to the contract and must wait until the date for performance has passed before instituting proceedings for breach. If in the meantime circumstances have arisen which provide the defendant with a good defence, he will be able to escape liability by taking advantage of the supervening circumstances.

Thus, in *Avery v. Bowden* (1856) 6 E. & B. 953, the defendant contracted to charter the plaintiff's ship and to load it at a Russian port within forty-five days. Not having a cargo available, the defendant informed the plaintiff that he was unable to fulfil his contract. The plaintiff refused to accept the repudiation, and remained at the port awaiting a cargo. While the plaintiff was there the Crimean war between Russia and England broke out, and it became unlawful to load any cargo at the port. It was held that this supervening circumstance terminated the contract, and that the defendant was not liable in damages. Had the plaintiff accepted the repudiation when it occurred he would have had a claim for damages notwithstanding the subsequent outbreak of war.

If, before the time of performance arrives, one of the parties renders the contract impossible of performance, the contract may be treated as repudiated by him and an action may be commenced immediately.

In *Lovelock v. Franklyn* (1846) 8 Q.B. 371, F agreed to assign a lease to L, but executed an assignment to another person prior to the date upon which the original assignment was to have been completed. It was held that F's conduct constituted an implied repudiation of his contract with L.

(2) *Failure of Performance*

When there has been a breach of contract by failure of performance, the injured party may bring an action for the breach, but whether or not he is himself discharged from further performance of the contract depends on the nature of the contract and the nature of the breach.

If the breach is so serious that it goes to the root of the whole contract, or if the act or conduct of one of the parties amounts to an intimation of an intention to abandon and altogether refuse performance of the contract, the other party will be discharged. If the breach is less serious, the injured party may claim damages, but will not be liberated from performance of his own promises. The distinction between conditions and warranties in this context has already been noted (*ante*, § 6 (d)).

Where the parties' promises are interdependent, a breach by one party will discharge the other. Thus, in a contract for the sale of goods, where payment and delivery are to take place at one and the same time, the failure by the vendor to deliver the goods will discharge the buyer from his obligation to pay for them. Where, on the other hand, the contract consists of a number of divisible promises, and there has been a partial failure of performance by one party, the other party will not always be discharged from further performance. Thus, where goods are to be delivered in certain instalments, a default in the quantity contained in one or more of the instalments will not discharge the injured party unless the default is so serious as to amount in fact to a repudiation of the whole contract (*Mersey Steel and Iron Co.* v. *Naylor, supra*).

§ 13. *Remedies for Breach of Contract*

In the event of a breach of contract the injured party may have one or more of the following remedies:

(a) He may accept the breach as discharging the contract, and refuse to do anything under it himself; and at the same time he may bring an action for damages for breach of contract.

(b) He may continue to act upon the contract (and must do so if the breach does not discharge the contract) and bring an action for damages.

(c) If he has performed part of his own obligations, he may sue on a *quantum meruit*.

(d) He may apply to the court in appropriate cases for a decree of specific performance, or an injunction.

(a) Rescission

Where the breach is such as to discharge the contract, the innocent party may regard himself as being relieved from any further liability under it, and, if he wishes, obtain judgment for its rescission, provided that the parties can be restored to their former position

(*Thorpe* v. *Fasey* [1949] Ch. 649). The question of restitution has already been considered in relation to misrepresentation (see *ante*, § 8 (b)). Thus, the injured party must return any money he has received from the party in default, if it was received in part payment of the contract price (*Dies* v. *British and International Mining Corpn.* [1939] 1 K.B. 724). But if money is deposited as earnest or as a guarantee for the due performance of the payer's obligation, the deposit is forfeited and cannot be recovered by the party in default (*Howe* v. *Smith* (1884) 27 Ch. D. 89), although equity may grant relief from forfeiture if it is unconscionable for the money to be retained (*Stockloser* v. *Johnson* [1954] 1 Q.D. 476).

(b) Damages

Damages for breach of contract may be nominal or substantial. Whether or not actual loss has been occasioned, a breach of contract is of itself actionable, and the awarding of nominal damages affirms that there has been an infringement of a legal right by the breach; but if actual loss as a result of the breach can be proved, the plaintiff is entitled to substantial damages.

Damages are awarded to put the party whose rights have been infringed in the same position, so far as money can do it, as if his rights had been duly observed. Damages are compensatory, not punitive, in character.

(1) *Remoteness of Damage*

Not every kind of loss actually suffered by the plaintiff as a result of the defendant's breach will entitle the plaintiff to claim damages. Losses arising from circumstances which are not within the reasonable contemplation of the parties may be regarded as too remote. The rules as to remoteness of damage are stated in *Hadley* v. *Baxendale* (1854) 9 Exch. 341, the facts of which were as follows:

The plaintiffs' mill was brought to a standstill by the breakdown of a shaft, which was sent away to the makers as a pattern for a new one. The defendant, a carrier, agreed to deliver the shaft, but owing to his neglect the shaft was delayed in transit, so that the mill was idle for a longer period than otherwise would have been the case had there been no breach of the contract of carriage. The plaintiffs sued in respect of the loss of profit which they had suffered owing to the delay.

Held: The defendant was not liable for the loss of profit. It was not in the usual course of things that the mill would cease work altogether for the lack of the shaft – the plaintiff might well have had one in reserve; and further, there were no circumstances disclosed to the defendant by which it was made apparent that a breach of the contract of carriage to deliver within a certain period would inevitably result in the loss of profits.

Two rules emerge from the judgment in this case:

'Where two parties have made a contract which one of them has broken, the damages which the other party ought to receive in respect of such breach of contract should be such as may fairly and reasonably be considered *either* arising naturally, *i.e.*, according to the usual course of things, from such breach of contract itself, *or* such as may reasonably be supposed to have been in the contemplation of both parties, at the time they made the contract, as the probable result of the breach of it.'

The first rule deals with the ordinary case where nothing exceptional is known to the party later in default. In such a case the defendant is liable for such loss as he ought, as a reasonable man, to have foreseen at the time of entering into the contract as a probable consequence of the breach.

The second rule concerns cases where there are exceptional circumstances, and the attendant loss arising from a breach of contract is greater than would otherwise be the case. Here, if it can be shown that the defendant had actual or constructive knowledge of the special circumstances, and should have foreseen the possibility of special loss arising in the event of a breach of contract by him, then he will be responsible for all such loss arising reasonably and naturally from a breach of the contract in those special circumstances.

Thus, in *Victoria Laundry (Windsor), Ltd.* v. *Newman Industries, Ltd.* [1949] 2 K.B. 528, the plaintiffs, who were dyers and cleaners, wished to extend their premises and deal with certain lucrative dyeing contracts. They required a larger boiler for this work and this was ordered from an engineering firm, who, as a result of certain mishaps, failed to deliver for a considerable period beyond the agreed date. In consequence the plaintiffs suffered loss of profits they would have earned from the extension of their business and also lost the exceptional profits from the 'lucrative' contracts.

Held: The defendants with their engineering experience and with knowledge of the facts in their possession were responsible for the normal profit lost to the plaintiffs arising from the dyeing contracts which they were unable to execute, but they could not be held liable for the loss of the 'lucrative' profits that the plaintiffs had hoped to make.

In *Diamond* v. *Campbell-Jones* [1961] Ch. 22, the plaintiff agreed to buy a house from the defendant which he intended to convert into offices and maisonettes. The defendant wrongfully repudiated the contract, and the plaintiff claimed to recover the profit that he would have made if the conversion had been carried out.

Held: The plaintiff was entitled to recover only the difference between the purchase price and the market value of the property at the date of the breach of contract. The defendant, although he knew that such conversion was a possible use of the premises, did not know that the plaintiff intended to convert them, and such knowledge could not be imputed to him.

(2) *Measure of Damages*

The measure of damages payable by the defendant in respect of the breach of contract is the amount required to put the plaintiff in the position he would have been in if the contract had been duly performed. Thus, where a seller of goods fails to deliver them, the damage which occurs in the usual course is the difference between the value of the goods to the buyer if the contract had been performed, less the price he would have paid for them; and all that is required to restore the plaintiff to the position he ought to be in is a sufficient sum of money to enable him to buy similar goods in the open market.

In accordance with this principle, where damages are claimed for loss of earnings or profits, allowance must be made for any incidence of taxation (*British Transport Commission* v. *Gourley* [1956] A.C. 185). It follows from this that the extent of the defendant's liability will vary according to the tax position of the plaintiff. This rule only applies where the damages will not be liable to taxation in the hands of the plaintiff. Thus, it was not applied where damages were awarded for loss of profits owing to injury to a vehicle used in a business, because the profits of the business, which would include such damages, would themselves be assessable to income tax (*Herring* v. *British Transport Commission* [1958] T.R. 401).

The fact that damages may be difficult to assess will not deprive an injured party of his right; and a claim may be made not only in respect of loss already sustained but also of prospective loss if such loss was reasonably within the contemplation of the parties.

Where the damages relate to some loss expressed in a foreign currency, a conversion into sterling must be effected, and this is taken as on the date when the loss or breach occurred and not as on the date when the action is brought (*Re British American Continental Bank, Ltd.* [1923] 1 Ch. 276).

(3) *Mitigation of Damage*

It is the duty of the injured party to minimise the loss which he has sustained. If A agrees to sell certain goods to B who before delivery repudiates the contract, the measure of loss for which A could claim would be the difference between the contract price and that at which he could dispose of the goods elsewhere. If he could have resold them at a certain price but neglected to do so and disposed of them at a lower price, the price at which he could have sold them will be that to be taken in ascertaining the damages sustained. So too, where a contract of employment is terminated, the employee must mitigate his loss by accepting a reasonable offer of fresh employment (*Brace* v. *Calder* [1895] 2 Q.B. 253).

Since the duty to mitigate only arises after the contract has been broken, a person who elects to treat a contract which has been wrongfully repudiated by the other party as still subsisting may complete his own obligation under the contract without making any attempt to mitigate the loss.

In *White and Carter (Councils), Ltd.* v. *McGregor* [1962] A.C. 413, W, Ltd. agreed to advertise the business of M on litter bins for three years from November 1957. Before that date and before W, Ltd. had incurred any expenditure, M repudiated the contract. W, Ltd. refused to accept the repudiation, and proceeded to carry out their part of the contract, making no attempt to minimise the loss by finding other customers for the allotted advertising space. They then sued for the full contract price.

Held: Since W, Ltd. had elected to treat the contract as still subsisting, and since they could complete their side without the co-operation of M, they were entitled to do so. They were under no duty to mitigate the loss, and could therefore recover the price in full.

(4) *Liquidated Damages and Penalties*

Damages may be 'liquidated' or 'unliquidated.' Liquidated damages are a sum *agreed* on by the parties to the contract as an assessment of the damage or loss which will result from a breach of the contract; all other damages are unliquidated. Such an assessment may be made where it would be difficult to estimate accurately the loss which might be sustained, and such a provision is commonly found in a contract which is to be completed within a certain time. Demurrage is in the nature of liquidated damages, and similar clauses are usual in contracts for the erection of buildings, engineering works, etc., where the provision is for a stated sum for every day or week of delay. In the event of a breach of a contract which provides for liquidated damages the sum specified can be recovered, whether this is greater or less than the actual damage suffered.

Liquidated damages must be carefully distinguished from a 'penalty,' which in this connection is a sum named in a contract to be forfeited on breach, not as an agreed valuation of the damages, but as a security for the due performance of the contract. The court will not enforce a penalty clause in a contract (*Kemble* v. *Farren* (1829) 6 Bing. 141); if the contract is broken only the actual loss incurred as a result of the breach can be recovered by way of damages, whether this is greater or less than the fixed penalty. A penalty is nonetheless such by being described in the contract as 'liquidated damages.'

Whether an agreed sum payable on breach of contract is a penalty or liquidated damages is a question of fact, to be determined according to whether, in the light of all the circumstances, the sum was fixed to deter non-performance, when it would be a penalty, or as a genuine pre-estimate of the damage likely to be suffered, when it would be liquidated damages. The circumstances are to be considered as at the date of the contract, not as at the date of the breach. Accordingly, the fact that the sum fixed turns out to be far in excess of the damage actually suffered is not evidence that the sum was a penalty, except in so far as what in fact occurred may throw light on what the parties, at the time of making the contract, might reasonably have anticipated.

In *Dunlop Pneumatic Tyre Co., Ltd.* v. *New Garage and Motor Co., Ltd.* [1915] A.C. 79, the following tests were laid down for distinguishing between liquidated damages and penalties:

(i) The prescribed sum is a penalty if it is extravagant and unconscionable in comparison with the greatest loss that *could* follow from the breach.

(ii) An agreement to pay a larger sum of money on breach of a contract to pay a smaller one implies that the sum is a penalty, for the fixing of a larger sum cannot be a genuine pre-estimate of damage.

(iii) Subject to the above rules, if there is only one event upon which the agreed sum is to be paid, the sum is liquidated damages.

(iv) If the sum agreed is the same for several breaches, some of which might cause severe damage and some slight damage, the sum is a penalty, for the varying amount of damage likely to be suffered precludes fixing a single figure as a genuine pre-estimate. But if it is difficult, at the time of making the contract, to estimate what damage is likely to be suffered by breach, the agreed sum, if reasonable, is presumed to be liquidated damages. So, in the *Dunlop* case, where the plaintiffs supplied tyres to the defendants on an agreement that the defendants should not sell below the listed prices and would pay £5 by way of liquidated damages for every tyre sold in breach of the agreement, this amount was held to be liquidated damages. But where a retailer agreed not to sell cars or any parts below the list price and to pay £250 for breach of the agreement, this was a penalty, as it was too large to be a genuine pre-estimate of the probable loss (*Ford Motor Co., Ltd.* v. *Armstrong* (1915) 31 T.L.R. 267).

The distinction is of considerable importance in relation to hire-purchase agreements falling outside the statutory limits.

In *Campbell Discount Co., Ltd.* v. *Bridge* [1962] A.C. 600, the plaintiffs let a car to the defendant under a hire-purchase agreement which provided that, if the hirer terminated the agreement, he should pay to the plaintiffs 'such sum as may be necessary to make the rentals paid and payable equal to two-thirds of the price by way of agreed compensation for depreciation.' The defendant wrongfully terminated the agreement, and the plaintiffs claimed two-thirds of the purchase price less the amount already paid.

Held: The payment claimed was a penalty, as it was not a genuine pre-estimate either of depreciation or of loss, and accordingly the plaintiffs were not entitled to recover the amount claimed, but only for the damage actually suffered.

(c) Quantum Meruit

A claim on a *quantum meruit* is a claim for the value of work done by a party to a contract. Generally speaking, a party who has failed completely to perform his part can make no claim to any payment for the work which he has done, for his right to payment does not arise until he has carried out his part of the bargain (*Cutter* v. *Powell* (1795) 6 Term Rep. 320).

In *Sumpter* v. *Hedges* [1898] 1 Q.B. 673, a builder who had contracted to erect buildings for a lump sum payable on completion of the work abandoned the work with the buildings uncompleted.

Held: The builder was not entitled to any payment for the work he had done.

But, exceptionally, a party to a contract who has not completely performed his part can claim on a *quantum meruit* in the following circumstances:

(1) Where the other party, by electing to accept the benefit of the work done, has impliedly promised to pay on a *quantum meruit*. This principle applies only when the other party has an option to accept or reject the benefit (*Munro* v. *Butt* (1858) 8 E. & B. 738), as where a lesser quantity of goods than that contracted for is delivered under a contract of sale of goods, and the buyer elects to accept delivery. It would not apply in a case like *Sumpter* v. *Hedges, supra*, where a landowner has no option to reject a building which has been partially erected on his land.

(2) Where, although the work is not entirely carried out, there has been substantially complete performance. In this case the party claiming is entitled to payment of the contract price, less a deduction for the loss caused by the defective execution of the work (*Dakin & Co., Ltd.* v. *Lee* [1916] 1 K.B. 566). This is not strictly a *quantum meruit* claim, but a claim under the contract which is reduced by a counter-claim for damages.

(3) Where the contract is divisible, as where goods are to be delivered in instalments. A contract to work materials into the property of another, *e.g.*, by repairing a ship, is divisible for this purpose, and payment may be recovered on a *quantum meruit* although the work is not completed (*Roberts* v. *Havelock* (1832) 3 B. & Ad. 404).

(4) Where complete performance has been prevented by the wrongful act of the other party (*Planché* v. *Colburn* (1831) 5 C. & P. 58). Here the claim on a *quantum meruit* is alternative to a claim for damages for breach of contract.

(d) Specific Performance

Specific performance is a decree of the court ordering a party to carry out his part of the contract. Such an order is made where the usual remedy of damages would not sufficiently compensate the injured party, whose rights can only be satisfied by the performance of the contract in its exact terms. Specific performance is an equitable remedy, and will only be awarded at the discretion of the court, if the following conditions are satisfied:

(1) The contract must be fair and just as between the parties.

(2) The contract must be enforceable by both parties. Thus, the remedy is not available to an infant who would have been able to avoid performance of his part of the contract by reason of his infancy, nor in respect of a gratuitous promise made under seal.

(3) The court must be able to supervise and enforce execution. Thus contracts of personal service do not fall within the ambit of the rule.

Specific performance is most commonly granted in respect of contracts involving land. Although under s. 52 of the Sale of Goods Act, 1893, such an order can be made in respect of a contract for the sale of specific or ascertained goods, it will only be granted if the goods are not readily available in the market (see Chap. III, § 1 (e) (2)).

(e) Injunction

An injunction is an order of the court restraining a party from doing a wrongful act.

Although a decree of specific performance of a contract for personal services cannot be obtained, an injunction may be sought in such cases where there is in the contract a negative term sufficiently distinct to enable the court to enforce the contract by restraining infringement of the negative term, for example, an agreement by an artiste to perform at a particular place *and nowhere else* during a particular period (*Lumley* v. *Wagner* (1852) 1 D.M. & G. 604). But the negative term must be expressed in the contract, and not simply implied by a promise, *e.g.*, to devote full time to the performance of duties (*Mortimer* v. *Beckett* [1920] 1 Ch. 571). Moreover, if the negative term is so wide as to preclude the doing of anything except the contracted services, no injunction will be granted, as it would amount in effect to compelling the defendant to perform the contract or be idle (*Whitwood Chemical Co.* v. *Hardman* [1891] 2 Ch. 416).

(f) Remedies against Third Party procuring Breach

For one person to induce another to break a contract already entered upon is an actionable wrong, if the object of the party inducing the breach was either to injure the person who suffers by the breach, or to obtain a benefit for himself (*Quinn* v. *Leathem* [1901] A.C. 495). But one or more members of a trade union may induce a person to break a contract without incurring liability, provided they are acting in contemplation of a trade dispute (Trade Disputes Act, 1906).

The underlying principle is that a contract is sacred to the parties to it, and no third party must interfere to the detriment of either of them. The leading case is *Lumley* v. *Gye* (1853) 2 E. & B. 216, where A induced B to break her contract to sing at a particular theatre. The right of action against A would be independent of that against B for the breach of the contract. So, too, when A persuaded X's clerk to give him a list of his master's customers, X could claim damages and could secure an injunction forbidding A from making use of the list (*Lowenadler* v. *Lee* (1924) 158 L.T. 372).

It is not actionable merely to induce a man not to enter into a contract or to terminate a contract in a lawful manner (*Allen* v. *Flood* [1898] A.C. 1); but if intimidation is used, or if two or more persons combine wilfully to injure a man in his trade, a wrong is committed and damages may be obtained (*Sorrell* v. *Smith* [1925] A.C. 700; *Rookes* v. *Barnard* [1964] A.C. 1129). A threat to procure or commit a breach of contract is not, however, actionable if made in contemplation or furtherance of a trade dispute (Trade Disputes Act, 1965). The whole subject is one of considerable difficulty and properly belongs to the law of torts.

(g) Limitation of Actions

(1) *Limitation Act, 1939*

It is considered expedient that any right to which a person is entitled should be enforced by action, if such action is necessary, within a reasonable time. By the Limitation Act, 1939, as amended by the Law Reform (Limitation of Actions) Act, 1954, and the Limitation Act, 1963, action must be brought within the following periods after the cause of action first arose:

(i) *Within one year*

Actions by moneylenders for the recovery of money lent and interest, and for the enforcement of securities (with exceptions).

(ii) *Within two years*

(*a*) Actions by tortfeasors to recover contribution from joint tort-feasors;

(*b*) Actions under statutes to recover sums by way of penalty or forfeiture.

(iii) *Within three years*

Actions in contract or in tort claiming damages for personal injuries.

In this case the court may give leave to bring an action after the expiration of the limitation period if the plaintiff was unaware of 'material facts of a decisive character' during that period, provided the action is brought within twelve months of his discovering those facts.

(iv) *Within six years*

(*a*) Actions on simple contracts;

(*b*) Actions in tort;

(*c*) Actions to recover rent, mortgage interest, interest on judgment debts, or interest on legacies;

(*d*) Actions by beneficiaries under trusts;

(*e*) Actions to enforce a recognisance, or an arbitrator's award when the submission is not by an instrument under seal;

(*f*) Actions under statutes (except to recover sums by way of penalty or forfeiture);

(*g*) Actions for an account.

(v) *Within twelve years*

(*a*) Actions on specialty contracts (except to recover rent or mortgage interest);

(*b*) Actions to enforce a judgment (except to recover interest on a judgment debt), or an arbitrator's award when the submission is by an instrument under seal;

(*c*) Actions to recover mortgage money secured on real or personal property, or the proceeds of sale of land;

(*d*) Actions to recover land;

(*c*) Actions in respect of any claim to the personal estate of a deceased person, or any share or interest in such estate (other than interest on a legacy).

(vi) *Equitable relief*

In actions for specific performance, injunction or other equitable relief, if the claim is analagous to a common law claim, the action must be brought within the same time as in the case of the corresponding common law claim. In the case of purely equitable claims, relief must be sought promptly, otherwise the claim will fail under the equitable doctrine of *laches* (delay). The application of this rule to the equitable remedy of rescission has already been observed (see *ante*, § 8 (b) (3)).

Time does not begin to run until the date when the cause of action first accrued, and this is not necessarily the same as the date when the contract was made. Thus, if money is left with a banker on current account and is not drawn upon for more than six years, the customer's right of repayment remains. The cause of action does not accrue until a demand for repayment has been made, because until then there is no obligation on the banker to repay the money.

The making of a winding-up order against a company or a receiving order in bankruptcy proceedings against an individual stops time running, so that if debts are not statute-barred at the time of the making of the order, the rights of the creditors to prove are not affected by subsequent lapse of time.

In the case of actions for the recovery of land or in respect of the conversion of goods, the title as well as the remedy is extinguished by lapse of time, but in other cases the liability of the defaulting party still remains and may be enforced in other ways than by action, and may be revived by an acknowledgment or part payment.

(2) *Acknowledgments and Part Payment*

An acknowledgment of the debt or part payment may start time running again from the date of the acknowledgment. An acknowledgment is sufficient to revive the debt or to start time running again if it amounts to an admission that the debt is owing; it is not necessary that a promise to pay should be implied. Thus, a letter acknowledging the debt but refusing to pay on the grounds that it was statute-barred would be sufficient. The acknowledgment must be *in writing* and made by the party to be charged or his duly authorised agent.

The inclusion of a debt in the balance sheet of a company, signed by the directors, is not normally a sufficient written acknowledgment for this purpose, as the acknowledgment must be of a liability existing at the date of signature, and a balance sheet merely shows the liabilities of the company at the date to which it was made up, the signatures usually being added at a later date (*Consolidated Agencies, Ltd. v. Bertram, Ltd.* [1964] 3 All E.R. 282).

Where there are two or more joint debtors, an acknowledgment by one of them will not start time running again against the other of them. Part payment by one of them, if made before the debt has become statute-barred will start time running again against both of them; but if made after the debt has become statute-barred, it will not revive the liability of the other.

(3) *Disabilities*

If at the date when the cause of action arose the claimant was an infant or a person of unsound mind, time does not begin to run against him until the disability ceases. Once time has started running, however, the occurrence of a disability will not interrupt it. Furthermore, if a person to whom a right of action accrued while under a disability dies, time begins to run as from his death notwithstanding that the person to whom the right of action has passed may himself be under a disability. The absence of the debtor beyond the seas does not prevent time running in his favour.

(4) *Fraud or Mistake*

Where an action is based on fraud, or a right of action is concealed by fraud, or an action is for relief from the consequences of a mistake, the period of limitation does not begin to run until the plaintiff has discovered the fraud or mistake, or could with reasonable diligence have discovered it. This rule will not, however, operate to the prejudice of a *bona fide* purchaser of an interest in property which his predecessor may have acquired by fraud or mistake.

Fraud, in this context, is not restricted to its common law meaning, but includes 'equitable fraud,' *i.e.*, conduct which, having regard to some special relationship between the two parties concerned, is an unconscionable thing for the one to do to the other (*Kitchen* v. *Royal Air Force Association* [1958] 2 All E.R. 241).

In *Clark* v. *Woor* [1965] 2 All E.R. 353, a builder used inferior quality bricks to those specified in the agreement when building a house for the plaintiff. Eight years after the plaintiff had gone into occupation the bricks began to flake. The builder knew that the plaintiff was inexperienced in building matters and was relying on him for the honest performance of the contract.
Held: The plaintiff's right of action had been concealed by the defendant, and the relationship between himself and the plaintiff was such that his conduct was unconscionable; the plaintiff could not by reasonable diligence have discovered his right of action earlier, and, accordingly, it was not statute-barred.

§ 14. *Quasi-Contracts*

In certain circumstances where there is a special relationship between two persons, analogous to a contract, the law imposes upon one person a liability to pay money to the other on the grounds of unjust benefit. These cases are known as quasi-contracts. The following are the most important types of quasi-contracts.

(a) Money paid by one Party to the Use of the other Party

This arises where one person is compelled to pay money for which another person is liable. In order to recover the money so paid the person paying it must prove (1) that he was legally constrained to pay the money, and (2) that it was money for which the other party was legally liable.

In *Brook's Wharf* v. *Goodman Bros.* [1937] 1 K.B. 534, the plaintiffs agreed to warehouse certain goods imported from Russia by the defendants. The goods were stolen from the warehouse without negligence on the part of the plaintiffs. The Customs demanded the payment of duty by the plaintiffs on the goods, and the plaintiffs paid, as they were obliged to do by law.
Held: The plaintiffs could recover the amount as money paid to the use of the defendants, as the defendants were legally liable for the payment of the duty.

The right of contribution between co-sureties and joint tortfeasors is based on this rule.

(b) Money paid under a Mistake of Fact

This has already been considered (*ante*, § 8 (a) (3)).

(c) Money paid in pursuance of a Void or Illegal Contract, or on a Total Failure of Consideration

If the contract is void or illegal, a party making a payment under it has no contractual rights on which he can sue. Nevertheless, subject to the rules already stated (*ante*, § 9 (c)), he is allowed to recover money so paid by an action in quasi-contract.

Failure of consideration means the failure by one party to perform his part of the contract. Where there has been a total failure of consideration by one party, the other party has an option. He may treat the contract as discharged, in which case he must sue in quasi-contract for moneys he has paid, or he may treat the contract as still subsisting and seek damages for its breach.

(d) Claims on a Quantum Meruit

A claim on a *quantum meruit* may be either contractual or quasi-contractual. The action is quasi-contractual if the contract in respect of which the claim is made has been discharged, *e.g.*, by the other party refusing to perform, or rendering himself incapable of performing, his part of the contract (*Planché* v. *Colburn, ante*, p. 80), or where services have been rendered in pursuance of a void contract (*Craven-Ellis* v. *Canons, Ltd.* [1936] 2 K.B. 403).

(e) Money Had and Received by one Party to the Use of Another

If X receives money from Y, or is otherwise in possession of money belonging to Y, which he is instructed by Y to pay over to Z, and he indicates to Z his willingness to pay the money over to him, then Z may bring an action in quasi-contract to recover the money from X (*Shamia* v. *Joory* [1958] 1 Q.B. 448). A common example of this situation arises where a servant or agent receives money which is to be paid to his master or principal. It may also arise where a person obtains money by the improper use of property belonging to another person; in such a case the owner of the property can sue to recover the money so obtained (*Reading* v. *Attorney-General* [1951] A.C. 507).

§ 15. *Conflict of Laws*

A contract may be affected by the laws of more than one country, and the question then arises as to which national law governs the contract. There is no conflict in the true sense, as the contract, or any particular part of it, can be subject to the law of one country only; but the validity of the contract might be governed by the law of one country and its enforcement by the law of another. Thus, in *Leroux* v. *Brown* (1852) 12 C.B. 501, the contract was unenforceable in this country (though an action might have been successfully brought in France) since the written memorandum required under s. 4 of the Statute of Frauds was not in existence.

Bills of exchange, by their negotiation, might cause the application of the law of more than one country. By s.72 of the Bills of Exchange Act, 1882, the validity as regards requisites in form of any contract on the bill is determined by the law of the country where that contract was made. Thus, if a bill of exchange is drawn in this country, payable in Germany, and indorsed in France, English law will apply in respect of the form and drawing of the bill, German law to the presentment for acceptance and for payment, and French law to the indorsement.

In the case of individual contracts of a specific character, the terms of the contract itself must be considered to ascertain the intention of the parties, where the conditions are subject, on the face of the contract, to the laws of two or more countries. If there is no express provision in the contract, it will be governed by the law of that country with which it is most closely connected (the 'proper law' of the contract). This is usually the country of performance (*Benaim & Co.* v. *Debono* [1924] A.C. 514).

Although the courts of this country will enforce a contract subject to the law of a foreign state (upon the production of evidence of what the legal provisions actually are), they will not do so if the contract is in conflict with generally accepted principles of morality or justice, nor where the contract would be illegal or otherwise invalid in the country where it is to be carried out, although the law of this country may not have been infringed (*Regazzoni* v. *Sethia* [1958] A.C. 301).

If a judgment has been obtained in a foreign country, and the judgment creditor wishes to enforce it in this country, he may apply to the High Court at any time within six years after the date of the judgment, or of the determination of an appeal, to have the judgment registered in the High Court, and registration will be effected upon satisfactory proof of the matters prescribed. The judgment will not, however, be registered if it has been wholly satisfied, or if it could not be enforced by execution in the country of the original court. Upon registration, the judgment can be enforced, including a claim for interest, in the same manner as if it had been originally obtained in the registering court (Foreign Judgments (Reciprocal Enforcement) Act, 1933).

For a judgment to be enforceable, it must be final and conclusive as between the parties thereto, and must involve the payment of a sum of money not being taxes or other charges of a like nature or in respect of a fine or other penalty.

AGENCY

§ 1. *Definition of Agency*

An *agent* is a person having express or implied authority to act on behalf of another person, who is called the *principal*, with the object of bringing the principal into legal relations with third parties.

The relationship between the principal and the agent is called *agency*. It is usually, though not necessarily, created by contract between the principal and agent and is then analogous to, but not identical with, the contract between master and servant. Apart from any express appointment of an agent, the law itself may impose the relationship of principal and agent with its attendant consequences as, for instance, where the doctrine of agency of necessity is applicable.

§ 2. *Capacity to Appoint, or Act as, Agent*

Any person capable of entering into a contract on his own behalf may do so by means of an agent. An act done by an agent, as such, is deemed to be the act of the principal who authorised it, the agent being looked upon merely as an instrument. For this reason, although an agent might, on account of infancy or for some other reason, be incapable of entering into a contract on his own behalf, he is able to contract on behalf of and so bind his principal. But a legal disability in the principal to contract personally cannot be surmounted by the appointment of an agent, for the power to be given to the agent must be possessed by the principal.

As between principal and agent full contractual capacity is, of course, required for the mutual rights and obligations to be legally enforceable.

§ 3. *Classification of Agents*

A UNIVERSAL AGENT is one who has unrestricted authority to contract on behalf of his principal. Such appointments are rare, but might arise under an unlimited power of attorney.

A GENERAL AGENT is one who has authority to act for his principal in all matters concerning a particular trade or business, or in some specified direction, such as the administration of an estate; or to do some act in the ordinary course of his trade, profession, or business as an agent, on behalf of his principal.

A SPECIAL AGENT is one who has authority to do some particular act, or represent his principal in some specific transaction.

A DEL CREDERE AGENT is one who, usually in return for extra remuneration, undertakes to indemnify his principal against any loss arising from the failure of persons with whom he contracts on his principal's behalf to carry out their contracts. An agreement by an agent to sell on a *del credere* commission is not a guarantee within the meaning of s. 4 of the Statute of Frauds, 1677, and it is therefore not necessary for such an agreement to be evidenced in writing; it is rather a promise to indemnify the employer against the agent's own inadvertence or ill-fortune in making contracts with persons who cannot perform them by reason of their insolvency (*Sutton* v. *Grey* [1894] 1 Q.B. 285).

§ 4. *Appointment of Agent*

The relationship of principal and agent may arise in one of the following ways:

(a) By express appointment by the principal.

(b) By implied appointment by the principal, the implication arising from the conduct of the parties or the circumstances of the case.

(c) By ratification by the principal of acts which the supposed agent has purported to do on his behalf.

(d) Of necessity, by operation of law, in certain narrowly defined circumstances.

(e) By the doctrine of estoppel or holding out.

The last of these cases strictly falls outside the relationship of principal and agent. Its feature is that no agency in fact exists, yet the principal is bound by his conduct in representing the other as agent to treat him, as regards the claims of third parties against the principal, as though he had in fact express authority to act as agent.

(a) Express Appointment

There is generally no particular form in which an express appointment need be made; but if the agent is authorised to contract under seal, his appointment must be under seal, *i.e.*, by power of attorney.

An agent to grant a lease for more than three years must be appointed by power of attorney, since such a lease must be under seal (Law of Property Act, 1925, s. 52); but an agent to let property for a period not exceeding three years may be appointed orally.

An agent to sign for his principal a declaration of willingness to act as director, or an agent to sign a copy of the prospectus, to be filed with the Registrar of Companies, must be appointed in writing (Companies Act, 1948, ss. 41, 181). A proxy must also be appointed in writing, at least where Table A applies.

An agent to enter into a contract within s. 40 of the Law of Property Act, 1925, may be appointed orally, and may then sign the written memorandum upon which the contract may be enforced (*Basma* v. *Weekes* [1950] A.C. 441; *Davies* v. *Sweet* [1962] 2 Q.B. 300).

(b) Implied Appointment

An agent may be appointed impliedly where the principal, without expressly conferring authority on him, places him in a situation in which, according to the ordinary usages of mankind, or according to the customs of the particular trade, it is understood, as between himself and the principal, that he is to have authority to contract on his principal's behalf. For example, a person appointed by an estate owner as his land agent may have implied authority to conclude letting agreements, although the owner may never have specifically authorised him to do so.

An example of an agency implied from the customs of a particular business is to be seen in the position of an auctioneer as agent for the buyer of land. An auctioner is expressly appointed as agent for the seller, but on the fall of the hammer he becomes also agent for the buyer for the purpose of signing a memorandum of the sale and purchase. This signature will then bind both parties (see *post*, § 12 (d)).

(c) Appointment by Ratification

Where an act is done in the name or on behalf of a person without his authority by another person purporting to act as his agent, the person in whose name or on whose behalf the act is done may ratify this act, and thereby make it as valid and effective as if it had been originally done on his authority, whether the person doing the act was an agent exceeding his authority, or was a person having no authority to act for him at all.

Ratification relates back to the time the contract was made by the agent, so that if an offer is made to an agent, and is accepted by him without authority, the acceptance may be ratified by the principal, and the contract thereby made binding on the person who made the offer, even if he has, in the meantime, given notice to the principal of the withdrawal of the offer.

In *Bolton Partners* v. *Lambert* (1889) 41 Ch. D. 295, A made an offer to B, the managing director of a company, by whom it was accepted, without authority, on behalf of the company. A then withdrew his offer, and gave the company notice to that effect, and the company subsequently ratified B's unauthorised acceptance. It was held that the ratification related back to the time of acceptance so that the withdrawal was ineffective.

But if an agent accepts an offer on behalf of his principal *subject to that principal's ratification*, the third party is entitled to withdraw the offer at any time before such ratification takes place, as the acceptance must be unconditional to be binding on the offeror (*Watson* v. *Davies* [1931] 1 Ch. 455).

To constitute a valid ratification, the following conditions must be satisfied:

(1) The contract must be expressed to be made on behalf of a named or ascertainable principal. A contract made by a person in his own name, which is intended to be made on behalf of an undisclosed principal, though without the principal's authority, cannot be ratified by the principal so as to confer upon him rights or liabilities under the contract.

> In *Keighley, Maxted & Co.* v. *Durant* [1901] A.C. 240, A was authorised by P to purchase wheat at 44s. 3d. a quarter. A, being unable to make a purchase at that price, in excess of his authority agreed to buy from D at 44s. 6d. a quarter. He contracted in his own name without disclosing that he was acting for P. P ratified the contract but failed to take delivery and was sued by D.
>
> *Held:* P could not ratify the contract, and was therefore not liable to D.

A contract made on behalf of a named principal can be ratified even though the agent acted fraudulently, intending to keep the benefit of the contract for himself (*Re Tiedemann* [1899] 2 Q.B. 66).

(2) The principal must have been in existence and have had full contractual capacity at the time the contract was made. Thus, a contract made on behalf of an alien enemy cannot be ratified by him after the cessation of hostilities (*Boston Deep Sea Fishing and Ice Co., Ltd.* v. *Farnham* [1957] 1 W.L.R. 1051). Nor can a company, after incorporation, ratify a contract entered into by the promoters on behalf of the company before its incorporation, since it was not in existence at the time the contract was made (*Kelner* v. *Baxter* (1866) L.R. 2 C.P. 174). If a person signs a contract on behalf of a company which has not yet been formed and there is nothing in all the circumstances to show that he contracted personally, the contract is a nullity because the person so signing is not converted into a principal merely because there is no other party capable of being bound (*Newborne* v. *Sensolid (Great Britain), Ltd.* [1954] 1 Q.B. 45). Such a company may, of course, when formed, enter into a new contract on the same lines if appropriate power exists (*Ashbury Railway Carriage and Iron Co.* v. *Riche* (1875) L.R. 7 H.L. 653).

(3) Ratification must take place within a reasonable time, and in any event before the expiration of the time which may be fixed for performance; and ratification must be of the whole contract.

(4) No person is deemed to ratify an act done without his authority unless at the time of so doing he had full knowledge of all the material circumstances under which the act was done (*Marsh* v. *Joseph* [1897] 1 Ch. 213).

(d) Agency of Necessity

In certain circumstances a person may become the agent of another without any express or implied appointment. Such a person is known as an *agent of necessity*. Thus, a master of a ship or a common carrier may, when so compelled by circumstances, pledge his employer's credit.

The doctrine of agency of necessity is not confined to certain classes of agents only; but the agent must prove such an emergency as compelled him to act as he did (*Prager* v. *Blatspiel, Stamp and Heacock, Ltd.* [1924] 1 K.B. 566). In such circumstances there is an inference that the agent must protect the interests of his principal and that he has, therefore, an implied authority to bind his principal in the performance of acts of an exceptional character and done in good faith.

In *Great Northern Railway Co.* v. *Swaffield* (1874) L.R. 9 Ex. 132, A had sent a horse from King's Cross to Sandy, and upon arrival at its destination the animal was not met, nor was an address available to which the horse could be delivered. It was held that the railway company were able to recover from the owner the livery stable charges necessarily incurred in the circumstances.

But a person who performs an unauthorised act in relation to another's property cannot claim the protection of the doctrine of agency of necessity merely because it was convenient to perform the act.

In *Sachs* v. *Miklos* [1948] 1 All E.R. 67, a gratuitous bailee of furniture, who found it inconvenient to retain the articles, and who was unable to communicate with the owner, sold them without the owner's authority. On being sued for conversion, the bailee failed to establish an agency of necessity, the sale of the furniture being no more than an act of convenience, and was held liable in damages.

For such an agency to exist the act must be performed in such circumstances as would render it impossible to obtain the presumptive principal's instructions.

In *Springer* v. *Great Western Railway Co.* [1921] 1 K.B. 257, S, in Jersey, had sent a consignment of tomatoes to London. They arrived at Weymouth three days late and, owing to a railway strike, a further two days' delay occurred in unloading. They were then found to be in poor condition and, to minimise the loss, the railway company decided to sell them locally. The railway company was held liable to S for the loss. S's instructions could and should have been obtained when the condition of the tomatoes was discovered.

It is probably correct to say that, before an agency of necessity can come into existence, there must be some existing relationship of agency, out of which the necessity to exceed the authority arises; it is highly improbable that the so-called principal would be bound by the act of some stranger who owed no duty to the principal but who took it upon himself to do some act in the principal's interest (*Jebara* v. *Ottoman Bank* [1927] 2 K.B. 254).

(e) Agency by Estoppel

Agency by estoppel arises when a person, who has not, either expressly or impliedly, appointed another as his agent, makes such representations or acts in such a way as to lead third persons to suppose that that other is his agent. The person who has so held out that other as being his agent is by his conduct estopped from denying the agency, that is to say, he is bound by what the so-called agent has purported to do on his behalf as though he had given express authority.

In *Soanes* v. *London and South Western Railway Co.* (1919) 88 L.J.K.B. 524, a railway company supplied a porter with uniform, thus holding him out as its agent. While off duty, and therefore not at the time the company's agent, the porter took charge of a passenger's luggage at a railway station. The luggage was stolen, and the passenger claimed for the loss against the railway company. It was held that the company was estopped from denying the porter's agency, and was therefore liable.

A good example of this kind of agency can be found in the law of partnership. Every partner is an agent of the firm and of his other partners for the purpose of the business of the partnership. A partner who has retired no longer has authority to bind the firm, but if he were to purport to enter into some contract on behalf of the firm with some person with whom he had been accustomed to deal while still in the firm, his co-partners would be bound to that third party, unless they had notified him of the retirement.

The same principle applies to the position of a wife as the agent of her husband. If she has been accustomed to pledge his credit with particular suppliers, whether for necessaries or luxuries, and he has met the bills, he has thereby held her out as his agent; a private withdrawal of her authority would not prevent his being liable to those suppliers on her continuing to pledge his credit, unless he had notified them specifically that her authority had been withdrawn.

Agency by estoppel arises through the representation of the principal, not through the representation of the agent. A person could not be liable by estoppel for the act of another who held himself out as the first person's agent, unless that first person had acted in some way to support the appearance of authority. When there is no holding out by the alleged principal, it is the agent alone who is liable to the third party.

§ 5. *The Authority of the Agent*

An agent has implied authority to do whatever is necessary for the effective execution of his express authority in the usual way; but the authority, whether express or implied, cannot exceed the limits of the powers of his principal (*Shrewsbury, &c., Railway Co.* v. *London and North Western Railway Co.* (1857) 6 H.L. Cas. 113).

A general agent has an implied authority to do anything which a person in his position is usually authorised to do. Even if the principal expressly restricts this authority, any act done by the agent within the ostensible scope of his employment will be binding upon the principal, unless the person dealing with the agent knows of this restriction.

Thus, in *Watteau* v. *Fenwick* [1893] 1 Q.B. 346, where the manager of a public house purchased cigars from W on credit, although he had been expressly forbidden to do so by his employer, it was held that the manager was acting within the scope of his ostensible authority, and the principal was bound to pay for the cigars; he could not rely on any secret limitation of that authority as against W.

But the principal is not bound where the agent does anything outside the scope of his ostensible authority unless the principal had in fact authorised the agent to do it; nor is a principal bound by any act of the agent which is not done as agent on the principal's behalf.

As a general rule, authority to sell does not confer on the agent authority to receive payment (*Butwick* v. *Grant* [1924] 2 K.B. 483). Such authority might, however, be implied from the circumstances, in which event payment to the agent would discharge the buyer even though the money were misappropriated by the agent.

In *Bradford & Sons, Ltd.* v. *Price Bros.* (1923) 39 T.L.R. 272, an agent had authority to receive payment for goods in cash. A purchaser who paid the agent by cheque was held discharged even though he had had notice that cheques were to be drawn payable to the principal, for a cheque which is met is practically equivalent to cash and the notice was not sufficient to withdraw the agent's authority.

An agent has an implied authority to conform, in the pursuance of his agency, with the usages and customs of the place of business in which he is employed (*Sutton* v. *Tatham* (1839) 10 A. & E. 27), unless the usage or custom is illegal or unreasonable (*Hamilton* v. *Young* (1881) 7 L.R. Ir. 289), or has the effect of changing the character of the agency (*Robinson* v. *Mollett* (1874) L.R. 7 H.L. 802).

§ 6. *Delegation by the Agent*

An agent has no power to delegate his authority to a deputy or substitute except with the express or implied assent of the principal. The agreement of the principal to the delegation is implied where:

 (i) it is customary in the trade or business concerned, or

 (ii) it is necessary to the proper carrying out of the agency.

So, where a professional man, *e.g.*, a solicitor or accountant, is appointed to act for a client, delegation of some of the duties to clerks is permissible, and the agent takes responsibility therefor. A country solicitor is also empowered to employ a London agent for the conduct of proceedings in the courts.

It is also considered that an agent has power to delegate his duties to another in the event of a sudden emergency, but, for this course to be justified, there must be extreme urgency, and the inability on the part of the agent to communicate with his principal (*Gwilliam* v. *Twist* [1895] 2 Q.B. 84).

If the agent himself delegates to a sub-agent, the agent is answerable to the principal for money received by the sub-agent on behalf of the principal, and is also responsible to the principal for any damage arising out of the negligence, want of skill, or breach of duty of the sub-agent (*Swire* v. *Francis* (1877) 3 App. Cas. 106). There is no general rule that privity exists between a principal and a sub-agent, such privity will only exist where the principal has authorised his agent accordingly. Consequently, a principal cannot sue a sub-agent for the negligent performance of his duties (*Calico Printers' Association* v. *Barclays Bank, Ltd.* (1930) 170 L.T. 469).

Where an agent delegates his entire employment to a substitute, with the knowledge and consent of the principal, privity of contract may arise between the principal and the substitute, so as to render the substitute responsible to the principal for the proper performance of his duties, if this was the intention of the agent and of the substitute (*De Bussche* v. *Alt* (1878) 8 Ch. D. 286). Where a sub-agent is appointed without the authority, express or implied, of the principal, the principal is not bound by his acts (*Schmaling* v. *Thomlinson* (1815) 6 Taunt. 147).

§ 7. *Duties of the Agent to the Principal*

(a) To Carry Out the Terms of the Employment

An agent must carry out the terms of his agreement in accordance with the authority conferred upon him, and he must follow his principal's instructions, except where they are illegal (*Smart* v. *Sanders* (1848) 5 C.B. 895).

In the absence of express instructions he must act according to usage, if any; otherwise he may exercise his discretion so long as this is consistent with the terms of his employment, and he acts solely on behalf of his principal (*Gray* v. *Haig* (1854) 20 Beav. 219).

He must exercise proper care, skill and diligence. A paid agent must always exercise the skill which is usual and necessary in such matters. A gratuitous agent need not perform the agency, but if he does, he must exercise the skill that he possesses. Where a person holds himself out as possessing the skill and intelligence necessary for the carrying out of a particular undertaking, he must exercise such skill as one so holding himself out might be expected to possess. Failure by the agent to exercise the proper degree of care, skill, and diligence constitutes negligence. As to whether there has been negligence is a question of fact depending upon the nature of the agency and the surrounding circumstances; the only general rule which can be laid down is that the agent must display such care and diligence as can reasonably be expected in the particular class of agency in which he is employed.

The agent must not act in any way that would be inconsistent with his agency, and therefore any custom which would give him the character of a principal, or which would give him an interest opposed to his duty as agent, is an unreasonable custom, and will not be binding.

The agent must not deny the title of the principal to goods entrusted to him by the principal, and he must not, when acting as agent, sell the goods of the principal to himself, or acquire any interest in them. If he does so, the principal is entitled to repudiate the contract (*Re Pemberton* (1840) Mont. & Ch. 667).

The agent must disclose to the principal any information he obtains which might influence the principal in making the contract (*Heath* v. *Parkinson* (1926) 42 T.L.R. 693). He must not disclose to third persons information of a confidential nature entrusted to him in the course of his duties, even after the termination of his agency.

In *Robb* v. *Green* [1895] 2 Q.B. 315, A, while in B's employment, extracted a list of customers from B's order book and used it in a business which he subsequently established. It was held that it was an implied term of the contract that the employee should exercise good faith in view of the confidential relationship between him and his employer, and the latter was therefore entitled to damages and an injunction.

The agent is liable to the principal for any loss suffered by the principal as the direct result of the agent's negligence or breach of duty. Thus, where a house agent obtained an offer from A, but, before the principal had accepted it unconditionally, received a higher offer from B which he negligently failed to communicate to the principal, he was liable for the difference between A's price and B's price (*Keppel* v. *Wheeler* [1927] 1 K.B. 577).

(b) To Account

The agent must pay over to his principal all money received on behalf of the latter, and must keep such money, and all other property of the principal, separate from his own money and property, or that of other persons. He must always be ready with accounts of transactions that have arisen in the course of his agency (*White* v. *Lincoln* (1803) 8 Ves. 363), and must preserve all documents relating to the affairs of his principal, and produce them when required.

When accounts have been settled, the principal has no right to have them re-opened, unless the agent has committed fraud. In the case of fraud, the accounts will be re-opened *ab initio*, and the agent cannot set up the Limitation Act, 1939. If, however, fraud has not been committed, he may plead, and is entitled to the benefit of, the Limitation Act, unless he is sued for property entrusted to him in his capacity of agent, or for the proceeds or value of any such property converted by him to his own use (*Re Land Allotments Co.* [1894] 1 Ch. 616).

(c) Secret Profits

The agent must not make any profit out of the exercise of his authority without the knowledge and consent of his principal. Any profit so acquired must be paid over to the principal.

In *Regier v. Campbell-Stuart* [1939] Ch. 766, an agent agreed to act for a principal in obtaining a house. He bought a house for £2,000 in the name of a nominee, and subsequently entered into a contract with the nominee to purchase it from him for £4,500. He then resold it to his principal for £5,000, representing that he had paid £4,500 for it. It was held that the agent was liable to account to the principal not only for the £500 profit, but also for the £2,500 profit on the previous transaction.

If the principal is aware that the agent receives a recompense from third parties for his work, but misunderstands the extent of it, the principal will have no right to claim such remuneration, unless the agent has wilfully misled him (*Great Western Insurance Co.* v. *Cunliffe* (1874) L.R. 9 Ch. 525).

Where an agent has received a bribe or secret commission, the principal may, on discovering the fact, repudiate the contract (*Bartram & Sons* v. *Lloyd* (1904) 20 T.L.R. 281); he may also recover the bribe or commission from the agent, and may refuse him any remuneration, or recover it back if he has already paid it (*Andrews* v. *Ramsay & Co.* [1903] 2 K.B. 635). If the commission has caused him to pay a higher price than he otherwise would have done, he may recover the excess from the agent (*Mayor of Salford* v. *Lever* [1891] 1 Q.B. 168), or from the other party (*Hovenden & Sons* v. *Millhoff* (1900) 16 T.L.R. 506). He may also dismiss the agent without notice (*Boston Deep Sea Fishing and Ice Co., Ltd.* v. *Ansell* (1888) 39 Ch. D. 339).

It is an offence, punishable by imprisonment for a term not exceeding two years and/or a fine not exceeding £500, for an agent to accept a bribe in relation to his principal's affairs, or for a person to offer or give such a bribe to an agent (Prevention of Corruption Act, 1906, s. 1). In order to prosecute under this Act it is necessary to obtain the consent of the Attorney-General or Solicitor-General.

If money received by way of bribery is invested, the money cannot be followed, and the remedy of the principal is by way of an account, the relation between an agent and principal in this respect being that of debtor and creditor.

§ 8. *Rights of the Agent against the Principal*

(a) Remuneration

An agent is entitled to remuneration only on the basis of an express or implied term providing therefor in his contract with his principal. The principal will be held impliedly liable to pay a reasonable remuneration if he employs an agent to do work of the kind from which the latter gains his livelihood, as where he employs a house agent to sell his property.

Where a contract of agency provides for commission being paid to the agent, it is a question of construction of the contract whether in any particular case events have occurred which entitle the agent to his commission.

In *Luxor (Eastbourne), Ltd.* v. *Cooper* [1941] A.C. 108, Luxor wished to dispose of two cinemas, and agreed to pay their agent a commission on the completion of the sale to any purchaser whom he could introduce. He produced a purchaser who was able and willing to complete, but the company then decided not to proceed with the sale of the property. The agent claimed his commission on the ground that there ought to be implied in his agency agreement a term to the effect that the company would not without just cause so act as to prevent him from earning his commission. It was held, on the construction of the contract, that no such term was implied, and the agent was not entitled to his commission.

The legal position was summarised thus by Viscount Simon, L.C.:

'The primary necessity in each instance is to ascertain with precision what are the express terms of the particular contract under discussion, and then to consider whether these express terms necessitate the addition, by implication, of other terms . . . In contracts made with commission agents, there is no justification for introducing an implied term unless it is necessary to do so for the purpose of giving to the contract the business effect which both parties to it intend that it should have. It may be useful to point out that contracts under which an agent may be occupied in endeavouring to dispose of the property of a principal fall into several obvious classes. There is the class in which the agent is promised a commission by his principal if he succeeds in introducing to his principal a person who makes an adequate offer, usually an offer of not less than the stipulated amount. If that is all that is needed in order to earn his reward, it is obvious that he is entitled to be paid when this has been done, whether his principal accepts the offer and carries through the bargain or not. No implied term is needed to secure this result. There is another class of case in which the property is put into the hands of the agent to dispose of for the owner, and the agent accepts the employment, and, it may be, expends money and time in endeavouring to carry it out. Such a form of contract may well imply the term that the principal will not withdraw the authority he has given after the agent has incurred substantial outlay, or, at any rate, after he has succeeded in finding a possible purchaser . . . There is a third class of case where, by the express language of the contract, the agent is promised his commission only upon completion of the transaction which he is endeavouring to bring about between the offeror and his principal . . . There seems to be no room for the implied term [that the principal will not without just cause so act as to prevent the agent from earning his commission] in such a case. The agent is promised a reward in return for an event, and the event has not happened. He runs the risk of disappointment but, if he is not willing to run the risk, he should introduce into the express terms of the contract the clause which protects him.'

As a consequence of this decision, estate agents, who are a very important class of agents paid by commission, revised their terms of business so as to provide for their remuneration to become payable on the introduction of a person 'ready, able and willing' to purchase property put into their hands for sale. Several decisions have since been reported on the meaning of these words in cases where pro spective vendors have backed out of sales after the conclusion of an agreement to sell subject to contract, but before the execution of a binding contract. In *Graham & Scott (Southgate)* v. *Oxlade* [1950] 2 K.B. 257, the Court of Appeal held that a person whose offer was conditional only ('subject to contract and satisfactory survey') had not been shown to be willing, but only willing upon a condition, and that the vendor was entitled to withdraw before the execution of a binding contract without being liable to pay his agent's commission. It appears that a similar construction will be put upon all such phrases as 'finding a purchaser,' 'a person ready to buy,' and so forth. Where, however, commission is expressed to be payable when a person introduced by the agent enters into a legally binding contract to purchase the property, there is no implied term that such a person shall be 'able and willing' to complete the purchase, and the agent is entitled to his commission once the contract is signed, even though the sale is not completed because of the purchaser's default (*Sheggia* v. *Gradwell* [1963] 1 W.L.R. 1049).

The agent, to claim his remuneration, must show that the transaction was due to his agency. He need not, however, actually com plete the transaction, nor is it absolutely necessary that he should be acting for the principal at the time of the completion. It is sufficient if he can show that he was concerned with the negotiations which led to the transaction, and that his agency was the effective cause of the deal (*Robinson* v. *Tuck* (1957) 107 L.J. 683).

An agent may, in certain cases, be entitled to commission in respect of transactions arising after his employment has ceased. This will depend entirely upon the actual terms of his employment as agent.

In *Bilbee* v. *Hasse* (1889) 5 T.L.R. 677, it was arranged that the agent should be allowed commission upon all orders executed by the principal and paid for by customers arising from his introduction. In consequence of this express agreement the agent was entitled to commission on orders received even after he had left the service of his principals.

In *Sellers* v. *London Counties Newspapers* [1951] 1 K.B. 784, the plaintiff was employed by the defendants as a commercial traveller. He was paid by salary and commission on orders obtained by him, or which he was instrumental in obtaining, for advertisement in the defendants' newspapers. The commission was only payable if and when the advertisements had actually appeared. After his dismissal it was held that he was entitled to commission on any orders obtained for the defendants while he was employed by them even if they were not in fact printed until after the date on which his employment would have been properly terminated, including orders which were to continue until cancelled.

If it can be shown that there is a well-known trade custom that the right to commission on business introduced ceases with the termination of the agency, there will then be no right to remuneration on orders executed subsequently (*Barrett* v. *Gilmour & Co.* (1901) 6 Com. Cas. 72); and this may also be the case by reason of the court's interpretation of the terms of the agreement (*Weare* v. *Brimsdown Lead Co.* (1910) 103 L.T. 429).

Where an agent has been instructed to sell property on commission, and, in default of a purchaser being found, agrees with the principal to buy the property himself, he is not then really acting as agent, and is not entitled to the commission unless the principal has expressly agreed thereto (*Hocker* v. *Waller* (1924) 29 Com. Cas. 296).

Where an agent purports to act in a capacity which he is not entitled to assume, he cannot recover remuneration in respect of the agency; nor can he recover payment for services in relation to transactions obviously or to his knowledge unlawful, or to any wagering contract or agreement which is rendered null and void by the Gaming Act, 1845.

Where a person is appointed 'sole agent' or is granted a right in some such terms, his position depends on the true construction of the contract. The description 'sole agent,' or 'sole selling agent,' is quite often applied to people who are not agents at all, but independent buyers of goods who have obtained a 'concession,' *i.e.*, the sole right to deal in the goods of a manufacturer in a particular district. In these circumstances it may well be a breach of contract for the manufacturer to sell his own goods in that area (*W. T. Lamb & Sons* v. *Goring Brick Co.* [1932] 1 K.B. 710). An estate agent who is appointed 'sole agent' for the sale of a house is not, however, entitled to commission if the owner himself effects a sale (*Bentall, Horsley and Baldry* v. *Vicary* [1931] 1 K.B. 253); to obtain commission the agent must have stipulated for the 'sole right to sell.'

(b) To be Indemnified in Respect of his Agency

Every agent has a right to indemnity from his principal against losses, liabilities and expenses incurred by him in the course of his agency; and he has a right, if sued, to set off the value of this indemnity against the amount due from him to his principal (*Cropper* v. *Cook* (1868) L.R. 3 C.P. 194). Estate agents, however, have no such right in the absence of express agreement. The right is lost if the loss arises by reason of the agent's own default (*Duncan* v. *Hill* (1873) L.R. 8 Ex. 242).

Where the customs and usages in any particular business are known to the principal, the principal is bound to indemnify the agent against losses incurred when acting within the scope of the agency. Even where the custom is illegal, such as the contravention of Leeman's Act (see *ante*, p. 50), the principal must indemnify the agent if he knew of the custom of contravention (*Seymour* v. *Bridge* (1885) 14 Q.B.D. 460), but not if he was unaware of the custom (*Coates* v. *Pacey* (1892) 8 T.L.R. 47).

An agent, as a rule, has no right of action against his principal in respect of any agreement made on the principal's behalf, even though the agent has made himself liable upon the contract to the third party. His remedy is simply by way of indemnity. But, by custom, an insurance broker may sue his principal for premiums in respect of insurances entered into by him on the principal's behalf.

(c) Lien

Where goods or chattels are legally obtained by an agent in that capacity, the agent has a particular or general possessory lien for what is due to him from the principal upon the goods (see Chap. V, § 8 (a)), provided there is no term in his agreement with the principal inconsistent with such lien, and provided also that the goods do not come into his possession with particular directions, or for some special purpose inconsistent with the lien.

(d) Stoppage in Transitu

If an agent has made himself personally liable for goods purchased on behalf of his principal, he may exercise the right of stoppage *in transitu*, in the same manner as he could have done if the relationship existing between him and his principal had been that of seller and buyer (see Chap. III, § 1 (d) (2)).

§ 9. *Principal and Agent and Third Parties*

Where an agent, acting within the authority conferred upon him by his principal, enters into contracts with third parties, the question whether agent or principal is the contracting party is to be determined by reference to the express or implied intention of the parties and the form of the contract made by the agent.

For the purpose of determining the position of the principal and agent in relation to third parties, contracts entered into by agents can be classified under three heads, to each of which certain principles are applicable, although these can be displaced if the parties show a contrary intention.

These three classes of contracts are:

(a) Where the agent expressly contracts as agent for a NAMED principal;

(b) Where the agent expressly contracts as agent without disclosing the IDENTITY of the principal ('unnamed principal');

(c) Where the agent discloses neither the EXISTENCE nor the IDENTITY of the principal ('undisclosed principal').

(a) Contracts for Named Principal

In such cases the principal alone can sue and be sued on the contract, and the agent incurs neither rights nor liabilities under it (*Montgomerie* v. *United Kingdom Steamship Association* [1891] 1 Q.B. 370). This rule is, however, excluded in the following cases, where the agent will incur personal liability on the contract:

(i) If the agent expressly or impliedly assumes personal liability.

(ii) If he signs a written contract in his own name and is held to be a party to the contract on the proper construction of the document.

(iii) By trade usage or custom.

(iv) If, though purporting to act as agent, he is actually contracting on his own behalf, or if there is no principal in existence who can and does take over the liabilities of the contract by ratification or otherwise.

(v) If he signs a negotiable instrument in his own name without making clear on the face of the document that he signs merely as agent.

(vi) If he is acting as an officer of the court, *e.g.*, as receiver.

(vii) If he executes a deed in his own name. A principal must generally be made a party to the deed if he is to sue or be sued under its terms, notwithstanding that it purports to be executed on his behalf (*Chesterfield Colliery Co.* v. *Hawkins* (1865) 3 H. & C. 677). But an agent who executes a deed *under a power of attorney* on behalf of a named principal may do so in his own name without incurring personal liability, and the principal will be in the same position as if it had been executed in his name (Law of Property Act, 1925, s. 123).

(viii) There was formerly a presumption that an agent who contracted in this country for a foreign principal was personally liable on the contract. In *Holt and Moseley* v. *Cunningham* (1949) 83 Ll. L.R. 141, it was stated that this presumption no longer applied, although a contrary view was subsequently expressed by Pearce, J., in *Rusholme, &c., Ltd.* v. *S. G. Read & Co., Ltd.* [1955] 1 W.L.R. 146. Whether or not the presumption now applies, the fact that the principal is a foreigner is still a factor to be taken into consideration in determining the intention of the parties.

Where the agent contracts personally, he may sue in his own name upon the contract entered into by him, if he has an interest in or lien upon the subject-matter. This right will be lost if the principal himself intervenes; and if the agent has no interest in or lien upon the property, a settlement with the principal will be a good defence against the agent.

(b) Contracts for Unnamed Principal

A contract made by an agent for a principal whose identity is not disclosed is a contract between the principal and the third party, for the third party is not led to believe that he is contracting with the agent. He knows that he is contracting with a principal although he does not know who the principal is. As a general rule, therefore, the agent can neither sue nor be sued on the contract (*Fleet* v. *Murton* (1871) L.R. 7 Q.B. 126) which differs little from a contract made by an agent for a named principal, although an intention on the part of the agent to assume personal liability will more readily be inferred.

If the agent declines to disclose the identity of his principal, or gives evidence as to his principal's identity which is not accepted by the court, he will become personally liable on the contract (*Hersom* v. *Bernett* [1955] 1 Q.B. 98).

If the agent buys, and the seller knew that there was a principal, credit would not be given exclusively to the agent, and it will be no defence to the principal to show that he has paid the agent, unless he can also show that he was led to do so by the conduct of the third party (*Irvine* v. *Watson* (1880) 5 Q.B.D. 414). If the agent sells, and the third party knew that there was a principal, he has no right of set-off in respect of money due to him from the agent.

(c) Contracts for Undisclosed Principal

If an agent enters into a contract without disclosing that he is an agent, either the principal or the agent may as a rule sue upon it. But if the agent has contracted in terms which import that he is the real and only principal, e.g., where the agent enters into a charter-party as 'owner' of the ship (*Humble* v. *Hunter* (1848) 12 Q.B. 310), he alone may sue. The third party, even though at the time of executing the transaction he may have thought he was dealing with the principal, may, upon discovering that the party dealt with was merely an agent, recover from the real principal (*Sims* v. *Bond* (1838) 5 B. & Ad. 393). But where the third party, after learning who was the real principal, has elected to hold either the principal or agent alone responsible, he is bound by such election and cannot afterwards sue the other. So, if the third party obtains judgment against the principal, the judgment, even if unsatisfied, will bar proceedings against the agent. The commencement of legal proceedings against one party is not, however, *conclusive* evidence of election.

In *Clarkson, Booker, Ltd* v. *Andjel* [1964] 3 All E.R. 260, the defendant, without disclosing that he was acting as an agent, purchased tickets from the plaintiffs on behalf of a travel agency, and was given credit for the price. On learning of the existence of the principal, the plaintiffs informed both principal and agent that if the money outstanding was not paid proceedings for its recovery might be commenced. They then issued and served a writ against the principal. Learning subsequently that the principal was insolvent and was going into voluntary liquidation, the plaintiffs did not proceed with the action, but brought a further action against the agent. The agent contended that the plaintiffs had made a binding election to pursue their remedy against the principal.

Held: The commencement of legal proceedings against the principal was *prima facie* evidence of election, but the issue of the writ was not necessarily an abandonment by the plaintiffs of their right of action against the agent, and on the facts there had not been any final election, so that the plaintiffs were entitled to recover from the agent.

If the contract is in writing, parol evidence is admissible for the purpose of identifying the real principal, so that he may be charged or may himself sue upon the contract; but any such parol evidence must not be inconsistent with the written agreement, so that if the agent expressly describes himself as a principal, the real principal is unable to bring an action in respect of the contract (*Epps* v. *Rothnie* [1945] K.B. 562).

An undisclosed principal sued for the price of goods bought on his account cannot plead that credit was given to his agent and that he had paid the agent on that basis (*Heald* v. *Kenworthy* (1855) 10 Exch. 739).

Where an agent sells for an undisclosed principal, the purchaser is entitled to treat the agent as a principal and to claim against the true principal a right of set-off in respect of any sum owing to him by the agent, before he became aware that the agent was not the principal (*Isberg* v. *Bowden* (1853) 8 Exch. 852). But the right will not arise where the third party knew the agent acted as such, even though he did not know in what capacity the agent was acting in that particular transaction (*Cooke* v. *Eshelby* (1887) 12 App. Cas. 271).

§ 10. *Wrongful Acts of Agent*

(a) Misrepresentation by Agent

Misrepresentation, whether innocent or fraudulent, or, in the case of contracts *uberrimae fidei*, non-disclosure by an agent, creates remedies against the principal to the same extent as if it had been committed by the principal himself.

In *Blackburn, Low & Co.* v. *Haslam* (1888) 21 Q.B.D. 144, the principal instructed his agent to reinsure an overdue ship at a certain rate. The agent received an offer at a higher rate and, after having heard that the vessel was actually lost, accepted this offer. It was held that, as the agent had not disclosed to the insurer his knowledge of the loss of the ship, his principal could not recover upon the policy.

If an agent makes a misrepresentation innocently, it does not rank as a fraudulent misrepresentation by reason only of the principal's knowledge of the facts which render the statement false. But if the principal deliberately concealed his knowledge from the agent with the dishonest intention that the agent should make the misrepresentation, or, *a fortiori*, if he authorised the making of the statement, the principal would then be guilty of fraud through his agent's misrepresentation.

In *Armstrong* v. *Strain* [1952] 1 K.B. 232, the owner of a bungalow placed it in an agent's hands for sale. The owner was aware that it was in a defective structural condition, but he did not communicate his knowledge to the agent, though his failure to communicate was not with the deliberate intention that the agent should deceive prospective purchasers. The agent made the innocent misrepresentation to a prospective purchaser that the bungalow was 'in splendid condition,' on the faith of which the latter completed his purchase. On discovering the structural defects, the purchaser claimed damages from the vendor for fraudulent misrepresentation. It was held that his action failed, as the agent had made the misrepresentation innocently, and the principal's knowledge could not be imputed to him.

A principal is liable for his agent's fraud although committed before appointment if thereafter the fraud continues to influence the other party (*Briess* v. *Woolley* [1954] A.C. 333).

(b) Torts of Agent

The principal is liable jointly and severally with the agent for the latter's torts, when the agent is acting in the ordinary course of his agency, or by the authority of the principal, even though the principal receives no benefit therefrom (*Lloyd* v. *Grace, Smith & Co* [1912] A.C. 716). But if the tort is committed outside the ordinary course of the agency, and without the principal's authority, or if the agent when committing a tort is not acting on the principal's behalf, the principal is under no liability (*Rayner* v. *Mitchell* (1877) 2 C.P.D. 357).

If the agent commits a tortious act as a result of which the principal incurs liability to a third party, the principal is entitled to recover either contribution or a complete indemnity from the agent except in circumstances where the tort was committed with the knowledge of, or under instruction from, the principal (Law Reform (Married Women and Tortfeasors) Act, 1935, s. 6).

The agent is always personally liable for a tort committed by him, whether or not liability also attaches to the principal.

(c) Breach of Warranty of Authority

Where an agent purports to act as agent on behalf of a principal who is in existence, and induces another to enter into a contract, when he had in fact no express or implied authority to do so, the alleged principal is under no liability on the contract; but the third party can sue the purported agent for damages for breach of warranty of authority in respect of loss suffered through absence of the supposed authority. It is immaterial for this purpose that the purported agent believed himself to have authority.

Thus, in *Starkey* v. *Bank of England* [1903] A.C. 114, a broker forwarded to the Bank of England a power of attorney, purporting to be signed by the owner, for the transfer of certain Consols. The broker believed that the power had been duly executed, but in fact the signature of the holder had been forged. It was held by the House of Lords that the broker had impliedly warranted that he had the authority he professed and that he was liable to the Bank for breach of that warranty.

Liability for breach of warranty of authority will also attach to an agent who contracts on behalf of a principal who has died prior to the date of the contract, even though the agent was unaware of the fact, for the principal being dead, the agent's authority has terminated.

If the agent knew that he had no authority, he is also liable for the tort of deceit (*Oxenham* v. *Smythe* (1861) 31 L.J. Ex. 110).

§ 11. *Termination of Agency*

An agency may be terminated by:

(a) Completion of the transaction for which the agency was formed.

(b) Destruction of the subject-matter.

(c) The death or insanity of the principal or agent, or in certain cases by the principal or agent becoming an alien enemy.

(d) The bankruptcy of the principal.

(e) Revocation by the principal.

(f) Renunciation by the agent.

(g) Effluxion of time.

(h) Agreement of the parties.

(i) Supervening illegality or frustration.

Prima facie, a principal has an indefeasible power to revoke the authority which he has given his agent, and this is so notwithstanding any breach of the contract with the agent the revocation may involve. The only limitation of this principle at common law is the rule that an authority is irrevocable if coupled with an interest, *i.e.* given for the purpose of securing the discharge of some liablity of the principal to the agent. If, for example, a principal owes his agent money and gives him a bill of exchange which he, the principal, has accepted, the agent's authority to fill in blanks in the bill will normally be an authority coupled with an inerest and so will not be revoked by the death of the principal (*Carter* v. *White* (1883) 25 Ch. D. 666).

Statute law has affected the common law position so far as powers of attorney are concerned. Section 126 of the Law of Property Act, 1925, provides that a power of attorney which is given for valuable consideration and expressed in the instrument creating it to be irrevocable cannot be revoked without the donee's consent. Section 127 applies a similar rule to any power of attorney, whether given for valuable consideration or not, which is expressed in the instrument creating it to be irrevocable for a definite specified period not exceeding one year.

Renunciation by the agent must be carried out in accordance with the terms of the contract otherwise a right of action for breach of contract will arise.

When the authority of an agent has been terminated, otherwise than by the death or bankruptcy of the principal, notice of such termination must be given to third parties who have dealt with the agent on the faith of any representation, express or implied, on the part of the principal that the agent is authorised to act on his behalf. Otherwise the principal will remain liable to the third party dealing with that agent to the same extent as he would have been if the authority had not been terminated.

Thus, in *Drew* v. *Nunn* (1879) 4 Q.B.D. 661, a wife was given authority by her husband to buy goods on credit from the plaintiff, and continued to do so after her husband became insane. The plaintiff was unaware of the husband's insanity.

Held: The husband was liable to pay for the goods.

§ 12. *Special Classes of Agents*

(a) Factors

Throughout legal history, the common law has endeavoured to preserve a balance between two leading principles, firstly, that a person cannot pass a title in property which he himself does not own (*nemo dat quod non habet*), and, secondly, that in the interests of the mercantile community a person buying goods from someone in possession of them and having the appearance of ownership should be able to acquire a title thereto. Within the law of agency, this approach is exemplified in the provisions of the Factors Act, 1889, s. 2 (1) of which provides that:

Where a mercantile agent is, with the consent of the owner, in possession of goods or of the documents of title to goods, any sale, pledge, or other disposition of the goods made by him, when acting in the ordinary course of business as a mercantile agent shall, subject to the provisions of this Act, be as valid as if he were expressly authorised by the owner of the goods to make the same; provided that the person taking under the disposition acts in good faith, and has not at the time of the disposition notice that the person making the disposition has not authority to make the same.

For this provision to apply, however, the person transferring the goods (or documents of title thereto) must be a factor, defined in s. 1 (1) of the Act as:

'a mercantile agent having in the customary course of his business as such agent authority either to sell goods, or to consign goods for the purpose of sale, or to buy goods, or to raise money on the security of goods.'

Authority for any of the activities mentioned above suffices; and a person is still a mercantile agent notwithstanding that his principal has limited his powers, *e.g.*, by entrusting the goods to him on 'sale or return' (*Weiner* v. *Harris* [1910] 1 K.B. 285); or that he acts for one customer or principal only (*Lowther* v. *Harris* [1927] 1 K.B. 393), provided he acts in his business capacity. Once it is established that a person is a mercantile agent the Act applies and it is irrelevant that in a particular trade certain transactions, *e.g.*, pledging goods, are not done by mercantile agents (*Oppenheimer* v. *Attenborough* [1908] 1 K.B. 221).

On the other hand the definition of a mercantile agent does not include ordinary shop assistants (their power to pass a title to goods depends on broader principles of agency), clerks or other employees who have no discretionary powers, *i.e.*, where the relationship is that of master and servant. Neither does the definition include agents employed merely to obtain orders but having no power to buy or sell; or a warehouseman or other ordinary bailee such as a friend to whom a piece of jewellery has been entrusted for sale (*Budberg* v. *Jerwood* (1934) 57 T.L.R. 99).

A person claiming title through a mercantile agent under s. 2 of the Act must show that:

(i) the owner of the goods consented to the mercantile agent having possession as a factor;

(ii) the agent acted in the ordinary course of business; and

(iii) the buyer acted in good faith and had no notice of lack of authority on the part of the agent.

(i) Consent to the fact of possession is presumed in the absence of evidence to the contrary (s. 2 (4)); and it is immaterial that the consent has been revoked or that the authority is restricted, unless the third party is aware of that fact.

In *Folkes* v. *King* [1923] 1 K.B. 282, F was the owner of a car which he delivered to X, a mercantile agent, for sale with instructions not to sell at less than £575 without F's authority. X sold the car to K for £340 and misappropriated the money.
Held: K obtained a good title to the car.

The goods need not be entrusted to the agent for sale, for it is enough that they are in his possession with the owner's consent.

In *Moody* v. *Pall Mall Deposit and Forwarding Co., Ltd.* (1917) 33 T.L.R. 306, the owner of a picture delivered it for exhibition purposes only. It was held that a good title to it was transferred by the exhibitor on a sale by him, as he was otherwise qualified as a mercantile agent.

The agent may have possession with consent although the circumstances amount to theft (*Du Jardin* v. *Beadman* [1952] 2 Q.B. 712); but where something is handed over, and intended to be immediately returned, there is no possession with consent if it is not taken back because it is forgotten (*Pearson* v. *Rose and Young, Ltd.* [1951] 1 K.B. 275).

(ii) The agent must act as a mercantile agent, duly authorised by the owner, would have acted. This probably means that he must act during business hours, at a proper place of business, and in other respects in the ordinary way lacking circumstances of suspicion (*Oppenheimer* v. *Attenborough, supra*). Hence, although a disposition is not taken out of the provisions of the Act merely by showing that such a disposition is not customary in the agent's particular business (*ibid.*), a departure from a well known custom would do so, *e.g.*, selling a car without a log-book; the disposal of a car without its registration book is not a disposition in the ordinary course of business for these purposes since the car and book are the goods (*Pearson* v. *Rose and Young, Ltd., supra*).

In *Stadium Finance, Ltd* v *Robbins* [1962] 2 Q.B. 664, the owner of a car left it with a car dealer to obtain inquiries with a view to sale by the owner. The owner took away the ignition key, but accidentally left the registration book in the glove compartment, which was locked. The dealer removed the book from the glove compartment with another key and sold the car with the registration book to the defendants.

Held: The defendants had not acquired a good title to the car, since a sale by a dealer of a car whose owner had not given him possession of the ignition key and registration book was not a sale by a mercantile agent in the ordinary course of his business as such agent; nor was possession of the car in the circumstances possession with the consent of the owner.

(iii) The good faith required on the part of the third party is probably the same as that required under s. 62 (2) of the Sale of Goods Act, 1893, whereby a thing is done in good faith when in fact it is done honestly, whether it is done negligently or not. There must not be actual notice that something is wrong; nor must the third party be aware of circumstances which would lead a reasonable man, applying his mind to them and judging from them, to the conclusion that something is unusual. An offer of a second-hand car without the log-book should put the buyer upon inquiry.

The Factors Act refers to goods or documents of title thereto; but it does not include stocks and shares, negotiable instruments and similar documents. Documents of title include (s. 1(4)):

'any bill of lading, dock warrant, warehouse-keeper's certificate, and warrant
or order for the delivery of goods, and any other document used in the ordinary
course of business as proof of the possession or control of goods, or authorising
or purporting to authorise, either by indorsement or delivery, the possessor of the
document to transfer or receive goods thereby represented.'

A factor has an implied authority, *inter alia*, to (i) sell goods in his
own name; (ii) sell at such times and at such prices as he thinks
suitable; (iii) sell on the usual terms of credit; (iv) warrant the goods
sold, if such is usual in the trade or for the particular class of
merchandise; and (v) receive payment of the price if he sells in his
own name.

A factor has a lien on goods that have come to him in his capacity
as such for the balance of his charges; and this lien extends to the
proceeds of sale of the goods (*Drinkwater* v. *Goodwin* (1775) Cowp.
251). He will lose the lien upon delivery of the goods to the owner,
but he does not lose it on account of the right of set-off which the
third party may have against his principal (*ibid.*).

(b) Brokers

A broker is a mercantile agent who in the ordinary course of his
business is employed to make contracts for the purchase or sale of
property or goods of which he is not entrusted with the possession or
documents of title. Special classes of brokers, such as insurance
brokers or stockbrokers, deal not in property or goods but in rights
or services. Brokers are usually remunerated by a commission called
brokerage.

Brokers as such are not subject to the provisions of the Factors Act,
and are distinguishable from factors in that they do not have possession of the goods or documents of title (*Stevens* v. *Biller* (1883) 25
Ch. D. 31), and also in that the factor may sell in his own name,
whereas the broker can merely sell in the name of his principal
(*Baring* v. *Corrie* (1818) 2 B. & Ald. 137).

If a broker is known to be contracting as such, he does not incur
personal liability, even though the name of the principal is not disclosed (*Southwell* v. *Bowditch* (1876) 1 C.P.D. 374), but he may make
himself liable by contract, express or implied, or by custom (as in the
case of a stockbroker).

A broker has implied authority, *inter alia*, to (i) sell on the usual
terms of credit; (ii) receive payment of the price where he sells on
behalf of an undisclosed principal; and (iii) act in accordance with the
usage, rules and regulations of the market in which he deals so far as
they are not illegal or unreasonable or inconsistent with the contract.

(1) *Stockbrokers*

Members of the London Stock Exchange have to declare whether
it is their intention to act as brokers or jobbers. A stock-jobber

always contracts as principal, but a stockbroker buys and sells as agent on behalf of a principal.

Where a broker is employed by a client, the client is presumed to give him such authority as will enable him to comply with the rules and regulations of the Stock Exchange, and with any reasonable custom. It does not matter whether or not the client is acquainted with the rules of the Exchange (*Sutton* v. *Tatham* (1839) 10 A. & E. 27), unless the custom is unreasonable (see *ante*, p. 94).

Although a stockbroker may put through dealings on behalf of several clients in one transaction, dividing them up in his own books, a contract between such clients and the jobber with whom the transaction was entered into will be established by the custom of the Exchange (*Scott* v. *Godfrey* [1901] 2 K.B. 726).

(2) *Insurance Brokers*

An insurance broker is an agent employed to arrange a contract of insurance with an underwriter on behalf of his principal. The broker is merely an agent in arranging the insurance, but he is a principal for the purpose of receiving payment of the money due from the insured, and of paying it to the underwriter (*Power* v. *Butcher* (1829) 10 B. & C. 329). He has a lien on the policy for the balance due (*Fisher* v. *Smith* (1878) 4 App. Cas. 1; Marine Insurance Act, 1906, s. 52 (2)). The underwriter cannot sue the insured for the premium, but the insured can sue the underwriter in the event of a claim.

(c) Bankers

As to the relationship between a banker and his customer, and his position as agent of the customer, see Chap. IV, § 3 (d).

(d) Auctioneers

An auctioneer is a person authorised to sell goods or land at a public auction or sale. The method of dealing is for the auctioneer to offer specified goods or property, and to sell them on behalf of his principal to the highest bidder. Primarily he is the agent of the seller, but after land has been knocked down to the highest bidder he is also the agent of the buyer, and by his signature he can bind both parties in order to bring into existence the memorandum necessary under s. 40 of the Law of Property Act, 1925 (see Chap. I, § 4 (e)). There must, however, be no undue delay, otherwise the agency will be deemed to have terminated.

In *Chaney* v. *Maclow* [1929] 1 Ch. 461, the purchaser, immediately after the auction, objected to one of the conditions of sale, and left without signing the memorandum. The auctioneer, being of the opinion that the purchaser would sign later, returned to his office, and as the purchaser did not appear, signed the memorandum on his behalf two hours later. It was held that the purchaser was bound thereby.

An auctioneer should only sell for cash; but where it is customary to accept a negotiable instrument, he may do so if he acts without negligence (*Farrer* v. *Lacey* (1885) 31 Ch. D. 42).

He has a lien on the goods to the extent of his charges while they are in his possession (*Williams* v. *Millington* (1788) 1 H. Bl. 84).

By s. 58 of the Sale of Goods Act, 1893:

(1) Where goods are put up for sale by auction in lots, each lot is *prima facie* deemed to be the subject of a separate contract of sale.

(2) A sale by auction is complete when the auctioneer announces its completion by the fall of the hammer, or in other customary manner. Until such announcement is made any bidder may retract his bid.

(3) Where a sale by auction is not notified to be subject to a right to bid on behalf of the seller, it is not lawful for the seller to bid himself, or to employ any person to bid at the sale, or for the auctioneer knowingly to take any bid from the seller or any such person. Any sale contravening this rule may be treated as fraudulent by the buyer.

(4) A sale by auction may be notified to be subject to a reserved or upset price, and a right to bid may also be reserved expressly by or on behalf of the seller.

Where goods are sold by auction and are known to be subject to a reserve price, the sale will not be binding should the auctioneer knock down a lot under the mistaken impression that the reserve has been reached, for each bid is a conditional offer, and the fall of the hammer a conditional acceptance, subject to the reserve being reached (*McManus* v. *Fortescue* [1907] 2 K.B. 1). But if in such a case the auctioneer actually signs a memorandum of the contract, the acceptance ceases to be conditional, and he will be liable to an action for breach of warranty of authority at the suit of the purchaser if he sells below the reserve price (*Fay* v. *Miller, Wilkins & Co.* [1941] Ch. 360).

An advertisement by an auctioneer of a sale by auction is not of the nature of a contract to sell, and the auctioneer will not be liable in damages for loss of time and expenses of a person who attended with a view to effecting a bid, if the auction does not take place (*Harris* v. *Nickerson* (1873) L.R. 8 Q.B. 286).

An auctioneer has no implied authority to warrant the goods sold by him (*Payne* v. *Leconfield* (1882) 51 L.J. Q.B. 642); nor does he warrant the principal's right to sell in the case of specific goods, but he must not be aware of any defect in the seller's title (*Benton* v. *Campbell, Parker & Co., Ltd.* [1925] 2 K.B. 410).

Auctions (Bidding Agreements) Act, 1927

It is an offence punishable by a fine not exceeding £100 and/or imprisonment for a term not exceeding six months for any dealer to give or agree to give any consideration to another person as an inducement to him to abstain from bidding at a sale by auction; and similar penalties are liable to be incurred by the recipient of such a gift. For the purposes of the Act, a dealer is defined as 'a person who

in the normal course of his business attends sales by auction for the
purpose of purchasing goods with a view to reselling them.'

Where any sale has been effected as a result of this practice, and a
prosecution and conviction have resulted therefrom, it may be treated
by the vendor, as against a purchaser who has been a party to the
agreement or transaction, as a sale induced by fraud. But a notice or
intimation by the vendor to the auctioneer that he intends to exercise
this power does not affect the obligation of the latter to deliver the
goods to the purchaser.

Mock Auctions Act, 1961

It is an offence punishable by a fine not exceeding £1,000 and/or
imprisonment for a term not exceeding two years to promote or
conduct or to assist in the conduct of a mock auction. For the purposes of the Act a sale of goods by way of competitive bidding is a
mock auction if, during the course of the sale:

(1) any lot to which the Act applies is sold to a person at a price lower than his
highest bid for it, or part of the price at which it is sold to him is repaid or
credited to him;
(2) the right to bid is restricted to persons who have bought or agreed to buy one
or more articles; or
(3) any articles are given away or offered as gifts.

The lots to which the Act applies comprise articles of household or
personal use or ornament or any musical or scientific instrument or
apparatus.

(e) Partners

The agency of partners is considered in Chap. VIII, § 2 (a).

(f) Married Women

A married woman has no authority by the mere fact of marriage to
contract on behalf of her husband, but in certain cases an authority
to pledge the credit of her husband for necessaries is presumed until
the contrary is proved. This implied authority arises partly from the
duty of the husband to provide her with the necessaries of life, and
partly from the position in which the husband places her in respect of
housekeeping matters, but it is strictly confined to the provision of
necessaries for herself and her household, and she has no power to
borrow money in his name. The presumption of authority to pledge
his credit may also be rebutted by showing that she was already properly provided with necessaries, and that she had no authority in fact.

Thus, if the husband's credit is pledged by the wife, and he can
show that he had actually forbidden her to pledge his credit, he is
under no liability, even though the person dealing with the wife had
no notice of the want of authority, unless the husband himself, in
spite of the other circumstances, had invested her with an appearance

of authority, or had done some act which estopped him from denying her authority (*Remmington* v. *Broadwood* (1902) 18 T.L.R. 270).

The word 'necessaries' signifies articles which are reasonably needed, and which are suitable to the station in life and the style of living fixed by the husband. Costs incurred by a wife in bringing proceedings for divorce against her husband are 'necessaries' for which the husband is liable (*Abrahams* v. *Hoffe-Miles* (1923) 40 T.L.R. 2).

If the husband forbids the wife to pledge his credit, he must make her an allowance for necessaries, or keep her fully supplied with them. It seems that the fact that a wife living with her husband has a separate income, however large, does not of itself exonerate her husband from the obligation to provide her with necessaries (*Callot* v. *Nash* (1923) 39 T.L.R. 291). This was doubted in *Biberfeld* v. *Berens* [1952] 2 All E.R. 237, and it may be that she must use her own resources for personal necessaries, confining her right to pledge her husband's credit to household necessaries.

Before 1971 it was possible for a wife who had been deserted by her husband to pledge his credit for the purchase of necessaries as his agent of necessity. This right was abolished by the Matrimonial Proceedings and Property Act, 1970, s. 41.

A husband is not liable if the wife pledges his credit after judicial separation, unless he has failed to pay alimony that has been ordered, in which case he would be liable for necessaries.

Advertisements are sometimes inserted in newspapers by which a husband repudiates liability for his wife's debts. Such advertisements are either unnecessary or insufficient. If the wife has not already been in the habit of pledging the credit of the husband they are unnecessary, since the husband can privately forbid the wife to pledge his credit, and keep her fully supplied with necessaries. If the wife has already been in the habit of pledging the husband's credit, with his consent, the advertisements are insufficient, since specific notice must be given to the persons with whom she has been in the habit of dealing. If it could be proved that the advertisement had come to the knowledge of a particular trader, this would be regarded as sufficient notice and the husband would not be liable in respect of his wife's subsequent transactions with that trader (*Hunt* v. *De Blaquiere* (1829) 5 Bing. 550).

CHAPTER III

SALE OF GOODS AND HIRE-PURCHASE

§ 1. *The Sale of Goods*

The law relating to the sale of goods is substantially codified in the Sale of Goods Act, 1893; but the general principles of contract law also apply except in so far as they are inconsistent with the Act.*

(a) The Contract of Sale

(1) *Nature of the Contract*

A contract of sale is defined by s. 1 (1) of the Sale of Goods Act as 'a contract whereby the seller transfers or agrees to transfer, the property in goods to the buyer, for a money consideration called the price.' 'Property' means the right of ownership, *i.e.*, a right which is good against all the world.

'Goods' include all chattels personal other than things in action and money. The term also includes emblements (*i.e.*, vegetable products which are the annual result of agricultural labour), industrial growing crops, and things attached to or forming part of the land, which are agreed to be severed before sale or under the contract of sale (s. 62). A ship is also 'goods' within the meaning of the Act (*Behnke* v. *Bede Shipping Co.* [1927] 1 K.B. 649).

Where under a contract of sale the property in the goods is transferred from the seller to the buyer the contract is called a *sale*; where the transfer of the property in the goods is to take place at a future time or subject to some condition thereafter to be fulfilled the contract is called an *agreement to sell* (s. 1 (3)). An agreement to sell becomes a sale when the time elapses or the conditions are fulfilled subject to which the property in the goods is to be transferred (s. 1 (4)).

The Act does *not* apply to a contract for WORK AND MATERIALS. It is sometimes difficult to distinguish a contract for work, which contemplates the ultimate transfer of the property in a chattel, from a sale, the test being whether the essential object of the agreement is the provision of materials or the exercise of skill. So an agreement to paint a portrait was held to be a contract for work notwithstanding that the result of its performance would be the transfer of the property in the finished portrait (*Robinson* v. *Graves* [1935] 1 K.B. 579); but a contract for the sale of a fur coat of special design and colour to a customer's requirements is a sale of goods, notwithstanding the degree of skill, work and labour involved in its production (*Marcel*

*Where goods are sold under 'credit-sale' or 'conditional sale' agreements the provisions of the Hire-Purchase Act, 1965, may also apply; see *post*, § 3(b).

Furriers v. *Tapper* [1953] 1 All E.R. 15). A contract by a dentist to make a set of false teeth was held to be a contract for the sale of goods in *Lee* v. *Griffin* (1861) 30 L.J.Q.B. 252, although the question was left open by the Court of Appeal in *Samuels* v. *Davis* [1943] K.B. 526. Where a contract involves the repair of a motor car and the supply of parts therefor, the contract is one for work and materials and not one for the sale of goods (*Myers* v. *Brent Cross Service Co.* [1934] 1 K.B. 46; *Stewart* v. *Reavell's Garage* [1952] 2 Q.B. 545).

Since the repeal of s. 4 (*infra*) the distinction has been of little practical importance, particularly as the courts will imply into a contract for work and materials a condition analogous to that in s. 14 (1) (see (8), *infra*) that the work will be properly done and that the materials supplied will be fit for the required purpose, if this is made known to the supplier (*Samuels* v. *Davis, supra*).

The distinction between sale of goods and hire-purchase is considered in § 3 of this Chapter.

(2) *Capacity to Contract*

The capacity to buy and sell is stated by s. 2 to be regulated by the law concerning capacity to contract (see Chap. I, § 7). The section expressly provides that where necessaries are sold and delivered to an infant or person who by mental incapacity or drunkenness is incompetent to contract, he must pay a reasonable price therefor.

(3) *Form of the Contract*

A contract of sale may be in writing, either with or without seal, or by word of mouth, or partly in writing and partly by word of mouth, or may be implied from the conduct of the parties (s. 3).

Section 4, which required written evidence of certain contracts of sale, was repealed by the Law Reform (Enforcement of Contracts) Act, 1954, and every contract of sale may now be made orally, if so desired.

(4) *Contract for Future Goods*

Section 5 provides that the contract of sale may be one for the sale either of existing or of future goods, future goods being those which are to be manufactured or acquired after the making of the contract of sale; and that there may be a contract for the sale of goods, the acquisition of which by the seller depends upon a contingency which may or may not happen. A contract for the sale of future goods operates as an agreement to sell the goods.

(5) *Existing Goods*

It is important to determine whether, in the case of existing goods, these are specific goods, unascertained goods or ascertained goods, because in many respects, *e.g.*, in relation to the passing of the property in the goods, different rules apply to each.

'Specific goods' are goods identified and agreed upon at the time a contract of sale is made (s. 62). Goods are not specific merely because the source of supply is identified, *e.g.*, '500 tons from the 1,000 tons on board' is not specific; but, on the other hand, 'the 500 tons in the hold' is specific (*Re Wait* [1927] 1 Ch. 606).

Unascertained goods are existing goods not specifically identified, but referred to by description. Ascertained goods are goods which are identified in accordance with the agreement after the contract is made.

(6) *Perishing of the Goods*

Section 6 provides that where, in a contract for the sale of *specific* goods, the goods, without the knowledge of the seller, have perished at the time when the contract is made, the contract is void.

This provision, which concerns a loss *prior* to the contract, is a statutory application of the common law rule relating to mistake; but whilst at common law it is the common mistake of the parties as to the existence of the subject-matter which renders the contract void, here it is the mistake of the seller alone which is material.

Section 7 provides that where there is an agreement to sell *specific* goods, and without any fault on the part of either the seller or the buyer the goods subsequently perish before the risk passes to the buyer, the agreement is avoided. (As to when the risk passes, see (b) (1), *infra*.)

This section, which concerns a loss arising *subsequent* to the contract, but before the risk has passed to the buyer, is a statutory application of the principle of frustration; but if the goods are not specific goods the general rules of the common law are to be applied, so that if, for instance, both parties contemplated that the goods should come from a certain source which fails, there is frustration; but where the seller alone had in mind certain goods or a particular source for the goods in question, there is no frustration. If, for example, the sale is of generic goods, *i.e.*, goods of a general description, the seller is not relieved from responsibility if the goods he had in mind turn out to be non-existent or otherwise unavailable. It will be up to him to secure other goods of a like description for delivery to the buyer.

In the case of specific goods, if the risk has passed to the buyer and the goods perish, he must pay for them although he cannot get delivery, and so he bears the loss; on the other hand, if the risk has not yet passed, the contract is avoided, and any loss will fall upon the seller. The provisions of the Law Reform (Frustrated Contracts) Act, 1943, are excluded in relation to this section.

Both sections apply to a total accidental loss; and they also apply to a partial loss if there is a sale of an indivisible parcel of goods for an entire price or under an entire contract. Thus, it may be impossible to give delivery on account of the misappropriation of the goods by a third party, or where only part of the goods contained in an indivisible contract have perished.

In *Barrow, Lane and Ballard, Ltd.* v. *Philip Phillips & Co., Ltd.* [1929] 1 K.B. 574, the plaintiff company purchased a load of 700 bags of nuts lying at a London wharf, and shortly afterwards resold them to the defendants at a time when, unknown to either of the parties, 109 bags had been misappropriated. In an action for the price, it was held that no load of 700 bags was in existence at the time of the sub-sale, and the plaintiffs were unable to recover, as the contract was void.

The 'perishing' of the subject-matter of the contract does not include the mere deterioration of the goods if they still answer the contract description (*Horn* v. *Minister of Food* [1948] 2 All E.R. 1036); but goods are said to 'perish,' not only where there is complete physical destruction, but also where the goods are so damaged or have so far deteriorated as to have ceased to exist commercially as goods of the description under which they were sold (*Asfar & Co.* v. *Blundell* [1896] 1 Q.B. 123).

(7) *The Price*

The price to be paid may actually be fixed in the contract, or may be left to be fixed in a manner thereby agreed, or may be determined by the course of dealing between the parties; otherwise the buyer must pay a reasonable price, and what is a reasonable price is a question of fact dependent on the circumstances of each particular case (s. 8).

If the terms of the contract provide that the price is to be fixed by the valuation of a third party, and such third party cannot or does not make the valuation, the agreement is avoided; but if the goods or any part thereof have been delivered to and appropriated by the buyer, he must pay a reasonable price therefor (s. 9 (1)); and if the valuation is impossible, owing to the fault of one of the contracting parties, the party not in fault may maintain an action for damages against the party in fault (s. 9 (2)).

The price must be a money price, otherwise the contract is one of barter and not of sale; but apparently part barter with an adjustment by way of money payment to even up the bargain is within the definition of a sale (*Simpson* v. *Connolly* [1953] 2 All E.R. 474). Apart from the fact that the consideration (price) must be in money, the general rules as to consideration apply, and the price need not be adequate for the contract to be enforceable.

(8) *Conditions and Warranties*

The distinction between conditions and warranties and the meaning of these terms have already been considered (see Chap. I, § 6 (d)). The Act defines a 'warranty' as an agreement with reference to goods which are the subject of a contract of sale, but *collateral to the main purpose* of such contract, the breach of which gives rise to a claim for *damages* but not the right to reject the goods and treat the contract as repudiated (s. 62). 'Condition' is not defined in the Act, but by necessary inference a condition is a term of a contract but for which the party would not have entered into the contract; so that the breach of a condition will entitle the injured party to *repudiate* the contract and claim damages. Whether a stipulation is a condition or a warranty depends in each case on the construction of the contract, and it is possible for a stipulation to be a condition though called a warranty in the contract (s. 11 (1) (*b*)).

Stipulations as to time of payment are not, in the absence of agreement to the contrary, of the essence of a contract of sale (s. 10) (see Chap. I, § 12 (b) (2)).

Where a contract of sale is subject to any condition to be fulfilled by the seller, the buyer may waive the condition, or may elect to treat its breach as a breach of warranty and not as a ground for treating the contract as repudiated (s. 11 (1) (*a*)). If the contract is not severable, and the buyer has accepted any part of the goods, then, unless otherwise agreed, any breach of condition on the part of the seller can only be treated as a breach of warranty, and not as a ground for repudiating the contract (s. 11 (1) (*c*)). In these cases the condition is said to become a 'warranty *ex post facto*.'

A contract is not severable merely because the seller has an option to make the contract one transaction or to divide it into two or more transactions by his mode of performance. If he chooses the former course, e.g., by delivering all the goods contracted for in a single shipment, the buyer, by accepting any part of the goods, is precluded by s. 11 (1) (*c*) from rejecting the remainder (*J. Rosenthal & Sons, Ltd.* v. *Esmail* [1965] 2 All E.R. 860, H.L.).

In the case of an unconditional contract for the sale of specific goods in a deliverable state, the property usually passes when the contract is made, in accordance with s. 18 (1) (see (b) (1), *infra*), so that in this and similar cases *it is never possible to repudiate the contract for breach of condition*, unless an express stipulation to that effect is made.

At common law the maxim *caveat emptor* ('let the buyer take care') applied, so that, in the absence of any express terms to the contrary, the seller was not liable to the buyer for any defects in the goods sold. The courts limited the operation of this principle by implying certain undertakings on the part of the seller, and these are now incorporated in the Sale of Goods Act, which provides that, unless the terms of the contract reveal a different intention, the following conditions and warranties are *implied* into every contract for the sale of goods:

(i) *Stipulations as to* TITLE

Under s. 12 there are:

(1) An implied CONDITION that the seller has a *right to sell* the goods, or, in the case of an agreement to sell, that he will have a right to sell at the time when the property is to pass;

(2) An implied WARRANTY that the buyer shall have and enjoy *quiet possession* of the goods;

(3) An implied WARRANTY that the goods shall be *free from any charge or incumbrance* in favour of any third party, not declared or known to the buyer before or at the time when the contract is made.

When goods are labelled in such a way that they cannot be resold without infringing the trade mark of a third party, the buyer will be entitled to reject the goods, as the seller has broken the implied condition contained in s. 12 (1) that he had a right to sell the goods (*Niblett* v. *Confectioners' Materials Co., Ltd.* [1921] 3 K.B. 387).

Although, on a sale of specific goods, the buyer may be unable to treat the breach of s. 12 (1) as a breach of condition because of the operation of s. 11 (1) (*c*) (*supra*), he may nevertheless be able to recover the full purchase price on the ground that there has been a total failure of consideration.

In *Rowland* v. *Divall* [1923] 2 K.B. 500, R bought a car from D which he used for some months. The car had in fact been stolen and R was obliged to return it to the true owner. R recovered the price he had paid for it as on a consideration which had wholly failed, although he had had the use of the car for a time, since he had bargained for the lawful property in it which he did not obtain.

(ii) *Sales by* DESCRIPTION

In a sale of goods by DESCRIPTION there is under s. 13 an implied CONDITION that the goods *shall correspond with the description*; and if the sale is by sample as well as by description, it is not sufficient that the bulk corresponds with the sample, if the goods do not also correspond with the description.

This section is strictly construed in favour of the buyer, and 'description' covers not only matters which go to the nature of the goods sold, but also such attributes as the origin of the goods or the mode of packing named in the contract, or the time of shipment. Every item is a description which constitutes a substantial ingredient in the 'identity' of the thing sold.

'If you contract to sell peas, you cannot oblige a party to take beans. If the description of the article tendered is different in any respect, it is not the article bargained for, and the other party is not bound to take it' (*per* Lord Blackburn in *Bowes* v. *Shand* (1877) 2 App. Cas. 455, at p. 480).

In *Re Moore & Co. and Landauer & Co.* [1921] 2 K.B. 529, there was a contract to purchase 3,000 tins of canned fruit, to be packed in cases each containing 30 tins. A substantial part was delivered in cases containing 24 tins. It was held that the buyer could reject the whole consignment, as it did not correspond with the description of the goods ordered.

In *Nichol* v. *Godts* (1854) 10 Ex. 191, a purchaser who had agreed to buy oil called 'foreign refined rape oil, warranted only equal to sample,' was held entitled to refuse the bulk, although it corresponded with the sample, because it was not 'foreign refined rape oil,' and therefore did not correspond with the description.

In all cases where the buyer has not seen the goods, and buys them relying entirely on the description, there is a contract for the sale of goods by description (*Varley* v. *Whipp* [1900] 1 Q.B. 513). And even when the buyer has seen the goods before purchase, there may, nevertheless, be a sale by description where any discrepancy between goods and description was not apparent.

In *Nicholson and Venn* v. *Smith Marriott* (1947) 177 L.T. 189, linen cloths about to be put up for auction were described in the sale catalogue as being seventeenth century lace. Antique dealers read the description, saw the lace and bought it, but it later transpired that the lace was in fact an eighteenth century product. Having relied on the catalogue description they were held entitled to succeed against the defendants for breach of implied condition notwithstanding physical inspection of the goods.

Apart from civil liability under the Sale of Goods Act it should be remembered that a person who applies a false trade description to goods may be criminally liable under the Trade Descriptions Act, 1968.

(iii) QUALITY *and* FITNESS

Under s. 14, subject to the provisions of the Sale of Goods Act, and of any statute in that behalf, there is no implied warranty or condition as to the quality or fitness for any particular purpose of goods supplied under a contract of sale except as follows:

(1) Where the buyer expressly or by implication makes known to the seller the PARTICULAR PURPOSE for which the goods are required, so as to show that the buyer relies on the seller's skill or judgment, and the goods are of a description which it is in the course of the seller's business to supply (whether he be the manufacturer or not), there is an implied CONDITION that the goods shall be reasonably fit for such purpose; provided that in the case of a contract for the sale of a specified article under its patent or trade name there is no implied condition as to its fitness for any particular purpose.

(2) Where goods are bought by description from a seller who deals in goods of that description (whether he be the manufacturer or not), there is an implied CONDITION that the goods shall be of a MERCHANTABLE QUALITY; provided that if the buyer has examined the goods there shall be no implied condition as regards defects which such examination ought to have revealed.

(3) An implied warranty or condition as to quality or fitness for a particular purpose may be annexed by the usage of trade.

(4) An express warranty or condition does not negative a warranty or condition implied by the Act unless inconsistent therewith.

Under s. 14 (1), where goods are ordered for a special purpose, and that purpose is disclosed to the vendor, so that in accepting the contract he undertakes to supply goods which are suitable for the object required, such a contract is enough to establish that the buyer has shown that he relies on the seller's skill or judgment (*Manchester Liners* v. *Rea* [1922] 2 A.C. 74). The buyer need not make known to the seller the purpose for which he requires the goods if it is obvious, for reliance upon the seller's skill or judgment may be inferred (*Preist* v. *Last* [1903] 2 K.B. 148 (bursting hot-water bottle); *Frost* v. *Aylesbury Dairy Co.* [1905] 1 K.B. 608 (milk containing typhoid germs); *Chapronière* v. *Mason* (1905) 21 T.L.R. 633 (bun containing stone which broke plaintiff's tooth)); and the buyer may be relying upon the seller's skill or judgment even though the goods are to be supplied according to the buyer's plans and specifications, *e.g.*, the manufacture and sale of propellors for a ship (*Cammell Laird & Co., Ltd.* v. *Manganese Bronze and Brass Co., Ltd.* [1934] A.C. 402).

Goods are of a description which it is in the course of the seller's business to supply if they are within the general ambit of his business, although the particular purpose is unusual, *e.g.*, the supply of special gum for fly-papers by manufacturers of general adhesives (*Spencer Trading Co.* v. *Devon (Fixol and Stickphast), Ltd.* [1947] 1 All E.R. 284).

The exception as to a trade name applies only to sales under the trade name simply, and not to cases where the name is used but it is clear that the seller's skill or judgment is relied upon.

In *Baldry* v. *Marshall, Ltd.* [1925] 1 K.B. 260, B informed the defendant car dealers that he required a comfortable car suitable for touring purposes. The firm recommended a 'Bugatti' which B bought. B found the car uncomfortable and unsuitable for the purpose for which he required it. It was held that he was entitled to reject the car and recover the price.

A name is a trade name only when particular goods have come to be identified with that name whether by usage or otherwise (*Bristol Tramways Co.* v. *Fiat Motors, Ltd.* [1910] 2 K.B. 831).

Section 14 (2) is wider in its terms than s. 14 (1), and may apply where the latter cannot do so, *e.g.*, where a trade name excludes its operation or where there is no reliance on the skill or judgment of the seller.

In *Wilson* v. *Rickett, Cockerell & Co., Ltd.* [1954] 1 Q.B. 598, the plaintiff suffered damage from the discharge of a piece of high explosive hidden in a ton of 'Coalite' supplied by the defendants. It was held that the load of fuel supplied was not reasonably fit for the purpose for which it was required, though probably the defendants could claim the benefit of the proviso to s. 14 (1); but in any event the ton of fuel was not of merchantable quality and the plaintiff was entitled to recover under s. 14 (2), notwithstanding that the danger was created by some extraneous piece of material and not by any part of the 'Coalite.'

The expression 'merchantable quality' is not given a statutory definition, but it appears to mean that the goods must be reasonably saleable under the contract description, that is, when a reasonable man, after full examination, would accept the goods in performance of his purchase (*Bristol Tramways Co.* v. *Fiat Motors, Ltd., supra*). Thus, a cargo of dates impregnated with sewage is not merchantable although capable of conversion into vinegar (*Asfar & Co.* v. *Blundell* [1896] 1 Q.B. 123; *ante*, p. 118). But goods are merchantable if they are reasonably fit for one of several purposes for which such goods would normally be used, even if unfit for the particular purpose intended by the buyer, *e.g.*, barley for the feeding of pigs (*Canada Atlantic Grain Exports Co.* v. *Eilers* (1929) 35 Com. Cas. 90). Where the goods are normally used for one purpose only, they may be merchantable if they are of some use, though not entirely efficient use, for that purpose (*Bartlett* v. *Sidney Marcus, Ltd.* [1965] 2 All E.R. 753).

The implied condition as to merchantability is excluded as regards defects which ought to have been revealed to the buyer on an examination of the goods by him prior to or on making the contract. Under s. 34 (see (c) (2), *infra*) there is a general right to examine the goods prior to acceptance of them.

In *Thornett and Fehr* v. *Beers & Sons* [1919] 1 K.B. 486, the buyer's representative, being pressed for time, did not inspect the contents of certain barrels of glue, but contented himself with their outward appearance. There were defects in the goods which a proper examination would have revealed. It was held that, having had an opportunity of examining the barrels, the buyer was estopped from denying that he had in fact examined them, and there was no condition as to merchantability.

The section applies to goods *supplied*, not only to goods *sold*, so that where, for example, mineral waters are supplied in bottles, both the contents and the bottles (although the property in the latter does not pass) are goods supplied within the meaning of s. 14, and a vendor will be liable in damages thereunder for personal injuries caused by the bursting of the bottle (*Geddling* v. *Marsh* [1920] 1 K.B. 688; *Morelli* v. *Fitch and Gibbons* [1928] 2 K.B. 636).

(iv) *Sales by* SAMPLE

Under s. 15 (2), when a sale is by SAMPLE there are three implied CONDITIONS:

(a) that the bulk shall correspond with the sample in quality;

(b) that the buyer shall have a reasonable opportunity of comparing the bulk with the sample; and

(c) that the goods shall be free from any defect rendering them unmerchantable, which would not be apparent on a reasonable examination of the sample.

In *Drummond* v. *Van Ingen* (1887) 12 App. Cas. 284, A ordered from a manufacturer a quantity of worsted coatings, weight and quality equal to sample; the coatings were equal to sample, but were unmerchantable owing to being 'slippery,' this defect not being apparent on a reasonable examination of the sample. A was allowed to reject the goods.

Bulk and sample do not correspond if some process, however small, is needed to make them do so (*Ruben, Ltd.* v. *Faire Bros. & Co., Ltd.* [1949] 1 K.B. 254).

The mere exhibition of a sample during negotiations does not make the sale one by sample; it must be a term of the contract that the sale is by sample (s. 15 (1)).

Where in a contract of sale by sample the goods are sold 'with all faults and imperfections,' the seller is not relieved from his duty to deliver goods corresponding with the sample, although he may be relieved from his liability for any defects not apparent to the buyer on a reasonable examination of the sample. Thus, an 'all faults clause' in a contract may relieve the seller from obligations under (c) above, but not under (a) or (b) (*Champanhac, Ltd.* v. *Waller, Ltd.* [1948] 2 All E.R. 724).

The operation of ss. 14 and 15 is well illustrated by the case of *Godley* v. *Perry* [1960] 1 All E.R. 36:

The defendant, a newsagent, sold a plastic toy catapult to the plaintiff, a boy of six. The catapult broke while the plaintiff was using it in the proper manner, due to the fact that the material used in its manufacture was unsuitable, and the boy was blinded in one eye.

Held: (1) The seller was liable under s. 14 (1) as the plaintiff had relied upon his skill and judgment and the catapult was not fit for its purpose. Such reliance is a matter of inference, and the inference is readily drawn where the customer is of very tender years.

(2) Since the child had merely asked for *a* catapult, and had not specified any particular one, the sale was by description, although made over the counter, so that the seller was also liable under s. 14 (2), as the catapult was not of merchantable quality.

(3) The contract under which the newsagent had acquired the catapult from the wholesaler was a sale by sample, and therefore the wholesaler, in turn, was liable to the newsagent under s. 15, since the defect was one which a reasonable examination of the sample would not have revealed.

Implied terms of a contract represent the presumed intention of the parties, but such terms may be negatived or varied by express agreement or by the course of dealing between the parties, or by trade usage (s. 55). As has already been observed, however (see Chap. I, § 6), the courts construe exclusion and limitation clauses strictly against the person seeking to rely on them. In particular, both conditions and warranties must be excluded if the terms implied under the Act are to be completely negatived.

In *Wallis* v. *Pratt* [1911] A.C. 394, seed was described as 'common English Sainfoin.' It was resold to a third person and proved to be 'giant Sainfoin,' which is commercially different from 'common English Sainfoin.' The plaintiffs claimed damages for breach of condition as to description under s. 13. The defendants relied on a clause excluding 'all warranties express or implied, as to growth and description,' and relied on s. 11 (1) (*c*), whereby a condition, in the circumstances, is to be treated as a warranty. It was held by the House of Lords that s. 11 (1) (*c*) affects remedies only and does not alter the status of the undertaking. Thus, since only warranties were expressly excluded, the clause was inadequate to protect the defendants, and the buyer was entitled to damages.

Further, a clause which excludes all *implied* terms will not protect a seller against a breach of an express term of the contract.

In *Andrews Brothers (Bournemouth), Ltd.* v. *Singer & Co., Ltd.* [1934] 1 K.B. 17, a contract for the sale by the defendant of 'new Singer cars' provided that 'all conditions, warranties, and liabilities, implied by statute, common law or otherwise' were to be excluded. The plaintiffs were held to be entitled to damages for breach of contract when the defendants later delivered a used car.

But a clause which provides that 'any express or implied condition statement or warranty, statutory or otherwise, is hereby excluded' is sufficiently comprehensive to give complete protection to the seller (*L'Estrange* v. *Graucob* [1934] 2 K.B. 394).

Numerous statutes make provision for the giving of warranties on a sale of specified articles. For instance, warranties as to quality or fitness are implied on a sale of food and drugs under the Food and Drugs Act, 1955; and where trading stamps are redeemed for goods, there are implied warranties as to title and quality of the goods under the Trading Stamps Act, 1964.

Apart from any contractual or statutory liability, a manufacturer of defective goods may be liable to a purchaser of the goods for the tort of negligence if the latter suffers damage as a result of the defect (*Grant* v. *Australian Knitting Mills, Ltd.* [1936] A.C. 85).

(b) The Transfer of the Property

(1) *The Passing of Ownership*

The ascertainment of the time at which the *property* in goods passes from seller to buyer is of the utmost importance in order to determine at whose risk they are at a given moment, who can pass a good title by resale or other dealing with them, and to whom they belong in the event of the bankruptcy of the buyer before payment of the price.

Unless otherwise agreed, the goods remain at the seller's *risk* until the property therein is transferred to the buyer, whereupon the goods are at the buyer's risk whether delivery has been made or not. But where delivery has been delayed through the fault of either buyer or seller, the goods are then at the risk of the party in fault as regards any loss which might not have occurred but for such fault (s. 20).

If the route involves sea transit, the seller must give such notice to the buyer as may enable him to insure the goods during their sea transit, otherwise they are at the seller's risk; that is to say, though property and possession have passed, the risk has not passed with them (s. 32 (3)). Although the seller agrees to deliver the goods at his own risk, at a place other than where they are when sold, the buyer, unless otherwise agreed, takes the risk of any deterioration in the goods necessarily incident to the course of transit (s. 33).

In *Bull* v. *Robinson* (1854) 10 Exch. 342, manufactured iron was sent by canal at the request of the buyer; it arrived in a rusty condition, the rusting being 'necessarily incident to the course of transit.'
Held: The buyer was bound to accept the goods.

If goods are UNASCERTAINED (see (a) (5), *supra*), no property passes till they are actually ascertained (s. 16). If the sale of a portion of a bulk is made, there is no transfer of the property in that portion until it is actually separated from the bulk and ascertained (*Laurie & Morewood* v. *Dudin & Sons* [1926] 1 K.B. 223).

If the contract is for the sale of SPECIFIC or ASCERTAINED goods the *intention* of the parties is the test as to the time at which the property will pass; this intention is to be ascertained in each case from the contract, the conduct of the parties, and the circumstances of the case (s. 17).

Section 18 lays down rules which are to be applied in order to ascertain the intention of the parties *in the absence of clear evidence to the contrary.*

Rule 1
Where there is an *unconditional* contract for the sale of *specific* goods *in a deliverable state*, the property in the goods passes to the buyer when the contract is made, even though the time of delivery or time of payment is postponed.

In *Tarling* v. *Baxter* (1827) 6 B. & C. 360, A purchased a haystack from B to be paid for on 4th February, the hay to stand on B's land until 1st May, and not to be cut until paid for. The hay was burnt, and the loss fell upon A, as the property had passed to him.

Rule 2

Where there is a contract for the sale of *specific* goods, and the seller is bound to do something to the goods to put them into a deliverable state, the property does not pass until this has been done, and the buyer has notice thereof.

By s. 62 goods are in a 'deliverable state' when they are in such a state that the buyer would, under the contract, be bound to take delivery of them.

In *Underwood* v. *Burgh Castle Brick and Cement Syndicate* [1922] 1 K.B. 343, the owners of a horizontal condensing engine agreed to sell it at a price 'free on rail' in London. It weighed 30 tons and was bolted to and embedded in a floor of concrete. Before it could be delivered on rail it had to be detached and dismantled. The sellers detached it, but in loading it on a truck they damaged it by accident, so that the buyers refused to accept it. In an action by the sellers, it was held that the property in the engine had not passed to the defendants, as the plaintiffs were bound to do something which they had not done for the purpose of putting the engine into a deliverable state.

Rule 3

Where there is a contract for the sale of *specific* goods in a deliverable state, but the seller has still something to do, such as weighing, measuring or testing, *in order to ascertain the price*, the property does not pass until such act is done, and the buyer has notice thereof.

Rule 4

Where goods are delivered on *approval* or on *sale or return* or other similar terms, the property therein passes to the buyer:

(*a*) When he signifies his approval or acceptance to the seller, or does any other act adopting the transaction; or

(*b*) If he retains the goods without giving notice of rejection within a fixed or reasonable time.

In *Kirkham* v. *Attenborough* [1897] 1 Q.B. 201, jewellery was sent by A to B 'on sale or return.' B pledged the jewellery with C. It was held that the pledge was an act adopting the transaction, so that the property passed to B, and C was entitled to retain the jewellery.

If goods are sent with an 'appro.' note showing that they are to remain the property of the sender until paid for in cash or invoiced, then the property does not pass until this condition has been satisfied; and if such goods are improperly dealt with, the sender may recover them (*Weiner* v. *Gill* [1906] 2 K.B. 574). But if the person to whom the goods are entrusted is a mercantile agent, for instance, a jeweller's traveller, then even if such restrictions are placed in the original contract note they are not effective against *bona fide* purchasers or pledgees for value who take without notice of the restrictions, since these persons get a good title under the Factors Act, 1889 (*Weiner* v. *Harris* [1910] 1 K.B. 285).

Goods may be delivered on sale or return where they are delivered to a person who intends not to buy them himself but to sell them to third parties.

In *Poole* v. *Smith's Car Sales* (*Balham*), *Ltd.* [1962] 2 All E.R. 482, the plaintiff, a car dealer, supplied two cars to the defendants, who were also dealers, at the end of August, on the understanding that if the latter did not sell them they should be returned to the plaintiff. Only one car was sold, and the plaintiff made repeated requests in October for the return of the other. On 7th November he wrote to the defendants saying that if the car had not been returned by 10th November it would be deemed to have been sold to the defendants. The car was returned some weeks later in a damaged condition. The plaintiff rejected it and sued for the price of the car.

Held: The contract was one for sale or return, notwithstanding that the defendants did not intend to buy the car themselves, so that the property would pass to the defendants on the expiration of a reasonable time, in the absence of rejection or any contrary intention being shown. In the circumstances, having regard to the seasonal decline in the second-hand car market, a reasonable time had expired without the car being returned, and the defendants were therefore liable to pay the price for it.

Rule 5

(1) Where there is a contract for the sale of *unascertained* or *future* goods sold by description, the property passes to the buyer when goods of that description and in a deliverable state are unconditionally appropriated to the contract by one party with the assent of the other. Such assent may be express or implied, and may be given either before or after the appropriation is made.

(2) Such unconditional appropriation can be made by the seller delivering the goods to the buyer, or to a carrier on his behalf, without reserving the right of disposal.

If the right of disposal is reserved, the goods will not pass to the buyer until the conditions imposed by the seller are fulfilled (s. 19 (1)). The seller is *prima facie* deemed to reserve the right of disposal if goods are shipped and are, by the bill of lading, deliverable to the order of the seller or his agent (s. 19 (2)); and if the seller sends a bill of exchange with bill of lading annexed to the buyer for acceptance, and the buyer does not honour the bill of exchange, he is bound to return the bill of lading, and if he wrongfully retains it the property in the goods does not pass to him (s. 19 (3)). (But the buyer may nevertheless be able to pass a good title by resale; see *Cahn* v. *Pockett's Bristol Channel Steam Packet Co., Ltd., post*, p. 131.)

(2) *The Title of the Seller*

As a rule only the owner, or a person acting under the authority or with the consent of the owner, can give a good title to a purchaser (*nemo dat quod non habet*). A buyer may, however, aquire a good title to goods from some person other than the owner in the following cases:

(i) *Estoppel*

The owner may be precluded by his conduct from denying the seller's authority to sell (s. 21 (1)). This will arise, for example, in the case of an agency by estoppel, where the owner of goods holds out a person as having authority to sell them, although such authority has not in fact been given (*Eastern Distributors, Ltd.* v. *Goldring* [1957] 2 Q.B. 600; see Chap. II, § 4 (e)).

(ii) *Sales by factors*

The power of a factor to pass a good title to goods placed with him (see Chap. II, § 12 (a)) is expressly preserved by s. 21 (2) (*a*).

(iii) *Sales under special common law or statutory powers*

The rule does not affect the validity of a contract of sale under any special common law or statutory power of sale or under the order of a court of competent jurisdiction (s. 21 (2) (*b*)). Persons who may pass a good title under such powers include sheriffs in respect of executions, landlords for goods distrained upon, pawnbrokers, innkeepers, and repairers of goods.

(iv) *Sales in market overt*

Where goods are sold in *market overt* (open market) according to the usage of the market, the buyer acquires a good title to the goods, provided he buys them in good faith and without notice of any defect or want of title on the part of the seller (s. 22 (1)).

In the City of London market overt is held every day except Sunday in all shops or markets which deal in goods of the kind in question. In the country, market overt is held only on special days provided for particular places by charter, by custom, or under statute (*Bishopsgate Motor Finance Corporation, Ltd.* v. *Transport Brakes, Ltd.* [1949] 1 K.B. 322).

In addition to the existence of good faith on the part of the buyer, the following conditions must be complied with in order that the buyer may rely upon the protection afforded by market overt:

(*a*) The goods must have been exposed *publicly* for sale.

(*b*) The bulk and not merely a sample must have been exposed for sale.

(*c*) The goods must have been of the class usually dealt in by the seller.

(*d*) The sale must have taken place between sunrise and sunset.

It is a question of fact in each case whether premises in the City of London in which goods are sold constitute a shop. It has been held that an auction room on the first floor was not such a shop as to

constitute market overt (*Clayton* v. *Le Roy & Fils* [1911] 2 K.B. 1031).
A sale *to* the shopkeeper does not obtain the protection of the
custom (*Hargreave* v. *Spink* [1892] 1 Q.B. 25).

Originally the Sale of Goods Act provided that where goods had
been stolen and the offender was convicted of larceny the property
in the goods re-vested in the original owner (notwithstanding that the
goods might, in the meanwhile, have been sold in market overt)
(s. 24 (1)). This section has now been repealed by the Theft Act, 1968
(s. 33) so that a purchaser who obtains a good title in market overt
cannot subsequently lose it by reason of the subsequent conviction of
the thief.

(v) *Sale under voidable title*

When the seller of goods has a voidable title to the goods, but his
title has not been avoided at the time of the sale, the buyer acquires
a good title to the goods, provided he buys them in good faith and
without notice of the seller's defect of title (s. 23).

The circumstances in which a contract is voidable have been considered in Chapter I. The rule does not apply in a case where the
seller has acquired the goods under a contract which is absolutely
void, *e.g.*, where it was induced by a material mistake of fact.

Where a seller has the right to avoid a contract for fraud, but is
unable to find the fraudulent purchaser and communicate with him,
he sufficiently exercises his right of avoidance if he takes all possible
steps to regain the goods immediately on discovering the fraud, *e.g.*, by
notifying the police (*Car and Universal Finance Co., Ltd.* v. *Caldwell*
[1964] 1 All E.R. 290). But, although this will prevent the fraudulent
purchaser from passing a good title to a third party under s. 23, the
latter may nevertheless obtain a good title to the goods under the
Factors Act or under s. 25 (2), *infra* (*Newtons of Wembley, Ltd.* v.
Williams [1964] 3 All E.R. 532).

(vi) *Sale by seller or buyer in possession*

When a person, after selling goods, continues to have possession
of the goods, or of the documents of title to them, the delivery or
transfer by him of the goods or documents of title under any sale,
pledge or other disposition thereof, to any person receiving the same
in good faith and without notice of the previous sale, confers a good
title upon that person (s. 25 (1)).

In *Staffordshire Motor Guarantee, Ltd.* v. *British Wagon Co., Ltd.*
[1934] 2 K.B. 305, it was held that possession under the section must
be possession by the seller as seller; so that where, for example, the
owner of a motor vehicle sells the vehicle to a finance company and
immediately hires it back under a hire-purchase agreement without
ever transferring possession of the vehicle (see Chap. V, § 6 (a)),

a further fraudulent sale by him to a third party will not pass a title under s. 25 (1), as he is merely in possession as a hirer, and not as the seller of the goods. In *Pacific Motor Auctions Pty., Ltd.* v. *Motor Credits (Hire Finance), Ltd.* [1965] 2 All E.R. 105, however, the Judicial Committee of the Privy Council held that this decision was incorrect. Provided the seller continues in physical possession of the goods, he can pass a good title to a third party, regardless of any private transactions between the seller and the original purchaser which might alter the legal title under which the possession is held. The latter interpretation of the section is likely to be preferred in future cases.

Section 25 (2) deals with the converse case, and provides that when a person having bought or agreed to buy goods obtains, with the consent of the seller, possession of the goods or documents of title to goods, the delivery or transfer by that person of the goods or documents of title under any sale, pledge, or other disposition to any person receiving the same in good faith, and without notice of any lien or other right of the original seller in respect of the goods, confers a good title on that person.

In *Cahn* v. *Pockett's Bristol Channel Steam Packet Co., Ltd.* [1899] 1 Q.B. 643, the seller of goods to a foreign buyer forwarded a bill of lading for the goods, indorsed in blank, together with a bill of exchange for the price of the goods for the buyer's acceptance. The buyer kept the bill of lading without accepting the bill of exchange, and transferred it to an innocent third party for value. The seller stopped the goods *in transitu*. It was held that, although the property in the goods had not been transferred to the buyer by virtue of s. 19 (3) (see *ante*, p. 128), nevertheless he had passed a good title to the third party under s. 25 (2).

(vii) *Sales of motor vehicles by hirer or buyer*

A hirer of goods under a hire-purchase agreement is not normally in possession as a person who has 'agreed to buy' so that he cannot pass a good title under s. 25 (2) (see *post*, § 3 (a)). But if the subject-matter of the hire-purchase agreement is a motor vehicle and the hirer sells it to a *private* purchaser who takes it in good faith and without notice of the hire-purchase agreement, the disposition takes effect as if the title of the owner had been vested in the hirer immediately before the disposition, so that the purchaser obtains a good title to the vehicle; and, where the hirer sells to a dealer or a finance company, the first private purchaser of the vehicle thereafter is similarly protected (Hire-Purchase Act, 1964, ss. 27-29). These provisions also apply where the seller is in possession of the vehicle under a conditional sale agreement (*ibid.*).

(c) **Performance of the Contract**

It is the duty of the seller to deliver the goods, and of the buyer to accept and pay for them, in accordance with the terms of the contract (s. 27).

Unless otherwise agreed, delivery and payment are concurrent conditions, that is to say, the seller must be ready and willing to give possession of the goods to the buyer in exchange for the price, and the buyer must be ready and willing to pay the price in exchange for possession of the goods (s. 28).

(1) *Delivery*

(i) *Rules as to delivery*

Whether it is for the buyer to take possession of the goods or for the seller to send them to the buyer is a question depending in each case on the contract, express or implied, between the parties. Apart from any provision in relation thereto, the place of delivery is the seller's place of business if he has one, and if not, his residence; but if the goods are specific, and to the knowledge of the other party are in some other place, that other place is the place of delivery (s. 29 (1)). If the goods are in the possession of a third person, there is no delivery until that third person acknowledges to the buyer that he holds the goods on his behalf (s. 29 (3)).

Where the seller has to send the goods, and no time for sending them is fixed, he must send them within a reasonable time (s. 29 (2)). Demand or tender of delivery must be made at a reasonable hour to be effectual (s. 29 (4)).

The cost of putting the goods into a deliverable state is, in the absence of agreement, to be borne by the seller (s. 29 (5)).

(ii) *Incorrect delivery*

If the seller delivers to the buyer either less or more than the quantity contracted for, the buyer is entitled to reject the whole; but where he accepts the whole or part, he must pay for them at the contract rate (s. 30 (1), (2)).

In view of the difficulty of exact delivery where the quantity of goods ordered is considerable, the expressions 'about' or 'more or less' are frequently incorporated in the terms of the contract to provide for a certain latitude and to prevent the buyer standing on the strict letter of the section. The difference between the quantity ordered and that delivered must, however, be reasonable, and if any other factor indicative of quantity is introduced, this will also be considered, e.g., where the contract was to load a full and complete cargo, say 1,100 tons, and the vessel was capable of taking 1,210 tons, a delivery of 1,080 tons would not satisfy the contract, although only 20 tons short of the quantity mentioned, for it was not a full and complete cargo (*Morris* v. *Levison* (1876) 1 C.P.D. 155).

When the seller delivers to the buyer goods he has contracted to sell, mixed with goods of a different description not included in the contract, the buyer may accept the goods which are in accordance with the contract and reject the rest, or he may reject the whole (s. 30 (3)).

(iii) *Delivery by instalments*

Unless otherwise agreed, the buyer of goods is not bound to accept delivery by instalments. Where there is a contract for the sale of goods to be delivered by stated instalments, which are to be paid for separately, and the seller makes defective delivery, or the buyer fails to take delivery of one or more instalments, it is a question in each case whether the breach of contract is a repudiation of the whole contract or whether it is a severable breach giving rise to a claim for compensation, but not to a right to treat the whole contract as repudiated (s. 31). Which is the position depends on the terms of the contract and the circumstances of the case. The chief considerations are first, the ratio quantitatively which the breach bears to the contract as a whole, and secondly, the degree of probability or improbability that such a breach will be repeated (*per* Hewart, C.J., in *Maple Flock Co., Ltd.* v. *Universal Furniture Products, Ltd.* [1934] 1 K.B. 148, at p. 157).

Where goods are to be delivered by instalments and the price is quoted for each article to be delivered, an action will lie for the payment of the goods delivered, even though other instalments have yet to be made (*Howell* v. *Evans* (1926) 42 T.L.R. 310).

(iv) *Delivery to carrier*

Where the seller is authorised or required to send the goods to the buyer, delivery of the goods to a carrier, whether named by the buyer or not, for the purpose of transmission to the buyer is *prima facie* deemed to be a delivery of the goods to the buyer (s. 32 (1)).

Unless otherwise authorised by the buyer, the seller must make such contract with the carrier on behalf of the buyer as may be reasonable, having regard to the nature of the goods and the other circumstances of the case. If the seller omits to do this, and the goods are lost or damaged in the course of transit, the buyer may decline to treat delivery to the carrier as a delivery to himself, or may sue the seller in damages (s. 32 (2)).

(2) *Acceptance*

A buyer is deemed to have *accepted* goods when he intimates to the seller that he has accepted them, or when the goods have been delivered to him and he does any act in relation to them which is inconsistent with the seller's ownership, as, for instance, if he resells them in whole or part, or retains the goods for longer than is reasonable without intimating to the seller that he has rejected them (s. 35).

When a buyer has accepted goods, or has accepted part of the goods under an indivisible contract, he cannot rescind the contract (s. 11 (1) (c)), but he is not deemed to have accepted them until he has had a reasonable opportunity of examining them to ascertain whether they conform to the contract, and the seller must afford this opportunity on tendering delivery if so requested (s. 34). Under the Misrepresentation Act, 1967 (s. 4 (2)) section 34 will prevail over section 35 and the decision in *Hardy* v. *Hillerns and Fowler* [1923] 2 K.B. 490 is overruled.

If the buyer refuses to accept goods delivered when he has a right to do so, he is not, unless it is otherwise agreed, bound to return them to the seller; it is sufficient if he intimates to the seller that he refuses to accept (s. 36). If the buyer otherwise refuses to take delivery within a reasonable time when requested to do so, he is liable to the seller for any loss occasioned by his neglect or refusal, and also for a reasonable charge for the care and custody of the goods (s. 37).

(d) Rights of Unpaid Seller against the Goods

In relation to the rights of an unpaid seller *against the goods*, the term 'seller' includes any person who is in the position of a seller, as, for instance, an agent to whom a bill of lading has been indorsed, or a consignor or agent who has himself paid, or is directly responsible for the price, or a surety who has paid the price. The seller is deemed to be unpaid when the whole price has not been paid or tendered, or when a bill of exchange taken *conditionally* has been dishonoured (s. 38). A person who has purchased goods and has rejected them after paying the purchase price is not in the position of an unpaid seller as regards the price repayable to him (*Lyons & Co., Ltd.* v. *May and Baker, Ltd.* [1923] 1 K.B. 685).

The unpaid seller has the following rights *against the goods*, notwithstanding that the property in the goods has passed to the buyer:

(1) a lien on the goods for the price while he is in possession of them;
(2) if the buyer becomes insolvent, a right of stopping the goods in transit after he has parted with possession;
(3) a right of resale as limited by the Act (s. 39 (1)).

(1) *Lien*

A lien is a right to retain goods which are in the possession of the person claiming the lien (see Chap. V, § 8). The unpaid seller of goods is entitled to retain possession of them until payment or tender of the price where:

(i) the goods have been sold without any stipulation as to credit, or

(ii) if credit has been given, the term has expired, or

(iii) the buyer becomes insolvent (s. 41).

The seller may exercise his right of lien notwithstanding that his possession of the goods is as agent or bailee for the buyer.

As a lien depends on possession, the right can only be exercised when the seller remains in possession of the goods. The lien is lost if the unpaid seller delivers the goods to a carrier for transmission to the buyer, without reserving the right of disposal, or when the buyer or his agent lawfully obtains possession of them, or if the right is waived; but it is not lost by reason only of the seller having obtained judgment for the price (s. 43).

Where part delivery has been made, the lien may still attach to the remainder of the goods, unless the circumstances show an agreement to waive it (s. 42).

The lien is not affected by any sale or other disposition of the goods which the buyer may make unless the seller assents thereto (s. 47). The assent must be so given as to show that the unpaid seller consented to the sub-purchaser's right to delivery free from the lien under the original contract (*Mordaunt* v. *British Oil and Cake Mills* [1910] 2 K.B. 502). If, however, a document of title (which here includes all documents used in the ordinary course of business authorising delivery (s. 62)) is lawfully transferred to any person as buyer or owner of the goods, he may defeat the right of lien (wholly or partly) by transferring the document to an innocent third party for value, whether by way of sale or pledge (s. 47, proviso).

In *Anton Jurgens Margarinefabrieken* v. *Louis Dreyfus & Co.* [1914] 3 K.B. 41, A sold a quantity of seed to B who paid by cheque, which was dishonoured upon presentment. A gave a delivery order to B for the goods, and B resold to C, indorsing the delivery order to him.

Held: A had lost his lien and, notwithstanding that payment by B had not been made, had to give delivery of the seed to C. (In *Mordaunt's* case (*supra*), the seller had not given a delivery order to the purchaser.)

If the property in the goods has not passed to the buyer, there is no lien in favour of the seller, for a man cannot have a lien on his own goods; but in the several circumstances in which a lien is enforceable, a right of withholding delivery is conferred on the seller, who thus secures an equivalent protection (s. 39 (2)).

(2) *Stoppage in Transitu*

After the seller has parted with possession of the goods to a carrier for transmission to the buyer, he has still the right of *stoppage in transitu*, i.e., a right to stop the goods and retake possession, *but only on the buyer becoming insolvent* (s. 44). A buyer is deemed to be insolvent if he has ceased to pay his debts in the ordinary course of business, or cannot pay his debts as they become due, whether or not he has committed an act of bankruptcy (s. 62). This right exists, even though the credit given has not expired, until the goods have reached the buyer or his agent. By exercising the right the seller does not rescind the contract, neither does the property in the goods become revested in him, but he is entitled to retain the goods until payment or tender of the price.

The right of stoppage *in transitu* may be exercised by taking possession either of the goods or of the documents of title.

In *Ex parte Watson* (1877) 5 Ch. D. 35, A sold goods to B, and B became insolvent while the goods were in course of transit to Shanghai. A demanded bills of lading from C, the shipowner in London, and B's trustee in bankruptcy also claimed them. It was held that the demand by A was effectual as a stoppage *in transitu*.

It may also be exercised by giving notice of the claim to the carrier or other bailee, or to his principal, who must pass the notice on to his servant, but he must be given a reasonable time to do so (s. 46 (1)). A notice is ineffectual if addressed to the consignee only, and not to the owner or master of the ship which carries the goods (*Phelps* v. *Comber* (1885) 29 Ch. D. 813).

The carrier receiving notice of stoppage must redeliver the goods according to the directions of the seller, who must bear the expenses of the redelivery (s. 46 (2)).

If part delivery has been made, stoppage *in transitu* can still be exercised on the remainder of the goods, unless the circumstances show an agreement to waive the right (s. 45 (7)).

The right is lost by the transit coming to an end, *i.e.*, by the goods coming into the actual or constructive possession of the buyer or his agent, or by the transfer of a bill of lading to the buyer.

The point at which transit ceases must be determined by the facts of each case. The transit of goods is determined, *inter alia*, in the following circumstances (s. 45 (2)–(6)):

(*a*) If the buyer or his agent obtains possession of the goods before their arrival at their appointed destination.

(*b*) If, when the goods have reached their appointed destination, the carrier acknowledges to the buyer or his agent that he holds the goods as bailee for the buyer or his agent; but it is not at an end if the carrier remains in possession after the buyer has rejected them, even if the seller has refused to receive them back.

(*c*) If the goods are delivered to a ship chartered by the buyer, it is a question depending upon the circumstances whether they are in the possession of the master as a carrier, or as the buyer's agent; but delivery to the buyer's own ship is a delivery to the buyer.

(*d*) If the carrier wrongfully refuses to deliver to the buyer.

(*e*) If the goods reach the hands of an agent who is to keep them pending further instructions from the buyer (*Kendall* v. *Marshall, Stevens & Co.* (1883) 11 Q.B.D. 356).

Section 47 protects the seller's right of stoppage *in transitu* in the event of a sub-sale or pledge by the buyer to the same extent as it protects his right of lien (*supra*).

(3) *Resale*

The exercise of the right of lien or stoppage *in transitu* does not rescind the contract; but if the unpaid seller resells the goods, the new buyer acquires a good title thereto as against the original buyer. The unpaid seller may resell the goods if they are of a perishable nature, or if the buyer does not, after notice from the unpaid seller of his intention to resell, tender the price within a reasonable time, and he may also recover damages for any loss occasioned by the breach of contract (s. 48).

Resale under the power conferred by the section may produce an excess over and above the contract price. If, however, a right of resale on default by the buyer is *expressly reserved* by the seller, its exercise *will* rescind the contract (s. 48 (4)), and any excess will then belong to the seller.

(e) Actions for Breach of the Contract

(1) *Remedies of the Seller*

(i) *Action for price*

Apart from the remedies against the goods, the seller can also sue the buyer for the price, if the property has passed to the buyer. If a date has been agreed for the payment of the price, irrespective of delivery, the seller may maintain an action for the price, although the property in the goods has not passed, and the goods have not been appropriated to the contract (s. 49).

(ii) *Damages for non-acceptance*

Where the buyer wrongfully refuses to accept and pay for the goods, the seller may maintain an action for damages for non-acceptance. The measure of damages is the estimated loss directly and naturally resulting, in the ordinary course of events, from the buyer's breach of contract. If there is an available market, the measure of damages is *prima facie* the difference between the contract price and the market price on the day when the goods ought to have been accepted, or, if no time was fixed for acceptance, at the time of refusal to accept (s. 50).

If, however, there is no available market, or for any reason it would be unjust to apply the *prima facie* rule laid down in s. 50, damages may be estimated on the general basis of the loss of the seller's bargain. So, where the defendants had refused to take delivery of a motor car, and it was proved that in the then state of the market the plaintiff vendor's only course was to return the vehicle to their suppliers, it was held that the true measure of damages was the plaintiff's loss of profit on the sale (*W. L. Thompson, Ltd.* v. *Robinson (Gunmakers), Ltd.* [1955] Ch. 177); but in *Charter* v. *Sullivan* [1957]

2 Q.B. 117, a similar refusal entitled the plaintiff to nominal damages only as he could find a purchaser for every car of that make which he could get from the manufacturers.

(2) *Remedies of the Buyer*
(i) *Damages for non-delivery*

If the seller wrongfully neglects or refuses to deliver the goods to the buyer, the buyer has a right of action against the seller for damages for non-delivery (s. 51). The measure of damages is the same as in the seller's action for non-acceptance.

Where there is no market in which the buyer can purchase, and to the actual or imputed knowledge of the seller the buyer has bought the goods with a view to resale, the buyer is entitled to recover the loss of profit on resale, the measure of damages being normally the difference between the contract price and the resale price (*Patrick* v. *Russo-British Grain Export Co.* [1927] 2 K.B. 535).

(ii) *Specific performance*

Where the contract is for the delivery of specific or ascertained goods, the court may, if it thinks fit, on the application of the buyer, direct that the contract shall be performed specifically without giving the seller the option of retaining the goods upon payment of damages. The decree may be unconditional, or upon such terms and conditions as to damages, payment of the price, and otherwise, as to the court may seem just (s. 52). This remedy will normally be granted only when the goods are unique in character or not obtainable elsewhere.

(iii) *Breach of warranty*

Upon a breach of warranty, or breach of a condition which the buyer elects, or is compelled, to treat as a breach of warranty, the remedy of the buyer is to set up against the seller a claim for damages in diminution or extinction of the price, or to maintain an action against him for damages for the breach of warranty. The fact that the buyer has set up the breach of warranty in diminution or extinction of the price does not prevent him from maintaining an action for the same breach of warranty if he has suffered further damage (s. 53).

The measure of damages for breach of warranty is the estimated loss directly and naturally arising in the ordinary course of events from the breach of warranty, and, if the contract is made under special circumstances to the knowledge of both parties, such additional loss as may reasonably be supposed to have been in the contemplation of the parties as the probable result of the breach.

In the case of a breach as to quality, the loss is *prima facie* the difference between the value of the goods at the time of delivery to the buyer and what that value would have been if they had answered to the warranty.

(3) *Interest*

If interest can be claimed at law, *e.g.*, where there is an agreement to pay interest, or where the debt is of a class upon which the court would allow interest to be charged, it is recoverable in the case of breach of contract for the sale of goods; and if the consideration has failed altogether, any sums paid under the contract may be recovered (s. 54).

(f) Sales by Auction

Sales by auction, which are subject to the provisions of s. 58 of the Act, have already been considered (see Chap. II, § 12 (d)).

(g) Contracts of Sale Involving Shipment of Goods

(1) *C.I.F. Contracts*

A contract of sale c.i.f. (*i.e.*, cost, insurance, freight) is best defined generally as a contract for the sale of goods to be carried by sea, which is performed by the delivery of certain documents representing the goods, called shipping documents (see *per* Bankes, L.J., in *Karberg* v. *Blythe* [1916] 1 K.B. 495, at p. 510). The distinctive feature of a c.i.f. contract is that the seller, in consideration of an increased price, has to arrange, at his own expense, for the carriage of the goods to the port of destination and for their insurance during transit. He is also responsible for procuring the shipping documents which, when in the hands of the buyer, give him a direct claim to the goods.

In *Biddell Brothers* v *F. Clemens Horst & Co.* [1911] 1 K.B. 214, Hamilton, J., defined the obligation of a seller under a c.i.f. contract as follows:

'The seller . . . has –
  (i) to ship at the port of shipment goods of the description contained in the contract;
  (ii) to procure a contract of affreightment under which the goods will be delivered at the destination contemplated by the contract;
  (iii) to arrange for an insurance upon the terms current in the trade which will be available for the benefit of the buyer;
  (iv) to make out an invoice . . . , and
  (v) to tender these documents to the buyer so that he may be able to obtain delivery of the goods, if they arrive, or recover for their loss if they are lost on the voyage.'

As an alternative to shipping the goods himself, the seller can perform his contract by purchasing goods afloat which have been shipped under a bill of lading or charter-party to the contractual destination.

The shipping documents which the seller has to tender ordinarily mean (i) a bill of lading, (ii) a policy of insurance, (iii) an invoice.

(i) The BILL OF LADING must conform to any express requirements in the contract, or if the contract does not expressly deal with the form of bill of lading to be tendered, the bill of lading must be in a form usual in the trade. It must cover the whole transit, and must be such as to enable the buyer to obtain delivery of the goods which he has contracted to buy, or, alternatively, to give him a right of action against the carrier in respect of any loss or damage which the goods have suffered *en route*.

(ii) Ordinarily a POLICY OF INSURANCE must be tendered, and not a cover note or certificate of insurance. If the buyer accepts a certificate of insurance the seller warrants that the statements in the certificate are true, and undertakes to procure a valid policy (*Harper & Co.* v. *MacKechnie & Co.* [1925] 2 K.B. 423). The policy must be tendered notwithstanding that the goods have arrived safely at their destination (*Orient Co.* v. *Brekke* [1913] 1 K.B. 531). The purchaser is entitled to demand a policy which covers all, and only, the goods mentioned in the bills of lading and invoice (*Manbre Saccharine Co.* v. *Corn Products Co.* [1919] 1 K.B. 198). The policy must cover all risks usually insured in the trade. Where the goods are deliverable by instalments, the acceptance of one instalment without objection by the buyer to the nature of the policy tendered does not estop him from raising objection on this account in respect of later instalments (*Malmberg* v. *H. J. Evans & Co.* (1924) 29 Com. Cas. 235).

(iii) The INVOICE must be in the form described by Blackburn, J., in *Ireland* v. *Livingstone* (1872) L.R. 5 H.L. 395, at p. 406, or in a similar form, that is to say, 'debiting the buyer with the agreed price (or the actual cost and commission, with the premiums of insurance and the freight, as the case may be) and giving him credit for the amount of freight which he will have to pay to the shipowner on actual delivery.'

The documents must be tendered within a reasonable time from the agreed date of shipment (*Groom, Ltd.* v. *Barber* [1915] 1 K.B. 316), and may be tendered by the seller even though he knows that in the meantime the goods have been lost (*Manbre Saccharine Co.* v. *Corn Products Co.*, *supra*).

The goods are usually at the buyer's risk after shipment, and he is obliged to pay against a tender of proper documents, whether or not the good have arrived, and whether or not they have been lost *en route*, and notwithstanding that he has had no opportunity of examining the goods. Since the contract is performed by the tender of proper documents the buyer's obligation to pay is irrespective of the position of the goods (*Biddell Brothers* v. *E. Clemens Horst & Co., supra*). The buyer does not, however, by accepting the documents, lose his right to reject the goods if they do not conform with the contract (*Kwei Tek Chao* v. *British Traders and Shippers, Ltd.* [1954] 2 Q.B. 459).

The question when the property in goods passes under a c.i.f. contract is a vexed one. Ultimately it is a question in each case of the intention of the parties as shown by the terms and circumstances of the contract. But apart from any clear evidence of intention, the property probably passes when the shipping documents are tendered to and accepted by the buyer (*Wait* v. *Baker* (1848) 2 Ex. 1; *The Miramichi* [1915] P. 71, at p.78; *Groom, Ltd.* v. *Barber, supra*). In the last case it was decided that, though the seller must be in a position to pass the property in the goods by the bill of lading if they are in existence, he need not have appropriated the particular goods in the particular bill of lading to the particular buyer until the moment of tendering the bill of lading.

(2) *F.O.B. Contracts*

An f.o.b. (free on board) contract is also a contract for the sale of goods to be carried by sea, but is distinguished from a c.i.f. contract by the fact that the buyer must see to the sea carriage and insurance of the goods himself. The seller's obligation under an f.o.b. contract is only to deliver the goods on board a ship at the agreed place of shipment. The buyer has to see that a ship is there ready to receive the goods. The seller has no concern with what happens to the goods after shipment, but, by s. 32 (3) of the Sale of Goods Act, the seller must give such notice to the buyer as will enable him to insure the goods during their sea transit, and if the seller fails to do so, the goods will be deemed to be at his risk during the sea transit. Section 32 (3) does not apply to c.i.f. contracts.

The expense of putting the goods on board ship falls on the seller, and the goods are at his risk until they are put on board. Thereafter his contractual liability as seller ceases, and delivery to the buyer is complete so far as he is concerned, and the goods are at the risk of the buyer (*per* Hamilton, L.J., in *Wimble* v. *Rosenberg* [1913] 3 K.B. 743, at p. 757).

The property in goods sold under an f.o.b. contract usually passes with the risk upon shipment (*Brown* v. *Hare* (1859) 4 H. & N. 822; *Carlos Federspiel & Co.* v. *Chas. Twigg & Co.* [1957] 1 Lloyd's Rep. 240); but the buyer might be able to reject the goods if they are not up to contract quality when he had no reasonable opportunity for examination until arrival at the port of delivery (*Bragg* v. *Villanova*

(1923) 40 T.L.R. 154). The question turns on the construction of each contract.

(3) *'Ex Ship'* Contracts

Where there is a contract for the sale of goods 'ex ship,' the position of the parties was stated by Lord Sumner in *Yangtsze Insurance Association* v. *Lukmanjee* [1918] A.C. 585, at p. 589, to be as follows:

'The seller has –

(i) to cause delivery to be made to the buyer from a ship which has arrived at the port of delivery, and has reached a place therein which is usual for delivery of goods of the kind in question . . .

(ii) to pay the freight or otherwise to release the shipowner's lien, and

(iii) to furnish the buyer with an effectual direction to the ship to deliver.

Till this is done the buyer is not bound to pay for the goods. Till this is done he may have an insurable interest in profits, but none that can directly be described as an interest 'upon goods,' nor any interest which the seller, as seller, is bound to insure for him.'

The goods are thus at the risk of the seller during the voyage, and he is not obliged to effect the policy of insurance on behalf of the buyer.

(4) *Letters of Credit*

The financing of transactions requiring payment against documents is usually effected by a banker's letter of credit. The buyer arranges with his bank to open a confirmed and irrevocable credit with that bank's branch or agent in the country of the seller available to the seller against delivery of documents. When the seller has been advised of the credit by the bank's branch or agent it cannot be cancelled, even on the buyer's instructions (*Urquhart, Lindsay & Co.* v. *Eastern Bank* [1922] 1 K.B. 318).

The credit must be available to the seller at the date of the first shipment (*Pavia & Co.* v. *Thurmann-Nielson* [1952] 2 Q.B. 84).

The credit will usually specify quantities, weights, prices and amounts, *i.e.*, all the details of the shipment that the buyer expects to receive. The bank or agent will pay the seller only when it receives documents which comply strictly with the terms of the credit (*Rayner & Co., Ltd.* v. *Hambro's Bank, Ltd.* [1943] K.B. 37).

§ 2. *Restrictive Trade Practices*

In commercial practice buyers and sellers frequently enter into contracts under which certain restrictions are imposed by one party upon the other, *e.g.*, as to the minimum prices at which goods are to be resold. These and similar restrictions were formerly covered by the common law doctrine of restraint of trade (see Chap. I, § 9 (b)); but now most restrictive trading agreements are subject to registration

with the Registrar of Restrictive Trading Agreements, and a considerable degree of control over the power of persons to implement
such contracts is exercised by the Restrictive Practices Court in
pursuance of the Restrictive Trade Practices Acts, 1956 and 1968
and the Resale Prices Act, 1964.

(a) Restrictive Trade Practices Acts, 1956 and 1968

These Acts provide for the registration and judicial investigation of
certain restrictive trading agreements, and for the prohibition of such
agreements as are found to be contrary to the public interest;
prohibit the collective enforcement of conditions regulating the
resale price of goods; and make further provision for the *individual*
enforcement of such conditions by legal proceedings (although the
practical importance of this last provision has been considerably reduced by the Resale Prices Act, 1964, *infra*).

(b) Registration of Agreements

Part I of the 1956 Act applies to any agreement between two or
more persons carrying on business within the United Kingdom in the
production or supply of goods, or in the application to goods of any
process of manufacture, whether with or without other parties, being
an agreement under which restrictions are accepted by two or more
parties in respect of the following matters (s. 6 (1)):

(i) the prices to be charged, quoted or paid for goods supplied, offered or
acquired, or for the application of any process of manufacture to goods;
(ii) the terms or conditions on or subject to which goods are to be supplied or
acquired or any such process is to be applied to goods;
(iii) the quantities or descriptions of goods to be produced, supplied or acquired;
(iv) the processes of manufacture to be applied to any goods, or the quantities
or descriptions of goods to which any such process is to be applied; or
(v) the persons or classes of persons to, for or from whom, or the areas or
places in or from which, goods are to be supplied or acquired, or any such
process applied.

An agreement within the meaning of the Act includes one which is
not intended (apart from the Act) to be enforceable by legal proceedings.

The expression 'persons' includes bodies whether incorporated or
not; and where an agreement is made by a trade association, all
persons who are members thereof are to be treated as parties to the
agreement and any restriction accepted under the agreement by the
association is treated as accepted by each of those members.

Agreements concerning exports, services or labour are excluded, as
also are agreements and licences concerning trade marks, patents and
registered designs. 'Sole distributor' agreements will usually also be
excluded.

Particulars of any agreement subject to the Act must be forwarded to the Registrar of Restrictive Trading Agreements before any restrictions in it take effect or within three months (whichever date is the earlier). The details required to be furnished are the names of all persons who are parties and the whole of the terms of the agreement, whether or not they all relate to restrictions which render it registrable, and whether or not the agreement is expressed in writing. Any registrable agreement which is not registered within due time is void. It is the duty of the Registrar to enter in the register prescribed by the Act particulars of all registrable agreements and to take all necessary proceedings before the Restrictive Practices Court in respect of agreements of which particulars are entered or filed in the register.

The Court may, on the application of any person aggrieved, order the register to be rectified by the variation or removal of particulars included therein in respect of any agreement; and any question as to whether an agreement is subject to registration or not must be referred to the Court.

If the Registrar has reasonable cause to believe that any person or trade association is or may be a party to any agreement subject to registration under the Act, he may require that person or association to give him information on the matter, and, if necessary, an application may be made to the Court for the examination on oath of any such person, or, in the case of a body corporate, of any director, manager, secretary or other officer.

(c) Judicial Investigation

On any application made to it, the Restrictive Practices Court has power to determine whether any restrictions in a registered agreement are contrary to the public interest; and if they are so found, the agreement is void in respect of those restrictions. This power extends to an agreement which has been terminated by the parties to it between registration and the reference to the Court (*Re Newspaper Proprietors' Agreement* [1964] 1 All E.R. 55, H.L.). The Court may make an order restraining all or any of the parties to the agreement who carry on business in the United Kingdom from (i) giving effect to, or enforcing or purporting to enforce, the agreement in respect of those restrictions; or (ii) making any other agreement (whether with the same parties or with other parties) to the like effect.

In proceedings before the Court, a restriction accepted in pursuance of any agreement is deemed to be contrary to the public interest unless the Court is satisfied as to any one or more of the following circumstances (s. 21 (1)):

(i) that the restriction is reasonably necessary, having regard to the character of the goods to which it applies, to protect the public against injury (whether to persons or premises) in connection with the consumption, installation or use of those goods;

(ii) that the removal of the restriction would deny to the public as purchasers, consumers or users of any goods other specific and substantial benefits or advantages enjoyed or likely to be enjoyed by them as such;

(iii) that the restriction is reasonably necessary to counteract measures taken by any person not party to the agreement with a view to preventing or restricting competition in the same trade or business;

(iv) that the restriction is reasonably necessary to enable the persons party to the agreement to negotiate fair terms for the supply of goods to, or the acquisition of goods from, any person not party thereto who controls a preponderant part of the trade or business of acquiring or supplying such goods;

(v) that the removal of the restriction would be likely to have a serious and persistent adverse effect on the general level of unemployment in an area, or in areas taken together, in which a substantial proportion of the trade or industry to which the agreement relates is situated;

(vi) that the removal of the restriction would be likely to cause a reduction in the volume or earnings of the export business which is substantial either in relation to the whole export business of the United Kingdom or in relation to the whole business (including export business) of the particular trade or industry; or

(vii) that the restriction is reasonably required for purposes connected with the maintenance of any other restriction accepted by the parties, being a restriction which is found by the Court not to be contrary to the public interest upon grounds other than those specified in this paragraph;

and is further satisfied (in any such case) that the restriction is not unreasonable having regard to the balance between those circumstances and any detriment to the public or to persons not parties to the agreement (being purchasers, consumers or users of goods produced or sold by such parties, or persons engaged or seeking to become engaged in the trade or business of selling such goods or of producing or selling similar goods) resulting or likely to result from the operation of the restriction.

An application for the variation of a previous decision may be made to the Court by the Registrar or by any person who is, or was at the time of the previous determination by the Court, subject to or entitled to the benefit of the restriction in question. No such application may be made except by leave of the Court, which will not be granted except upon *prima facie* evidence of a material change in the relevant circumstances.

(d) Resale Price Maintenance

(1) *Enforcement of Resale Price Conditions under the 1956 Act*

By s. 24 of the Act, it is unlawful for any two or more persons carrying on business in the United Kingdom as suppliers of any goods to make or carry out any agreement or arrangement by which they undertake:

(i) to withhold supplies of goods for delivery in the United Kingdom from dealers (whether party to the agreement or arrangement or not) who resell or have resold goods in breach of any condition *as to the price at which those goods may be sold*;

(ii) to refuse to supply goods for delivery in the United Kingdom to such dealers except on terms and conditions which are less favourable than those applicable in the case of other dealers carrying on business in similar circumstances; or

(iii) to supply goods only to persons who undertake or have undertaken to withhold supplies of goods, or to refuse to supply goods, as aforesaid.

Agreements or arrangements authorising the recovery of penalties from dealers who resell goods in breach of any such conditions, and the conduct of any domestic proceedings in connection therewith, are also unlawful. There are similar provisions affecting agreements between dealers in goods.

On the other hand, where goods are sold by a supplier subject to a condition as to the minimum price at which the goods may be resold, s. 25 *extends* the right of the supplier to enforce that condition, by enabling him to take legal proceedings for such enforcement, not only against the buyer of the goods, but also against any person who subsequently acquires the goods with notice of the condition. Such notice need not be express; it is sufficient that the purchaser knows of the existence of conditions, and how details thereof can be obtained (*Goodyear Tyre and Rubber Co. (Great Britain), Ltd.* v. *Lancashire Batteries, Ltd.* [1958] 3 All E.R. 7). (As to the effect of this section on the rule of privity of contract, see Chap. I, § 11 (a).)

Section 25 now applies only to resale price conditions in respect of goods which are 'exempted goods' under the Resale Prices Act, 1964. This includes goods registered under the 1964 Act pending a reference to the Restrictive Practices Court (*E.M.I. Records, Ltd.* v. *Marcus* [1965] 2 All E.R. 781).

(2) Resale Prices Act, 1964

This Act was introduced to abolish resale price maintenance except where it could be shown to be in the public interest.

Under s. 1, except as provided by the Act, any term or condition of an agreement relating to the sale of goods by a supplier to a dealer is void in so far as it purports to provide for the establishment of minimum prices to be charged on the resale of those goods in the United Kingdom; and it is unlawful for any supplier of goods:

(i) to include in any agreement for the sale of goods any such term or condition;

(ii) to require, as a condition of supplying goods to a dealer, the inclusion in any contract or agreement of any such term or condition, or the giving of any undertaking to the like effect;

(iii) to notify to dealers or otherwise publish minimum prices which may be charged on the resale of the goods (although publication of a *recommended* price is permitted).

Indirect enforcement of minimum resale prices by the withholding of supplies of goods from a dealer who sells, or is likely to sell, goods obtained from the supplier below the resale price, or who supplies goods to a third party who has done so or is likely to do so, is also unlawful. A supplier of goods is to be treated as withholding supplies of goods if he refuses or fails to supply the goods to the order of the dealer, or if he refuses to supply them except at unfavourable prices, or if, although he contracts to supply the goods, he treats the dealer less favourably than he normally treats other such dealers in respect of times or methods of delivery or other matters arising in the execution of the contract (s. 2).

A supplier may, however, withhold goods if he has reasonable cause to believe that within the previous twelve months the dealer has been using the goods as 'loss leaders.' 'Loss leaders' are goods which are sold not for the purpose of making a profit, but for the purpose of attracting custom to the dealer's premises or otherwise of advertising his business; but the term does not include goods which are so sold with the consent of the manufacturer or, in certain circumstances, the supplier, nor does it include goods sold at genuine seasonal or clearance sales (s. 3).

The remedy for breach of these provisions is a civil action which may be brought by any person affected by that breach or by the Crown. Where a supplier has withheld goods from a dealer whom he knew to have sold, or to have intended to sell, his goods below the resale price, it is presumed, unless the supplier proves to the contrary, that he withheld the supplies on the ground that the dealer had so acted or was likely so to act (s. 4).

(3) *Exempted Goods*

The Act prescribed a period of three months from 16th August to 15th November, 1964, during which any supplier who supplied goods under arrangements for resale price maintenance could give notice to the Registrar of Restrictive Trading Agreements claiming registration in respect of the goods so supplied. The Act requires the Registrar to compile a register containing particulars of goods so notified, and from time to time to publish lists of the classes of goods of which particulars are entered in the register. Such goods are to be treated as exempt from the provisions of ss. 1 and 2 of the Act until the Restrictive Practices Court makes, or refuses to make, an order in respect of them. The Registrar must refer to the Court all goods on the register, and must from time to time publish lists of the classes of goods in respect of which the Court has made or refused to make orders under the Act (s. 6).

Under s. 5, the Restrictive Practices Court may, on a reference made by the Registrar, direct that goods of a particular class shall be permanently exempt if it appears to the Court that in default of a system of maintained minimum resale prices applicable to those goods:

(i) the quality of the goods available for sale, or the variety of the goods so available, would be substantially reduced; or

(ii) the number of establishments in which the goods are sold by retail would be substantially reduced; or

(iii) the prices at which the goods are sold by retail would in general and in the long run be increased; or

(iv) the goods would be sold by retail under conditions likely to cause danger to health in consequence of their misuse; or

(v) any necessary services actually provided in connection with or after the sale of the goods by retail would cease to be so provided or would be substantially reduced;

and in any such case that the resulting detriment to the public as consumers or users of the goods in question would outweigh any detriment to them as such consumers or users resulting from the maintenance of minimum resale prices in respect of the goods.

Late application for the exemption of goods which were not registered during the prescribed three months' period may be made to the Court by the Registrar or by any supplier of goods of the class in question or by any trade association whose members include suppliers of such goods. Leave of the Court must be obtained and there must be *prima facie* evidence of facts upon which an order could be made in accordance with s. 5 in respect of the goods (s. 7).

Application to the Court may also be made with leave for the discharge of any order previously made by the Court directing that goods of any class are to be exempted goods, or for an order in respect of goods which the Court has previously refused to make or has previously discharged, provided that *prima facie* evidence is shown of a material change in the relevant circumstances (*ibid.*).

(e) Monopolies

A monopoly arises where at least one-third of a market, either local or national, is controlled by one person or by a group of persons working in combination. Provision for the control of monopolies was made by the Monopolies and Restrictive Practices (Inquiry and Control) Act, 1948, which created a Commission, known as the Monopolies Commission, to investigate and report on certain types of monopolies referred to it by the Board of Trade. The powers of the Monopolies Commission were reduced by the Restrictive Trade Practices Act, 1956, but have now been substantially increased by the Monopolies and Mergers Act, 1965.

. Under the Monopolies and Mergers Acts, 1948 and 1965, as the Acts are collectively known, the Commission may consist of not less than four nor more than twenty-five regular members appointed by the Board of Trade, the Board having power to increase this number by statutory instrument if it thinks fit. The functions of the Commission may be delegated to groups consisting of not less than five regular members. The Board of Trade may require the Commission to investigate and report on apparent monopoly situations in connection with the production or supply of goods or the supply of commercial services, unless these arise out of agreements registrable under the Restrictive Trade Practices Act, 1956; to report on restrictive practices to which the 1956 Act does not apply, whether or not these arise out of monopoly situations; and to investigate and report on certain mergers between two or more enterprises.

A merger or proposed merger may be referred to the Commission if it will, or is likely to, result in the creation or strengthening of a monopoly situation, or if the value of the assets taken over exceeds five million pounds. The reference must be made within six months of the merger, and the Commission must make its report within six months of the reference or such further time, not exceeding three months, as the Board of Trade may allow. Newspaper mergers which result in a proprietor controlling an average daily circulation of 500,000 or more copies must, subject to certain limited exceptions, be referred to the Commission, and are unlawful and void unless the Board of Trade gives its written consent after receiving the Commission's report.

If the Board of Trade is of opinion that a monopoly situation or merger, on which the Commission has reported, operates or is likely to operate against the public interest, it is empowered to declare any such agreement or arrangement, or the means by which it is put into effect, to be unlawful and require it to be terminated. It may also make orders for the publication of price lists and the regulation of prices; prohibit or restrict the acquisition by one person of the business of another; and require the division of any trade or business by the sale of part of the business, and make orders for the carrying out of this division.

§ 3. *Hire-Purchase*

(a) Nature of Hire-Purchase Agreement

A hire-purchase agreement is defined by s. 1 of the Hire-Purchase Act, 1965, as:

an agreement for the bailment of goods under which the bailee may buy the goods, or under which the property in the goods will or may pass to the bailee.*

Usually one person, called the owner, lets goods on hire to another, called the hirer, on the condition that the hirer pays instal-

*As to bailments generally, see Chap. V, § 1.

ments to the owner until a certain agreed sum has been paid, when the hirer either becomes the owner of the goods automatically, or exercises an option to purchase by the payment of a small agreed sum. When a person agrees to take goods from a trader on hire-purchase, the form of transaction commonly adopted is that the trader sells the goods outright for cash to a finance company, which becomes the owner of the goods, and the finance company thereupon lets the goods to the hirer, whose intention it is to acquire the goods in accordance with the terms of the agreement, by exercising an option to purchase for a nominal sum, *e.g.*, £1, when all instalments have been paid. At the same time the finance company frequently enters into a 'recourse agreement' with the dealer, whereby the dealer agrees to repurchase the goods from the finance company if the hirer defaults.

Three different kinds of contract may fall within the statutory definition. A person may agree to hire goods for a specified period, paying regular instalments, the property in the goods to pass to him on payment of the last instalment; or he may make the same contract, except that the property is not to pass until he exercises an option to acquire it by paying some final nominal sum; or he may make either arrangement without binding himself to continue the hire for the specified period.

The importance of the distinction is that a buyer who makes the first kind of agreement is *a person in possession of goods with the seller's consent under an agreement to buy*, within the meaning of s. 25 (2) of the Sale of Goods Act, 1893, and can therefore pass a good title by a sale, pledge or other disposition to a party who takes in good faith, even though the instalment payments have not been completed. A person who has made one of the other types of contract, however, cannot pass a good title in such circumstances, since he is not in possession under an agreement to buy, either because he has a mere *option* to buy after payment of the instalments (*Belsize Motor Supply Co.* v. *Cox* [1914] 1 K.B. 244), or because he is under no obligation to continue the hiring (*Helby* v. *Matthews* [1895] A.C. 471). But the title of the owner could nevertheless be defeated by a sale in *market overt* (*Bishopsgate Motor Finance Corporation, Ltd.* v. *Transport Brakes, Ltd.* [1949] 1 K.B. 322), or under ss. 27-29 of the Hire-Purchase Act, 1964 (see *ante*, § 1 (b) (2)). And where a hirer who cannot pass a good title in fact sells the goods in breach of his agreement, the buyer – or a subsequent transferee – may nevertheless obtain a title if the wrongful seller later acquires one.

In *Butterworth* v. *Kingsway Motors* [1954] 2 All E.R. 694, a hire-purchaser of a car wrongfully sold it to an innocent buyer before all instalments under the hire-purchase agreement had been paid. A series of sales ensued, and the hire-purchaser completed the payments at a time when the defendants had the apparent right to possession.

Held: The legal title acquired by the hire-purchaser went to 'feed' the defective titles of the various buyers and vested a good title forthwith in the defendants.

(b) Hire-Purchase Act, 1965

(1) *Scope of the Act*

The Hire-Purchase Acts, 1938 and 1954, and the greater part of the Hire-Purchase Act, 1964, were repealed and re-enacted by the Hire-Purchase Act, 1965. The Act applies to hire-purchase and conditional sale agreements under which the hire-purchase price or total purchase price, excluding any penalty, damages or compensation payable for a breach of the agreement, does not exceed £2,000, and to credit-sale agreements under which the total purchase price exceeds £30, but does not exceed £2,000 (s. 2). The limit of £2,000 may be increased by Order in Council (s. 3). The Act does not apply to such agreements where the hirer or buyer is a body corporate (s. 4).

The statutory definition of a hire-purchase agreement has already been given (*ante*, p. 150). A credit-sale agreement is defined by s. 1 as:

an agreement for the sale of goods under which the purchase price is payable by five or more instalments, not being a conditional sale agreement.

A conditional sale agreement is defined by s. 1 as:

an agreement for the sale of goods under which the purchase price or part of it is payable by instalments, and the property in the goods is to remain in the seller (notwithstanding that the buyer is to be in possession of the goods) until such conditions as to the payment of instalments or otherwise as may be specified in the agreement are fulfilled.

Credit-sale and conditional sale agreements are also subject to the provisions of the Sale of Goods Act, 1893; but ss. 11 (1) (c), 12-15, and 25 (2) of that Act are not to apply to conditional sale agreements which fall within the statutory limit (ss. 20, 54).

(2) *Requirements on Formation of Agreement*

An owner or seller is not entitled to enforce an agreement to which the Act applies or any security or guarantee relating thereto, or to enforce any right to recover the goods from the hirer or buyer, unless the following requirements are complied with (ss. 5-9):

(i) The cash price of the goods must be stated in writing before the agreement is entered into. This requirement is sufficiently complied with if a ticket clearly stating the price is attached to the goods when the hirer or buyer inspects them, or the price is stated in a catalogue or advertisement by reference to which the hirer or buyer has selected the goods.

(ii) The agreement must be signed by the hirer or buyer and by or on behalf of all other parties thereto.

(iii) The agreement must contain a statement of the hire-purchase or total purchase price, the cash price, the amount and date of the instalments, and a list of the goods to which the agreement relates.

(iv) The agreement must, when the hirer or buyer signs it, comply with any regulations made by the Board of Trade as to the form and legibility of the document which constitutes the agreement.

(v) The agreement must contain a notice, at least as prominent as the rest of its contents, of the rights of the hirer or buyer to terminate the agreement and the restriction of the owner's or seller's right to recover the goods, in the terms prescribed in Schedules 1 and 2 to the Act. (This provision does not apply to credit-sale agreements.)

(vi) If the agreement is signed by the hirer or buyer at appropriate trade premises, and is signed by or on behalf of all other parties either immediately before or immediately after it is signed by the hirer or buyer, a copy must there and then be delivered to him. In any other case there must immediately be delivered or sent to him a copy of the document which is presented or sent to him for his signature in the form in which it then is ('the first statutory copy'), and, within seven days of the making of the agreement, there must also be delivered or sent to him a copy of the completed agreement ('the second statutory copy'). Where the agreement is signed by the hirer or buyer at a place other than appropriate trade premises, the second statutory copy must be sent to him by post, and both copies must contain a statement in the prescribed form of his right to cancel the agreement, and the name and address of a person to whom notice of cancellation may be sent.

'Appropriate trade premises' means premises at which the owner or seller normally carries on a business, or at which goods of the description to which the agreement relates, or of a similar description, are normally offered or exposed for sale in the course of a business carried on at those premises (s. 58).

If in any action the court is satisfied that a failure to comply with any of the above requirements (other than (ii)) has not prejudiced the hirer or buyer, and that it would be just and equitable to dispense with the requirement, the court may, subject to any conditions that it thinks fit to impose, dispense with that requirement for the purpose of the action (s. 10). This power is not, however, exercisable where, in the case of an agreement signed by the hirer or buyer at a place other than appropriate trade premises, the second statutory copy has not been sent to him, or either copy fails to state his right of cancellation (*ibid.*).

(3) *Right of Cancellation*

Where the hirer or buyer signs the agreement at a place other than appropriate trade premises, he may within four days of receiving the second statutory copy serve notice of cancellation on the owner or seller or his agent and thereby rescind the agreement or withdraw his offer, as the case may be (s. 11). If notice of cancellation is sent by post to a person at his proper address, it is deemed to be served at the time when it is posted (s. 12).

If any goods have been delivered to the hirer or buyer under the agreement, his only obligation is to make the goods available at his own premises upon receipt of a written request to do so, and to take reasonable care of the goods for a period of twenty-one days from the date of service of the notice of cancellation. If the goods are not collected within that period through no fault of his own, he is under no further obligation to take care of the goods (s. 13). Any sum paid by him under the agreement is recoverable, and he has a lien on the goods while they are in his possession for any such sum (s. 14). If he has delivered goods in part exchange these must be returned to him in good condition within ten days of service of the notice of cancellation or a sum paid to him equal to the part exchange allowance, and he is entitled to a lien on goods in his possession for this sum (s. 15).

These provisions cannot be excluded or restricted by agreement (s. 29).

(4) *Dealer as Agent of Owner or Seller*

Where a dealer negotiates an agreement between a hirer or buyer and an owner or seller (usually a finance company), any representations made to the hirer or buyer by the dealer in respect of the goods to which the agreement relates, whether orally or in writing, are deemed to be made by him as agent of the owner or seller (s. 16). The dealer is also deemed to be the agent of the owner or seller for the purpose of receiving any notice of cancellation served by the hirer or buyer (s. 12 (3)), or other notice of withdrawal of the offer or rescission of the agreement, other than notice of termination under s. 27 (see (7), *infra*) (s. 31). Sections 16 and 31 apply to all credit-sale agreements where the total purchase price does not exceed £2,000 even where this is less than £30. These provisions cannot be excluded or restricted by agreement (s. 29).

(5) *Implied Conditions and Warranties*

The following conditions and warranties are implied in hire-purchase and conditional sale agreements to which the Act applies:

(i) *Title*

(*a*) A CONDITION that the owner or seller shall have a right to sell the goods at the time when the property is to pass.

(*b*) A WARRANTY that the hirer or buyer shall have and enjoy quiet possession of the goods.

(*c*) A WARRANTY that the goods shall be free from any charge or incumbrance in favour of any third party at the time when the property is to pass (s. 17 (1)).

(ii) *Quality*

A CONDITION that the goods will be of merchantable quality, except, where the hirer or buyer has examined the goods or a sample of them, in respect of defects which the examination ought to have revealed (s. 17 (2), (3)).

(iii) *Fitness for purpose*

Where the hirer or buyer, either expressly or by implication, has made known to the owner or seller, or to a servant or to an agent of the owner or seller, the particular purpose for which the goods are required, or in the course of antecedent negotiations has made that purpose known to the person conducting the negotiations, or to a servant or agent of such a person, a CONDITION that the goods will be reasonably fit for that purpose (s. 17 (4)).

(iv) *Hire or sale by reference to sample*

Where goods are let or agreed to be sold by reference to a sample:

(*a*) A CONDITION that the bulk will correspond to the sample in quality.

(*b*) A CONDITION that the hirer or buyer will have a reasonable opportunity of comparing the bulk with the sample (s. 19 (1)).

(v) *Hire or sale by description*

Where goods are let or agreed to be sold by description, a CONDITION that the goods will correspond with the description; and, if the goods are let or agreed to be sold by reference to a sample as well as by description, a CONDITION that the goods will correspond with both the sample and the description (s. 19 (2)).

The conditions and warranties under (i), (iv) and (v) above cannot be excluded by express agreement (ss. 18, 29). The condition as to merchantable quality may only be excluded where the goods are let or agreed to be sold as second-hand goods or as goods which are subject to specified defects and the agreement contains a statement to that effect together with a provision expressly excluding the implied condition in relation to those goods or in respect of those defects, and it is proved that before the agreement was made this provision was brought to the notice of the hirer or buyer and its effect made clear to him (s. 18). The condition as to fitness for purpose may be excluded or modified provided it is proved that before the agreement was made the provision excluding or modifying the condition was brought to the notice of the hirer or buyer and its effect made clear to him (*ibid.*).

(6) *Contracts of Guarantee*

A contract of guarantee relating to an agreement to which the Act applies, and any security given by a guarantor in respect of money payable under such a contract, is not enforceable unless, within seven days of the making of the contract of guarantee or of the agreement to which it relates, whichever is the later, there is delivered or sent to the guarantor a copy of the agreement, and a copy of a note or memorandum of the contract of guarantee signed by the guarantor or his agent. The court may, however, dispense with these requirements if it is satisfied that a failure to comply with them has not prejudiced the guarantor (s. 22).

For the purposes of the Act 'contract of guarantee' includes a contract of indemnity (s. 58) (see Chap. V, § 4).

(7) *Right of Hirer or Buyer to Terminate Agreement*

At any time before the final payment under a hire-purchase or conditional sale agreement falls due, the hirer or buyer may terminate the agreement by giving written notice to the person entitled or authorised to receive the sums payable under the agreement (s. 27). He must allow the owner or seller to retake possession of the goods, pay all instalments then due, and a further sum if necessary to bring his total payments up to one-half of the hire purchase or total purchase price, or any lesser sum which may be specified in the agreement. The court may itself substitute a lesser sum which it considers to be equal to the actual loss sustained by the owner or seller. The hirer or buyer will also be liable in damages if he has failed to take reasonable care of the goods (s. 28). Any provision in the agreement purporting to exclude or restrict this right of termination or to impose a greater liability upon the hirer or buyer than that imposed by the Act is void (s. 29).

(8) *Restrictions on Right of Owner or Seller to Terminate Agreement or Recover Possession of Goods*

Where a hire-purchase or conditional sale agreement provides that the owner may determine the agreement or recover possession of the goods upon the hirer's failure to pay any instalment or other sum payable by him, the owner or seller is not entitled to exercise this right unless he serves a 'notice of default' upon the hirer requiring payment within a specified period not less than seven days thereafter, and the payment is not made or tendered before the end of that period (s. 25).

Any provision in a hire-purchase or conditional sale agreement that, on the death of the hirer or buyer, the agreement is to terminate or the owner or seller is to have the right to recover possession of the goods, or that the liability of the hirer or buyer shall be increased or accelerated in any way, or his rights restricted or postponed in any way, is void (s. 30).

After one-third of the hire-purchase price or, in the case of a conditional sale agreement, the total purchase price has been paid or tendered, then, provided that the hirer or buyer has not himself determined the agreement, the owner or seller of the goods cannot enforce any right to recover possession of the goods from the hirer or buyer otherwise than by action in a county court (s. 34). Contravention of this provision terminates the agreement, and the hirer or buyer is released from all liability, and is entitled to recover all sums paid, under the agreement (*ibid.*). The section does not, however, apply if possession is retaken with the consent of the hirer or buyer.

In *Mercantile Credit Co., Ltd.* v. *Cross* [1965] 1 All E.R. 577, a hirer of goods who had paid more than one-third of the hire-purchase price fell into arrears of payment. The owners wrote a letter to him stating that they thereby terminated the hiring and required him to give up possession of the goods. The hirer thereupon returned the goods to the owners. It was held that the hirer had consented to the return of the goods, and that the owners had not enforced a right to recover possession contrary to the Act.

Upon an application to the court for possession the court may order:

(i) the specific delivery of all the goods to the owner or seller;

(ii) the specific delivery of all the goods to the owner or seller, the operation of the order to be postponed on condition that the hirer or buyer or any guarantor pays the unpaid balance of the price at such times and in such amounts either as are agreed by the parties or as the court thinks just; or

(iii) the specific delivery of a part of the goods to the owner or seller and for the transfer to the hirer or buyer of the title of the owner or seller to the remainder of the goods (ss. 35–45).

(9) *Appropriation of Payments*

For the provisions of the Act relating to the appropriation of payments, see Chap. I, § 12 (b) (5).

(c) Law Apart from Statute

Most hire-purchase agreements now fall within the scope of the Hire-Purchase Act, 1965. It is still necessary, however, to examine the common law rules, not only because of their application to contracts falling outside the Act, but also because these rules apply to all hire-purchase agreements in so far as the Act is silent. Generally speaking, the parties are free to make whatever terms they choose, but in the absence of agreement to the contrary, the following rules apply.

(1) Duties of Owner and Hirer

It is the duty of the owner to deliver possession to the hirer, and to transfer ownership to him if he exercises his option to purchase the goods in accordance with the agreement. It is the duty of the hirer to take the same care of the goods while in his possession which a reasonable and prudent man would take; and he will be liable for damage caused by his negligence, though not for that attributable to fair wear and tear.

(2) Implied Conditions and Warranties

As has already been observed (see Chap. I, § 6 (e)), the courts imply into hire-purchase agreements falling outside the Hire-Purchase Act conditions and warranties similar to those implied by the Act. Where the Act does not apply, the following conditions and warranties are implied:

(i) Title

There is an implied CONDITION that the owner will be able to pass a good title to the goods when the option to purchase becomes exercisable; and an implied WARRANTY that the hirer shall have and enjoy quiet possession of the goods.

In *Karflex, Ltd.* v. *Poole* [1933] 2 K.B. 251, the purported owners entered into a hire-purchase agreement in respect of a motor car, which unknown to them was a stolen car. The hirer defaulted. The purported owners retook the car, which the true owner now discovered and claimed from them. The hirer was held to be entitled to a return of the instalments which he had paid.

(ii) Fitness for purpose

There is an implied WARRANTY by the owner that the goods are and will remain as fit and suitable for the purpose for which they are required as care and skill can make them, except where the defect is apparent, or where the hirer does not rely on the skill and judgment of the owner. Implied terms as to fitness may be, and usually are, excluded by express terms in the contract. Such exemption clauses, however, will not excuse a breach of the fundamental obligation imposed by the contract (*Karsales (Harrow), Ltd.* v. *Wallis, ante,* p. 29).

(iii) Letting by description

Where goods are let under a hire-purchase agreement by description there is an implied term, which is normally a fundamental term which cannot be excluded, that the goods hired will correspond to the description (*Astley Industrial Trust, Ltd.* v. *Grimley* [1963] 2 All E.R. 33).

(3) *Liability of Dealer*

Where a dealer arranges for goods to be let to a customer by a finance company to which the dealer sells the goods for that purpose, the dealer does not become a party to the hire-purchase agreement, and cannot therefore be sued by the customer for any breach of that agreement. But if the dealer, with a view to inducing the customer to enter into the agreement, makes an express warranty relating to the goods which turns out to be false, the dealer is liable to the customer for breach of this *collateral* warranty (*Andrews* v. *Hopkinson, ante*, p. 23).

The dealer may be regarded for certain purposes as agent of the finance company so as to bind the company by his actions, *e.g.*, where he accepts notice of revocation of the hirer's offer to the finance company (*Financings, Ltd.* v. *Stimson* [1962] 3 All E.R. 386).

(4) *Termination of Agreement*

The agreement normally provides that the owner may terminate the agreement and retake possession of the goods on default in payment of any instalment by the hirer. Where the agreement provides in addition that the hirer shall pay a sum of money to the owner as damages on default, it is a question of construction whether this sum is liquidated damages or a penalty. If it is the former, the whole sum can be recovered; if the latter, the owner can only recover in respect of the damage which he has actually suffered (*Campbell Discount Co., Ltd.* v. *Bridge, ante*, p. 79).

If the hirer gives notice to the owner of his inability to pay any further instalments, and of his desire to terminate the agreement, this may constitute, not a breach of the agreement, but the exercise of a power contained therein whereby the hirer may terminate the agreement by giving such notice. If so, the hirer will be liable to pay any sum prescribed in the agreement, as he is acting in performance of the contract and is bound by its terms; since there is no breach the question of a penalty will not arise (*ibid.*). If the hirer's conduct constitutes a breach of the agreement, the notice will normally be treated as a repudiation of the whole agreement, and the owner will be entitled to repossess the car and to recover damages, the measure of which will be the total hire-purchase price less all amounts already paid, the amount recovered by resale of the goods, and a rebate for accelerated payment (*Overstone, Ltd.* v. *Shipway* [1962] 1 All E.R. 54).

Where the hirer has failed to pay any instalments without giving notice that he does not intend to make any further payments, the owner is entitled to retake possession of the goods, but his right to damages is limited to any unpaid instalments to date with interest thereon, as a mere failure to pay instalments does not constitute repudiation (*Financings, Ltd.* v. *Baldock* [1963] 2 Q.B. 104).

(5) *Rights of Third Parties*

The following are the rights of third parties in relation to goods which are the subject of a hire-purchase agreement:

(i) *Sureties*

The ordinary law of suretyship applies (see Chap, V, § 4); and in particular, the surety will be released from liability if the owner terminates the agreement by retaking the goods, unless the contract of guarantee otherwise provides.

(ii) *Assignees*

In the absence of agreement to the contrary, either the owner or the hirer may assign his rights under the hire-purchase agreement; but the owner cannot assign his personal right to enter and retake the goods. The assignee will then assume all the rights and liabilities of the assignor, though the assignor will still remain liable for the performance of his obligations.

In *Whiteley, Ltd.* v. *Hilt* [1918] 2 K.B. 808, a hirer of a piano, who had paid all instalments due to date, purported to sell the piano to a purchaser who believed that it was the property of the hirer. The owners, on becoming aware of the sale, sued the purchaser for its return. The purchaser paid into court all the instalments remaining unpaid. It was held that there had been a valid assignment of the hirer's rights, and the purchaser was entitled to exercise the option to purchase.

An assignee from the hirer will not get any title to the goods themselves unless and until he is able to and in fact does exercise the option to purchase, and if the agreement forbids assignment by the hirer, the supposed purchaser or assignee can obtain no rights, even if he was unaware of the terms of the agreement.

(iii) *Landlords*

A landlord has a right of distress over goods held on hire-purchase by a tenant on the premises (Law of Distress Amendment Act, 1908, s. 4). Even if the terms of the hire-purchase agreement provide that the agreement, and the owner's consent to the hirer's possession of the goods, are to determine if the landlord levies or threatens to levy a distress, the landlord will still be able to distrain on the goods, as they will be in the possession, order or disposition of the tenant, by the consent and permission of the true owner, under such circumstances that the tenant is the reputed owner, and goods in such circumstances are not protected against a distress (*ibid.*). The only remedy for the owner appears to be expressly to withdraw his consent and to demand the return of the goods prior to the levy of the distress.

(iv) *Execution creditors*

Goods held under a hire-purchase agreement cannot be taken in execution of a judgment against the hirer.

If, however, the sheriff seizes and sells the goods, the purchaser receives a good title thereto (Bankruptcy and Deeds of Arrangement Act, 1913, s. 15); but the owner can recover the proceeds of sale from the judgment creditor (*Curtis* v. *Maloney* [1951] 1 K.B. 736).

(v) *Trustees in bankruptcy*

If the owner becomes bankrupt, all his rights under the agreement vest in his trustee in bankruptcy. If the hirer becomes bankrupt, his trustee becomes entitled to the benefit of the hire-purchase agreement, but if its burdens are more onerous than its benefits, he may disclaim and allow the owner to retake the goods and prove in the hirer's bankruptcy for any damage he may have suffered (Bankruptcy Act, 1914, s. 54). If, however, the hire-purchase goods are at the commencement of the bankruptcy in the possession, order or disposition of the hirer, by the consent and permission of the owner, in his trade or business, under such circumstances that he is the reputed owner thereof, his trustee in bankruptcy may claim them for the benefit of the general body of creditors, leaving the owner to prove in the bankruptcy for his loss (*ibid.*, s. 38). The owner's consent can be withdrawn only by express notice before the commencement of the bankruptcy. The reputed ownership of the hirer may be rebutted by showing a trade custom to the contrary; in some cases, such custom must be expressly proved; in other cases, it is so well established that judicial notice will be taken without express proof, as in the hotel business, where it is customary for a hotel-keeper to have his furniture on hire-purchase.

(d) Advertisements (Hire-Purchase) Act, 1957

Any advertisement of goods available on hire-purchase or credit-sale (which for this purpose includes conditional sale) which states:

(1) the amount of the deposit payable, or that no deposit is payable, or

(2) the amount of any one or more of the deposits payable, or

(3) a fraction representing the rate of interest payable, or

(4) the hire-purchase or total purchase price of the goods,

must (unless it relates solely to credit-sales of goods at a price not exceeding £5 per article) comply with the provisions of the Advertisements (Hire-Purchase) Act, 1957, as amended by the Hire-Purchase Act, 1964, ss. 30–32, as to the information included therein.

In most cases, the information to be included is:

(*a*) either –

    (i) the amount of the deposit directly expressed, or

    (ii) a statement that the amount of the deposit is a fraction specified in the advertisement of a sum the amount of which is directly expressed therein, or

    (iii) a statement that no deposit is payable;

(*b*) the amount of each instalment directly expressed;

(*c*) the total number of instalments payable;

(*d*) the length of the period in respect of which each instalment is payable;

(*e*) if any instalments are payable before delivery of the goods, the number of instalments so payable;

(*f*) a sum stated as the cash price of the goods; and

(*g*) a sum stated as the hire-purchase or total purchase price of the goods and being the amount (directly expressed) of the aggregate of the amount of the deposit (if any) and of all the instalments payable.

If the advertisement includes a fraction representing the rate of interest the fraction must be expressed as a specified amount per cent. per annum and must be not less than an amount calculated in accordance with the formula prescribed in Schedule 3 of the Hire-Purchase Act, 1964.

CHAPTER IV

NEGOTIABLE INSTRUMENTS

§ 1. *Negotiability*

It has already been observed (Chap. I, § 11 (c)) that certain documents are recognised in law as having the characteristic of negotiability. The essential features of such negotiable instruments may be summarised as follows:

(1) the property and rights in the instrument pass by delivery, with or without indorsement according to circumstances, and no further evidence of the transfer is required;

(2) the holder of the instrument for the time being possesses a right of action in his own name;

(3) notice to the person liable in respect of the instrument is not required;

(4) consideration is *presumed* to have been given for the instrument;

(5) a transferee who takes in good faith and for value is unaffected by equities, *i.e.*, defences that might be available against the transferor, and can obtain a good title to the instrument despite any defect in the title of the transferor.

The whole question of negotiability is one of the *law merchant*, and any instrument will be recognised by law as negotiable *if it is so treated by the custom of merchants*. It was at one time thought that the list of negotiable instruments was definitely closed, and was confined to documents of the nature of bills of exchange and promissory notes, and that there was no custom by which any other documents could be indorsed over so as to have the character of negotiability; but in *Goodwin* v. *Robarts* (1875) L.R. 10 Ex. 337 it was held that foreign scrip might be rendered negotiable by custom; and in *Bechuanaland Exploration Co.* v. *London Trading Bank* [1898] 2 Q.B. 658 it was decided that the debentures to bearer of a limited company are negotiable by mercantile custom. In the case of bills of exchange, promissory notes and cheques, the law has recognised the custom of merchants by statute, provisions as to these being now contained in the Bills of Exchange Act, 1882, and the Cheques Act, 1957.

At the present time, in addition to bills of exchange, cheques and promissory notes, exchequer bills, circular notes, dividend warrants and certain debenture bonds and share warrants are negotiable; whilst amongst instruments possessing somewhat analogous features, but which are not recognised by law as negotiable, are bills of lading, dock warrants and wharfingers' certificates.

§ 2. *Bills of Exchange*

(a) Definition and Form of Bill of Exchange

The Bills of Exchange Act, 1882, s. 3 (1), defines a bill of exchange as:

> An *unconditional* order in writing, addressed by one person to another, signed by the person giving it, requiring the person to whom it is addressed to *pay on demand, or at a fixed or determinable future time, a sum certain* in money, to, or to the order of, a specified person, or to bearer.

An order which does not comply with these conditions, or which requires an act to be done in addition to the payment of money, is not a bill of exchange (s. 3 (2)).

(1) *Order must be Unconditional*

An order to a banker to pay a sum of money 'provided the receipt form at foot hereof is duly signed' is not a bill of exchange, because the order is not unconditional (*Bavins* v. *London and South Western Bank* [1900] 1 Q.B. 270). But if the order has words such as 'the receipt at the back hereof must be signed, which signature will be taken as an indorsement of this cheque,' the document will be a bill of exchange, because the words are not addressed to the banker, who is at liberty to pay without signature of the receipt, but are simply a request by the drawer to the payee to sign the receipt (*Nathan* v. *Ogdens* (1905) 93 L.T. 553).

In *Roberts & Co.* v. *Marsh* [1915] 1 K.B. 42, a person drew a cheque on a blank sheet of paper, and wrote on it the words 'to be retained,' telling the payee not to present it for payment, as he would send him a cheque on a proper form to replace it. He did not send the promised cheque in substitution, and the payee therefore presented the original cheque for payment. It was dishonoured, and the payee sued the drawer on the cheque. It was held that the order for payment was unconditional, and the document was a cheque within the meaning of the Act on which the payee was entitled to sue. The words 'to be retained' were not addressed to the banker, but were simply a condition between drawer and payee.

An order to pay out of a particular fund is not unconditional; but an unqualified order to pay is unconditional although coupled with an indication of a particular fund out of which the drawee is to reimburse himself or a particular account to be debited with the amount, or a statement of the transaction which gives rise to the bill (s. 3 (3)).

(2) *Time for Payment*

A bill is payable 'on demand':

(i) which is expressed to be payable on demand, or at sight, or on presentation; or

(ii) in which no time for payment is expressed (s. 10 (1)).

A bill is payable at a 'determinable future time' when it is expressed to be payable:

(i) at a fixed period after date or sight;

(ii) on or at a fixed period after the occurrence of a specified event which is certain to happen, though the time of happening may be uncertain (s. 11).

Thus, a bill payable 'three months after the death of A' would be valid, but one payable 'three months after my [the drawer's] marriage' would be irregular, as the marriage is an event which is not certain to happen. The happening of an uncertain event does not cure the defect (s. 11). A bill which is payable 'on or before' a given date does not fall within the definition, as the option to pay at an earlier date creates an uncertainty in the time of payment (*Williamson* v. *Rider* [1963] 1 Q.B. 89).

(3) *Sum Certain*

The sum payable is a sum certain, although it may be required to be paid with interest, or by stated instalments, or by instalments with a provision that upon default in payment of any instalment the whole sum shall become due, or according to an indicated or ascertainable rate of exchange (s. 9 (1)). Where a bill is expressed to be payable with interest, then, unless the instrument otherwise provides, the interest runs from the date of the bill, and if the bill is undated from the date of issue thereof (s. 9 (3)). If the rate of interest is not stated, 5 per cent. is taken.

If the words and figures do not agree, the sum denoted by the words is the amount payable (s. 9 (2)).

(4) *Payee to be Specified*

A bill must be drawn to or to the order of a specified person or to bearer. A document in the form of a cheque drawn 'Pay Cash or Order' does not fall within the definition (*Cole* v. *Milsome* [1951] 1 All E.R. 311), nor, presumably, does a document drawn in favour of an impersonal object such as 'wages,' 'office' and so forth. Such a document could not be interpreted as a bill payable to a fictitious payee (see (e) (4), *infra*), as an impersonal object is not a payee at all.

A document which does not fall within the definition of a bill of exchange is not negotiable, and cannot in itself confer any rights on the parties to it. It must not be supposed, however, that such documents have no legal effect whatsoever. They may constitute a good authority, or mandate, to the banker to pay the money to the bearer of the document, and confer the protection given by s. 4 of the Cheques Act, 1957, upon the collecting banker (*Orbit Mining & Trading Co., Ltd.* v. *Westminster Bank, Ltd.* [1963] 1 Q.B. 794; see *post*, § 3 (e) (3)). And, although the parties cannot sue on the document itself, they may be able to sue on the contract in respect of which the document was given, and use the document as evidence of that contract.

(5) *Parties to a Bill*

The person who draws the bill is called the *drawer*, the person on whom the bill is drawn is called the *drawee*, and the person to whom the bill is payable is called the *payee*. When the drawee has accepted the bill he is called the *acceptor*. Thus, in the example of an inland bill which follows (see (9), *infra*), J. Black is the drawer, W. Brown & Co. are the drawees, and F. White is the payee. The person who indorses a bill is called the *indorser*, and the person to whom the bill is indorsed the *indorsee*. In some instances, the bill may be drawn payable 'to my order,' in which case the drawer is himself the payee. The payee or indorsee of a bill who is in possession of it, or the person in possession of a bearer bill, is called the *holder* (s. 2).

The drawee of the bill must be named or indicated in the bill with reasonable certainty (s. 6 (1)); and the same applies to the payee when the bill is not payable to bearer (s. 7 (1)). The bill may be addressed to two or more drawees, whether partners or otherwise, but not alternatively or successively (s. 6 (2)). There may be two or more joint payees, or an alternative payee, or the holder of an office for the time being may be the payee (s. 7 (2)).

A bill may be drawn payable to, or to the order of, the drawer or the drawee (s. 5 (1)). Where in a bill drawer and drawee are the same person, or where the drawee is a fictitious person or a person not having capacity to contract, the holder may treat the instrument, at his option, either as a bill of exchange or as a promissory note (s. 5 (2)). The reason for this option is no doubt because, in a bill of this kind, the liability of the drawee or acceptor is illusory, so that the bill strongly resembles a promissory note, which is simply a promise by the maker of the note unaccompanied by any order on a drawee.

(6) *Date of Bill*

The validity of a bill is not affected by reason that it is not dated, or that the value given for it is not specified, or that it does not state the place where it is drawn, or the place where it is payable (s. 3 (4)).

The date on the bill is deemed to be the true date, unless the contrary is proved; and a bill is not invalid because it is ante-dated, post-dated, or bears date on a Sunday (s. 13).

Where a bill expressed to be payable at a fixed period after date is issued undated, or where the acceptance of a bill payable at a fixed period after sight is undated, the holder may insert therein the true date of issue or acceptance, and the bill is payable accordingly. If a wrong date is inserted by mistake and in good faith, and in *every case* where, a wrong date having been inserted, the bill subsequently comes into the hands of a holder in due course (see (c) (3), *infra*), the bill operates and is payable as if the date inserted had been the true date (s. 12).

(7) *Inland and Foreign Bills*

An *inland bill* is defined by the Act as one 'both drawn and payable within the British Islands, or drawn within the British Islands upon some person resident therein.' Any other bill is a *foreign bill*. Unless the contrary appears on the face of the bill, the holder is entitled to treat it as an inland bill (s. 4).

Foreign bills are generally drawn in triplicate, *i.e.*, in a set of three bills identical in terms, except that each is expressed to be payable only on condition that the other parts or either of them have not been paid. The first two parts being forwarded separately, the inconvenience resulting from the bill being lost is greatly diminished. The third part is usually retained by the drawer.

If a bill is drawn in a set, each part thereof being numbered, and containing a reference to the other parts, the whole of the parts constitute one bill; but if the holder indorses two or more parts to different persons he is liable on every such part. The acceptance may be written on any part, and must be on one part only; if the drawee accepts more than one part, he is liable to a holder in due course for every such part. Upon payment he should require the accepted part to be delivered up or he may incur further liability upon it (s. 71).

Where only one copy of a foreign bill is drawn, this is called a 'Sola of Exchange.'

(8) *Stamping of Bills*

Formerly most bills had to be stamped. The stamp duty of 2d payable on bills of exchange and promissory notes drawn, payable or negotiated in the United Kingdom was abolished as from 1st February, 1971. No stamp duty is payable under English law on a foreign bill which is drawn and payable abroad, merely because it is accepted in the United Kingdom, as an acceptance does not constitute 'negotiation.'

(9) *Forms of Bills*

INLAND BILL

London,
£100   1st Feb., 19 .....

Three months after date pay to F. White or order the sum of One hundred pounds for value received.

To W. Brown & Co., Liverpool.   J. BLACK

FOREIGN BILL DRAWN AND PAYABLE OUTSIDE THE
UNITED KINGDOM

	Capetown,
£500	1st Feb., 19......

Three months after sight pay this First of Exchange (second and third of even tenor and date unpaid) to J. Smith or order the sum of Five hundred pounds for value received.

To Emile Leblanc,
　　Paris.　　　　　　　　　　　　　　　　　　J. RHODES

(10) *Inchoate Instruments*

Where a simple signature on a blank stamped paper is delivered by the signer in order that it may be converted into a bill, it operates as a *prima facie* authority to fill it up as a complete bill. The signature may be used for that of drawer, acceptor or indorser. In like manner, when a bill is wanting in any material particular, the person in possession of it has a *prima facie* authority to fill up the omission in any way he thinks fit (s. 20 (1)). In order that any such instrument when completed may be enforceable against any person who became a party thereto prior to its completion, it must be filled up within a reasonable time and strictly in accordance with the authority given. What is a reasonable time is a question of fact (s. 20 (2)). But even a bill which is filled up without authority or after the lapse of a reasonable time is valid and effectual for all purposes in the hands of a holder in due course (s. 20 (2), proviso).

But it is otherwise if, although a blank stamped paper is signed, it has not been delivered for the purpose of being converted into a bill, as when it is stolen.

In *Baxendale* v. *Bennett* (1878) 3 Q.B.D. 525, the defendant signed a blank acceptance on a stamped paper, intending to make an accommodation bill. Circumstances arose in which the bill was not required, and the defendant put the document into an unlocked drawer of his desk. From there it was stolen by C, completed by him and negotiated for value to a holder who took it in good faith.

Held: The holder obtained no rights, as the document was never delivered in order that it might be converted into a bill.

(b) Capacity to Contract by Bill

The capacity to incur liability upon a bill is co-extensive with the capacity to contract (s. 22 (1)) (see Chap. I, § 7). But the incapacity of one party in no way diminishes the liability of other parties.

An infant incurs no liability by drawing, indorsing or accepting a bill (Infants Relief Act, 1874), even though it is given for necessaries (*Re Soltykoff* [1891] 1 Q.B. 413). But the holder may enforce it against any other party (s. 22 (2)). It seems, however, that an infant, who after attaining his majority accepts a bill for debts contracted while an infant, may be liable on such a bill to a holder in due course (*Belfast Banking Co.* v. *Doherty* (1879) 4 Ir. L.R. Q.B.D. 124). This decision cannot be said to command universal acceptance, but has been supported on the ground that a fresh promise is implicit in the acceptance. But where a bill is accepted after attaining majority for a *loan* obtained during infancy, the bill is void as against all parties whomsoever (Betting and Loans (Infants) Act, 1892, s. 5).

(c) Consideration

(1) *What Constitutes Value*

Valuable consideration for a bill may be constituted by (i) any consideration sufficient to support a simple contract, or (ii) *an antecedent debt or liability* (s. 27 (1)).

It is not essential that the nature of the consideration should appear on the face of the bill. As the bill may be negotiated, it may not be desirable to communicate this information to third parties. As an indication that consideration has been given, the words 'for value received' are generally included, but the absence of these words has no effect upon the validity of the bill (s. 3 (4) (*b*)). It is always *presumed* that a bill has been made for consideration (s. 30 (1)), but this may be rebutted by evidence that no value has at any time been given.

The antecedent consideration must move from a party to the bill; an antecedent consideration moving from a person who is not a party to the bill will not be sufficient to support it.

In *Oliver* v. *Davis and Woodcock* [1949] 2 K.B. 727, D engaged himself to marry W's sister, 'a thing which he should not have done seeing that he was already married to a wife in Gloucester.' He signed a contract to buy a house as the matrimonial home, and borrowed money from O. He then approached W and told her that unless he could pay O the money he owed, the house would be taken away from him. W thereupon wrote a cheque for £400 in favour of O, which was left at O's house. Shortly afterwards W discovered D's character to be unsatisfactory and stopped payment of her cheque. O sued her on the cheque, contending that his loan to D was an antecedent debt or liability sufficient to support the cheque. It was held, in the circumstances, that W was not liable on the cheque, as the antecedent debt or liability was not due from her, and, therefore, there was no consideration to support the cheque.

(2) *Accommodation Bill or Party*

A person signing a bill whether as drawer, acceptor, or indorser, without receiving value therefor, and for the purpose of lending his name to some other person, is an *accommodation party* (s. 28 (1)). He is in substance merely a surety for the person accommodated, and is entitled to be indemnified by him for any liability incurred on the bill. He is liable to a holder for value, and it is immaterial whether the holder, when he took the bill, knew him to be an accommodation party or not (s. 28 (2)). An *accommodation bill* (which must be distinguished from a bill with an accommodation party) is a bill the *acceptor* of which is an accommodation party.

(3) *Holder in Due Course*

A *holder in due course* is a holder who has taken a bill:

(i) complete and regular on the face of it,

(ii) before it was overdue,

(iii) without notice that it had been previously dishonoured, if such was the fact,

(iv) in good faith and for value, and

(v) without notice of any defect in the title of the person who negotiated it (s. 29 (1)).

A bill is complete and regular although it has not been accepted, but not if the name of the payee or drawer is absent; and a cheque is regular although post-dated, but apparently an undated bill is not complete. If by reason of mutilation a bill may be taken to have been cancelled it cannot be regular; and a discrepancy between the name of the payee and that of the indorsement will render the bill irregular (*Arab Bank, Ltd.* v. *Ross* [1952] 2 Q.B. 216).

A bill which is overdue ceases to have the characteristics of negotiability and may be transferred only subject to defects affecting it at maturity.

What amounts to 'good faith' is a matter of fact and must be considered in relation to the circumstances of the case; a thing is deemed to be done in good faith where it is in fact done honestly, whether it is done negligently or not (s. 90). The value or consideration given need not be adequate although inadequacy may, in the circumstances, be evidence of bad faith. There must, of course, be no knowledge of a defect in the title of the person from whom the bill is taken, nor must the holder close his eyes to facts which, from their nature, call for inquiry. Mere negligence will not disentitle the holder to recover on the bill so long as his suspicions were not aroused. It is not so much a question as to whether he *ought* to have suspected that his transferor's title was defective but as to whether he *did* suspect and did not pursue his inquiries. In particular, the title of a person who negotiates a bill is defective when he obtained the bill, or the acceptance thereof, by fraud, duress, or force and fear, or other unlawful means, or for an illegal consideration, or when he negotiates it in breach of faith, or under such circumstances as amount to fraud (s. 29 (2)).

Every holder of a bill is *prima facie* deemed to be a holder in due course, but if it is shown that the bill is affected by fraud, illegality, etc., the burden shifts to the holder to prove that, subsequent to the fraud or illegality, value has been given in good faith for the bill (s. 30 (2)). The original payee of a bill cannot, as such, be a holder in due course (*R. E. Jones & Co., Ltd.* v. *Waring & Gillow, Ltd.* [1926] A.C. 670).

The position of a holder in due course is a strong one. He may sue on the bill in his own name and enforce payment against all parties liable on the bill, and he holds free from any defect of title of prior parties, as well as from mere personal defences available to prior parties among themselves (s. 38).

(4) *Holder for Value*

A holder who has taken a bill in circumstances which do not constitute him a holder in due course is deemed to be a *holder for value*. A holder for value need not himself have given value for the bill. If value has at any time been given, the holder is deemed to be a holder for value as regards the acceptor, and all parties to the bill who became parties prior to such time (s. 27 (2)). If the holder has a lien upon the bill, he is a holder for value to the extent of the sum for which he has a lien.

A holder for value may find himself confronted by defences of fraud, illegality, etc., by any persons who became parties to the bill at the time of or prior to the fraud or illegality. He may also find himself confronted by the defence that no consideration was given for the bill since the time when the person against whom he is claiming became a party to the bill. A holder who is not even a holder for value, by reason of no consideration having at any time been given on the bill, is unable to enforce it at all.

But a holder for value is by no means without any remedy on the bill. In the first place, if he derives his title through a holder in due course, and is not himself a party to any fraud or illegality affecting it, he has all the rights of that holder in due course as regards the acceptor and all parties to the bill prior to that holder (s. 29 (3)). For example, if a holder in due course were to make X a present of the bill, X would be able to sue all parties except the holder in due course who had transferred it to him. The prior parties would not be able to raise the defence that X had not given value, because that defence would not have been available against the holder in due course. If X himself were to negotiate the bill to a holder in due course, the latter would obtain rights superior to those of X, as he would be able to sue all parties, including the earlier holder in due course who had transferred the bill to X by way of gift (on the assumption that the earlier holder had become a party by indorsing the bill).

Moreover, the claim of a holder for value cannot be defeated on the grounds of defects of title, such as fraud or illegality, by those who became parties to the bill subsequently to the defect.

A party cannot defend himself against a claim under the bill by a holder for value (or, *a fortiori*, by a holder in due course) by showing that he himself received no consideration for a bill, if consideration has been given, even though not by the holder, at some time subsequent to the time when the person sued became a party to the bill. Thus, if A, the acceptor of an accommodation bill, is sued by B, who received the bill as a present from K, who had himself given value for it, B can recover from A the amount of the bill, for A is not entitled to raise any question whether or not B has given value, since consideration had been given on the bill after A became a party thereto.

(d) Obligations of the Parties

The acceptor of a bill is primarily liable on it; the drawer and indorsers are sureties for him. If the bill is dishonoured by the drawee or acceptor, the holder may have recourse to drawer or indorsers as he chooses. But as between the drawer and the indorsers themselves, the primary liability is upon the drawer, and that of the indorsers follows in the order in which they have become parties to the bill. The detailed rules as to the liability of the parties are as follows:

(1) *The Acceptor*

The *acceptor* of a bill, by accepting it, engages that he will pay it according to the tenor of his acceptance. He is precluded from denying to a holder in due course the existence and capacity of the drawer or payee and the genuineness of the signature of the drawer as such, but is not precluded from denying the genuineness of any indorsement (s. 54). This means that the acceptor could not refuse payment on the ground, for example, that the drawer's signature was forged, but he would be acting properly in refusing on the ground that indorsements were forged.

(2) *The Drawer*

The *drawer* of a bill by drawing it engages that it will, on due presentment, be accepted and paid according to its tenor, and that if it is dishonoured he will compensate the holder or any indorser who is compelled to pay it, if proper proceedings have been taken. He is precluded from denying to a holder in due course the existence and capacity of the payee (s. 55 (1)).

(3) *The Indorser*

The *indorser* of a bill by indorsing it engages that it will, on due presentment, be accepted and paid according to its tenor, and that if it is dishonoured he will compensate the holder or a subsequent indorser who is compelled to pay it, provided the proper proceedings have been taken. He is precluded from denying to a holder in due course the genuineness of the drawer's signature and all previous indorsements, and, to a subsequent indorsee, the validity of the bill or his own title thereto at the time of his indorsement (s. 55 (2)).

(4) *Indorsement of a Stranger*

A person who signs a bill otherwise than as drawer or acceptor thereby incurs the liabilities of an indorser to a holder in due course (s. 56). Strictly speaking, an indorser is a holder of a bill who receives value for indorsing it over to a new holder. This section extends the liability of an ordinary indorser to a person who 'backs' a bill by indorsing it without receiving value at the request of the drawer or payee, or of a party who is subsequently asked to take the instrument, in order to lend the strength of his credit to that person.

(5) *Transferor by Delivery*

A *transferor by delivery* is the holder of a bill payable to bearer who negotiates it without indorsement. A transferor by delivery is not liable on the instrument but, by negotiating the bill, he warrants to his immediate transferee, being a holder for value, that the bill is what it purports to be, that he has a right to transfer it, and that at the time of the transfer he is not aware of any fact which renders it valueless (s. 58). For a breach of these warranties he would be liable to refund to his transferee whatever the transferee paid to him for the bill.

(e) Signature of Parties

(1) *Signature Essential to Liability*

No person is liable as drawer, indorser, or acceptor of a bill who has not signed it as such. A person who signs a bill in a trade or assumed name is liable thereon as if he had signed it in his own name. The signature of the name of a firm is equivalent to the signature by the person so signing of the names of all persons liable as partners in that firm (s. 23).

(2) *Signature by Agent*

It is not necessary that a party to a bill should sign the bill himself; it is sufficient if the bill is signed by an agent duly authorised on his behalf (s. 91).

If an agent signs *by procuration* ('*per pro.*'), the signature operates as a notice that the agent has only a limited power to sign, and the principal is only bound if the agent in so signing was acting within the *actual* limits of his authority (s. 25). A person taking such a bill ought to exercise due caution, and it would be only reasonable to require the production of the authority.

In *Gompertz* v. *Cook* (1903) 20 T.L.R. 106, the manager of a business had authority to indorse cheques *per pro.*, for the purpose of paying them into the bank, but for no other purpose. He indorsed certain cheques *per pro.*, and obtained payment from the bank. It was held that the banker could not retain the money from the true owners; the mere fact that the indorsement was *per pro.* should have put him upon inquiry, when he would have ascertained that the agent was not acting within the scope of his authority.

A person who signs a bill as drawer, indorser or acceptor, and adds words to his signature, indicating that he signs for or on behalf of a principal, or in a representative character, is not personally liable thereon. But the mere addition to his signature of words describing him as an agent, or as filling a representative character, does not exempt him from personal liability (s. 26 (1)). Thus, for example, a bill signed by directors of a company must show clearly that it is signed for or on behalf of the company, and that the director or other person signing only intends to sign as agent of that company. The use of such words as 'director,' 'secretary,' etc., will not *in itself* enable the person signing the bill to avoid personal liability.

In *Chapman* v. *Smethurst* [1909] 1 K.B. 927, a note was signed: 'J. H. Smethurst's Laundry and Dye Works, Limited. J. H. Smethurst, Managing Director.' It was held that J. H. Smethurst was not personally liable, as the juxtaposition of his name and the name of the company made it reasonably clear that he had signed as agent only.

In *Landes* v. *Marcus and Davids* (1909) 25 T.L.R. 478, a cheque drawn in favour of the plaintiff was stamped near the top with the words 'B. Marcus & Co., Limited,' and was signed by the two defendants: 'B. Marcus, Director; S. H. Davids, Director.' The name of the company did not appear anywhere except at the top of the cheque. The defendants were held personally liable on the cheque.

Where there is an ambiguity as to whether a signature is that of the signatory personally or is that of the signatory for and on behalf of the principal, the construction most favourable to the validity of the instrument will be adopted (s. 26 (2)). Thus, if a bill is accepted by directors for and on behalf of the company, and the drawer, doubting the company's ability to meet its obligation, requests an indorsement by the directors as additional security, the latter must be regarded as having indorsed in their personal capacity and would be so liable (*Elliott* v. *Bax–Ironside* [1925] 2 K.B. 301).

(3) *Forged or Unauthorised Signature*

Where a signature on a bill is forged, or placed thereon without the authority of the person whose signature it purports to be, the forged or unauthorised signature is wholly inoperative; and no right to retain the bill, or to give a discharge therefor, or to enforce payment thereof against any party thereto, can be acquired through or under that signature, unless the party against whom it is sought to retain or enforce payment of the bill is precluded from setting up forgery or want of authority (s. 24).

As has been observed (see (d), *supra*), the acceptor and any indorsers are precluded from denying the genuineness of the signature of a *prior* party to the bill, but the section protects them against liability to a person relying on a *subsequent* signature which is not genuine. Thus, for example, a person who gives value for an indorsement in his favour which is not genuine cannot enforce the bill against a person who became a party prior to the forgery, but if he himself indorses the bill for value to a further holder, he becomes liable on the bill to that holder, and his only remedy is against the forger.

A forged indorsement on a bill payable to bearer does not affect the title of a subsequent holder, since the title to such a bill passes by mere delivery, and the holder's title is not dependent upon the genuineness of the indorsement.

The position where a person signs a bill without authority is very similar, except that such a signature may be ratified provided that it does not amount to a forgery. Since the signature is otherwise completely ineffective, the person signing it does not himself incur any liability on the bill, but he may be liable to the transferee for breach of warranty of authority. To sign the name of a person to a bill '*per pro.*' without authority and with intent to defraud is a forgery (Forgery Act, 1913, s. 1).

(4) *Fictitious Payee*

A payee is regarded as fictitious where the name inserted is that of a non-existent person or where the name of a real person has been inserted to whom there is no intention on the part of the drawer that payment should be made. Such a course may be resorted to for purposes of fraud or to hide the true identity of the person to whom the bill has been delivered. Where the payee is a fictitious or non-existent person, the bill may be treated as payable to bearer (s. 7 (3)).

A person to whom such a bill is subsequently negotiated may not be aware of the position, and would naturally require the bill to be indorsed. Such an indorsement could not be genuine, but, as the bill would be regarded as payable to bearer, this would not affect the holder's title.

In *Clutton & Co.* v. *Attenborough* [1897] A.C. 90, a clerk of the plaintiffs, fraudulently representing to them that work had been done on their account by B, induced them from time to time to draw cheques payable to the order of B in payment of the pretended work. There was, in fact, no such person as B. The clerk forged B's indorsement to the cheques, and negotiated them to the defendant, who gave value for them in good faith. The cheques were duly honoured by the plaintiffs' bankers.

Held: B was a fictitious or non-existent person within the meaning of s. 7 (3), though at the time of drawing the cheques the plaintiffs supposed him to be a real person; and consequently the defendant was entitled to treat the cheques as payable to bearer. The defendant did not, therefore, hold the cheques under or through the forged indorsements, as no indorsement was necessary to complete his title. Consequently s. 24 did not operate to prevent him having the ordinary rights of a holder in due course, and he was not liable to the plaintiffs for the amount of the cheques.

In *Bank of England* v. *Vagliano Bros.* [1891] A.C. 157, a bill purporting to be drawn by Vucina to the order of Petridi & Co., and to be indorsed by them, was accepted by Vagliano Bros., payable at their bankers. The bankers paid it at maturity. The names and signatures of the drawer and payee had, in fact, been forged by a clerk of the acceptors who obtained the money.

Held: Petridi & Co., though really existent, were fictitious for the purposes of the bill, because their name was inserted without any intention on the part of the persons who actually drew the bill that payment should be made to them, and the bill being therefore payable to bearer, the bank was allowed to debit the acceptors' account with the sum so paid.

But if the drawer intends that payment should be made to an existing person, the payee cannot be regarded as fictitious, even though nothing is due to him (*North and South Wales Bank* v. *Macbeth* [1908] A.C. 137).

In *Vinden* v. *Hughes* [1905] 1 K.B. 795, a clerk of the plaintiffs induced his employers to draw cheques in favour of persons to whom in fact nothing was due, and, having forged the payees' signatures, cashed the cheques with the defendant. It was held that as the drawer did intend that payment should be made to the payees named, and the payees were actually existing persons, the payees were not fictitious, so that no title could pass under the forged indorsement to the defendant.

The position is the same where the payee's name is subsequently altered.

In *Goldman* v. *Cox* (1924) 157 L.T. 531, A had been in the habit of drawing cheques in favour of A. Cohen. A's clerk obtained some of these cheques after A had signed them, altered the payee's name to A. S. Cohen, forged an indorsement and obtained cash from X. It was held that the payee was not a fictitious person and A was therefore able to recover the amount from X.

(f) Delivery

Delivery is defined by the Act as the 'transfer of possession, actual or constructive, from one person to another' (s. 2). No liability can be incurred by either drawer, acceptor or indorser, until delivery by him of the instrument he has signed. At any time before delivery he is free to revoke the contract. In the case of the acceptor, however, the acceptance becomes complete and irrevocable if, after signing, the acceptor gives notice to or according to the directions of the person entitled to the bill that he has accepted it (s. 21 (1)).

In *Bank of Van Diemen's Land* v. *Victoria Bank* (1871) L.R. 3 P.C. 526, a bill was left with the drawee for acceptance. The drawee, having written his acceptance upon it, kept it in his possession, and two days later, having in the meantime heard that the drawer had failed, cancelled the acceptance and returned the bill to the holder.

Held: The drawee was entitled to cancel his acceptance, and had incurred no liability upon the instrument.

As between immediate parties, and as regards a remote party other than a holder in due course, the delivery:

(i) in order to be effectual must be made either by or under the authority of the party drawing, accepting or indorsing, as the case may be;

(ii) may be shown to have been conditional or for a special purpose only, and not for the purpose of transferring the property in the bill.

But if the bill is in the hands of a holder in due course, a valid delivery of the bill by all parties prior to him so as to make them liable to him is *conclusively presumed* (s. 21 (2)).

(g) Acceptance

(1) *Meaning of Acceptance*

Acceptance is the signification by the drawee of his assent to the order of the drawer. It must be written on the bill and signed by the drawee or his agent. The signature alone is sufficient without any other words. It must not stipulate that payment is to be made in any form other than money (s. 17). The bill may be accepted while incomplete, or unsigned by the drawer, or even if it has been previously dishonoured or is overdue (s. 18). Delivery is necessary to complete the acceptance (s. 2).

It is customary, in the case of inland bills, for the drawer to forward the bill to the drawee for acceptance before negotiating it. The acceptance by the drawee enables the drawer to negotiate the bill with more freedom as there are then two parties, instead of one, liable upon it. There is, however, nothing in law to prevent the drawer from negotiating the bill before it has been accepted, so that the duty of presenting for acceptance then falls on a subsequent holder.

The drawee incurs no liability on the bill until he accepts it (s. 53 (1)). But if he refuses to accept it when it is presented for that purpose, he may be liable to the drawer for breach of contract, if he had for valuable consideration agreed with the drawer that he would accept.

(2) *Presentment for Acceptance*

As a general rule it is not *necessary* for a bill to have been accepted before it is presented to the drawee for payment. Presentment for acceptance is, however, necessary in the following three cases:

(i) where it is payable after sight;

(ii) where the bill expressly so stipulates; or

(iii) where it is drawn payable elsewhere than at the residence or place of business of the drawee (s. 39).

Where a bill is payable after sight, presentment for acceptance is necessary in order to fix the maturity of the bill. Where such a bill is negotiated, except in those cases where presentment for acceptance is excused (see *infra*), the holder must either present it for acceptance or negotiate it within a reasonable time, and if he does not do so the drawer and all prior indorsers are discharged. In determining what is a reasonable time, regard must be had to the nature of the bill, the usage of trade with respect to similar bills, and the facts of the particular case (s. 40).

Where the holder of a bill drawn payable elsewhere than at the place of business or residence of the drawee has not time, with the exercise of reasonable diligence, to present the bill for acceptance before presenting it for payment on the day that it falls due, the delay caused by presenting the bill for acceptance before presenting it for payment is excused, and does not discharge the drawer and indorsers (s. 39 (4)).

Although not required by the Act in other cases, a bill should nevertheless be presented for acceptance, except where it is payable on demand, on sight, or on presentation, since the drawee is under no liability until he does accept; and if the bill is not accepted on presentment, there is an *immediate* right of recourse against the drawer and prior indorsers, even though the bill has not matured or been presented for payment (s. 43 (2)).

A bill is duly presented for acceptance which is presented in accordance with the following rules (s. 41 (1)):

(i) The presentment must be made by or on behalf of the holder to the drawee, or to some person authorised to accept or refuse acceptance on his behalf, at a reasonable hour on a business day, and before the bill is overdue.

(ii) Where a bill is addressed to two or more drawees, who are not partners, presentment must be made to them all, unless one has authority to accept for all, then presentment may be made to him only.

(iii) Where the drawee is dead, presentment may be made to his personal representative.

(iv) Where the drawee is bankrupt, presentment may be made to him or to his trustee.

(v) Where authorised by agreement or usage, a presentment through the post office is sufficient.

Where a bill is required to be presented for acceptance, presentment is excused, *and the bill may be treated as dishonoured by non-acceptance* (s. 41 (2)):

(i) Where the drawee is dead or bankrupt, or is a fictitious person or a person not having capacity to contract by bill.

(ii) Where, after the exercise of reasonable diligence, such presentment cannot be effected.

(iii) Where, although the presentment has been irregular, acceptance has been refused on some other ground.

The fact that the holder has reason to believe that the bill will be dishonoured on presentment does not excuse presentment (s. 41 (3)).

The person presenting the bill to the drawee for acceptance must deliver it up to him if required to do so. The drawee may retain possession of it for the customary time of twenty-four hours, and must then return it accepted or non-accepted. If he does not do so, the holder must treat it as dishonoured by non-acceptance, otherwise he will lose his rights against the drawer and indorsers (s. 42).

(3) *Qualified Acceptance*

An acceptance is either general or qualified. A general acceptance assents without qualification to the order of the drawer. A qualified acceptance in express terms varies the effect of the bill as drawn (s. 19).

A *qualified acceptance* may be:

(i) *Conditional: i.e.*, accepted payable subject to the fulfilment of a condition stated therein; *e.g.*, payable on giving up bills of lading.

(ii) *Partial: i.e.*, accepted for part only of the sum specified.

(iii) *Local: i.e.*, payable only at a particular place; but an acceptance to pay at a particular place is a general acceptance, unless it expressly states that the bill is to be paid there *only* and not elsewhere.

(iv) *Qualified as to time: e.g.*, accepted payable in six months instead of three months.

(v) *Acceptance by some only of the drawees.*

A qualified acceptance only affects the rights of those who have rendered themselves liable on the bill prior thereto. As most inland bills are forwarded by the drawer for acceptance, whatever variation the drawee wishes to make affects the drawer only, who can agree or not at his discretion. But if the bill has previously been negotiated and a holder presents it for acceptance, he is entitled to assume that the acceptance will be in the exact terms in which the bill has been drawn. He is not bound to take a qualified acceptance, and if he does not obtain an unqualified acceptance, he may treat the bill as dishonoured (s. 44 (1)).

If the holder takes a qualified acceptance without the assent of the drawer and previous indorsers, he releases them from their liability (s. 44 (2)). This is in accordance with the ordinary rules of suretyship, the drawer and indorsers being sureties for the acceptor; a surety is always freed from liability by any change in the terms without his assent. Assent is assumed after the lapse of a reasonable time from notice being given, if the party concerned does not dissent (s. 44 (3)).

When a *partial* acceptance is offered, the holder may, as in the case of any other qualified acceptance, refuse to take it and treat the bill as dishonoured. But a partial acceptance differs in its effect from the other kinds of qualified acceptance in that, if the holder takes it, previous parties are not thereby discharged, if due notice thereof is given to them (s. 44 (2), proviso).

The bill is normally payable at the address of the drawee appearing thereon, but for the sake of convenience it is customary for the drawee, upon acceptance, to 'domicile' the bill at his bank, *i.e.*, he accepts the bill payable at a specified branch of his bank. By doing so, he does not restrict the rights of a holder, for the latter can if he wishes still present the bill at the drawee's address; in fact, this method of acceptance benefits the holder, as he can pay the bill in to his own bank for collection through the ordinary channels. If, however, the acceptor so qualifies his acceptance that the bill is payable *only* at a bank or some place other than his specified address, the position of the holder might be adversely affected. Such qualification, therefore, may be rejected by the holder.

(4) *Referee in Case of Need and Acceptance for Honour*

In order to avoid any damage to his credit by reason of dishonour by the drawee, the drawer may insert the name of some person to whom application may be made in case the bill is dishonoured by non-acceptance or non-payment, and the same may be done by any indorser. The person so indicated is known as the *referee in case of need* (s. 15). The holder is not obliged to refer the bill to the 'case of need,' and the latter is not obliged to accept it. If he does accept, he must do so '*supra* protest,' *i.e.*, after the bill has been protested for non-acceptance by the drawee (see (j) (3), *infra*).

Apart from the referee in case of need, any stranger to the bill may accept *for honour* with the consent of the holder after the bill has been protested for non-acceptance. The acceptor for honour usually states for whose honour he accepts, and if he does not do so, is deemed to accept for the honour of the drawer (s. 65).

By accepting the bill the acceptor for honour engages that he will, on due presentment, pay the bill according to the tenor of his acceptance, if it is not paid by the drawee, provided it has been duly presented for payment and protested for non-payment, and that he receives notice of these facts (ss. 66 (1), 67 (1)). Thus the acceptor for honour incurs no liability until the bill has been protested twice: first, on acceptance being refused, before it can be presented to him for acceptance, and, secondly, after it has been presented to the original drawee for payment on maturity and such payment has been refused. Once these conditions have been complied with, the acceptor for honour is liable to the holder and to all parties to the bill subsequent to the party for whose honour he has accepted (s. 66 (2)).

This is the only case in which protest is absolutely necessary in the case of an inland bill.

The above provisions relate to an *acceptance* for honour. Where a bill has been *protested for non-payment*, any person, whether a party to the bill or not, may intervene and pay it *supra* protest for the honour of any party liable thereon or for the person for whose account the bill is drawn (s. 68).

(h) Negotiation

(1) *Bearer and Order Bills*

A bill is *negotiated* when it is transferred from one person to another in such manner as to constitute the transferee the holder of the bill (s. 31 (1)). The method of negotiation depends upon whether the bill is payable to *bearer*, or to *order*.

A bill is payable to bearer when it is expressed to be so payable, or when the only or last indorsement is an indorsement in blank (s. 8 (3)). A bill payable to bearer is negotiated by delivery only (s. 31 (2)). A bill is payable to order when it is expressed to be so payable, or it is expressed to be payable to a particular person and there are no words prohibiting transfer or indicating an intention that it should not be transferable (s. 8 (4)). A bill payable to order is negotiated by indorsement and delivery (s. 31 (3)). If a bill is made payable, either originally or by indorsement, 'to the order of A,' A has the option either of claiming payment himself or of transferring the bill to another person (s. 5 (5)).

If a bill payable to order is transferred for value without indorsement, the transfer gives no better title to the transferee than the transferor had; but the transferee acquires the right to have the bill indorsed by the transferor (s. 31 (4)).

If a bill contains words prohibiting transfer, it is valid as between the parties thereto, but is not negotiable (s. 8 (1)).

(2) *Requisites of a Valid Indorsement*

An indorsement consists of two distinct contracts; it transfers the property in the bill, and it involves a contingent assumption of liability on the part of the indorser.

In order to operate as a negotiation, an indorsement must comply with the following conditions (s. 32):

(i) The indorsement must be written on the bill itself, signed by the indorser, or on an *allonge*.

An *allonge* is a slip of paper attached to the bill. The first indorsement on the allonge should begin on the bill and end on the allonge, in order to prevent an allonge being taken from one bill and attached to another.

(ii) The indorsement must be of the entire bill. A partial indorsement, *i.e.*, an indorsement for part only of the sum named, or to two or more indorsees severally, does not operate as a negotiation of the bill.

(iii) Where a bill is payable to the order of two or more payees or indorsees who are not partners, all must indorse, unless the one indorsing has authority to indorse for the others.

(iv) Where, in a bill payable to order, the payee or indorsee is wrongly designated, or his name is mis-spelt, he may indorse the bill as therein described, adding, if he thinks fit, his proper signature.

(v) Where there are two or more indorsements on a bill, each indorsement is deemed to have been made in the order in which it appears on the bill, until the contrary is proved.

The mere fact that an indorsement has been placed above, instead of below, a prior indorsement will not affect the liability of the parties, if their real intention can be shown by extraneous evidence (*Lombard Banking, Ltd.* v. *Central Garage and Engineering Co., Ltd.* [1963] 1 Q.B. 220).

(3) Types of Indorsement

An indorsement may be made in blank or special, and may also contain terms making it restrictive (s. 32 (6)).

(i) A bill which is indorsed *in blank*, that is, without specifying an indorsee, becomes payable to bearer (s. 34 (1)).

(ii) A *special* indorsement specifies the person to whom or to whose order, the bill is to be payable (s. 34 (2)). The bill is then payable to the specified indorsee or to his order, and can only be negotiated subject to his indorsement. If a bill has been indorsed in blank, the holder may convert the blank indorsement into a special indorsement by writing above the indorser's signature a direction to pay the bill to the order of himself or some other person (s. 34 (4)).

(iii) A *restrictive* indorsement, as 'Pay D only,' puts an end to the negotiability of the instrument. If the restrictive indorsement authorises further transfer, all subsequent transferees take the bill subject to equities, that is, to any defences which might have been set up against the transferor (s. 35).

(iv) An indorsement may negative or limit any liabilities on the part of the indorser (s. 16 (1)). For instance, an indorsement may be '*sans recours*,' which negatives liability, or '*sans frais*,' which exempts the indorser from liability for expenses. A transferee is not bound to take such an indorsement, since he is, if he has given value, entitled to the security of the transferor.

(v) A *facultative* indorsement waives some of the holder's duties towards the indorser (s. 16 (2)). It takes some such form as 'Notice of dishonour waived.' No subsequent party is obliged to give notice of dishonour to this indorser.

(vi) Where a bill is indorsed *conditionally*, as 'Pay to the order of A on his marriage with B,' the condition may be disregarded by the payer, and payment to the indorsee is valid, whether the condition has been fulfilled or not (s. 33). But the Act does not *compel* the payer to ignore the condition and he can therefore insist upon its fulfilment.

(4) *Overdue Bills*

An overdue bill can only be transferred subject to any defect of title affecting it at its maturity, and thenceforward no person who takes it can acquire or give a better title than that of the person from whom he took it (s. 36 (2)). In effect it ceases to be a negotiable instrument. A bill payable on demand is deemed to be overdue for this purpose if it appears on the face of it to have been in circulation for an unreasonable time. What is an unreasonable length of time is a question of fact (s. 36 (3)). A cheque negotiated eight days after date has been held not to be overdue (*London and County Bank* v. *Groome* (1881) 8 Q.B.D. 288).

Except where an indorsement bears a date after the maturity of the bill, every negotiation is *prima facie* deemed to have been effected before the bill was overdue (s. 36 (4)).

(5) *Circuity of Action*

Where a bill is negotiated back to the drawer, or to a prior indorser or to the acceptor, that party may, subject to the provisions of the Act, re-issue and further negotiate the bill, but he is not entitled to enforce payment of the bill against any intervening party to whom he was previously liable (s. 37).

Thus, A indorses a bill to B. It passes on through the hands of C and others, and again comes into the hands of A who re-issues it. A has no remedy against holders between his first and second indorsements; the two sets of rights cancel one another. The intermediate indorsers are, however, not released against a holder taking subsequent to A's second indorsement.

(i) Presentment for Payment

On maturity of the bill, the holder, or some person duly authorised on his behalf, must present it for payment. If, on presentation, payment is refused, the holder has an immediate right of recourse against other parties to the bill (s. 47 (2)), although the extent of this right depends on whether he is a holder in due course or a holder for value or otherwise (see (c), *supra*). It is imperative that the bill be presented for payment, the drawer and indorsers being otherwise freed from liability should the bill not be met. But if the bill has been accepted generally, presentment for payment is not necessary to render the *acceptor* liable; his liability is not discharged by failure to present for payment nor by failure to give notice of dishonour (s. 52). He is freed from liability only on expiry of the six-year time limit applying to contracts under the Limitation Act, 1939.

(1) *Rules as to Presentment for Payment*

Presentment for payment must be in conformity with the following rules (s. 45).

(i) Where the bill is not payable on demand, presentment must be made on the day it falls due.

(ii) Where the bill is payable on demand, then presentment must be made within a reasonable time after its issue in order to render the drawer liable, and within a reasonable time after its indorsement in order to render the indorser liable.

(iii) Presentment must be made by the holder or by some person authorised to receive payment on his behalf at a reasonable hour on a business day, at the proper place as hereinafter defined, either to the person designated by the bill as payer, or to some person authorised to pay or refuse payment on his behalf, if with the exercise of reasonable diligence such person can be found.

(iv) A bill is presented at the proper place:

(*a*) Where a place of payment is specified in the bill and the bill is there presented.

(*b*) Where no place of payment is specified. but the address of the drawee or acceptor is given on the bill, and the bill is presented there.

(*c*) Where no place of payment is specified and no address given, and the bill is presented at the drawee's or acceptor's place of business if known, and if not, at his ordinary residence if known.

(*d*) In any other case if presented to the drawee or acceptor wherever he can be found, or if presented at his last known place of business or residence.

(v) Where a bill is presented at the proper place, and after the exercise of reasonable diligence no person authorised to pay or refuse payment can be found there, no further presentment to the drawee or acceptor is required, and the bill can be treated as dishonoured.

(vi) Where a bill is drawn upon or accepted by two or more persons who are not partners, and no place of payment is specified, presentment must be made to them all.

(vii) Where the drawee or acceptor of a bill is dead, and no place of payment is specified, presentment must be made to a personal representative, if there is one, and with the exercise of reasonable diligence he can be be found.

(viii) Where authorised by agreement or usage a presentment through the post office is sufficient.

(2) *Excuses for Delay or Non-Presentment*

Delay is excused and presentment is dispensed with in the following circumstances (s. 46):

(i) *Delay* in making presentment for payment is excused when the delay is caused by circumstances beyond the control of the holder, and not imputable to his default, misconduct or negligence. When the cause of delay ceases to operate, presentment must be made with reasonable diligence.

(ii) Presentment for payment is *dispensed with:*

    (*a*) Where, after the exercise of reasonable diligence, presentment cannot be effected.

    The fact that the holder has reason to believe that the bill will, on presentment, be dishonoured does not dispense with the necessity for presentment.

    (*b*) Where the drawee is a fictitious person.

    (*c*) As regards the drawer, where the drawee or acceptor is not bound, as between himself and the drawer, to accept or pay the bill, and the drawer has no reason to believe that the bill would be paid if presented.

    (*d*) As regards an indorser, where the bill was accepted or made for the accommodation of that indorser, and he has no reason to expect that the bill would be paid if presented.

    (*e*) By waiver of presentment, express or implied.

The consequence of presentment being dispensed with is that the holder can treat the bill as dishonoured, and enforce his rights against other parties, notwithstanding that he has not presented the bill for payment.

(3) *Time for Payment*

Where a bill is not payable on demand or at sight, the day on which it falls due is determined as follows (s. 14) as amended:

(i) Days of grace on bills of exchange were abolished with effect from January 16th 1972 by the Banking and Financial Dealings Act 1971. A bill is now payable on the last day fixed by the bill or, if that is a non-business day (i.e. Saturdays, Sundays and Bank Holidays) on the succeeding business day.

(ii) Where a bill is payable at a fixed period after date, after sight, or after the happening of a specified event, the time of payment is determined by excluding the day from which the time is to begin to run and by including the day of payment, *e.g.*, a bill drawn on 1st January payable one month after date would fall due on 1st February, and not on 31st January.

(iii) If a bill is payable at a fixed period after sight, the time begins to run from the date of the acceptance if the bill is accepted, and from the date of noting or protest if the bill is noted or protested for non-acceptance or for non-delivery.

(j) Dishonour

A bill may be dishonoured either by (1) non-acceptance, where it has been duly presented for acceptance and is not unconditionally accepted within the customary time (usually twenty-four hours) (s. 42); or (2) non-payment, when it is duly presented for payment and payment is refused or cannot be obtained, or where presentment is excused and the bill is overdue and unpaid (s. 47). A bill can also be treated as dishonoured where a receiving order in bankruptcy is made against the acceptor prior to the due date of the bill.

(1) *Notice of Dishonour*

If a bill is dishonoured, notice must be given by or on behalf of the holder to all parties to the bill whom it is intended to charge (s. 48). It is not wise to be content with giving notice to the immediate indorser, since, if he in his turn fails to transmit the notice, the parties entitled to notice will be freed from liability.

Notice of dishonour must be given in accordance with the following rules (s. 49):

(i) The notice must be given by the holder of the bill, or an indorser liable on the bill, or the agent of either of them.

(ii) Notice given by the holder or any indorser enures for the benefit of any person who is entitled to enforce the bill against the party to whom notice is given.

(iii) No particular form of notice is necessary, although it is advisable that it should be in writing as evidence of the fact. The return of a dishonoured bill to the drawer or an indorser is, in point of form, deemed a sufficient notice of dishonour.

(iv) Notice must be given within a reasonable time, that is, either on the day after the dishonour, if the person giving and the person to receive notice reside in the same place; or, if they live in different places, it must be sent off by post either on the day after dishonour, or by the next post thereafter.

(v) Even though the drawer or indorser is dead or bankrupt, notice of dishonour must still be given; in the former case to the personal representative, and in the latter case to the party himself or his trustee.

(vi) If there are two or more drawers or indorsers who are not partners, notice should be given to all, unless one has authority to receive notice for the others.

(vii) If notice is sent by post, it is not necessary in order to fix a person with liability that notice should reach him. It is sufficient to prove that it was addressed and posted with reasonable diligence.

(2) *Excuses for Non-Notice or Delay*

Delay in giving notice is excused, and notice may be dispensed with, under the following circumstances (s. 50):

(i) Where the *delay* is caused by circumstances beyond the control of the party giving notice, and not imputable to his default, misconduct or negligence. When the cause of the delay ceases to operate, the notice must be given with reasonable diligence.

(ii) Notice of dishonour is *dispensed with*:
   (a) When, after the exercise of reasonable diligence, notice cannot be given to, or does not reach, the drawer or indorser sought to be charged.

(b) By waiver, express or implied. Notice of dishonour may be waived before the time of giving notice has arrived or after the omission to give due notice.

(c) As regards the *drawer*, in the following cases:
   (1) where drawer and drawee are the same person;
   (2) where the drawee is a fictitious person, or a person not having capacity to contract;
   (3) where the drawer is the person to whom the bill is presented for payment;
   (4) where the drawee or acceptor is as between himself and the drawer under no obligation to accept or pay the bill;
   (5) where the drawer has countermanded payment.

(d) As regards the *indorser*, in the following cases:
   (1) where the drawee is a fictitious person, or a person not having capacity to contract, and the indorser was aware of the fact at the time he indorsed the bill;
   (2) where the indorser is the person to whom the bill is presented for payment;
   (3) where the bill was accepted or made for his accommodation.

(3) *Noting and Protest*

Where a bill is required to be noted or protested, it is handed to a notary public* who, either by his clerk or personally, re-presents it on the day of dishonour or on the next succeeding business day (s. 51 (4), as amended by the Bills of Exchange (Time of Noting) Act, 1917), enters all the facts in his register, and 'notes' on the bill, or on a slip attached thereto, the date, his noting charges, a folio or similar reference to the entry in the register, and appends his initials. He should also indicate the reason given for the dishonour.

This process is known as 'noting' the bill and is a preliminary to the more formal 'protest,' which is a document signed by the notary containing an exact copy of the bill and specifying:

(i) the person at whose request the bill is protested, and

(ii) the place and date of protest, the cause or reason for protesting the bill, the demand made, and the answer given, if any, or a statement that the drawee or acceptor could not be found (s. 51 (7)).

If the services of a notary public cannot be obtained at the place where the bill is dishonoured, protest may be made by any householder or substantial resident in the presence of two witnesses (s. 94).

When protest is necessary, it must be made at the place where the bill was dishonoured, provided that (s. 51 (6)):

---

* A notary public is a person, usually a solicitor, specially appointed for dealing with such matters as presenting bills of exchange, attesting deeds, etc., so as to provide evidence in a foreign court.

(i) when presentment has been made by post, and the bill has been returned by post dishonoured, it may be protested at the place to which it has been returned and on the day of its return if received during business hours, or otherwise on the next business day;

(ii) when a bill drawn payable at the place of business or residence of some person other than the drawee has been dishonoured by non-acceptance, it must be protested for non-payment at the place where it is expressed to be payable, and no further presentment for payment to, or demand on, the drawee is necessary.

Protest is required when a *foreign* bill has been dishonoured by non-acceptance or non-payment (s. 51 (2)), and where such a bill has been accepted as to part only (s. 44 (2)). Protest is not required in the case of an inland bill, except as a preliminary to acceptance or payment *for honour*, and, even so, 'noting' alone would be sufficient, the formal protest being subsequently extended (s. 93).

Except in the above cases 'noting' is not a condition precedent to the right of enforcement of the bill (s. 51 (1)). Noting may be of advantage, however, where legal action on the bill is contemplated, since it affords satisfactory evidence that the statutory provisions with regard to presentment have been complied with.

(4) *Measure of Damages*

The measure of damages recoverable if the bill is dishonoured is: (i) the amount of the bill; (ii) interest at 5 per cent. per annum (the rate allowed by the courts) from the date of maturity, or where the bill is payable on demand from the date of presentment; (iii) the expenses of noting, and of protest when protest is necessary and has been extended (s. 57 (1)).

In the case of a bill which has been dishonoured abroad, a party entitled may recover from any party liable to him, in lieu of the above damages, the amount of the *re-exchange* with interest until the time of payment (s. 57 (2)). *Re-exchange* represents the sum for which a sight bill could be drawn at the time and place of dishonour at the rate of exchange of the day so as to produce the amount of the dishonoured bill and any expenses incurred upon dishonour.

(k) Discharge of Bill

(1) *Payment in Due Course*

The bill may be discharged by payment in due course by or on behalf of the drawee or acceptor. Payment in due course means payment made at or after the maturity of the bill to the holder thereof in good faith and without notice that his title to the bill is defective (s. 59 (1)).

When a bill is paid by the drawer or an indorser, it is not discharged (s. 59 (2)). The drawer will be able to claim on the bill against the acceptor, and the indorsers will be able to claim against the acceptor, the drawer and prior indorsers.

If the drawer or indorser of a bill pays it, he is entitled to the benefit of any securities which may have been deposited by the acceptor with the holder, and retained by the holder at the time of dishonour of the bill (*Duncan, Fox & Co.* v. *North and South Wales Bank* (1880) 6 App. Cas. 1). When a bill is paid, the holder must deliver it to the party paying it (s. 52 (4)).

Where the drawer has paid a bill which was payable to or to the order of a third party, he may not re-issue it (s. 59 (2) (*a*)). But where the drawer pays a bill payable to his own order, or where an indorser pays the bill, the party paying may strike out his own and subsequent indorsements and again negotiate the bill (s. 59 (2) (*b*)). In this way a drawer or indorser who has paid the bill may reimburse himself by subsequent negotiation (though it may, of course, not be easy to find persons who will give value for such a bill), and leave it to subsequent holders to enforce the bill against the parties who have defaulted.

Where an accommodation bill is paid in due course by the party accommodated, the bill is discharged (s. 59 (3)). Thus, if a bill is accepted for the accommodation of the drawer, and the drawer, after negotiating the bill, takes it up at maturity, the bill is discharged. If the drawer subsequently re-issues it, the holder cannot sue the acceptor (*Cook* v. *Lister* (1863) 32 L.J. C.P. 127).

(2) *Negotiation to Acceptor*

A bill is discharged if the acceptor becomes the holder of it in his own right at or after maturity (s. 61).

(3) *Waiver*

A bill may also be discharged by express waiver or renunciation on the part of the holder. The renunciation must be in writing, unless the bill is delivered up to the acceptor. If the holder releases in writing one of the parties to a bill, he also releases all those who would have had recourse to the party released, so far as the person giving the release is concerned; but this does not affect the rights of any subsequent holder in due course, who had no notice of the renunciation (s. 62).

(4) *Cancellation*

Where a bill is intentionally cancelled by the holder or his agent, and the cancellation is apparent, the bill is discharged (s. 63 (1)); and if the signature of any party liable is similarly cancelled, that party, and any party having a right of recourse against him, is also discharged (s. 63 (2)). If the cancellation was unintentional, or made without the consent of the holder, or by mistake, it is inoperative, but the burden of proof is on the party alleging this (s. 63 (3)).

(5) *Discharge of Surety*

If between the parties to a bill there exists the relationship of principal and surety, and if the holder of the bill, knowing this, makes a binding agreement, founded on consideration, to give the principal time, or if he discharges him, the surety is discharged unless the holder expressly reserves his rights against the surety. As renewing a bill or note is the granting of an extended time for payment, the assent of all parties liable on the bill as sureties must be obtained to any renewal, or they will be discharged (*Tindal* v. *Brown* (1786) 1 T.R. 167).

(6) *Alteration of Bill*

Where a bill or acceptance is materially altered without the assent of all parties liable on the bill, the bill is avoided except as against a party who has himself made, authorised or assented to the alteration, and subsequent indorsers (s. 64 (1)). But where the bill is in the hands of a holder in due course, and the alteration is not apparent, he may enforce payment of the bill according to its original tenor as if it had not been altered (s. 64 (1), proviso).

In particular the following alterations are material: date, sum payable, time of payment, place of payment, and, in the case of a general acceptance, the addition of a place of payment without the acceptor's assent (s. 64 (2)).

The fact that a bill is carelessly drawn so as to facilitate alteration does not render the acceptor liable to a holder in due course for a greater sum than the amount of the bill as originally accepted.

In *Scholfield* v. *Earl of Londesborough* [1896] A.C. 514, the drawer of a bill for £500 left room for insertions in front of the amounts written in words and figures. The defendant accepted the bill for £500 and returned it to the drawer, who fraudulently wrote in words and figures increasing the amount to £3,500. The drawer then negotiated the bill for value to a holder in due course, the alteration not being apparent. The holder sued the defendant for the sum of £3,500, alleging that he was negligent in accepting a bill in a form facilitating alteration, and so was liable to the holder for the full amount. It was held that the defendant's liability was limited to £500, as he owed no duty to be careful towards the plaintiff.

The rule that carelessness in drawing or accepting a bill involves no liability does not apply in the case of cheques, owing to the special duties attaching to the relationship of banker and customer (see *post*, § 3 (d)).

(l) **Lost Bill**

When the holder of a bill loses it before it is overdue, he may require the drawer to give him another bill of the same tenor; but if required he must give security to indemnify the drawer, in case the lost instrument should be found again (s. 69). There is no power to obtain a new acceptance or indorsement.

§ 3. *Cheques*

(a) Definition and Form of Cheque

A cheque is a bill of exchange drawn on a banker payable on demand (s. 73).

It is consequently subject to the same rules applicable to bills of exchange generally which are payable on demand. Acceptance is not necessary, and the cheque must be presented within a reasonable time.

The following is a form of cheque commonly in use:

No................   1st Feb., 19......

MIDLAND BANK
Lower Street, Whitemoor

Pay John Jones .... or Order

One hundred and five pounds. | £105·00p |

W. REDMOND

(b) Presentment for Payment

Cheques may be presented for payment either at the counter of the branch of the bank on which they are drawn, or, where they have been crossed, by a collecting banker through the medium of the Bankers' Clearing House, or by direct application, according to circumstances.

If the holder of a cheque neglects to present it for payment within a reasonable time of its issue, and the drawer had a credit balance sufficient to meet the cheque when drawn, and suffers actual damage from the delay, he is discharged, as against the holder, to the extent of such damage (s. 74 (1)). In other words, if the customer has available funds at the time when the cheque should have been presented, but the banker has failed before the presentment was actually made, the drawer is discharged from liability. In such a case the holder becomes a creditor of the bank, in place of the drawer, to the extent of such discharge (s. 74 (3)).

If the bank is continuing business (and failures are now happily only of historical interest), the cheque would be met if the customer's account was sufficiently in credit, but if the cheque had been in circulation for a considerable time, the banker would regard it as 'stale' and would generally require confirmation of the order to pay before he honoured it. If, however, he refused to honour the cheque, he should take care so to mark it that the customer's credit is not injured thereby.

The usual practice of a banker is to pay a cheque that is presented at any time within six months of its date. A transferee of an overdue cheque may fail to obtain a good title, but it does not follow that the bank will refuse payment if it is presented within the customary six months.

(c) Crossings

A cheque may be 'crossed' in one or more of four ways:

(1) *General Crossing*

A *general crossing* consists of two parallel transverse lines drawn across the face of the cheque with or without the addition of the words '& Co.' (which addition has now no legal significance), and with or without the words 'not negotiable' (s. 76(1)). A general crossing has the effect of precluding payment over the counter, presentment by a collecting banker being essential.

(2) *Special Crossing*

If the name of a banker is inserted between the transverse lines or written across the face of the cheque without the lines, this constitutes a *special crossing* (s. 76 (2)), and its effect is to make the cheque payable only to the banker specified in the crossing.

(3) *'Not Negotiable'*

Where a person takes a crossed cheque which bears on it the words *'not negotiable'* he shall not have and shall not be capable of giving a better title to the cheque than that which the person from whom he took it had (s. 81). In other words, the negotiable character of the instrument ceases to exist.

The words do not restrict the *transferability* of the instrument, nor do they prevent the transferor from giving a good title if he has one. But, if a cheque so marked is stolen, a person taking it is unable to retain it against the true owner even though he has no notice of the defect in title of his transferor; for the cheque being marked 'not negotiable,' the transferor is unable to give a better title than he himself possessed, *i.e.*, he can give no title at all.

A cheque is the only form of bill of exchange which can be crossed 'not negotiable.' In the case of a bill other than a cheque, if it is desired to make it non-negotiable this must appear in the body of the instrument; where a bill is negotiable in its origin, it continues to be negotiable until it has been restrictively indorsed, or discharged by payment or otherwise (s. 36 (1)).

(4) *'Account Payee'*

The words 'a/c payee' or 'a/c payee only' are sometimes placed in the crossing, and operate as notice to the collecting bank that only the account of the payee is to be credited. This is not a statutory provision, and does not affect the negotiability of the cheque (*National Bank* v. *Silke* [1891] 1 Q.B. 435). It is, however, the custom of bankers to give effect to this crossing, and the collecting banker may be liable for negligence if he fails to do so (*House Property Co.* v. *London County and Westminster Bank* (1915) 31 T.L.R. 479). The position of the paying banker is, however, not affected, as he would not know to which account the proceeds of the cheque were to be credited, and, moreover, he is only bound to obey the mandate of his customer, the drawer of the cheque, and the words may not have been inserted by him.

Crossings may take one of the following forms:

GENERAL CROSSINGS

SPECIAL CROSSINGS

The crossing is a material part of the cheque, and it is not lawful for any person to obliterate, add to, or alter the crossing, except as provided by the Act, *i.e.*:

  (i) The holder may cross an uncrossed cheque;

  (ii) He may turn a general crossing into a special crossing;

  (iii) He may add the words 'not negotiable';

  (iv) A banker may cross an uncrossed cheque, or a cheque crossed generally, specially to himself; or, if crossed specially to himself, he may again cross it specially to another banker for collection (ss. 77, 78).

If the paying banker pays the crossed cheque over the counter or, in the case of a special crossing, pays the cheque otherwise than to the banker named, he is liable to the true owner of the cheque for any loss he may thereby sustain, unless the cheque does not appear to be crossed, or to have had a crossing which has been obliterated, or to have been added to or altered otherwise than as authorised by the Act, and the banker has paid the cheque in good faith and without negligence (s. 79).

(d) Relationship of Banker and Customer

The relationship existing between a banker and his customer is normally that of debtor and creditor, the latter depositing with the former funds from time to time out of which demands for payment in the form of cheques can be met. Where the customer has made arrangements for an overdraft, the banker becomes the creditor, but he cannot refuse to honour cheques properly drawn, so long as the limit of the overdraft has not been reached.

A banker may not close his customer's account which is in credit without giving reasonable notice (*Prosperity, Ltd.* v. *Lloyds Bank, Ltd.* (1923) 39 T.L.R. 372); and if the banker dishonours a cheque regularly drawn, where the funds to the credit of the customer's account are sufficient, the customer can recover damages for injury to his credit. In the case of a business customer the effect of such dishonour is regarded so seriously that it is not necessary for the customer to prove the extent of the damage that he has suffered by the banker's action; and as a general rule the smaller the amount of the cheque, the greater the damage to credit sustained. But a private customer can only recover nominal damages.

The banker is not bound to honour an undated cheque, and the authority of the holder (under s. 20) to fill in the date must be exercised within a reasonable time to render the banker liable. A year's delay has been held to be unreasonable (*Griffiths* v. *Dalton* [1940] 2 K.B. 264).

If the words and figures on the cheque disagree, the banker should return the cheque unpaid, although, since the words form the essential part of the instrument, the figures being merely supplementary, he would be entitled to honour the cheque on the basis of the words. He does not usually adopt this course, however, although he would not incur risk if the amount expressed to be payable by the words was less than that indicated by the figures.

If there are alterations on the cheque, they must be authenticated by the initials of the customer. Where a crossed cheque has been 'opened,' the full signature of the drawer must be appended to the 'opening,' but even so, bankers will refuse payment over the counter unless the cheque is presented by the drawer or by his known agent.

The banker should assure himself that the customer's signature as drawer is genuine, for in the event of forgery, he will be liable to the customer for the amount paid (*Orr* v. *Union Bank* (1854) 1 Macq. H.L. 513). The customer is, however, under an obligation to inform the banker immediately he becomes aware of the irregularity, so as to enable the banker to be in a position to enforce his rights against the delinquent party. Neglect on the part of the customer would relieve the banker of his liability (*Greenwood* v. *Martins Bank, Ltd.* [1933] A.C.1).

The banker is entitled to rely upon the exercise of due care by his customer in drawing cheques, and if the customer has been negligent in signing a cheque, so as to enable a dishonest holder to alter the amount and obtain a greater sum from the bank, without the alteration being apparent, the banker is not obliged to refund to the customer the difference so paid (*London Joint Stock Bank* v. *Macmillan* [1918] A.C. 777). For the banker to be protected the forgery or alteration must be a natural and direct result of the negligence of the customer in drawing the cheque. But where the alteration of a cheque is effected by an addition to the name of the payee, liability will attach to the banker if he pays it without inquiry.

In *Slingsby* v. *District Bank, Ltd.* [1932] 1 K.B. 544, A drew a cheque payable to B or order and handed it to C at whose request the cheque was drawn. C inserted after B's name 'per C' and indorsed the cheque merely as C, paying it into his bank for collection. The cheque was duly paid by A's bank. It was held that there was no negligence on the part of A in not drawing a line after the name of the payee so as to preclude any subsequent insertion, as a drawer does not contemplate an alteration in this direction in the same way as in the words or figures. The bank could not, therefore, debit A's account with the amount of the cheque.

It is an implied term of the contract between a banker and his customer that the banker will not without consent divulge to third persons information concerning the customer's account, unless he is compelled to do so by order of a court, or a public duty of disclosure arises, or the protection of the banker's own interests requires it, or the customer has authorised disclosure, expressly or by implication, as regards the customer's general financial position and character, *e.g.*, by giving the bank as a reference. As to the liability of a banker for giving an inaccurate reference, and for giving negligent advice to a customer on, *e.g.*, financial matters, see Chap. I, § 8 (b) (3).

A banker's authority to pay a cheque drawn on him is revoked by:
(1) Countermand of payment by the customer (s. 75 (1)). It is not, however, necessarily revoked by an unauthenticated telegram (*Curtice* v. *London City and Midland Bank* [1908] 1 K.B. 293).

(2) Notice of the customer's death (s. 75 (2)).

(3) Notice of the presentation of a bankruptcy petition against the customer or the making of a receiving order against him, or notice of the winding up of a corporate customer.

(4) Notice that the customer is drawing cheques for an unlawful purpose, or, if a trustee, in breach of trust.

(5) Notice of the customer's insanity.

(6) Service of a garnishee order on the banker attaching the customer's balance.

(7) Notice that the customer is an undischarged bankrupt.

(8) Injunction or order of the court restraining the banker from making payments.

(e) Cheques Act, 1957

(1) *Purpose of the Act*

The main purpose of the Cheques Act, 1957, was to abolish the former requirement that cheques should be indorsed by the payee on delivery to a banker for collection. At the same time the Act extended the protection given by the Bills of Exchange Act, 1882, to the paying and collecting bankers.

Section 3 of the Act provides that an unindorsed cheque which appears to have been paid by the banker on whom it is drawn is evidence of the receipt by the payee of the sum payable by the cheque. This section is commonly thought to have dispensed with the need to give a receipt when required. In fact, a paid indorsed cheque has always been *evidence* of receipt by the payee of the sum payable; and the section merely puts an unindorsed cheque in the same position. The drawer is still entitled to a receipt on request.

(2) *Protection of Paying Banker*

While a banker is expected to know the signatures of his customers, and will therefore incur liability if he pays a cheque drawn on himself on which the drawer's signature is forged, he cannot ordinarily be acquainted with the signatures of other persons. He is protected in this respect by s. 60 of the 1882 Act, which provides that if a banker pays a cheque drawn on himself in good faith and in the ordinary course of business, he is deemed to have paid the bill in due course, although the indorsement has been forged or made without authority. This is an important exception in favour of the banker to the rule that a forged indorsement on a bill is wholly inoperative.

The practical importance of s. 60 has been reduced by s. 1 of the

Cheques Act, 1957, which provides that a banker who in good faith and in the ordinary course of business pays a cheque drawn on him which is not indorsed or is irregularly indorsed does not by so doing incur any liability *by reason only* of the absence of, or irregularity in, indorsement and he is deemed to have paid it in due course. This protection is extended to the payment by him of any document issued by a customer which, though not a bill of exchange, is intended to enable a person to obtain payment of the sum mentioned in the document, and of a banker's draft.

A payment which is made within a reasonable margin after the bank's advertised time of closing is regarded as being made in the ordinary course of business (*Baines* v. *National Provincial Bank* (1927) 96 L.J. K.B. 801). Payment contrary to the crossing of a cheque would not be in the ordinary course of business (*Smith* v. *Union Bank of London* (1875) 1 Q.B.D. 31), as, for example, if a bank were to pay a crossed cheque in cash across the counter.

Apart from the particular protection afforded to bankers under s. 60 of the 1882 Act, they are protected generally by virtue of s. 80 which, subject to the extended protection now given by s. 1 of the 1957 Act, provides that where the banker, on whom a crossed cheque is drawn, pays it in good faith and without negligence, if crossed generally, to a banker, and if crossed specially, to the banker to whom it is crossed, or his agent for collection being a banker, the banker paying the cheque, and, if the cheque has come into the hands of the payee, the drawer shall respectively be entitled to the same right, and be placed in the same position, as if payment of the cheque had been made to the true owner thereof. Although limited to *crossed* cheques, this section is in general wider in its application than is s. 60, which confers protection in respect of forged indorsements only. But in one respect s. 80 is narrower: to obtain the protection of the section absence of negligence must be shown; whereas under s. 60 a banker who pays a cheque bearing a forged indorsement is protected even if he is negligent, provided that he acts in the ordinary course of business.

What constitutes negligence for this purpose is a question of fact. A banker has been held to be negligent where he paid a cheque bearing an irregular indorsement (*Slingsby* v. *District Bank, Ltd.*, *ante*, p. 194), but s. 1 of the Cheques Act now precludes liability in such a case, except, perhaps, where the irregularity is obvious.

(3) *Protection of Collecting Banker*

Section 82 of the Bills of Exchange Act, 1882, was repealed by the Cheques Act, 1957, and its provisions reproduced in wider form in s. 4 (1) of that Act, which provides:

Where a banker, in good faith and without negligence:

(*a*) receives payment for a customer of an instrument to which this section applies; or

(*b*) having credited a customer's account with the amount of such an instrument, receives payment thereof for himself;

and the customer has no title, or a defective title, to the instrument, the banker does not incur any liability to the true owner of the instrument *by reason only* of having received payment thereof.

This protection given to a banker against the claims of the true owner for conversion of the amount of the instrument was previously confined to a cheque crossed generally or specially to the banker concerned, but is now extended to all documents specified in s. 4 (2) of the 1957 Act, *viz.*:

(i) all cheques;

(ii) any document issued by a customer of a banker which, though not a bill of exchange, is intended to enable a person to obtain payment from that banker of the sum mentioned in the document;

(iii) any document issued by a public officer which is intended to enable a person to obtain payment from the Paymaster General or the Queen's and Lord Treasurer's Remembrancer of the sum mentioned in the document but is not a bill of exchange;

(iv) any draft payable on demand drawn by a banker upon himself, whether payable at the head office or some other office of his bank.

Thus, a banker who collects payment of a document containing a direction to 'pay cash or order' is entitled to the protection of the section (*Orbit Mining & Trading Co., Ltd.* v. *Westminster Bank, Ltd., ante*, p. 164).

If the banker is to succeed in his defence there must be (i) good faith, (ii) absence of negligence on the part of the banker, and (iii) a transaction for a 'customer.'

(i) A thing is done in good faith where it is in fact done honestly, whether it is done negligently or not (Bills of Exchange Act, 1882, s. 90).

(ii) The courts have on numerous occasions been called upon to decide whether, in collecting cheques for a customer, the banker concerned had acted without negligence under the earlier Act; and similar principles would apply to cases subject to the 1957 Act.

In *Midland Bank, Ltd*, v. *Reckitt* [1933] A.C. 1, a client had given a solicitor a power of attorney entitling him to draw cheques on the former's banking account and apply the moneys for the purposes of the client. The solicitor fraudulently drew fifteen cheques, signing as attorney of the client, and paid them into his own account with the Midland Bank with whom he had an overdraft. It was held that the bank was negligent in not making inquiry, having regard to the method of signature and the destination of the proceeds, as to the solicitor's authority to pay these cheques into his own account.

In *Marquess of Bute* v. *Barclays Bank, Ltd.* [1955] 1 Q.B. 202, a farm manager who had applied on his employer's behalf for certain subsidies received warrants for the amounts payable to him 'for' the plaintiff employer after he had left the latter's service. He opened an account with the defendant bank and paid in the warrants, which the bank collected.

Held: The warrants were meant to be the property of the plaintiff, and the defendants had been negligent in crediting the proceeds to the manager's personal account.

Since a limited company possesses an entity apart from that of its constituent members, cheques drawn in favour of the company should not be collected on account of the managing director or other officer of the company personally, even though the company is virtually a 'one-man' company (*Underwood, Ltd.* v. *Bank of Liverpool and Martins, Ltd.* [1924] 1 K.B. 775).

It is now provided by s. 4 (3) of the 1957 Act that a banker who collects payment of an instrument is not to be treated as having been negligent *by reason only* of his failure to concern himself with the absence of, or irregularity in, the indorsement of the instrument. It follows that the payee of a cheque need not indorse it on paying it into his bank, and a person who pays a cheque into his bank for another person need not himself indorse it, although in that case the indorsement to him is still necessary.

(iii) To become a customer, a person need not have habitual dealings with a banker. Having a current account, for however short a time, constitutes a person a customer (*Lacave & Co.* v. *Crédit Lyonnais* [1897] 1 Q.B. 148). But although a bank may show that a person for whom it collected cheques was a customer, yet it may have been negligent in opening an account for that customer without obtaining references or making inquiries as to his standing, including inquiries as to who are his employers (*Lloyds Bank, Ltd.* v. *Savory* [1933] A.C. 201; *Baker* v. *Barclays Bank, Ltd.* [1955] 2 All E.R. 571).

By s. 2 of the Cheques Act, a banker who gives value for, or has a lien on, a cheque payable to order which the holder delivers to him for collection, without indorsing it, has such (if any) rights as he would have had if, upon delivery, the holder had indorsed it in blank. This enables a collecting banker to plead that he is a holder for value of an unindorsed cheque (but not of an irregularly indorsed one).

In *Midland Bank, Ltd.* v. *R. V. Harris, Ltd.* [1963] 2 All E.R. 685, the plaintiff bank permitted a customer to draw on his current account against uncleared cheques that had been credited to his account. Two of these cheques were dishonoured and the bank sued the drawers, who contended that the bank was not a 'holder' of the cheques as they were not indorsed and that s. 2 of the Cheques Act did not confer on the bank the status of holder.

Held: The bank was holder in due course of the cheques because (i) the description 'indorsee' in the definition of 'holder' in s. 2 of the Bills of Exchange Act, 1882, included the plaintiff bank, as the 1957 Act had conferred upon it the rights it would have had if the customer had indorsed the cheques in blank on delivery to the bank; or (ii) the two cheques were, by virtue of s. 2 of the 1957 Act, payable to bearer in the hands of the bank, and thus the bank was a 'holder' of them within s. 2 of the 1882 Act.

In *Westminster Bank, Ltd.* v. *Zang* [1965] 1 All E.R. 1023, T, the managing director and controlling shareholder of a 'one-man' company lent the defendant £1,000 of the company's money, in return for a cheque for the same sum drawn in favour of T personally. T handed the cheque to the plaintiff bank without indorsing it, together with several other cheques drawn in favour of the company, to be credited to the company's account, and for this purpose filled in a paying-in slip at the foot of which was a note stating that the bank reserved the right to postpone payment of cheques drawn against uncleared effects. The bank credited the cheque to the company's account which was heavily overdrawn. The cheque was twice dishonoured on presentation. The bank subsequently returned the cheque to T at his request in order to enable him to commence proceedings against the defendant, but these proceedings were not pursued, and the cheque was returned to the bank, which then itself brought an action against the defendant, founding its right to do so on s. 2 of the Cheques Act.

By way of defence the defendant claimed (i) that the cheque was not delivered to the bank by the holder; (ii) that the cheque was not delivered for collection for the holder; (iii) that the bank did not give value for the cheque; and (iv) that the bank ceased to be a holder and also lost its lien by returning the cheque to T.

Held:

(i) The delivery of the cheque to the bank was delivery by T as the holder, and not delivery by an agent on behalf of T's company, as the cheque had not been negotiated to the company;

(ii) T delivered the cheque 'for collection' within s. 2 of the Cheques Act, as the section does not apply only where the cheque is delivered for collection for the account of the holder;

(iii) The bank had not given value for the cheque, as no agreement by the bank to allow the company to draw against uncleared effects could be inferred; and

(iv) The redelivery of the cheque by the bank to T caused the bank to lose its lien and T again became holder of the cheque, and the bank did not become holder on its subsequent return, unindorsed, to the bank.

The bank was, therefore, not entitled to sue on the unindorsed cheque.

(4) *Effect of the Act*

As a result of the Cheques Act, 1957, the banks have intimated that they will not require indorsement where (*a*) cheques are paid in to the account of the payee; or (*b*) cheques are paid in for the credit of a joint or partnership account. Indorsement is still required, however, on (i) cheques cashed or exchanged over the counter; (ii) negotiated cheques, *i.e.*, those tendered for the credit of an account other than that of the ostensible payee; (iii) cheques payable to joint payees, if tendered for the credit of an account to which all are not parties; and (iv) bills of exchange (other than cheques) and promissory notes. In all except the last of these cases the banker is protected if the indorsement is not genuine, but the statutory protection does not extend to bills other than cheques, so that, for example, where the drawee of a bill 'domiciles' the bill at his bank, the banker will be liable to the drawee if he pays the bill on a forged indorsement.

§ 4. *Promissory Notes*

(a) Definition and Form of Promissory Note

A promissory note is defined by s. 83 (1) of the Bills of Exchange Act as:

An unconditional promise in writing, made by one person to another, signed by the maker, engaging to pay, on demand or at a fixed or determinable future time, a sum certain in money to, or to the order of, a specified person, or to bearer.

The following is a form of promissory note:

London,
1st Feb., 19......

Three months after date I promise to pay J. Black or order the sum of One thousand five hundred pounds for value received.

W. JONES

£1,500 · 00p

A promissory note is inchoate and incomplete until delivery thereof to the payee or bearer (s. 84).

The maker of a note engages that he will pay it according to its tenor, and is precluded from denying to a holder in due course the existence of the payee and his then capacity to indorse (s. 88).

(b) Joint and Several Notes

A promissory note may be made by two or more makers, and they may be liable thereon jointly, or jointly and severally, according to its tenor. Where a note runs, 'I promise to pay,' and is signed by two or more persons, it is deemed to be their joint and several note (s. 85). The holder of such a note may sue the makers jointly or severally; judgment against one party only does not prevent a subsequent action against the others so long as satisfaction has not been obtained.

But a note which runs, 'We promise to pay,' and which is signed by two or more persons, is deemed to be a joint note only. The holder of such a note must sue the makers jointly, since judgment against one party, even without satisfaction, bars the remedy against the others.

(c) Presentment for Payment

If a note payable on demand has been indorsed, it must be presented for payment within a reasonable time. If it is not so presented the indorser is discharged (s. 86 (1)). In determining what is a reasonable time, regard shall be had to the nature of the instrument, the usage of trade and the facts of the particular case (s. 86 (2)). Where a note payable on demand is negotiated, it is not deemed to be overdue, for the purpose of affecting the holder with defects of title of which he had no notice, by reason that it appears that a reasonable time for presenting it for payment has elapsed since its issue (s. 86 (3)).

Where a promissory note is made payable at a particular place, it must be presented for payment at that place, in order to render the maker or an indorser liable. In any other case presentment for payment is not necessary in order to render the maker liable, but in order to render an indorser liable it is always necessary to present a note for payment (s. 87).

(d) Application of Bills of Exchange Act

The provisions of the Act relating to bills apply *mutatis mutandis* to promissory notes, except as to (1) presentment for acceptance, (2) acceptance, (3) acceptance *supra protest*, and (4) bills in a set (s. 89 (1)–(3)).

In applying these provisions, the maker of the note is deemed to correspond to the acceptor of a bill, and the first indorser of the note is deemed to correspond with the drawer of an accepted bill, payable to the drawer's order (s. 89 (1)).

Protest of a foreign note is unnecessary (s. 89 (4)).

§ 5. *Bank Notes*

A bank note is a promissory note issued by a banker, payable to bearer on demand.

Stamp duties on bank notes are now payable only on notes issued by banks in Scotland or Northern Ireland, for in England the sole note-issuing authority is the Bank of England whose notes are exempt from stamp duty.

§ 6. *I.O.U.s*

An I.O.U. is merely a memorandum of indebtedness to the holder by the person signing it. It is evidence of an account stated between the parties, but not of money lent; it is not a negotiable instrument, and does not require to be stamped.

§ 7. *Payment by Bill or Cheque*

It is the duty of a debtor, when his debt is due, in the absence of any different agreement, to seek out his creditor and tender him the exact amount of his debt in legal tender (see Chap. I, § 12 (b) (4)). The debtor is not bound to honour a bill drawn on him by a creditor, unless he has accepted it or contracted to do so; but on the other hand the creditor is under no obligation to take a negotiable instrument in discharge of the sum due to him.

If a bill or note is taken as payment, such payment may be absolute or conditional, the presumption being that the payment is conditional. In the latter case, if the instrument is dishonoured, the original debt revives, and the holder of the instrument has a right of action both upon the original consideration, and upon the dishonoured bill or note. This applies to a cheque payable on demand as well as to a bill or note maturing at a date subsequent to that upon which it was drawn. Where, however, a cheque or bill is taken by way of absolute discharge (as is presumed to be the case where, for instance, a creditor *asks* for payment to be made in this way), the right of action upon the original debt is lost and cannot be revived, so that the creditor is confined to whatever remedy may be available to him under the instrument.

In *Bolt & Nut Co. (Tipton), Ltd.* v. *Rowlands, Nicholls & Co., Ltd.* [1964] 1 All E.R. 137, the plaintiffs were in a position to enter judgment in default of appearance in an action against the defendants for a sum payable in respect of goods sold and delivered. The plaintiffs took a cheque from the defendants for part of this sum and then, before the cheque had been cleared, entered judgment for the whole sum claimed, without making allowance for the amount of the cheque. The cheque was cleared and paid in due course.

Held: The defendants were entitled to have the judgment set aside, as the acceptance of the cheque by the plaintiffs amounted to a conditional satisfaction of that part of the debt, and thus suspended the plaintiff's remedies during the currency of the cheque, so that during that time the plaintiffs were not entitled to enter judgment for a sum which included the amount of the cheque.

If a bill is taken for the price of goods sold, the lien of the seller is, in general, lost during the currency of the bill, which is equivalent to a term of credit; but the lien revives on dishonour of the bill, if the goods are still in the seller's possession.

§ 8. *Limitation of Actions*

Action on a bill or note is barred, as against any party to the bill, at the expiration of six years from the time when a right of action first accrued to the then holder against that party.

As against the acceptor, time begins to run from the date of maturity; for example, in the case of a bill or note payable three months after date or sight, time begins to run from three months and three days after date or sight.

In the case of a bill payable on demand, time begins to run from the date of the bill.

In the case of a promissory note payable on demand, time begins to run, as against the maker, from the date of issue. Thus, as regards a note payable on demand dated 1st January, but not issued until 1st July, time begins to run from 1st July (*Savage* v. *Aldren* (1817) 2 Stark. 232).

As regards the drawer or indorser of a bill, time begins to run from the date that notice of dishonour is received.

CHAPTER V

BAILMENTS AND SECURITIES

§ 1. *Bailments*

(a) Definition and Classification of Bailments

A *bailment* is a delivery of goods by one person to another on the terms, express or implied, that the goods will be redelivered in either their original or an altered form as soon as the purpose for which they were bailed has been completed.

The person delivering the goods is called the *bailor*, and the person to whom they are delivered is called the *bailee*.

There are many different forms of bailment and they can be classified in a number of ways. Perhaps the simplest classification is:

(1) bailments for the benefit of the bailor alone;

(2) bailments for the benefit of the bailee alone;

(3) bailments for the mutual benefit of the bailor and the bailee.

A bailment of the first type would arise, for example, where a person volunteers to look after a friend's goods while he is away; and a bailment of the second type where property is lent gratuitously for the bailee's use. Examples of the third type of bailment are the hiring of goods for reward, the pledging of goods as security for a loan, and the delivery of goods for repairing or warehousing on the terms that the bailor will pay for such services. Bailments of the first and second types are sometimes described as 'gratuitous bailments,' and those of the third type as 'bailments for reward.'

An ordinary bailment is constituted by the mere delivery and acceptance of the possession of a chattel, quite independently of any contract. An infant may, therefore, be a bailee of goods and be sued in tort therefor (*Ballett* v. *Mingay, ante,* p. 35). The legal position as between bailor and bailee, so far as their respective rights, duties and liabilities are concerned, is governed by the ordinary common law relating to bailment, although a contract between the parties usually alters the common law position by creating contractual rights and duties over and above those normally applicable to ordinary bailments. This situation is very common in mercantile transactions, and the general effect of such a superimposed contract is usually to reduce or extinguish the common law liability of the bailee. In such a case, subject to any special terms of the contract, liability may arise either in contract or in tort.

203

(b) Duties of Bailee

The bailee is under an implied obligation to take reasonable care of the goods while they are in his possession, and to redeliver the goods when the purpose of the bailment has been completed. It has long been considered that the standard of care required of the bailee varies according to the nature of the bailment, greater care being required in the case of a bailment for reward or a gratuitous bailment for the benefit of the bailee than in the case of a bailment for the benefit of the bailor alone. In *Houghland* v. *R. R. Low* (*Luxury Coaches*), *Ltd.* [1962] 1 Q.B. 694, Ormerod, L.J., stated that the standard of care required must be determined according to the circumstances of each particular case, regardless of the type of bailment involved; but the traditional view has subsequently been re-affirmed by the Court of Appeal in *Morris* v. *C. W. Martin & Sons, Ltd.* [1965] 2 All E.R. 725, although the *dictum* of Ormerod, L.J., was not there considered.

The bailor must prove that a bailment existed and that the chattel was lost or damaged during the bailment. When this has been done, the onus of proof is upon the bailee to disprove the inference of negligence which then arises, and he must show that he took reasonable and proper care of the chattel (*Houghland* v. *R. R. Low* (*Luxury Coaches*), *Ltd., supra*).

In *Martin* v. *L.C.C.* [1947] K.B. 628, the plaintiff entered the defendants' hospital as a patient, and handed over to the hospital authorities some jewellery stated to them to be valuable, but which, nevertheless, was stored in a room to which a burglar could have easy access. The jewellery was stolen. The defendants were held liable since they had not taken a reasonable degree of care in the circumstances.

A bailee may be guilty of negligence in failing to fulfil his own requirements of care.

In *Newman* v. *Bourne and Hollingsworth* (1915) 31 T.L.R. 209, the plaintiff visited the defendants' shop on a Saturday morning, and, in order to try on coats, took off a valuable brooch and placed it on a show case. She forgot the brooch and left the premises. A shop assistant later discovered the brooch and handed it to the shopwalker, who placed it in his desk. According to the defendants' rules the brooch ought to have been deposited in their lost property office. On Monday morning the brooch could not be found. It was held that the defendants were liable for the loss of the brooch.

If the situation or profession of the bailee is such that skill on his part is implied, he will be liable for negligence if he does not use such skill, even if the bailment is solely for the benefit of the bailor (*Wilson* v. *Brett* (1843) 11 M. & W. 113).

Where a bailee proves that he has used proper care, he need go no further, for he is not bound to show how, in fact, the loss or damage occurred without negligence on his part (*Bullen* v. *Swan Electric Engraving Co.* (1907) 23 T.L.R. 258), so that if the subject-matter of the bailment is stolen while in the possession of the bailee, he will only be liable if want of reasonable care on his part is established.

A bailee is not responsible for reasonable wear and tear unless the contract expressly so provides, nor, except in special circumstances where the bailee exercises a public calling such as that of a common carrier of goods (see Chap. VII, § 1), is he liable for accidents or losses which happen to the bailed chattels, as by fire, without his privity or negligence. The bailee is not responsible, as a rule, for loss or damage occasioned by the negligence of an independent contractor properly employed by him. But he cannot avoid his duty to take care of the goods by delegating it to a servant or agent, and he will be liable if the servant or agent negligently damages or loses the goods or steals them, even though, in the case of a bailment for reward, he had no reason to doubt the servant's competence or honesty (*Morris* v. *C. W. Martin & Sons, Ltd., supra*).

A person does not incur liability as a bailee merely because he allows others to leave goods on his premises, *e.g.*, by providing car parking facilities, even for reward (*Ashby* v. *Tolhurst* [1937] 2 K.B. 242). Thus, no bailment is created by a person hanging his coat on a hook in a restaurant; but there is a bailment if the coat is taken from him by a waiter without request (*Ultzen* v. *Nicols* [1894] 1 Q.B. 92), and possibly also if a separate cloakroom is provided. There is no bailment where goods are deposited with a person (sometimes called an 'involuntary bailee') without his consent, though a bailment will arise if he uses the goods. The only duty of the person receiving the goods in such cases is to refrain from intentionally damaging them.

(c) Bailment subject to Special Contract

Where the bailment takes the form of a special contract, the terms of it, express or implied, may make the bailee liable to a degree beyond that of mere negligence; although it is more usual, where persons in the course of their business receive the goods of others for custody, or to do work thereon, for the terms of the contract to limit or exclude the bailee's liability for negligence and other defaults. The strict rules governing the operation and effect of such terms have already been considered (see Chap. I, § 6 (f)).

Notwithstanding any exclusion clause, a bailee will be liable for loss or damage where he deviates from the contract or exceeds the terms of the bailment, even where there is no actual fault on his part.

In *Lilley* v. *Doubleday* (1881) 7 Q.B.D. 510, goods were warehoused with the defendant at a particular repository, but without authority the bailee transferred part of them to another place where, without negligence on his part, they were destroyed by fire. The bailee was held to be liable for the loss on the ground that he had departed from the terms of the contract.

There is a deviation where the bailee wrongfully retains the goods after the bailment has terminated, or lends the goods to another (unless with authority), or misuses a chattel bailed to him for use, or otherwise uses goods which have been entrusted to him merely for safe custody. The principle applies to a gratuitous bailment as well as one for reward. Deviation is now regarded as a breach of the fundamental obligation imposed by the contract (see Chap. I, § 6 (g)).

In *Alexander* v. *Railway Executive* [1951] 2 K.B. 882, the plaintiff deposited luggage in the defendants' cloakroom. The defendants allowed an unauthorised person to enter the cloakroom, who opened the luggage and removed certain articles. It was held that the defendants' conduct constituted a breach of a fundamental term in the contract of bailment, and the defendants were liable, notwithstanding a condition excluding liability for misdelivery of luggage.

(d) Liability of Bailor

Where a chattel is bailed gratuitously, the bailor's duty is to warn the borrower of any defect in the chattel of which he is aware (*Coughlin* v. *Gillison* [1889] 1 Q.B. 145), and perhaps also of any defects of which he ought reasonably to have been aware.

Where the chattel is bailed for reward, as in the case of a contract of hire, there is an implied warranty on the part of the bailor that the title is such that the bailee's possession shall remain undisturbed and that the chattel is reasonably fit and suitable for the purpose for which it is bailed. Thus, where there was no apparent reason for an outbreak of fire on a hired motor launch, it was held that there was a presumption that the craft was not reasonably fit for use (*Reed* v. *Dean* [1949] 1 K.B. 188).

(e) Right of Bailee to Dispose of Goods

In the absence of a statutory or common law power, or a term in a contract, a bailee is not justified in selling or otherwise disposing of chattels bailed with him, and if he does so he will be liable to the bailor for the tort of conversion (*Sachs* v. *Miklos* [1948] 2 K.B. 23).

Under the Disposal of Uncollected Goods Act, 1952, a bailee who has accepted goods *in the course of his business* for repair or other treatment is given a statutory right in certain circumstances to sell those goods if the bailor fails to collect them. At the time of acceptance of the goods there must be a notice conspicuously displayed at the bailee's business premises that acceptance is subject to the provisions of the Act and that the Act confers a right of sale in certain circumstances. If the bailor fails both to pay for and to take delivery of the goods, the bailee must give the bailor notice that the goods are ready for redelivery, and, if the bailor fails to collect within twelve months of the notice, the bailee must give a second notice by registered post of his intention to sell. If the charges remain unpaid and the goods remain uncollected for fourteen days after the second notice, the bailee can sell the goods by public auction. After deducting his charges from the proceeds of sale, he must pay the balance to the bailor.

§ 2. *Innkeepers*

The question of what premises constitute an inn is one of fact and the name by which the premises are called is immaterial. Broadly speaking, an inn is what is nowadays more generally called an hotel, the latter expression being defined by the Hotel Proprietors Act, 1956, as:

'an establishment held out by the proprietor as offering food, drink, and, if so required, sleeping accommodation, without special contract, to any traveller presenting himself who appears able and willing to pay a reasonable sum for the services and facilities provided and who is in a fit state to be received.'

An establishment, such as a boarding-house, where the proprietor enters into special contracts with persons who seek accommodation is not within the statutory definition.

(a) Duties and Liabilities of Innkeeper at Common Law

The common law duty of an innkeeper to receive and entertain only extends to the provision of such accommodation as he has, and a guest cannot insist upon having any particular room. Drunkenness, or other misbehaviour of an applicant for accommodation, or uncleanliness, but not, it seems illness, may be good reason for refusing admission when the house is not full.

Length of stay at an inn may change the character of a guest from that of a traveller to that of a lodger, in which case he may be turned out by reasonable notice. An innkeeper is not bound to provide accommodation for an unreasonably prolonged period.

An innkeeper whose house is not full and who refuses to receive a guest without lawful excuse may be liable to an action in damages without proof of special damage, even though the plaintiff was accommodated in some other establishment in the same ownership (*Constantine* v. *Imperial London Hotels, Ltd.* [1944] K.B. 693). The innkeeper may also be criminally liable in respect of the refusal, and also if, having received a guest, he charges excessive prices.

The innkeeper is bound to provide food within a reasonable time upon payment therefor, unless he has a proper excuse. He is not bound to send out for food if he has none in the house, nor is he obliged to allow the whole of his provisions to be consumed during the day, if he reasonably expects other travellers to be arriving later. He may book tables for guests, and refuse to serve anyone who has not booked a table even if he has food in the house, unless, having regard to all the facts, such a refusal is unreasonable (*R.* v. *Higgins* [1948] 1 K.B. 165).

At common law the innkeeper cannot contract out of his strict liability in respect of the goods of his guest. His liability is that of an insurer of the goods unless loss is occasioned by:

(1) act of God, *e.g.*, flooding of the premises;

(2) act of the Queen's enemies, *e.g.*, an air raid;

(3) negligence of the guest himself.

In *Shacklock* v. *Ethorpe, Ltd.* [1939] 3 All E.R. 372, the plaintiff left jewellery in a locked receptacle in her hotel bedroom. She did not lock the door and the jewellery was stolen.

Held: Her failure to lock the bedroom door or to deposit the jewels with the innkeeper for safe custody was not sufficient evidence of negligence on her part, and the innkeeper was liable.

It is common practice for hotel proprietors to post notices in bedrooms requiring articles of value to be deposited with the proprietor. Such a notice does not operate to terminate the liability of the proprietor (in his capacity of innkeeper) in the event of loss. There is no obligation on the part of the guest to lodge his valuables for safe custody; if the goods are lost, negligence of the guest must still be proved for the innkeeper to avoid liability (*Carpenter* v. *Haymarket Hotel, Ltd.* [1931] 1 K.B. 364).

(b) Hotel Proprietors Act, 1956

Although liable for loss, the innkeeper was not formerly responsible for *damage* to his guests' goods unless he was negligent in regard to them. Now, however, by s. 1 (2) of the Hotel Proprietors Act, 1956:

'the proprietor of an hotel shall, as an innkeeper, be under the like liability, if any, to make good to any guest of his any damage to property brought to the hotel as he would be under to make good the loss thereof.'

Under the Act, an innkeeper may limit his liability to a total of £100 in the case of any one guest. In order that he may claim the statutory protection, a copy of the notice as set out in the Schedule to the Act must be conspicuously displayed in a place where it can conveniently be read by guests at or near the reception office or desk, or, where there is no reception office or desk, at or near the main entrance to the hotel at the time when the property in question is brought to the hotel.

The prescribed notice is as follows:

NOTICE
LOSS OR DAMAGE TO GUESTS' PROPERTY

Under the Hotel Proprietors Act, 1956, an hotel proprietor may in certain circumstances be liable to make good any loss of or damage to a guest's property even though it was not due to any fault of the proprietor or staff of the hotel.

This liability however –

(a) extends only to the property of guests who have engaged sleeping accommodation at the hotel;

(b) is limited to £50 for any one article and a total of £100 in the case of any one guest, except in the case of property which has been deposited, or offered for deposit, for safe custody;

(c) does not cover motor cars or other vehicles of any kind or any property left in them, or horses or other live animals.

This notice does not constitute an admission either that the Act applies to this hotel or that liability thereunder attaches to the proprietor of this hotel in any particular case.

The hotel proprietor is not liable, as an innkeeper, to make good to any traveller any loss or damage to property brought to the hotel except where:

(1) at the time of the loss or damage sleeping accommodation at the hotel had been engaged for the traveller; and

(2) the loss or damage occurred during the period commencing with the midnight immediately preceding, and ending with the midnight immediately following, a period for which the traveller was a guest at the hotel and entitled to use the accommodation so engaged (Hotel Proprietors Act, 1956, s. 2 (1)).

Section 2 (2) of the Act relieves the hotel proprietor, as such, from liability for loss or damage to motor cars, bicycles, horses, or other live animal or its harness or other equipment; although he may still be liable under the ordinary law of negligence. On the other hand the Act deprives the hotel proprietor of any lien he formerly enjoyed over such property in respect of an unpaid hotel bill (see (c), *infra*).

Failure to display the notice as required will render the proprietor liable without limit. He will also be so liable where the property is lost, stolen or damaged through the default, neglect or wilful act of himself or his servants; or if the property is deposited for safe custody, and in a container fastened or sealed by the depositor, if so required by the proprietor or his servant, or if, after the guest has arrived at the hotel, either the property in question is offered for deposit and the proprietor or his servant refuses to receive it, or the guest wishes to offer the property for deposit but, through the default of the proprietor or his servant, is unable to do so.

(c) Innkeeper's Lien

An innkeeper, has, at common law, a lien on all such goods of his guest as he is bound to receive at the inn, and this is so whether or not the goods belong to the guest or some other person. Thus, the inn-keeper's lien has been held to attach to sewing machines sent to a commercial traveller for sale, or to a piano which was hired by a guest; and even to stolen goods (*Marsh* v. *Commissioner of Police*

[1945] K.B. 43). But if the innkeeper knows that the property does not belong to the guest, and the property is sent to the guest to be used for a particular purpose, *e.g.*, a piano sent by the manufacturer to a professional pianist to play during his stay at the inn, the lien will not attach to such property (*Broadwood* v. *Granara* (1854) 10 Ex. 417). Certain property is now excluded by the Hotel Proprietors Act, 1956 (see (b), *supra*).

A lien attaches in respect of the whole sum due from the guest to the innkeeper, and not merely for the amount due in respect of the goods detained. If the innkeeper takes security, the lien is not thereby lost. In the exercise of the lien the innkeeper is not required to be more careful of the goods which form the subject of the lien than he is of his own goods.

Under the Innkeepers Act, 1878, in addition to the lien at common law, an innkeeper with whom goods have been left by a guest who has not paid his bill may sell the goods by public auction after they have been in his possession for six weeks without payment having been made. Notice of the sale must be given by advertisement in a London and local newspaper at least one month before it is to take place.

§ 3. *Securities Generally*

Securities are rights given to a creditor, in addition to his right of action against a debtor, which the creditor can exercise if the debtor makes default in repayment of the debt. Securities may be either personal guarantees given by one or more third parties, or rights over property. Securities over property may be created by mortgage, pledge or lien.

§ 4. *Guarantees*

(a) Essentials of a Guarantee

(1) *Definition*

A *guarantee* is an undertaking to be answerable for the debt, default or miscarriage of another.

This definition covers three different kinds of liability: that arising from a failure to pay a debt already existing; that arising from a failure to pay a debt to be afterwards incurred; and that arising from a failure to perform some obligation other than the payment of money. The debt or obligation guaranteed may be founded either in contract or in tort.

The following are examples of guarantees:

(i) A agrees with a bank that, in consideration of the bank's undertaking not to take steps to call in B's overdraft, A will repay the amount owing with interest when called upon (guarantee of an existing debt).

(ii) A agrees with a bank that, in consideration of the bank's advancing money to B, A will repay the amount with interest in the event of B's default (guarantee of a future debt).

(iii) A director of a company agrees with a prospective landlord that, in consideration of the landlord's granting a lease to the company, the director will pay the rent in the event of the company's default (guarantee of a future debt).

(iv) A agrees with B that, in consideration of B's refraining from suing C, who has incurred liability in tort towards him, A will pay the amount of the damage (guarantee of an existing debt arising from a tort).

(2) *Parties to a Guarantee*

There are three persons concerned in a guarantee: the guarantor or *surety* by whom it is given; the creditor or guaranteed party to whom it is given; and the principal debtor in respect of whom it is given.

(3) *Nature of Guarantor's Liability*

A guarantor accepts only a secondary liability in the event of the default of another person. There is no guarantee where the so-called guarantor accepts primary liability (*Birkmyr* v. *Darnell* (1705) 1 Salk. 27). Thus, if A, at the request of B, enters into a joint promissory note to repay to C money which C advances to B, A has a primary liability, and is not a guarantor, because he can be sued by C irrespective of B's default, notwithstanding that the substance of the transaction may have been that A would guarantee repayment of B's debt.

Similarly, there is no guarantee where the contract by the so-called guarantor has the effect of releasing the principal debtor from liability, for then there is no default of a third party for which the guarantor is to be responsible. Thus, if A owes £100 to B, and C agrees with B to pay the amount owing in consideration of B's releasing A from liability, C is not a guarantor but a primary debtor under a contract of novation.

(4) *Guarantor's Interest Limited to Guarantee*

The guarantor must have no interest in the contract in respect of which the guarantee is given, except through his promise to make good any losses arising from the principal debtor's default. A contract is not a true guarantee which has some wider object as its main purpose.

Thus, if a principal appoints a person as his *del credere* agent, one of the terms of the contract being that the agent will undertake personal liability in the event of non-payment by customers whom he introduces to his principal, this is not a guarantee, as it is only collateral to the main contract of agency (*Couturier* v. *Hastie* (1852) 8 Ex. 40). Similarly, if goods are sold by A to B, and then by B to C, and C, to release the lien for the purchase price which A has over the goods, agrees to pay A if B defaults, C is not a guarantor, as the primary purpose of the contract is to obtain the goods and not to give a guarantee (*Fitzgerald* v. *Dressler* (1859) 29 L.J.C.P. 113).

(5) *Written Evidence of Guarantee Necessary*

By s. 4 of the Statute of Frauds, 1677, no action may be brought against a person on a promise to answer for the debt, default, or miscarriage of another, unless the agreement upon which the action is brought, or some memorandum or note thereof, is in writing, and signed by the party to be charged, or some other person authorised by him. The written evidence may be brought into existence at any time before the action is commenced. The consideration for the contract need not be mentioned in writing (Mercantile Law Amendment Act, 1856, s. 3), but consideration must exist (unless the guarantee is under seal), and may be proved by oral evidence. (As to the position where there is no written evidence, see Chap. I, § 4 (e)).

(6) *Distinction between Guarantees and Indemnities*

An indemnity is a contract whereby one party agrees to keep another immune from loss. This loss may arise through the default of another person or through some entirely extraneous cause, *e.g.*, fire, or through some cause attributable to the promisee himself. The word 'indemnity' covers a wide field which includes guarantees and insurance; but it is often used in a narrower sense as excluding contracts of guarantee and being in contrast thereto.

Examples of indemnities other than guarantees and insurance are:

(i) A agrees with B that, in consideration of B's contracting to build a house for C for £2,000 to be paid by C, A will pay to B any sum in excess of £2,000 which the building costs him. Although there are three persons concerned in this transaction, it is not a guarantee, because A is not agreeing to be responsible for any default of C, but is agreeing to indemnify B against any loss in which the contract will involve him.

(ii) A promises B, in consideration of B's accepting a bill of exchange, that he will meet the bill when it is presented for payment. This is not a guarantee, for A has made no promise to the holder of the bill to be responsible for B's default.

A contract of indemnity, in the narrower sense, may be distinguished from a guarantee in the following ways:

(i) there need be only *two* persons concerned in the contract;

(ii) the promisor assumes a *primary* liability;

(iii) the promisor *may* have some interest in the transaction apart from his indemnity; and

(iv) the contract may be made *orally*.

The need to distinguish between a guarantee and an indemnity usually arises where the contract is made orally, since, by the Statute of Frauds, an oral guarantee is unenforceable. The distinction may also be of importance in order to determine the extent of the promisor's liability (*Western Credit, Ltd.* v. *Alberry* [1964] 2 All E.R. 938; see (b), *infra*).

Whether a contract is one of guarantee or of some other form of indemnity must be determined by looking at the terms of the contract itself; the words used by the parties are not in any way decisive (*Guild & Co.* v. *Conrad* [1894] 2 Q.B. 885).

(b) Liability of the Surety

The extent and nature of the liability of a surety depend primarily upon the instrument creating the liability. Thus, if the instrument shows that the surety only intended to assume a joint liability with another, he can only incur liability to that extent (*Other* v. *Iveson* (1855) 3 Drew. 177).

The liability of the surety does not arise until the principal debtor has made default. When default is so made, a right of action at once arises against the surety, and in the absence of express agreement to the contrary the creditor is not bound to sue the principal debtor before taking action against him; nor is the creditor precluded from suing the surety merely because he holds securities from the principal debtor.

If there is no stipulation to the contrary, the creditor can sue the surety without demanding payment from him, or even informing him of the default of the principal debtor. But if the operation of the guarantee is dependent upon the happening of a particular event, the creditor must inform the surety that the event has taken place before he can sue.

Where the guarantee is given subject to the fulfilment of some condition precedent, *e.g.*, that others should join as co-sureties, the surety will only be liable if this condition is satisfied.

In *National Provincial Bank of England* v. *Brackenbury* (1906) 22 T.L.R. 797, a guarantee to a bank for an overdraft was, on its face, intended to be a joint and several guarantee by four guarantors. Three out of the four signed the guarantee, but the fourth did not sign, though willing to do so, and died without doing so. The three who signed were not liable on the guarantee.

In *Rickaby* v. *Lewis* (1906) 22 T.L.R. 130, a debtor promised to repay to the plaintiff an advance within three months of the receipt by him of a written notice requiring payment, and the defendant agreed to guarantee the repayment of the advance as arranged. The principal debtor died leaving no estate, and neither probate nor letters of administration were taken out. No written notice requiring payment was ever given. The guarantor was not liable, because the condition on which the money became payable had not been fulfilled.

The surety is liable for the amount due from the principal debtor at the time default is made. Thus, credit must be given to the surety for any sums already paid by the principal debtor (*Bardwell* v. *Lydall* (1831) 7 Bing. 489). If the debtor is liable to pay interest on the debt, the surety is liable to pay such interest himself (*Ackerman* v. *Ehrenspengen* (1846) 16 M. & W. 99). If the debt is not legally binding upon the principal debtor then the surety is not himself liable, *e.g.*, where the principal debtor is an infant (*Coutts & Co.* v. *Browne-Lecky* [1947] K.B. 104).

The surety is not necessarily liable for the whole of the creditor's loss. Thus, if in a contract of hire-purchase the hirer determines the agreement in accordance with a provision in the contract that he may do so on payment of a specified proportion of the total hire-purchase price, a surety will only be liable for that specified amount, even though this does not entirely cover the owner's loss of profit (*Western Credit, Ltd.* v. *Alberry, supra*).

In the case of the bankruptcy of the surety, proof may be made against his estate on the contingent liability. If at the time of lodging his proof the creditor has received payment on account, he can only prove for the net balance. But the proof is not reducible by a dividend received from the estate of the principal debtor after proving against the surety (*Re Blakeley* (1892) 9 Morrel 173). Nor is any reduction in the proof effected by reason of the receipt by the creditor of sums from co-sureties, but the creditor cannot recover in all more than twenty shillings in the pound (*Re Houlder* [1929] 1 Ch. 205).

If the surety receives security from the principal debtor, and afterwards both these parties become insolvent, the creditors of the surety are entitled to regard the security as part of the property of the surety, and are entitled to the benefit of it in discharge of their debts (*Loder's Case* (1868) L.R. 6 Eq. 491).

(c) Continuing Guarantees

The transactions to which the liability of a surety extends will depend on whether or not the guarantee is 'continuing.' A continuing guarantee is one which covers a series of transactions, *e.g.*, a bank overdraft; a non-continuing guarantee is one which is confined to a single transaction. Subject to the terms of the agreement, a continuing guarantee which is divisible and given for a consideration provided from time to time, such as a guarantee given in respect of goods supplied on a current account, may be revoked as to future transactions upon the account; and notice of the guarantor's death given to the creditor is a constructive revocation as to future transactions; but a non-continuing guarantee cannot be revoked unless otherwise provided.

In the case of a guarantee for goods supplied or for money advanced, the surrounding circumstances as well as the language of the guarantee itself must be looked at to ascertain whether the guarantee is continuing or non-continuing, since each case must be governed by its own circumstances (*Heffield* v. *Meadows* (1869) L.R. 4 C.P. 595).

In certain circumstances the liability of a surety may be seriously affected after the execution of a guarantee by changes occurring, which were not, at the time of execution, in any way contemplated by the parties, as in cases where guarantees have been given to a firm, or to a third person in respect of the dealings of a firm, and a change takes place in the constitution either of the firm to which, or of the firm in respect of which, the guarantee is given. Section 18 of the Partnership Act, 1890, provides that any such change has the effect of revoking a continuing guarantee, in the absence of agreement to the contrary, as regards future transactions. Agreement to the contrary will not be implied merely from the fact that the guarantee was given to, or in respect of, the 'firm'; the guarantee will still be presumed, until the contrary is shown, to apply only to the firm as then constituted.

(d) Rights of the Surety

(1) *Against the Principal Debtor*

Before making any payment under the guarantee, the surety can compel the principal debtor to pay the debt, and so free himself from liability. It is possible for the surety to take proceedings for this purpose the moment that his liability has arisen, even before he has himself been called upon to pay.

After payment, the surety is entitled to be indemnified by the principal debtor to the extent of any loss sustained under the guarantee, provided that he became surety with the knowledge and consent of the principal debtor. Any such payment is treated as being made to the use of the principal debtor, and can, therefore, be recovered from him by an action, or may be proved for in his bankruptcy. The amount recoverable by the surety is the principal sum which he has paid, together with interest at 4 per cent. per annum on this sum; and if he can prove that he has suffered further damage by the non-payment of the debt, he will be entitled to claim for this also. The surety cannot recover from the debtor the costs of defending an action brought upon the guarantee by the creditor unless it was defended with the authority of the debtor and upon reasonable grounds. He may, however, in such an action issue a third party notice against the debtor joining him as co-defendant and claiming an indemnity against him.

(2) *Against the Creditor*

From the time he becomes a surety, the surety has rights against the creditor; they do not arise only when the obligations of the debtor are discharged by him.

After the guaranteed debt has become payable and before being asked to pay it, the surety may at any time request the creditor to call upon the debtor to pay, and, upon an undertaking to indemnify the creditor against the costs and risk of loss, to proceed against the debtor. On the other hand the surety himself may pay the debt, and thereafter sue the debtor in the creditor's name, or, it seems, in his own name if he obtains an assignment to himself of the guaranteed debt. The creditor is not bound, however, to sue the debtor before suing the surety (*Wright* v. *Simpson* (1802) 6 Ves. 714).

On being sued by the creditor, the surety may plead any set-off or counterclaim which the debtor has against the creditor; and he may compel the creditor who has a claim on two funds, one of which is not available to the surety, to resort first to that fund.

Where the surety pays what is due under the guarantee, he is entitled to be subrogated to all the rights of the creditor in respect of the debt and to have assigned to himself every judgment or security held by the creditor in respect of the debt, whether known to him or not, and whether created before or after the guarantee (Mercantile Law Amendment Act, 1856, s. 5); and if any portion of such security is lost by the act of the creditor, the surety is to that extent discharged (*Taylor* v. *Bank of New South Wales* (1886) 11 App. Cas. 596).

The creditor is not, however, bound to preserve securities for the benefit of the surety if the principal debtor is bankrupt, since he may elect to surrender the security and prove for the full amount of the debt (*Rainbow* v. *Juggins* (1880) 5 Q.B.D. 138).

If a surety has paid only a proportion of the debt, he is *pro tanto* entitled to the same rights.

(3) *Against Co-Sureties*

A surety who has been compelled to pay under the guarantee has, as against his co-sureties, a right of contribution.

Before payment, if one surety is called upon to pay the whole debt, or more than his true proportion, he is entitled to call upon his co-sureties for their due proportion of the common debt. He has the right to force his co-sureties, by action, to contribute their proportion, even before he has himself paid; and this even if judgment has been obtained against him personally (*Wolmershausen* v. *Gullick* [1893] 2 Ch. 514).

After payment, the right to claim contribution does not arise until one surety has paid more than his proportion of the whole of the common debt (*Re Snowdon* (1881) 17 Ch. D. 44).

It does not make any difference to the right to enforce contribution whether the surety did or did not know at the time of incurring the liability that he was to be co-surety with others; even if he were unaware of this fact, the right to enforce contribution exists where the amount paid represents more than his rateable proportion of the debt for which the co-sureties are responsible. There is a right of contribution whether the sureties are bound jointly or jointly and severally; and whether they are bound by the same or by different instruments, provided it is the same principal and the same engagement; but if there is a contract that each surety shall be answerable only for a given portion of one sum of money, there is no right of contribution among the sureties. If one surety has become surety jointly with another, at the request of that other, the surety at whose request the liability was undertaken cannot enforce the right of contribution (*Turner* v. *Davies* (1796) 2 Esp. 479). If two or more persons indorse a bill for the accommodation of the acceptor or drawer, as between themselves they are co-sureties, not sureties in succession in the order of their names on the bill (*Macdonald* v. *Whitfield* (1883) 8 App. Cas. 733).

As regards the amount which may be recovered by way of contribution, the general rule is that sureties contribute equally. If, however, two or more persons join as sureties for a common principal, but in different amounts, they are only liable, upon default of the principal, to contribute proportionately to their respective liabilities, and not equally (*Ellesmere Brewery Co.* v. *Cooper* [1896] 1 Q.B. 75).

If one of the co-sureties is unable to pay, the surety claiming contribution after payment of the principal debt can claim from the sureties who are solvent their respective shares of the whole amount paid, together with interest from the date of payment, *i.e.*, each solvent surety must contribute his respective share of the proportion due by the insolvent surety (*Hitchman* v. *Stewart* (1855) 3 Drew. 271). If a co-surety has become bankrupt, proof can be made against his estate for the necessary contribution, and even if the actual amount due is not yet ascertained, proof can be made on the contingent liability.

The right of the surety to contribution will be barred after six years by the Limitation Act, 1939; but since the right to contribution does not arise until the surety has paid more than his share, the time does not begin to run until this has been done, or until the claim against him by the creditor has been established. If a surety has paid part of a debt more than six years before the bringing of an action, and the debtor has paid the remainder of the debt within six years, time only runs from the latter payment, because until it was made the liability of the co-surety was not determined (*Davies* v. *Humphries* (1840) 6 M. & W. 153; *Re Snowdon, supra*).

Sureties are entitled, in addition to the right of contribution, to the benefit of all securities taken by any co-surety to indemnify himself against liabilities under the guarantee.

If a surety has obtained a collateral security from the principal debtor, he is bound to bring it into hotchpot for the benefit of his co-sureties, and this even though he only agreed to assume liability upon the terms that he was to have such security, and despite the fact that his co-sureties did not know of its existence (*Steel* v. *Dixon* (1881) 45 L.T. 142). On the other hand, the creditor is not entitled to the benefit of collateral securities given in this manner by the principal debtor (*Re Walker* [1892] 1 Ch. 621).

(e) Discharge of Surety

A surety may avoid the contract of guarantee or be discharged from liability thereunder in the same way as any other party to a contract (see Chap. I). In addition, a surety is entitled to insist that the creditor will adhere strictly to the terms of the contract and at all times have regard to the interests of the surety as well as his own, and may become discharged from liability by some act of the creditor, whether inadvertent or otherwise, which operates adversely to the surety's interest.

(1) *Concealment of Material Facts*

A contract of guarantee is not, before it is entered into, a contract *uberrimae fidei* in the same sense as are certain other contracts (see Chap. 1, § 8 (b) (2)), in which even an innocent suppression of a material fact will vitiate the contract.

There are, however, certain matters which it is the duty of the creditor to disclose to the surety. If the creditor wilfully and intentionally conceals one of these matters, the contract may be avoided by the surety; but if the surety fails to ask a question on a point which it is not the duty of the creditor to make known to him, then concealment of the matter, though wilful and intentional on the part of the creditor, does not relieve the surety from liability.

'The concealment must be of some material part of the transaction itself between the creditor and his debtor to which the suretyship relates. The creditor is under no obligation to inform the intended surety of matters affecting the credit of the debtor, or of any circumstances unconnected with the transaction in which he is about to engage, which will render his position more hazardous' (*per* Lord Chelmsford in *Wythes* v. *Labouchere* (1858) 3 De G. & J. 593, at p. 607).

Thus, in *Cooper* v. *National Provincial Bank, Ltd.* [1946] K.B.1, it was held that the bank was under no obligation voluntarily to disclose to a surety the fact that the debtor's husband was an undischarged bankrupt, and had authority to draw on her account. On the other hand the creditor is bound to inform the surety of any private bargain between the debtor and the creditor by which the degree of liability of the surety is affected, as, for instance, in a guarantee for the payment of goods supplied, that the goods are to be charged at an

increase on the market price in order to liquidate an old debt
(*Pidcock* v. *Bishop* (1825) 3 B. & C. 605). Where the guarantee is for
the due performance of the duties of an office, *i.e.*, a fidelity guarantee,
the employer is bound to communicate misconduct already committed in the same office (*Smith* v. *Bank of Scotland* (1812) 1 Dow
272), or misconduct subsequently committed, if the guarantee is
continuing.

(2) *Variation of Agreement*

The surety may be discharged from liability if the creditor alters or
departs from the terms of his contract with the principal debtor or
with the surety himself, without the surety's consent. The alteration
must materially affect the surety's obligations, although it need not
in fact, prejudice his position.

In *Ellesmere Brewery Co.* v. *Cooper* [1896] 1 Q.B. 75, a joint and several bond o
suretyship was entered into by four persons, the liability of two of them being
limited by the instrument to £50 each, and that of the others to £25 each. After
three of them had duly executed the bond, the fourth, who should have been liable
to the extent of £50, executed the bond with an addition to his signature of the
words 'liable for £25 only.' This was held to be a material alteration as a result of
which the first three executants were discharged, and the other party himself was
not bound, since he executed the bond as a joint and several instrument only.

In *General Steam Navigation Co.* v. *Rolt* (1859) 6 C.B.N.S. 550, B contracted to
build a ship for A, the contract money to be paid by instalments as the work
reached certain stages of completion, and C became surety for the due performance of the work by B. A allowed B to draw a large portion of the last two
instalments before they were due. C was in consequence held to be discharged
from liability.

In *Bacon* v. *Chesney* (1816) 1 Stark. 192, it was held that if A guarantees payment for goods supplied by B to C, upon condition that 18 months' credit is given,
A is discharged if B only gives 12 months' credit.

For the same reason the surety is discharged if the creditor releases
any security held by him or takes a fresh security in lieu of the
original one (but not if additional security is given).

(3) *Agreement to give Time to Principal Debtor*

If the creditor, without the consent of the surety, enters into a
binding agreement with the principal debtor to give further time for
payment, the surety is discharged. Such an agreement must be enforceable at law, *i.e.*, under seal or for valuable consideration. Mere
omission to enforce payment from the principal debtor will not
operate to release the surety. Nor is he released if the creditor, while
giving time to the principal debtor, reserves his rights against the
surety, as the giving of time does not then affect the surety's rights
against the debtor.

In the case of a continuing guarantee, the giving of time for a single
payment will discharge the surety from liability only in respect of that

one payment if the contract is divisible (*Croydon Gas Co.* v. *Dickinson* (1876) 2 C.P.D. 46); but it will discharge him from all further liability if the contract is entire and indivisible, as in the case of a hire-purchase contract.

In *Midland Motor Showrooms, Ltd.* v. *Newman* [1929] 2 K.B. 256, A obtained a motor car from B under a hire-purchase agreement, the due performance of the agreement being guaranteed by C. B for valuable consideration gave A further time for payment of one of the instalments. It was held that the giving of time to A discharged C from any further liability under the guarantee.

(4) *Discharge of Principal Debtor*

If the creditor discharges the debtor absolutely, he also discharges the surety (*Commercial Bank of Tasmania* v. *Jones* [1893] A.C. 313).

In *Hewison* v. *Ricketts* (1894) 63 L.J.Q.B. 711, the defendants guaranteed the payment by G of certain instalments under a hire-purchase agreement. Upon default, the plaintiffs seized the goods, and so determined the hire-purchase contract. It was held that the surety was also discharged.

The reason for this is that the creditor, by releasing the debtor, destroys the surety's right of recourse against the debtor.

The surety may, by express contract, remain liable, even though the principal debtor is discharged. But if the creditor, in releasing the debtor, expressly reserves his rights against the surety, the surety still has his rights against the principal debtor, and may have recourse to him. There is, in such a case, really no discharge of the principal debtor; it is not a release, but an undertaking by the creditor that he himself will not sue the debtor (*Maltby* v. *Carstairs* (1828) 24 L.J.Q.B. 130).

Valid payment by the principal debtor will, of course, discharge the surety; and where the debtor in paying has made no appropriation it is possible for the surety to obtain the benefit of the doctrine of the appropriation of payments, by claiming that payments made by the debtor were on account of the debt for which the surety was liable.

If a bankrupt debtor obtains his discharge, this does not release any person who was a surety for him at the date of the receiving order (Bankruptcy Act, 1914, s. 28 (4)). But disclaimer of a lease by the trustee in bankruptcy releases a surety for payment of rent from any liability for the rent after the date of disclaimer (*Stacey* v. *Hill* [1901] 1 K.B. 660).

(5) *Discharge of Co-Surety*

If the creditor discharges a co-surety, or releases a security given by him, or does any other act which prejudices the right of contribution between co-sureties, without consent, the other co-sureties are discharged, unless the creditor expressly reserves his rights against the others (*Mercantile Bank of Sydney* v. *Taylor* [1893] A.C. 317).

(6) *Negligence of Creditor*

The surety may be discharged by the negligence of the creditor in not doing something which he is bound to do for the protection of the surety.

In *Watts* v. *Shuttleworth* (1860) 7 H. & N. 353, in the agreement between the plaintiff and the principal debtor there was a condition imposing upon the plaintiff the duty to insure against fire the work which was being done for him by the debtor. When the surety assumed liability for the due performance of the work, he was informed of this stipulation. The plaintiff did not insure, and the surety was discharged by the plaintiff's omission to do so.

The omission by the creditor of some act which he is not legally bound to do does not operate to discharge the surety.

The surety being entitled, on payment, to the benefit of all securities held by the creditor against the principal debtor, it follows that if, through the fault of the creditor, such securities are lost, the surety will be discharged to the extent thereof. It must be shown, however, that there has been an actual loss, and that the loss arose from the fault of the creditor. A similar position would arise if the creditor's actions caused the surety to lose a lien to which he was entitled.

In the case of a fidelity guarantee the surety is discharged if the employer retains the servant in his employment after discovering that he has been guilty of some dishonesty, unless the servant is retained with the consent of the surety (*Phillips* v. *Foxall* (1872) L.R. 7 Q.B. 666).

(7) *Revocation*

A surety may in some cases revoke the guarantee. Before actual acceptance the offer of a guarantee may always be revoked; after acceptance it can only be revoked if there is a provision to that effect in the contract. In the case of a continuing guarantee, where the consideration for the guarantee is to take the form of separate advances of money or goods, the offer may be at any time revoked as regards future advances; but where the consideration has been given once and for all, as in the case of a fidelity guarantee, there is no power to revoke (*Lloyd's* v. *Harper* (1880) 16 Ch. D. 290).

(8) *Death of Surety*

The death of a surety does not affect liability for *past* transactions. As regards its effect on subsequent transactions, this will depend on whether the surety had himself the power of revocation. If he could himself have revoked his guarantee by giving notice, then, but not otherwise, express or constructive notice of his death will operate as revocation (*Coulthart* v. *Clementson* (1879) 5 Q.B.D. 42). Under a joint and several continuing guarantee, the death of one co-surety does not of itself determine the future liability of the survivors.

(9) *Lapse of Time*

The surety may be released from liability by the operation of the Limitation Act, in the case of a parol contract after six years, and in the case of a guarantee under seal after twelve years. A payment made by one co-surety will not keep the debt alive against the others (*Re Wolmershausen* (1889) 62 L.T. 541); but if a payment of interest in respect of a loan to a firm is made by one of several partners, after the retirement of one of them, the debt is prevented from becoming barred as against the retired partner, since the continuing partners are assumed to have been acting for him and as his agents (*Re Tucker* [1894] 3 Ch. 429).

§ 5. *Mortgages*

A mortgage is a transaction whereby, as security for a loan of money, the borrower transfers to the lender an interest in some property of the borrower, real or personal, on the condition that the lender's interest in the property will be terminated on repayment of the loan. The person borrowing the money and giving the security is called the mortgagor, and the person lending the money and receiving the security is called the mortgagee.

(a) Mortgages of Land

(1) *Legal Mortgage*

By the Law of Property Act, 1925, a legal mortgage of land may be created in one of two ways:

(i) *By lease*

Where the mortgagor owns the fee simple or 'freehold,' he may grant the mortgagee a lease of the land for a specified number of years, with a proviso that the term shall cease when the money secured has been repaid. A second mortgage may be granted for the unexpired portion of the term plus one day, and any subsequent mortgage for a time one day longer than its immediate prior mortgage (s. 85).

Where the interest of the mortgagor in the property is leasehold, the mortgage is granted for the unexpired term of the lease, less ten days, a second mortgage for a period one day longer, and so on (s. 86).

(ii) *By charge*

Alternatively, the mortgagor may effect a charge by way of legal mortgage, by which he charges the land by deed with payment of the principal money and interest (s. 87); the effect is precisely the same as a mortgage created for a term of years, but the document has the advantage of being shorter and simpler.

Even though the time agreed upon for repayment has expired, the mortgagor is allowed to redeem his property on payment of the principal money, interest, and costs. This right of redemption is called the *equity of redemption*, and any provision which attempts to fetter or clog this right will be void. If a mortgagee enters into possession of the land, and retains possession for twelve years without acknowledging the title of the mortgagor, the equity of redemption is barred; similarly, if a mortgagor retains possession of the land for twelve years without paying interest or acknowledging the title of the mortgagee, he becomes entitled to the land free from the mortgage (Limitation Act, 1939).

A mortgagee can enforce his claim for payment in the following ways:

(a) He may sue on the personal covenant to repay contained in the mortgage deed.

(b) He may take possession of the land, though this is not usually done, because a mortgagee in possession must account very strictly, not only for rents and profits which he actually receives, but also for those which he might have received if he had exercised proper care.

(c) He may apply for foreclosure, which is an order of the court fixing the time within which the mortgagor must pay off the debt, with interest and costs, or in default lose his equity of redemption. If the order of foreclosure is not complied with within the time stated therein, the land becomes the property of the mortgagee.

(d) He may appoint a receiver when the statutory power of sale has arisen, by writing under his own hand, to receive the rents and profits of the land and apply them in payment of interest due under the mortgage.

(e) He may sell the property under an express power in the instrument, or under an implied power given by s. 101 of the Law of Property Act, 1925, which gives him power to sell not only the term of years vested in him, but the whole estate, whatever it may be, vested in the mortgagor. Before this power can be exercised the principal money must have been due, and have remained unpaid for at least three months after notice in writing to the mortgagor demanding payment had been given; or some interest must have been two months in arrear; or some covenant in the mortgage deed, other than the covenant to pay principal and interest, must have been broken (s. 103).

In the case of a sale, any other mortgagee, or, if none, the mortgagor, is entitled to any surplus realised.

(2) *Equitable Mortgage*

An equitable mortgage is an agreement or declaration in writing, not necessarily in the form of a deed, which demonstrates an intention to give a legal mortgage of the borrower's property as security for the loan. A deposit of the title deeds relating to the property with the same intention also creates an equitable mortgage.

Equitable mortgages are more simply effected than legal mortgages; and possession of the title deeds, or registration of the mortgage at the Land Registry, will prevent other mortgagees from obtaining priority. An equitable mortgagee's remedies are to sue for the amount of the debt or to apply to the court for the appointment of a receiver, a judicial sale, or foreclosure. If he has made the contract by deed he may, by virtue of the Law of Property Act, 1925, s. 101, appoint a receiver or sell the property without application to the court.

(b) Mortgages of Personal Property

(1) *Mortgage of Choses in Action*

Certain types of choses in action, *e.g.*, book debts and policies of life assurance, can be mortgaged by legal or equitable assignment to the mortgagee with a proviso for re-assignment on repayment of the loan. (As to assignments generally, see Chap. I, § 11 (b).) In other cases special rules apply. Thus, a legal mortgage of shares in a limited company may be effected by transferring the ownership of the shares to the mortgagee with a proviso for re-transfer on repayment; and an equitable mortgage by delivering the share certificate to the mortgagee with or without a blank instrument of transfer.

(2) *Mortgage of Personal Chattels*

A mortgage of personal chattels may be effected orally or, more usually, by an instrument setting out the terms of the mortgage. In the latter case, the instrument must be in the form prescribed by the Bills of Sale Acts (*infra*), and is subject to the rules laid down therein.

§ 6. *Bills of Sale*

(a) Definition and Purpose of Bills of Sale

A bill of sale is a document whereby the property in chattels is transferred to a grantee, either absolutely or conditionally by way of mortgage, possession of the chattels comprised in the bill of sale remaining with the grantor. To afford some protection to persons who might otherwise be persuaded to give credit on the strength of the possession of assets already sold or mortgaged, and also to ensure the proper treatment of needy borrowers, the law requires all bills of sale to be registered and certain other formalities to be observed.

By the Bills of Sale Acts, 1878 and 1882, the expression 'bill of sale' includes:

(1) Bills of sale as specifically understood;
(2) Assignments;
(3) Transfers;
(4) Declarations of trust without transfer;
(5) Inventories of goods with receipts thereto attached;
(6) Receipts for purchase moneys of goods, and other assurances of personal chattels;
(7) Powers of attorney, authorities, or licences to take possession of personal chattels as security for any debt;
(8) Any agreement, whether intended or not to be followed by the execution of any other instrument, by which a right in equity to any personal chattels, or to any charge or security thereon, shall be conferred.

The following classes of instruments do not fall within the definition:

(1) Assignments for the benefit of the grantor's creditors;
(2) Marriage settlements;
(3) Transfers or assignments of any ship or any share thereof;
(4) Transfers of goods in the ordinary course of business,
(5) Bills of sale of goods in foreign parts or at sea;
(6) Bills of lading, warehouse-keepers' certificates, delivery orders used in the ordinary course of business;
(7) An instrument charging or creating any security on or declaring trusts of imported goods given or executed at any time prior to their deposit in a warehouse, factory, or store, or to their being reshipped for export, or delivered to a purchaser not being the person giving or executing such instrument;
(8) Debentures issued by any incorporated company;
(9) Agricultural charges on farming stock and other agricultural assets.

The expression 'personal chattels' in this context means goods, furniture, and other articles capable of complete transfer by delivery, and (when separately assigned or charged) fixtures or growing crops. Trade machinery, with specified limitations, is also so regarded. A bill of sale cannot be given in respect of any chose in action.

In determining whether a document is a bill of sale the court will look beyond the document to the reality of the transaction. Thus, although a genuine hire-purchase contract is not a bill of sale, since it does not transfer the ownership of the goods hired, nevertheless, if the transaction described as a hire-purchase agreement is in substance a loan of money on the security of the goods, it will be invalid unless it complies with the provisions of the Bills of Sale Acts (*Polsky* v. *S. and A. Services* [1951] 1 All E.R. 185).

In *Madell* v. *Thomas* [1891] 1 Q.B. 230, A, wishing to borrow money on the security of chattels, assigned them absolutely to B, who thereupon hired the chattels back to A. It was held that the transaction was a bill of sale and void for want of registration.

In *North Central Wagon Finance Co., Ltd.* v. *Brailsford* [1962] 1 All E.R. 502, Cairns, J., summarised the principles for determining whether a hire-purchase agreement is a bill of sale as follows:

(i) If a person deliberately, with a clear understanding of what he is doing, and with all the proper formalities, sells his property to a finance company and then hires it back under a hire-purchase agreement, the agreement is not a bill of sale.

(ii) If the purpose of the transaction is to enable the hirer to dispose of the property to a customer, the courts will the more readily hold that the agreement is not a bill of sale.

(iii) If the agreement is a mere device to cloak a loan, the document is a bill of sale.

(iv) In considering whether the real transaction is a loan it is necessary to look behind the documents to discover its true nature.

(v) If the facts are not truly stated in the documents, this is a circumstance tending to show that the documents are a mere cloak.

Bills of sale as generally understood may be divided into two classes, namely, absolute and conditional bills.

(b) Absolute Bills of Sale

Absolute bills of sale are governed by the Bills of Sale Act, 1878. In transfers by way of an absolute bill of sale there is an absolute parting with the property in the chattels by the grantor, who has no right of redemption.

An absolute bill of sale need not be in any specified form, but it must show the consideration, if any, for the transaction, and must be explained to the grantor by a solicitor, and witnessed by a solicitor. The grantee may insert any conditions he pleases as to when he shall be entitled to take possession.

(c) Conditional Bills of Sale

A conditional bill of sale is one given as security for the repayment of money, the grantor having the right to have the property in the chattels reconveyed to him upon fulfilling the conditions. Such bills are governed by the Bills of Sale Act (1878) Amendment Act, 1882.

A conditional bill of sale need not be explained by a solicitor, but it must be witnessed by at least one credible witness. It must also be in the exact form given in the Schedule to the Act (s. 9), and must show the consideration, which must not be less than £30 (s. 12), also the rate of interest, the date of repayment, and any condition on the fulfilment of which the bill is to be void. An inventory of the personal chattels comprised in the bill must be attached, each of the chattels being specifically described.

The grantee can only take possession of the goods comprised in a conditional bill of sale where the grantor:

(1) fails to perform any of the covenants contained in the bill;

(2) becomes bankrupt, or allows the goods to be distrained for rent, rates or taxes;

(3) fraudulently removes the goods from the premises;

(4) fails without reasonable excuse to produce his last receipts for rent, rates or taxes after written demand;

(5) allows execution to be levied against the goods under a judgment at law (s. 7).

Even after seizure the goods cannot, without the consent of the grantor, be removed from the premises or sold for five days, and within that period the grantor may apply to the court for relief if by payment or otherwise the cause of seizure no longer exists (s. 13).

The following is the form of a conditional bill of sale:

THIS INDENTURE made the   day of
One thousand nine hundred and   BETWEEN
                                    of

of the one part and
of
of the other part WITNESSETH that in consideration of the sum

(a) Or whatever of (a)
the consideration
may be.

the receipt of which the said   hereby acknowledges
He the said   doth hereby assign unto
                                      his executors administrators and assigns
All and singular the several chattels and things specifically des-
scribed in the schedule hereto annexed by way of security for the
payment of the sum of   Pounds

(b) Insert the and interest thereon at the rate of (b)   per cent. per annum.
rate.   And the said   doth further agree
and declare that he will duly pay to the said
the principal sum aforesaid together with the interest then due by
equal   payments of
on the
in each and every

(c) Insert terms
as to insurance
payment of rent And the said
or otherwise doth also agree with the said
which the parties that he will (c)
may agree to for
the maintenance
or defeasance of
the security.

Provided always that the chattels hereby assigned shall not be
liable to seizure or to be taken possession of by the said
for any cause other than those specified in s. 7 of the Bills of Sale
Act (1878) Amendment Act, 1882. IN WITNESS whereof the
parties to these presents have hereunto set their hands and seals the
day and year first above written.
Signed and sealed by the said

(d) Add wit-   in the presence of me (d)
ness's name, ad-
dress and descrip-
tion.
                    THE SCHEDULE ABOVE REFERRED TO

_____

_____

_____

(d) Registration of Bills of Sale

Every bill of sale, whether absolute or conditional, must be filed with the Registrar of Bills of Sale at the Central Office of the Supreme Court within seven days of execution, and re-registered every five years. There must be produced to the Registrar the original bill, with a true copy of it and every schedule or inventory attached to it; an affidavit of due execution, stating the time it was given, and a description of the residence and occupation of the grantor and all other attesting witnesses. A conditional bill of sale must have attached a schedule specifically enumerating the chattels comprised in it, and chattels afterwards acquired cannot be included, except by way of substitution (s. 6). If the omission to register arises from accident or inadvertence, the court may make an order extending the time for registration.

(e) Avoidance of Bills of Sale

(1) *Absolute Bills*

An absolute bill of sale which is not registered or which does not otherwise comply with the statutory requirements is void against the trustee in bankruptcy or execution creditor of the grantor. It remains perfectly valid, however, as between grantor and grantee.

(2) *Conditional Bills*

A conditional bill of sale which does not comply strictly with the statutory form is altogether void, even as between the parties to the bill (s. 9). Thus, the bill will be void if the name, address, and description of the grantor, grantee, or witness are omitted; or if the receipt clause is absent, or if the copy filed discloses even a trifling error. A term introduced to enable the grantee to retain a bill of sale after payment of the debt will also avoid the bill; and so also will any term which has the effect of introducing covenants not contained in the statutory form, such as, for instance, incorporating terms by reference to another document.

A conditional bill is similarly void if it is given in consideration of a sum under £30 (s. 12).

In the above cases, although the grantee cannot recover payment of principal and interest under the bill, he can recover the principal as money lent, together with interest at 5 per cent. (*Davies* v. *Rees* (1886) 17 Q.B.D. 408).

If the bill is in the proper form, but is not attested or registered, or the consideration is not truly stated, the bill is void against all persons *in respect of the personal chattels comprised therein* (s. 8). But in other respects the bill remains valid, so that the covenants contained therein are enforceable (*Heseltine* v. *Simmons* [1892] 2 Q.B. 547).

If any of the chattels comprised in the bill are not specifically described in the schedule to the bill, or the schedule includes chattels of which the grantor was not the true owner at the time of the execution of the bill, the bill is void, *except as against the grantor*, in respect of any chattels so omitted or included (ss. 4, 5). A person is the 'true owner' if he is the legal owner of the goods even though he holds the goods on trust for another (*Re Sarl* [1892] 2 Q.B. 591). A person who holds goods under a hire-purchase agreement giving an option to purchase but imposing no obligation to do so is not the true owner of the goods (*Lewis* v. *Thomas* [1919] 1 K.B. 319); nor is a person the true owner who has already assigned the chattels by an absolute bill of sale, even though the bill has not been registered (*Tuck* v. *Southern Counties Deposit Bank* (1889) 42 Ch. D. 471). But a person who has granted a conditional bill of sale over the goods remains the true owner for this purpose, as he still has the equity of redemption in the goods (*Thomas* v. *Searles* [1891] 2 Q.B. 408). These provisions do not apply to growing crops separately assigned, or to fixtures, plant, or trade machinery afterwards substituted for the like articles which were specifically described in the schedule (s. 6).

The inclusion in the schedule of chattels to be acquired subsequently to the execution of the bill, other than those specified in s. 6, will render the whole bill void under s. 9, since such chattels are not 'personal chattels' within the meaning of the Act, and the bill is not, therefore, in the statutory form (*Thomas* v. *Kelly* (1888) 13 App. Cas. 506).

Apart from avoidance under the Act itself, if the bill contains any condition on the fulfilment of which the bill is to be avoided, this will be effective if the condition is set out in the statutory form.

§ 7. *Pledges*

A pledge is a bailment of goods as security for a loan. It involves an actual delivery by the pledgor of the article pledged, either to the pledgee or to a warehouse for him, in either case a receipt being given for the pledge.

Where actual delivery of possession is impossible, it may be given constructively, *e.g.*, by the delivery of a key, under such circumstances that full control of the place where the goods are stored is given by the delivery of the key. The actual property in the goods pledged remains with the pledgor, but a special property passes to the pledgee, in order that he may dispose of the goods if and when he becomes entitled to do so.

A pledgee impliedly undertakes to deliver back the property to the pledgor upon repayment of the sum advanced upon the property, and the pledgor impliedly warrants his own title to the property.

As in the case of other bailments, the pledgee is answerable for any negligence in respect of the goods pledged while they are in his possession; and he must not use the goods, unless to do so would be for the benefit of the goods.

Upon default in payment being made by the pledgor, the pledgee may sell the property at the stipulated time or after giving proper notice.

The distinction between a mortgage and a pledge is that, in the case of a mortgage, the legal ownership or an equivalent interest is transferred to the person lending the money, possession remaining with the borrower; whereas, in the case of a pledge, the legal ownership remains with the borrower, possession being transferred to the person lending the money.

Pledges are frequently effected with pawnbrokers, who are persons licensed to carry on the business of lending money on goods taken into pawn. Such pledges are governed by the Pawnbrokers Acts, 1872 and 1960, if they are for loans of £50 or less. Pledges above that amount are governed by the rules of common law. Special contracts may be made in respect of loans exceeding £5, but in such cases a special pawn-ticket must be given by the pawnbroker and signed by him, a duplicate being also signed by the pledgor.

The rate of interest that may be charged in respect of loans not exceeding £5 is limited to one halfpenny for every 10p or part per month. After the first month, less than fourteen days is counted as half a month, fourteen days or more up to one month as one month. On pledges above £5 the interest is limited to one halfpenny per month for each 12½p or part.

The goods pledged are made redeemable within six months from the day of pawning, including that day, with seven days of grace added. If the pledge is for £2, or under, it becomes the absolute property of the pawnbroker at the expiration of the time when it ceases to be redeemable; if the pledge is for more than £2, it is redeemable until sale, which must be by public auction. The pawnbroker must account for surplus receipts on sales within three years where the pledge is for over £2.

A pawnbroker must give a pawn-ticket in respect of each pledge, and the holder of the ticket is presumed to be the person entitled to redeem the property. The pawnbroker must deliver the property to him on payment of the loan and interest; but where a person's goods have been pledged without his authority, he may recover from the pawnbroker, so long as the person making the pledge could give no title to the property (see Chap. III, § 1 (b) (2)).

If a pawn-ticket is lost, a new ticket may be obtained by a declaration before a magistrate; the form of declaration must be shown to the pawnbroker within three days, after which the pawnbroker must not deliver to the holder of the original ticket.

If the goods pawned are destroyed by accidental fire, the pawn-broker is responsible for the loss. If he purchases, except at a public auction, any article pledged to him, he commits an offence under the Acts.

§ 8. *Liens*

(a) Possessory Liens

A *possessory* lien is the right of a person in possession of goods which belong to another to retain the goods until his pecuniary de-mands against that other are satisfied. Possessory liens are either general or particular.

(1) *General Lien*

A *general* lien is the right which arises by custom in particular trades or professions, or by contract, to retain goods not only until any sum due in respect of them is paid, but also until payment of any other sum which may be owing by the owner to the person in possession.

By custom a solicitor has a general lien over all the papers of his client, except his will; a factor over the goods of his principal; and other classes of persons who have a general lien are bankers, stock-brokers, insurance brokers, wharfingers, dyers, and calico printers. A banker has no lien over documents deposited with him for safe custody only, as he is not regarded as having legal possession of them.

(2) *Particular Lien*

A *particular* lien is the right to retain goods until payment of any sum due to the possessor by the owner *in respect of those goods*.

A particular lien arises in favour of a person who has by contract bestowed labour, skill or expense in improving or repairing goods, though not for merely maintaining a chattel, *e.g.*, for feeding a horse or servicing a motor car (*Hatton* v. *Car Maintenance Co.* (1915) 30 T.L.R. 275). An unpaid seller of goods, an unpaid carrier of goods, and an unpaid warehouseman also have rights of lien at common law or by statute.

For a lien to arise, the possession must be lawful and continuous. Thus, a garage proprietor has no lien on a car garaged with him, as the car can be taken away whenever the owner wishes (*Hatton* v. *Car Maintenance Co.*, *supra*).

There is no lien for services until the work contracted for is actually performed; but if the owner prevents completion of the work, the lien attaches for the work actually done. If the owner has not authorised the work, the lien cannot be enforced against him, but subject to his rights it can be enforced against the person at whose request the work was done.

A hirer of goods will normally have an implied authority to have the goods repaired, if necessary, and the repairer will therefore have a lien over the goods against the owner, even where the contract of hire purports to limit the hirer's power to create a lien (*Albemarle Supply Co., Ltd.* v. *Hind & Co.* [1928] 1 K.B. 307). But the lien cannot be enforced against the owner if the goods were not delivered to the repairer until after the contract of hire was determined (*Bowmaker, Ltd.* v. *Wycombe Motors, Ltd.* [1946] K.B. 505).

An innkeeper's lien (see *ante*, § 2 (c)) is of a special character: it is not particular, for the debt does not necessarily arise in respect of the goods detained but from the supply of accommodation and refreshment, and it is not general, inasmuch as the innkeeper is not entitled to exercise the right in regard to charges incurred by the guest upon the occasion of a previous visit.

(3) *Enforcement of Lien*

A lien confers only a passive right of detention until a debt is paid. No claim may be made for storage or keep, and there is no right of sale unless this arises by trade usage, or is expressly provided for by agreement or statute, *e.g.*, under the Sale of Goods Act, 1893, and the Disposal of Uncollected Goods Act, 1952 (*q.v.*). Where there is no right of sale, an application may be made to the court for an order for sale.

(4) *Discharge of Lien*

A lien is discharged by payment of the debt, or balance of account, as the case may be; or by giving credit for the amount due; or by lawfully losing possession of the property; or by acceptance of security, if the intention is to discharge the lien.

(b) Maritime Liens

A maritime lien is a right which consists of the power to have a ship or cargo and certain interests therein realised, and the proceeds applied in satisfaction of the sum due to the person having the lien. Maritime liens do not depend on possession, but attach to the subject-matter, wherever it may be.

The principal maritime liens so arising are those of:

(1) bottomry bondholders;

(2) master for wages and disbursements;

(3) sailors for services rendered;

(4) seamen for wages;

(5) ship damaged by collision, against the ship in default.

When the master borrows money upon the ship, or upon the ship and cargo, the instrument by which he engages to repay the sum borrowed is called a bottomry bond. He must not raise money on bottomry unless it is absolutely necessary for the completion of the voyage and then only if he cannot obtain it on the shipowner's personal credit, or from the owner's agent, and he is unable to communicate with the owner. It is a peculiarity of the bottomry bond that if the ship is lost the lender loses the whole of his money, but if it returns in safety then he recovers the principal and interest agreed upon.

The claim of a bottomry bondholder ranks for payment out of the security in priority to any mortgage but subsequently to any sum due for wages after the issue of the bottomry bond or salvage. As between several bottomry bondholders in relation to the same vessel, the order of payment is the reverse order in which the bonds were created, *i.e.*, the last bond given is the first for payment, and so on.

Since the holder of a bottomry bond has a lien on the vessel, the vessel cannot be disposed of without discharge of the bond. If the sum secured is not paid by the shipowner, the court may order the ship to be sold with a view to discharging the liability, subject to the claims of those who may have a prior right.

The cargo can only be hypothecated if it receives some actual or possible benefit from the transaction; and the master can only bind the cargo owner after communicating with the owner, or endeavouring to do so, unless such notice is not required by the law of the country in which the ship is registered. The bond by which a cargo alone is hypothecated is known as a *respondentia bond*.

(c) Equitable Liens

An equitable lien is a right conferred by equity upon a person to have certain property applied in a particular manner. It differs from a possessory lien in that it exists irrespective of possession and confers on the holder the right to a judicial sale. The partnership lien is one example (see Chap. VIII, § 4 (e)); others are the lien of a vendor of land for unpaid purchase money, and the lien of a purchaser for prematurely paid purchase money, such as a deposit paid by him on the signing of the contract to purchase.

In general, a person who has expended money for the benefit of another or on another's property has no lien in respect of such expenditure, but, when all parties interested in property act in the mistaken belief that one of them is the true owner and allow him to spend money for the preservation of the property, that one is entitled to an equitable lien on the property for the sums so spent by him.

In *Re Foster* [1938] 3 All E.R. 610, a father took out a policy of life assurance on the life of his son. The father paid the premiums until his death, and thereafter the son continued to pay them under an arrangement between all parties interested in the policy, in the belief that the policy belonged to him. The son died, and the insurance company, without raising any question as to whether the father had such an insurable interest in his son's life as to make the policy valid, paid out the proceeds on the joint receipt of the personal representatives of the father and son, and questions arose as to how the moneys should be applied.

Held: The father had created no trust in favour of the son, and accordingly the policy moneys belonged to the father's estate, subject to a lien in favour of the personal representatives of the son for the amount of the premiums paid by him subsequent to the father's death.

CHAPTER VI

INSURANCE

§ 1. *Nature of Contract of Insurance*

(a) Definition of Insurance

A contract of insurance is one having for its object the indemnification against loss, or the payment of a specified sum upon the happening of a certain event. The principal forms of insurance are life, fire and marine; fire and marine insurance being contracts of indemnity, and life insurance being a contract for a specified sum. Almost any risk, however, can be made the subject of a contract of insurance, and, in particular, accidents, employers' liability, and burglary are very commonly insured against.

The parties to a contract of insurance are the *insurer*, who is sometimes known as the assurer or underwriter, and the *insured*. The insurer is the person taking the risk, and agreeing to indemnify or pay a fixed sum on the happening of a particular event; and the insured is the person paying the premium for the consideration that he may be indemnified or receive payment. The contract is generally evidenced by an instrument known as a policy.

(b) Insurable Interest

It is important to distinguish between a contract of insurance and a mere wagering contract. A wagering contract is of no legal effect, so that if policies are merely wagering agreements, the court will not enforce them (*Gedge* v. *Royal Exchange Assurance Corporation* [1900] 2 Q.B. 214), and the premiums paid cannot be recovered, unless the parties are not *in pari delicto* (see Chap. I, § 9). *Prima facie* there is very little difference between speculating as to whether a horse will win a certain race, or whether a particular ship will be lost upon a given voyage. The difference is that, as regards a wager, the parties to the agreement suffer no loss or detriment, apart from the stake, whatever the result may be; whereas in the case of a valid contract of insurance the insured must have an *insurable interest* in the thing insured.

An insurable interest exists where a person 'is so circumstanced with respect to the subject-matter of the policy as to have benefit from its existence or prejudice from its destruction' (*Lucena* v. *Craufurd* (1806) 2 Bos. & P.N.R. 269). Save in some forms of life assurance the interest must be a pecuniary one, so that a contract of insurance is as a rule a contract of indemnity against pecuniary loss.

(c) Uberrima Fides

A contract of insurance is one of the class *uberrimae fidei* (see Chap. I, § 8 (b) (2)), because it is a type of contract in which, as a rule, one party is peculiarly in possession of facts unknown to the other at the time the contract is negotiated. The result is that all material facts within the knowledge of the parties must be disclosed, otherwise the contract may be avoided by the party to whom disclosure should have been made. This rule applies to all classes of insurance contracts. The test as to the materiality of a particular fact is whether or not the fact, if disclosed, would have influenced a reasonable underwriter to decline the risk, or to have stipulated for a higher premium (*Mutual Life Assurance Co. of New York* v. *Ontario Metal Products Co., Ltd.* [1925] A.C. 344).

The rule as to disclosure is binding upon an agent as well as a principal, so that if the contract is entered into by an agent of the insured, non-disclosure by the agent will render the contract void, even though the principal did not know of the particular fact which ought to have been disclosed (*Blackburn, Low & Co.* v. *Haslam* (1888) 21 Q.B.D. 144). But disclosure to an agent of the insurer is not sufficient to bind the latter if the particular fact is not disclosed in the proposal form which forms the basis of the contract (*Newsholme Bros.* v. *Road Transport and General Insurance Co., Ltd.* [1929] 2 K.B. 356).

A false statement in a proposal form for a fire insurance policy that the proposer's insurance had not previously been refused by any other office has been held to be a concealment of a material fact which would render the policy void, even though the proposal previously refused was one for a motor policy (*Locker and Woolf, Ltd.* v. *Western Australian Insurance Co.* [1936] 1 K.B. 408). The refusal of a proposal made by one of the partners in a firm on his own behalf is a material fact which must be disclosed in any proposal on behalf of the partnership (*Glicksman* v. *Lancashire and General Assurance Co.* [1937] A.C. 139).

If a material alteration of the risk arises between the date of the proposal and the issue of the policy, this must be disclosed to the insurer, otherwise he will be entitled to avoid the contract (*Looker* v. *Law Union and Rock Insurance Co., Ltd.* [1928] 1 K.B. 554).

The contract is voidable whether non-disclosure of a material fact is innocent or fraudulent. If it is fraudulent the insurer may retain all premiums paid; if innocent, he must repay them unless the contract expressly provides for forfeiture.

When it is expressly stated that the validity of the contract is conditional upon the truth of the statements contained in the proposal, the insurer incurs no liability if a proposal contains an untrue statement, whether or not the statement is material (*Dawsons, Ltd.* v. *Bonnin* [1922] 2 A.C. 413).

(d) Reinsurance

Reinsurance is the act of insuring a risk by an insurer who has already made himself liable in respect of it. Misrepresentation of any facts for the purpose of obtaining a reinsurance will vitiate the contract.

Reinsurance is resorted to for the purpose of spreading the risk over a number of insurers, and arrangements are made by means of 'treaties' with other insurance companies or underwriters for a specified proportion of the risk to be taken over by the latter in consideration of payment of a part of the premium received. Certain companies restrict their activities to undertaking reinsurance business. Risks of considerable magnitude are thus undertaken directly or indirectly by several insurers. In such cases the person originally insured has rights only against the insurer who has issued the policy; it is for the latter to recover from the reinsurers the due proportion of the amount of the loss sustained.

If the insurer successfully resists a claim by the insured, but is unable to recover his costs, he cannot claim to be reimbursed proportionately by the reinsurer unless there is a special term in the treaty to that effect, as the loss was not one for which the insurer (and consequently the reinsurer) was liable (*Scottish Metropolitan Assurance Co., Ltd.* v. *Groom* (1923) 157 L.T. 511).

(e) Double Insurance

Double insurance arises where a person effects more than one insurance with different insurers for the same risk and interest. If a loss is incurred, he can only recover to the extent of such loss, so far as the contract of insurance is a contract of indemnity. He may, however, recover from whichever of the insurers he chooses, and the one who pays him will have a right of contribution against the other insurer (see *post*, § 4 (o)(3)). If the insured receives any excess, he must hold it in trust for the insurers to whom it is due (*Kidston* v. *Empire Insurance Co.* (1866) L.R. 1 C.P. 535). This does not apply to life assurance, which is not a contract of indemnity, so that a person can insure his life for any amount with any number of insurers and the sums due under the various policies will all be recoverable in full.

(f) Insurance Companies Act, 1958

Companies which carry on the business of insurance in the United Kingdom are subject to the provisions of the Insurance Companies Act, 1958 and to the Companies Act, 1967 which is designed to ensure the solvency of such companies. The Act does not apply to the Corporation of Lloyd's, nor to any other association of underwriters approved by the Board of Trade, except in certain minor respects, *e.g.*, that accounts must be subjected to a yearly audit by a professional accountant.

§ 2. *Life Assurance*

(a) Nature of Contract

In a contract of life assurance the insurer undertakes to pay to the person for whose benefit the contract is entered into a sum of money or an annuity, upon the death of the person whose life is insured, in consideration of either a single premium or a number of periodical premiums paid to him.

In the case of an *endowment* policy, the liability of the insurer accrues either on the death of the insured or at a specified date, whichever is first in point of time.

(b) Insurable Interest

The Life Assurance Act, 1774, makes statutory the rule that a person may not insure another's life unless he has an insurable interest in it, and he cannot recover under any life assurance policy a greater amount than the value of his interest. The policy must state the name of the person interested therein or for whose benefit it is taken out.

It is not essential that the interest should exist except *at the time the policy is made* (*Dalby* v. *India and Life Assurance Co.* (1854) 15 C.B. 365). Moreover, provided that the sum assured at the outset was supported by an insurable interest of equivalent amount, the full amount assured can be recovered on the death, even if the insurable interest has declined in value.

The following rules have been laid down by the courts as to persons who have an insurable interest:

(1) A creditor may insure his debtor's life for a sum equal to the debt owing to him, and he will have an insurable interest to that extent (*Godsall* v. *Boldero* (1807) 9 East 72); and the insurance will hold good even though the debt itself is extinguished before the maturity of the policy.

(2) A wife has an insurable interest in the life of her husband, and a husband in that of his wife (*Griffiths* v. *Fleming* [1909] 1 K.B. 805).

(3) A man may always insure his own life for his own benefit (*McFarlane* v. *Royal London Friendly Society* (1886) 2 T.L.R. 755).

(4) A parent has not as a rule an insurable interest in the life of his child (*Halford* v. *Kymer* (1830) 10 B. & C. 724); nor a child in the life of his parent, unless the parent is supporting the child (*Howard* v. *Refuge Friendly Society* (1886) 54 L.T. 644).

(5) A sister has normally no insurable interest in the life of her brother, but may have to the extent of his funeral expenses, if she

has a *bona fide* expectation of having to meet those expenses (*O'Brien* v. *Irish National Insurance Co*. (1932) Ir. Rep. 532).

(c) Suicide of Assured

In *Beresford* v. *Royal Insurance Co*. [1938] A.C. 586, it was held that life assurance policy moneys could not be claimed from an assurance company by the assured's personal representatives if he committed suicide while sane, even if the policy provided that the moneys should be payable in such an event, for to allow the personal representatives to recover the fruits of the deceased's crime would be against public policy. Although, by the Suicide Act, 1961, suicide is no longer a crime, it is considered that this decision would still apply on general grounds of public policy (see Chap. I, § 9 (h)). If, however, the assured killed himself during a period of temporary insanity, the sum due may be recovered by his personal representatives unless the policy otherwise provides (*Horn* v. *Anglo-Australian Co*. (1861) 30 L.J. Ch. 511).

(d) Married Women's Property Act, 1882

A policy effected by a man on his own life and expressed to be for the benefit of his wife or children creates a trust in favour of the persons therein named. The policy moneys do not form part of his estate and are not subject to his debts unless the policy was effected with intent to defraud creditors. The position is similar if a woman effects a policy on her life for the benefit of her husband or children (Married Women's Property Act, 1882, s. 11).

If the wife for whose benefit a Married Women's Property Act policy is effected predeceases the assured, the policy forms part of her estate, and when the assured dies the policy moneys will be paid to her personal representatives (*Cousins* v. *Sun Life Assurance Society* [1933] 1 Ch. 126).

A policy effected by a person on his own life and expressed to be for the benefit of a person other than his spouse or children does not, unless so expressed, create any trust in favour of that person, and accordingly the beneficiary, as a stranger to the contract, has no right to claim the policy moneys, which will belong to the deceased's estate (*Re Sinclair's Life Policy* [1938] Ch. 799). If a person for whose benefit a policy is taken out pays the premiums under the mistaken belief of all parties that he has a legal right to the policy moneys, he will have a lien on the policy moneys for the premiums so paid by him (*Re Foster, ante*, p. 234).

(e) Assignment of Policy

A life policy may be assigned under the provisions of the Policies of Assurance Act, 1867, by indorsement of the policy or by a separate instrument. Written notice must be given to the insurer, and the insurer must give a certificate acknowledging receipt of such notice. An assignment for value which does not comply with the statutory requirements may nevertheless take effect as a valid equitable assignment (*Thomas* v. *Harris* [1947] 1 All E.R. 444). The assignee takes subject to equities in any case, *i.e.*, any defence which would have been good against the assignor is good against him.

By means of the assignment of the policy a person may insure his life, and transfer the policy to a third party who could not have insured the assignor himself because he had no insurable interest. So long as the insurable interest exists when the contract is entered into, the assignee is not bound to prove any interest of his own (*Ashley* v. *Ashley* (1829) 3 Sim. 149).

§ 3. *Fire Insurance*

(a) Nature of Contract

A contract of fire insurance is a contract whereby the insurer agrees to indemnify the insured against loss by fire, in respect of the subject-matter of the policy, for a consideration consisting of a premium paid by the insured. The contract is purely one of indemnity, and the party suffering the loss can only recover to the extent of the loss, so far as it does not exceed the sum insured.

In *Castellain* v. *Preston* (1883) 11 Q.B.D. 380, a house which was contracted to be sold was burnt down between the dates of the contract and the conveyance. The vendor recovered under the insurance policy, and subsequently received the full purchase money from the buyer, who remained bound. The vendor was held obliged to return to the insurance company the sum received under the policy, as he had suffered no loss by reason of the fire.

It is now provided by s. 47 of the Law of Property Act, 1925, that money which becomes payable in respect of damage to property the subject of a contract of sale under a policy of insurance maintained by the vendor is to be paid by the latter to the purchaser on completion. This rule is subject to any contrary stipulation in the contract, to any necessary consents of insurers, and to payment by the purchaser of a proportionate part of the premium.

By the Fires Prevention (Metropolis) Act, 1774, s. 83, if a building is burned down, *any interested person* (*e.g.*, a tenant) may require the insurance money to be laid out in rebuilding the premises. The provisions of this section of the Act are not confined to the Metropolitan area, but have universal application in England. By s. 108 of the Law of Property Act, 1925, a mortgagee may require all money received on an insurance of mortgaged property against loss or damage by fire to be applied by the mortgagor in making good the loss or damage in respect of which the money is received, or, in the absence of agreement (or obligation) to the contrary effect, that such money be applied in or towards the discharge of the mortgage.

(b) Insurable Interest

The insured must have an insurable interest, and this will generally exist to the extent of any right or interest in respect of the subject-matter of the insurance.

The insurable interest must exist *at the time of the loss* if a claim is to be supported, and it is generally considered that in the case of buildings the interest must also have existed at the time the contract of insurance was entered into.

A man can always insure his own property; a trustee may insure the trust property; and a mortgagee may insure the mortgaged property (*Westminster Fire Office* v. *Glasgow Provident Investment Society* (1888) 13 App. Cas. 699). Neither a shareholder of a company, even though he holds practically the whole of the shares, nor an unsecured creditor has any insurable interest in the property of the company (*Macaura* v. *Northern Assurance Co., Ltd.* [1925] A.C. 619).

(c) Ratification of Policy

If a contract of fire insurance is entered into by an agent without authority, the insured cannot ratify after he becomes aware of the loss of the subject-matter of the insurance (*Grover* v. *Matthews* [1910] 2 K.B. 401).

(d) Average Clause

If the policy contains an *average clause*, the assured can only recover such proportion of any loss as the amount insured bears to the whole value of the property insured, so that if the property is insured for less than its true value, the whole loss, even though less than the total sum insured, cannot be recovered. For example, suppose A insures buildings worth £10,000 for £1,000 and suffers damage to the extent of £1,000. If the policy contains an average clause, A can only recover £100. But if there is no average clause, A can recover the whole loss he has suffered up to the extent of the amount insured, *i.e.*, £1,000.

(e) Subrogation

Where the insurer has paid what is due from him under the policy, upon the occasion of a loss, he is entitled by the *doctrine of subrogation* to every legal and equitable right of the insured, whether the right arises out of contract or tort. If, for example, an insurer pays the owner of a burnt-out vehicle on the basis of a total loss, he is entitled to the wreck to make from it what he can; and if the fire was caused by the negligent act of a third party, the insurer is entitled to maintain an action in tort against that party and recover damages.

(f) Assignment of Policy

A fire insurance policy may be assigned *only with the consent of the insurer* (*Saddlers' Company* v. *Badcock* (1743) 2 Atk. 554); and if this is not obtained, the insurance will not follow the property upon a change of ownership. But a mortgage of property together with the benefit of a fire insurance policy is not an assignment requiring the consent of the insurer.

§ 4. *Marine Insurance*

The law relating to marine insurance has been codified by the Marine Insurance Act, 1906.

(a) Definition and Extent of Marine Insurance

The Act defines a contract of marine insurance as a contract whereby the insurer undertakes to indemnify the insured, in manner and to the extent thereby agreed, against the losses incident to a marine adventure (s. 1).

A contract of marine insurance may, by its express terms, or by usage of trade, be extended so as to protect the insured against losses on inland waters or against any land risk incidental to a sea voyage (s. 2 (1)).

(b) Insurable Interest

Every person has an insurable interest who is interested in a marine adventure, and particularly where he stands in any legal or equitable relation to the adventure, or any insurable property at risk therein, in consequence of which he may benefit by the safety or due arrival of insurable property, or may be prejudiced by its loss, damage, or detention, or may incur liability in respect thereof (s. 5).

The insured must be interested in the subject-matter insured *at the time of the loss*, though he need not be interested when the insurance is effected. Where the subject-matter is insured 'lost or not lost,' he may recover, although he may not have acquired his interest until after the loss, unless at the time of effecting the contract of insurance the insured was aware of the loss, and the insurer was not.

The following persons have an insurable interest:

(1) The lender of money on bottomry or respondentia (see Chap. V, § 8 (b)), in respect of the loan (s. 10).

(2) The master or any member of the crew, in respect of his wages (s. 11).

(3) A person advancing freight, in so far as the freight is not repayable in case of loss (s. 12).

(4) A mortgagor, to the full value of the property; and the mortgagee, in respect of any sum due under the mortgage (s. 14 (1)).

(5) The owner of insurable property, in respect of the full value thereof, notwithstanding that some third person may have agreed, or be liable, to indemnify him in case of loss (s. 14 (3)).

The underwriter has an insurable interest in his risk, and may re-insure in respect of it; but unless the policy otherwise provides, the original insured has no right or interest in respect of such reinsurance (s. 9).

(c) Gaming and Wagering Policies

Every contract of marine insurance by way of gaming or wagering is void; and such a contract is deemed to be a gaming or wagering contract (s. 4):

(1) Where the insured has not an insurable interest, and the contract is entered into with no expectation of acquiring such an interest; or

(2) Where the policy is made 'interest or no interest,' or 'without further proof of interest than the policy itself,' or subject to any other like term.

(3) Where the policy is made 'without benefit of salvage to the insurer,' unless there is no possibility of salvage.

By the Marine Insurance (Gambling Policies) Act, 1909, if any person effects a contract of marine insurance without having a *bona fide* interest direct or indirect, or a *bona fide* expectation of acquiring such an interest, or if any person in the employment of the owner of a ship, not being a part-owner thereof, effects a contract of marine insurance in relation to the ship, which is made 'interest or no interest,' or 'without further proof of interest than the policy itself,' or 'without benefit of salvage to the insurer,' or subject to any other like term, the person effecting it is guilty of an offence for which, on summary conviction, he may be imprisoned for a term not exceeding six months, or fined a sum not exceeding £100; and in either case any money received under the contract is forfeited to the Crown.

(d) Disclosure by the Insured

The contract being *uberrimae fidei*, if the utmost good faith is not observed by one party the contract may be avoided by the other party (s. 17). It is therefore essential that all material circumstances within the knowledge of the insured be disclosed by him to the insurer before the contract is concluded. But in the absence of inquiry he need not disclose any circumstances diminishing the risk, or as to which information is waived by the insurer, or which are a matter of notoriety, and therefore presumably known to the insurer, or which it is superfluous to disclose by reason of any express or implied warranty (s. 18).

The insured is deemed to know every material fact which, having regard to the nature of his business, he ought to know, and if he fails to disclose such facts the underwriters are not liable, even though they also might have been aware of such facts in the ordinary course of their business (*London General Insurance Co.* v. *General Marine Underwriters' Association* [1921] 1 K.B. 104).

Where an insurance is effected for the insured by an agent, the agent must disclose to the insurer every material circumstance which is known to himself, and every material circumstance which the insured is bound to disclose, unless it comes to the knowledge of the insured too late to communicate it to the agent (s. 19).

Every material representation made by the insured or his agent to the insurer during the negotiations for the contract, and before the contract is concluded, must be true. If it is untrue the insurer may avoid the contract. A representation as to a matter of fact is true if it is substantially correct, and a representation as to a matter of expectation or belief is true if it is made in good faith. A representation may be withdrawn or corrected before the contract is concluded (s. 20).

(e) Ratification of Policy

Where a contract of marine insurance is in good faith effected by one person on behalf of another, the person on whose behalf it is effected may ratify the contract *even after he is aware of a loss* (s. 86).

(f) Form of Policy

Particulars of the insurance are first entered upon a 'slip,' which is the foundation of the contract. The slip does not itself form any legal contract; but if there is a stamped policy in existence, the slip may be referred to in legal proceedings in order to arrive at the true terms of the contract (s. 90).

A contract of marine insurance must be incorporated in a marine insurance policy (s. 22), and signed by or on behalf of the insurers (s. 24). If must specify (s. 23):

(1) the name of the insured or some person who effects the insurance on his behalf;
(2) the subject-matter insured and the risk insured against;
(3) the voyage or period of time covered by the insurance;
(4) the sum insured; and
(5) the name of the insurers.

The nature and extent of the insured's interest in the subject-matter need not be specified in the policy (s. 26 (2)).

The Act contains a form of policy in its First Schedule.

(g) Classification of Policies

(1) *Voyage and Time Policies*

Where the contract is to insure the subject-matter 'at and from,' or from one place to another or others, the policy is called a *voyage policy*; and where the contract is to insure the subject-matter for a definite period of time, the policy is called a *time policy*. A contract for both voyage and time may be included in the same policy (s. 25 (1)), this being described as a *mixed policy*.

(2) Valued Policy

A *valued policy* is one which specifies the agreed value of the subject-matter insured (s. 27 (2)). If a total loss occurs, the amount recoverable under a valued policy is the sum for which the ship is so insured, without having regard to her actual value at the time of the loss; and in the absence of fraud or other circumstances vitiating the whole policy, the question of value cannot be re-opened.

(3) Unvalued Policy

An *unvalued policy* is a policy which does not specify the value of the subject-matter insured, but, subject to the limit of the sum insured, leaves the insurable value to be subsequently ascertained (s. 28).

(4) Floating Policy

A *floating policy* is a policy which describes the insurance in general terms, and leaves the name of the ship or ships and other particulars to be defined by subsequent declaration. The subsequent declaration or declarations may be made by indorsement on the policy, or in other customary manner.

Unless the policy otherwise provides, where a declaration of value is not made until after notice of loss or arrival, the policy must be treated as an unvalued policy as regards the subject-matter of that declaration (s. 29).

(h) The Premium

Where an insurance is effected at a premium to be arranged, and no arrangement is made, a reasonable premium is payable; and where an insurance is effected on the terms that an additional premium is to be arranged in a given event, and that event happens but no arrangement is made, then a reasonable additional premium is payable (s. 31).

(i) Double Insurance

The rule as to double insurance applies as in the case of other insurances for indemnity (s. 32).

(j) Warranties

A warranty, which may be expressed or implied, is an undertaking by the insured that some particular thing shall or shall not be done, or that some stipulation shall be fulfilled, or that a particular state of facts does, or does not, exist. Such an undertaking must be exactly complied with, whether it is material to the risk or not. If it is not so complied with, then subject to any express provision in the policy, the insurer is discharged from liability as from the date of the breach of warranty, but without prejudice to any liability incurred by him before that date (s. 33). A warranty, therefore, in a contract of marine insurance, is substantially the same as a condition in any other contract, and gives the injured party the right to avoid the contract as well as to bring an action for damages.

Non-compliance with a warranty is excused when, by reason of a change of circumstances, the warranty ceases to be applicable to the circumstances of the contract, or when compliance with the warranty is rendered unlawful by any change in the law. If a warranty is broken, the insured cannot avail himself of the defence that the breach has been remedied, and the warranty complied with, before loss; but a breach of warranty may be waived by the insurer (s. 34).

(1) *Express Warranties*

An express warranty may be in any form of words from which the intention to warrant is to be inferred; it must be included in, or written upon, the policy, or must be contained in some document incorporated by reference into the policy. An express warranty does not exclude an implied warranty, unless it is inconsistent therewith (s. 35).

(2) *Implied Warranties*

The Act makes the following provisions as to implied warranties (ss. 36–41):

(i) There is no implied warranty as to the nationality of a ship, or that her nationality shall not be changed during the risk, but where a ship is expressly warranted 'neutral,' there is an implied condition that the property shall have a neutral character at the commencement of the risk, and that the insured will do his best to preserve it, and that if the subject-matter is a ship, she shall carry the necessary papers to establish her neutrality.

(ii) In a voyage policy there is an implied warranty that at the commencement of the voyage the ship shall be seaworthy for the purpose of the particular adventure insured.

(iii) Where the policy attaches while the ship is in port, there is an implied warranty that she shall, at the commencement of the risk, be reasonably fit to encounter the ordinary perils of the port.

(iv) Where the policy relates to a voyage which is performed in different stages, during which the ship requires different kinds of, or further, preparation or equipment, there is an implied warranty that at the commencement of each stage the ship is seaworthy in respect of such preparation or equipment for the purposes of that stage.

(v) In a time policy there is no implied warranty that the ship shall be seaworthy at any stage of the adventure; but where, with the privity of the insured, the ship is sent to sea in an unseaworthy state, the insurer is not liable for any loss attributable to unseaworthiness.

(vi) In a policy on goods or other movables there is no implied warranty that the goods or movables are seaworthy, but there is an implied warranty that at the commencement of the voyage the ship is not only seaworthy as a ship, but also that she is reasonably fit to carry the goods or other movables to the destination contemplated by the policy.

(vii) There is an implied warranty that the adventure insured is a lawful one, and that, so far as the insured can control the matter, the adventure shall be carried out in a lawful manner.

A ship is deemed to be seaworthy if she is reasonably fit in all respects to encounter the ordinary perils of the seas of the adventure insured. In the case of a voyage policy, if the ship is lost from some cause totally unconnected with seaworthiness, the policy will nevertheless be avoided if in fact the ship was not seaworthy at the commencement of the voyage; and the fact that the insured had no knowledge that the ship was unseaworthy will not avail him (*Quebec Marine Insurance Co.* v. *Commercial Bank of Canada* (1870) L.R. 3 P.C. 234).

In the case of a time policy, the insurer can only avoid liability if the loss was due to the unseaworthiness to which the insured was privy.

In *Thomas* v. *Tyne and Wear S.S. Freight Insurance Association* [1917] 1 K.B. 938, a ship, insured under a time policy, put to sea with her hull in a defective condition, and with an insufficient crew. The insured owner was aware of the latter but not of the former defect. The ship was lost as a result of the defective hull. The insurers were held to be liable.

If, in this case, the insurance had been effected under a voyage policy where the warranty of seaworthiness is absolute, the insurers could have successfully repudiated liability.

(k) Rules as to the Voyage

Where the subject-matter is insured by a voyage policy 'at and from' or 'from' a particular place, it is not necessary that the ship should be at that place *when the contract is made;* but there is an implied condition that the adventure will be commenced within a reasonable time, unless the delay is caused by circumstances known to the insurer before the contract was concluded, or he waives the condition (s. 42). If the ship, instead of sailing from the place of departure specified by the policy, sails from any other place, or, instead of sailing for the destination specified in the policy, sails for any other destination, the risk does not attach (ss. 43, 44).

Where, after the commencement of the risk, the destination of the ship is voluntarily changed from the destination contemplated by the policy, the insurer is discharged from liability as from the time when the determination to change it is manifested; and it is immaterial that the ship may not in fact have left the course of voyage contemplated by the policy when the loss occurs (s. 45).

Where a ship, without lawful excuse, *deviates* from the voyage contemplated by the policy, the insurer is discharged from liability as from the time of deviation, and it is immaterial that the ship may have regained her route before any loss occurs. There is a deviation from the voyage contemplated by the policy:

(1) where the course of the voyage is specifically designated by the policy, and that course is actually departed from; or

(2) where the course of the voyage is not specifically designated by the policy, but the usual and customary course is actually departed from (s. 46).

Where several ports of discharge are specified by the policy, the ship may proceed to all or any of them, but in the order designated by the policy. Where the policy is to 'ports of discharge' within a given area, which are not named, the ship must proceed to them, or such of them as she goes to, in their geographical order. Failure in either case amounts to a deviation (s. 47).

In the case of a voyage policy, the adventure insured must be prosecuted throughout its course with reasonable dispatch, and if without lawful excuse it is not so prosecuted, the insurer is discharged from liability as from the time when the delay became unreasonable (s. 48).

Deviation or delay in prosecuting the voyage contemplated by the policy is *excused*:

(i) Where authorised by any special term in the policy;
(ii) Where caused by circumstances beyond the control of the master and his employer;
(iii) Where reasonably necessary in order to comply with an express or implied warranty;
(iv) Where reasonably necessary for the safety of the ship or subject-matter insured; but when the insurance is effected on the ship alone, and not on the cargo, a deviation to save the cargo will not be excused;
(v) For the purpose of saving human life, or aiding a ship in distress where human life may be in danger;
(vi) Where reasonably necessary for the purpose of obtaining medical or surgical aid for any person on board the ship;
(vii) Where caused by the barratrous conduct of the master or crew, if barratry* is one of the perils insured against.

When the cause excusing the deviation or delay ceases to operate, the ship must resume her course, and prosecute her voyage with reasonable dispatch (s. 49).

(l) Assignment of Policy

A marine policy is assignable by indorsement, or in other customary manner, unless it contains terms expressly prohibiting assignment. It may be assigned either before or after a loss has occurred,

* Barratry is any wrongful act wilfully committed by the master or crew to the prejudice of the owner or charterer.

subject to any contrary terms contained in the policy; but an assignment of a policy by a person subsequent to his parting with or losing his interest in the subject-matter is inoperative. The assignee can sue in his own name, but takes subject to equities (ss. 50, 51).

(m) Losses

The insurer is liable for any loss proximately caused by a peril insured against. The perils insured against usually correspond to the 'excepted risks' in a charter-party (see Chap. VII, § 3 (a) (2)).

Unless the policy otherwise provides, the insurer is liable even though the loss would not have happened but for the misconduct or negligence of the master or crew, but he is not liable for any loss attributable to the wilful misconduct of the insured.

Unless the policy otherwise provides, he is not liable for any loss caused by delay, nor for ordinary wear and tear, ordinary leakage and breakage, inherent vice or nature of the subject-matter insured, or for any loss caused by rats or vermin, or for any injury to machinery not proximately caused by maritime perils (s. 55).

A loss may be either total or partial. A total loss may be either an *actual total loss* or a *constructive total loss*. A partial loss may be either a *general average loss* or a *particular average loss*.

(1) *Actual Total Loss*

Where the subject matter insured is destroyed, or so damaged as to cease to be a thing of the kind insured, or where the assured is irretrievably deprived thereof, there is an actual total loss. In the case of an actual total loss no notice of abandonment need be given (s. 57).

Where the ship concerned in the adventure is missing, and after the lapse of a reasonable time no news of her has been received, an actual total loss may be presumed (s. 58).

(2) *Constructive Total Loss*

There is a constructive total loss where the subject-matter insured is reasonably abandoned on account of its actual total loss appearing to be unavoidable, or because it could not be preserved from actual total loss without an expenditure which would exceed its value when the expenditure had been incurred (s. 60).

Where there is a constructive total loss, the insured may either treat the loss as a partial loss, or abandon the subject-matter insured to the insurer, and treat the loss as if it were an actual total loss (s. 61). If the insured elects to abandon the subject-matter insured to the insurer, he must give notice of abandonment, otherwise the loss can only be treated as a partial loss.

Notice of abandonment may be given in any manner, but must indicate the intention of the insured to abandon his insured interest in the subject-matter insured unconditionally to the insurer. It must be given with reasonable diligence after the receipt of reliable information of the loss; but where the information is of a doubtful character, the insured is entitled to a reasonable time to make inquiry.

The acceptance of an abandonment may be either express or implied from the conduct of the insurer; but the mere silence of the insurer after notice is not an acceptance. Where notice of abandonment is accepted, the abandonment is irrevocable. The acceptance of the notice conclusively admits liability for the loss and the sufficiency of the notice.

Notice of abandonment is unnecessary where, at the time when the insured receives information of the loss, there would be no possibility of benefit to the insurer if notice were given to him; or when it has been waived by the insurer, or in respect of a reinsurance (s. 62).

Where there is a valid abandonment, the insurer is entitled to take over the interest of the insured in whatever may remain of the subject-matter insured, and all proprietary rights incidental thereto (s. 63).

(3) *General Average Loss*

A *general average loss* is a loss caused by or directly consequential on a general average act. A general average act consists in:

(i) any *extraordinary* sacrifice (it must be a *real* sacrifice), or expenditure;

(ii) voluntarily and reasonably made or incurred;

(iii) in time of imminent peril;

(iv) for the purpose of *preserving* the property imperilled in the common adventure.

The peril must actually exist, and a mistaken belief that it exists, even if such belief is reasonable under the circumstances, is not enough (*Joseph Watson & Sons, Ltd.* v. *Firemen's Fund Insurance Co. of San Francisco* [1922] 2 K.B. 355).

The danger must be common to all those who are called upon to contribute.

Examples of general average are:

(a) The cutting or casting overboard of a mast or rigging to lighten the ship during a storm and the jettison of cargo for a similar purpose. In both these cases no claim can be supported if the property jettisoned is already worthless.

(b) The cost of pilotage, towing, etc., incurred in putting into a port of refuge.

(c) The cost of unloading and reloading cargo at a port of refuge in order to allow necessary repairs to be undertaken.

(d) The beaching of a damaged vessel to avoid sinking.

Where there is a general average loss, the party on whom the loss falls is entitled to a rateable contribution from the other parties interested, and such contribution is called a *general average contribution*. There is no right of contribution when the danger which gave rise to the claim was brought about by a breach of duty on the part of the person making the claim.

The parties benefiting may be:

  (i) The shipowner for the value of the ship, and in respect of freight payable by the charterer or under bills of lading as the case may be.

 (ii) The owners of the cargo.

(iii) The charterer (if any) for freight payable under bills of lading.

Subject to any express provision in the policy, where the insured has incurred a general average expenditure he may recover from the insurer in respect of the proportion of the loss which falls upon him; and, in the case of a general average sacrifice, he may recover from the insurer in respect of the whole loss without having enforced his right of contribution from the other parties liable to contribute. Where the insured has paid or is liable to pay a general average contribution in respect of the subject matter insured, he may recover therefor from the insurer; but the insurer is not liable for any general average loss or contribution where the loss was not incurred for the purpose of avoiding, or in connection with the avoidance of, a peril insured against (s. 66).

Where a claim for general average has arisen, the amounts of contribution are usually ascertained at the port of first discharge. The duty of having the account made up, and of collecting the contributions, lies on the shipowner, and he has a lien on the cargo until all contributions are paid. In order to avoid delay in discharging goods and consequent loss, it is usual for the owners of cargo or their underwriters to deposit a sum with the shipowners or their underwriters, or to enter into a bond to be responsible for all claims for general average on condition that the cargo is released.

(4) Particular Average Loss

A particular average loss is a partial loss of the subject-matter insured, caused by a peril insured against, and which is not a general average loss (s. 64). It falls entirely upon the party interested in the subject-matter.

If a fire breaks out on board a ship and damage results to part of the cargo, both by fire and by the water used for putting the fire out, the loss by fire is a particular average loss, to be borne entirely by the party concerned; but the damage by water to other cargo is a general average loss, incurred for the safety of all parties, who must contribute even though their own goods are not damaged.

(n) Measure of Indemnity

Where there is a loss recoverable under the policy, the insurer, or each insurer if there is more than one, is liable for such proportion of the measure of indemnity as the amount of his subscription bears to the value fixed by the policy in the case of a valued policy, or to the insurable value in the case of an unvalued policy (s. 67 (2)).

The Act provides the following rules for the ascertainment of the measure of indemnity (ss. 68–71):

(1) Where there is a total loss of the subject-matter insured, the measure of indemnity, subject to any express provision in the policy, is:
    (i) If the policy is a valued policy, the sum fixed by the policy.
    (ii) If the policy is an unvalued policy, the insurable value of the subject-matter insured.

(2) Where a ship is damaged, but is not totally lost, the measure of indemnity, subject to any express provision in the policy, is as follows:
    (i) Where the ship has been repaired, the reasonable cost of the repairs, less the customary deductions, not exceeding the sum insured in respect of any one casualty.
    (ii) Where the ship has been only partially repaired, the reasonable cost of such repairs, and an indemnification for the reasonable depreciation, if any, arising from the unrepaired damage, provided that the aggregate amount shall not exceed the cost of repairing the whole damage.
    (iii) Where the ship has not been repaired, and has not been sold in her damaged state during the risk, indemnification for the reasonable depreciation arising from the unrepaired damage, not exceeding the reasonable cost of repairing such damage.

(3) Subject to any express provision in the policy, where there is a partial loss of freight, the measure of indemnity is such proportion of the sum fixed by the policy in the case of a valued policy, or of the insurable value in the case of an unvalued policy, as the proportion of freight lost by the insured bears to the whole freight at the risk of the insured under the policy.

(4) Where there is a partial loss of goods, merchandise, or other movables, the measure of indemnity, subject to any express provision in the policy, is as follows:
    (i) Where part of the goods, merchandise, or other movables insured by a valued policy is totally lost, such proportion of the sum fixed by the policy as the insurable value of the part lost bears to the insurable value of the whole.
    (ii) Where part of the goods, merchandise, or other movables insured by an unvalued policy is totally lost, the insurable value of the part lost.
    (iii) Where the whole or any part of the goods or merchandise insured has been delivered damaged at its destination, such proportion of the sum fixed by the policy in the case of a valued policy, or of the insurable value in the case of an unvalued policy, as the difference between the gross sound and damaged values at the place of arrival bears to the gross sound value.

Where the insurer limits his liability by a 'free from particular average' clause, the insured cannot recover for a loss of part, other than a loss incurred by a general average sacrifice, unless the contract contained in the policy is apportionable; but if the contract is apportionable, the insured may recover for a total loss of any apportionable part (s. 76 (1)).

(o) Rights of Insurer on Payment

(1) *Average*

Underwriters when paying are entitled to the benefit of 'average,' that is to say, if the owner insures for a portion only of the value or policy valuation, he is held to be his own insurer for the balance, and if a loss takes place, the underwriters are only liable for such a proportion as the amount of the insurance bears to the true value of the subject-matter (s. 81).

(2) *Subrogation*

Where the insurer pays for a total loss, either of the whole, or in the case of goods of any apportionable part, of the subject-matter insured, he thereupon becomes entitled to take over the interest of the insured in whatever may remain of the subject-matter so paid for, and he is thereby subrogated to all the rights and remedies of the insured in and in respect of that subject-matter as from the time of the casualty causing the loss.

Where the insurer pays for a partial loss, he acquires no title to the subject matter insured, or such part of it as may remain, but he is thereupon subrogated to all rights and remedies of the insured in and in respect of the subject-matter insured as from the time of the casualty causing the loss in so far as the insured has been indemnified by such payment for the loss (s. 79).

(3) *Contribution*

Where the insured is over-insured by double insurance, each insurer is bound, as between himself and the other insurers, to contribute rateably to the loss in proportion to the amount for which he is liable under his contract; and if any insurer pays more than his proportion of the loss, he is entitled to maintain an action for contribution against the other insurers, and is entitled to the like remedies as a surety who has paid more than his proportion of the debt (s. 80).

(p) Return of Premium

The premium, or a proportionate part of it, is returnable to the insured (ss. 83, 84):

(1) Where the policy contains a stipulation for the return of the premium, or a proportionate part thereof, on the happening of a certain event, and that event happens.

(2) Where the consideration, or an apportionable part thereof, for the payment of the premium totally fails, and there has been no fraud or illegality on the part of the insured or his agents.

(3) Where the policy is void, and there has been no fraud or illegality on the part of the insured.

(4) Where the risk has never been undertaken, except in the case of 'lost or not lost' policies. In a 'lost or not lost' policy the premium is returnable if the insurer knew that the vessel had arrived safely at the time when the contract was concluded.
(5) Where the insured had no insurable interest throughout the currency of the risk, so long as the policy is not a gaming or wagering policy.
(6) Where an unvalued policy has been over-insured.
(7) Where a double insurance has been unknowingly effected; but if that earliest in point of time has borne the entire risk, or if a claim has been paid on the policy in respect of the full sum insured thereby, no return may be claimed in respect of that policy.

The premium is not returnable in any case where the insurer has been induced to enter into the contract by the fraud of the insured or his agent, or where the policy is a gaming or wagering policy.

§ 5. *Third Party Insurance*

Where a person who is insured against liabilities to third parties becomes bankrupt or makes a composition or arrangement with his creditors, the rights of the insured against the insurance company in respect of any claim are transferred to and vest in the third party (Third Parties (Rights against Insurers) Act, 1930). The effect of this is to enable the third party to have his claim met out of the insurance money, so far as it is sufficient for the purpose, instead of having to prove in the bankruptcy or claim in the composition or arrangement. Similar rules apply when the insured, being a company, goes into liquidation (other than a voluntary one for the purposes of reconstruction or amalgamation), or has a receiver or manager appointed, or possession taken, by or on behalf of the holders of debentures secured by a floating charge.

By the Road Traffic Act, 1960, every user of a motor vehicle must insure against liability in respect of the death or bodily injury of any persons caused by the use of the vehicle on the road. If a third party obtains judgment against the assured in respect of such liability, he may enforce the judgment against the insurer; and, although not a party to the contract of insurance, the third party may sue the insurer directly on the policy.

If the driver is not adequately insured, the third party can recover compensation from the Motor Insurers' Bureau. The fact that the driver would be precluded by his own wrongful act from claiming under the policy does not defeat the third party's right to sue the insurer or the Bureau (*Hardy* v. *Motor Insurers' Bureau* [1964] 2 All E.R. 742).

CHAPTER VII

CARRIAGE

§ 1. *Common Carriers*

(a) Common Carriers and Private Carriers

There are two types of carrier at common law, *common* carriers and *private* carriers. A *common* carrier is one who holds himself out as willing to transport the goods of any person who chooses to employ him for the purpose. He may limit his terms in various ways, *e.g.*, he may hold himself out as a common carrier of certain goods only, or of goods of a certain size only, or may profess to carry only between certain places: but so long as he holds out that he will carry for anyone who asks him he is a common carrier. A *private* carrier is a carrier who makes no general offer, but restricts himself to working for particular persons with whom he negotiates special terms. The distinction is analogous to that between an innkeeper and the proprietor of a boarding house.

Since the delivery of goods to a carrier is a form of bailment, the general law relating to bailments will apply in the case of private carriers, subject to the express terms of the contract of carriage. Common carriers, however, are subject to special common law rules; and most forms of carriage, whether by land, sea or air, are governed to some extent by statute.

(b) Duties of Common Carrier

(1) *Duty to Carry Goods*

A common carrier is *bound* to carry goods of the class which he holds himself out as being ready to carry, for any person offering to pay the hire, unless his vehicle is already full, or there is some extraordinary risk attaching to the goods, or the destination is not one to which he usually carries goods. He must carry them without unnecessary delay and by his ordinary route, or such other route as may be specifically agreed upon.

The common carrier must charge a reasonable price for his services, but is not bound under common law to charge a uniform price. He has a lien on the goods for his charges for carriage, which he can enforce against both the consignor and the consignee. As a rule this is only a particular lien, although by usage or the course of dealing the lien may extend in respect of a general account due to the carrier.

(2) *Duty as Insurer of Goods*

At common law the carrier is an *insurer* of the goods in the sense that he warrants to carry and deliver the goods safely and securely.

A common carrier is therefore liable for any loss of, or damage to, the goods, even though he has not been negligent; but he is not liable if such loss or injury arises from:

(i) act of God; or

(ii) act of the Queen's enemies; or

(iii) negligence of the consignor, *e.g.*, bad packing; or

(iv) inherent vice of the goods carried.

For a loss to be attributable to an act of God it must arise from a direct, violent, sudden and irresistible act of nature which could not be foreseen, or, if foreseen, could not be prevented (*Nugent* v. *Smith* (1876) 1 C.P.D. 423). If, however, the carrier has omitted to take reasonable and necessary care, or if he does not provide a proper carriage, he will be liable in any case (*Steinman & Co.* v. *Angier Line* [1891] 1 Q.B. 624).

A carrier will not be liable where the goods are lost or damaged through neglect attributable to the owner without neglect on his own part, nor will he be liable if damage arises through inherent vice or natural deterioration of the goods themselves. And even if the defect is obvious at the time they are delivered to the carrier, as, for instance, if they are not properly packed, the carrier can set this up as a defence against the claim in respect of such damage, and he will succeed if he can show that the cause of the damage was in fact the bad packing (*Gould* v. *S.E. and C. Rly. Co.* [1920] 2 K.B. 186).

A contract of carriage not being *uberrimae fidei*, non-disclosure by the consignor of material facts (apart from the dangerous character of the goods) will not relieve the carrier of liability if he has committed a misfeasance in respect of it (*Sleat* v. *Fagg* (1822) 5 B. & Ald. 342). If the carrier has been negligent, only fraudulent concealment of value would be sufficient to discharge him from liability, even apart from the Carriers Act, 1830 (*infra*).

In *Long* v. *District Messenger Co.* (1916) 32 T.L.R. 596, A employed B to carry a packet from a bank, without stating, although the omission was not wilful, that the packet contained bank notes, and B made no inquiry. B was held liable for the loss.

Where, however, the goods are of a dangerous character, it is the duty of the consignor to give notice to the carrier of this fact.

In *Bamfield* v. *Goole and Sheffield Transport Co.* [1910] 2 K.B. 94, ferro-silicon was forwarded by barge, the consignors describing it to the carrier as general cargo. Neither the consignors nor the carrier knew that the goods were dangerous. In consequence of gases given off by the substance, the carrier died, and his widow sued the consignors for damages. She was held to be entitled to recover, on the ground that the defendants, when they forwarded the goods, impliedly warranted that they were safe to be carried.

The carrier should also be informed if damage will be caused by delay, otherwise he will not be liable if in ordinary circumstances delay would not damage the goods (*Baldwin* v. *London, Chatham and Dover Railway Co.* (1882) 9 Q.B.D. 582).

(3) Duty to Deliver Goods

Upon completion of the transit the carrier must deliver the goods to the consignee, as instructed by the consignor, unless he is ordered by the consignee to deliver the goods at a different address.

The consignor may change the address to which goods are to be delivered, during the transit, by a notice to the carrier, and he will be responsible if he does not deliver accordingly.

Where it is customary for the consignee to send for his goods at a wharf or other place of arrival of the carrier, the carrier must keep the goods for a reasonable length of time at his own risk, until the consignee or his assigns take delivery, and his liability as a common carrier will continue until such reasonable time has elapsed (*Bourne* v. *Gatliffe* (1844) 11 Cl. & F. 45).

Where the goods are refused when tendered to the consignee, the carrier ceases to be liable as a common carrier, his only liability then being that of an involuntary bailee.

After the liability of the carrier, as such, has ceased, he may render himself liable as warehouseman, if he keeps the goods in his possession. Where he does this, either expressly as warehouseman or in respect of his lien for charges, he must exercise reasonable care in respect of the goods, even though he may have notified the consignee that he holds them at the owner's sole risk; he is, however, entitled to all reasonable expenses incurred by him in the exercise of such care (*Great Northern Railway Co.* v. *Swaffield* (1874) L.R. 9 Ex. 132).

(c) Limitation of Carrier's Liability at Common Law

A common carrier is under no *duty* to carry on terms of strict liability, and can make a special contract with his customer limiting his liability. The special contract can be made by means of a public notice or declaration which limits liability and which is brought to the customer's notice at or before the time when the contract of carriage is made. In general, the courts will hold that terms and conditions are brought to a customer's notice if the notice containing them is put up in a conspicuous place in the carrier's depôt and the customer has the opportunity of reading them when he deposits his goods (see Chap. I, § 6 (f)). Carriers' practice in the early nineteenth century of imposing stringent conditions which were held to bind customers who had not in fact read them caused considerable public disquiet, to remedy which the Carriers Act, 1830, was passed.

(d) Carriers Act, 1830

This Act, which applies only to common carriers *by land*, provides that a carrier may not (except as stated below) limit his liability *by public notice*. Carriers are nevertheless left entirely free to make special contracts by other means, *e.g.*, by a written or printed instrument. The Act further provides that carriers are not to be liable for loss of or injury to certain specified articles of more than £10 in value unless, at the time of delivery of the articles to the carrier, the nature and value of the goods have been declared by the person sending them, and an increased charge paid. Such articles include gold or silver coin, manufactured or unmanufactured gold or silver, jewellery, precious stones, watches and clocks, silk, and furs.

In order that the carrier may obtain the protection of the Act, he must cause a legible notice of the increased charge to be posted in a conspicuous place in his office or warehouse, and such publication is deemed to be sufficient notice to the customer. In the event of an action in respect of the goods, the carrier is not bound by the declared value thereof, but may demand proof of the actual value.

The carrier is protected, where the value is not declared and the increased charge paid, in the case of a loss arising even from negligence. But he is not protected if the loss arises by felony on the part of his servant; nor does the protection extend to damage caused by delay for which the carrier is responsible.

§ 2. *Carriage by Land*

(a) Carriage by Rail

In 1947 the carriage of goods and passengers by rail in Great Britain was brought under the control of the British Transport Commission. By the Transport Act, 1962, the functions and powers of the Transport Commission were transferred to a new Transport Holding Company and four Transport Boards, *viz.*, the British Railways Board (operating through a number of Regional Railway Boards); the London Transport Board; the British Transport Docks Board; and the British Waterways Board.

Prior to the passing of this Act, carriers by rail could act as common carriers, and were subject to statutory restrictions as to the extent to which they could contract out of their strict liability. Section 43 (6) of the Act now provides that none of the Boards are to be regarded as common carriers by rail or inland waterway, and s. 43 (3) gives the Boards power 'to demand, take and recover such charges for their services and facilities, and to make the use of those services and facilities subject to such terms and conditions, as they think fit.' The Carriers Act, 1830, thus no longer applies to carriage by rail.

Goods are now normally carried subject to the Railways Board's 'General Conditions for the Carriage of Merchandise (other than Dangerous Goods and Merchandise for which Conditions are specially provided) when carried at the Board's Risk.' By these terms the Board undertakes a strict liability for the goods analagous to that of the common carrier, but imposes a maximum limit on its liability of £800 per ton if the consignment is totally lost, and, if there is a partial loss, of that proportion of £800 per ton as the value of the part lost bears to the value of the whole consignment.

Goods may also be carried at Owner's Risk for a lower charge. In this case the liability of the Board is much more restricted, the Board not being generally liable for loss or damage except upon proof that this arose from the wilful misconduct of the Board or its servants; although in certain cases, e.g., the non-delivery of the whole consignment, the Board is liable unless it can prove that it was not negligent.

As regards the carriage of passengers, s. 43 (7) provides that the Board may not carry passengers by rail on terms or conditions which:

(1) purport, whether directly or indirectly, to exclude or limit their liability in respect of the death of, or bodily injury to, any passenger other than a passenger travelling on a free pass; or

(2) purport, whether directly or indirectly, to prescribe the time within which or the manner in which such liability may be enforced.

The charges made by the Board in respect of the carriage of passengers must be approved by the Transport Tribunal, the constitution and powers of which are now laid down in the Transport Act, 1962.

The Board accepts liability for loss of, or damage or delay to, passengers' luggage in the event of the negligence or wilful misconduct of the Board or its servants or agents, but limits its liability to £50 per passenger.

(b) Carriage by Road

There are no statutory provisions relating to contracts for the carriage of goods by road within Great Britain, and such carriers may act as common carriers, but almost invariably enter into special contracts. A carrier of goods in a motor vehicle must, however, hold a proper licence if he carries goods for hire or reward, or for or in connection with a trade or business.

A carrier of passengers by road in a public service vehicle must also be licensed. In this case the contract of carriage is subject to s. 151 of the Road Traffic Act, 1960, which provides that any provision in the contract of carriage negativing or restricting the liability of the carrier in respect of claims arising out of the death of or bodily injury to any passenger in the vehicle is void.

By an International Convention in 1956 rules were laid down governing contracts for the carriage of goods by road for reward between two different countries. Provision is made by the Carriage of Goods by Road Act, 1965, for the incorporation of the Convention into English law on a day to be appointed by Order in Council. The Convention imposes liability on the carrier, except in certain limited cases, for loss of, or damage or delay to, the goods, but limits his liability to 25 gold francs per kilo, unless the sender declares a higher value for, or a special interest in delivery of, the goods, and pays an agreed surcharge, or the loss is caused by the wilful misconduct of the carrier.

§ 3. Carriage by Sea

The law of carriage by sea will be more easily understood if the terms used in the export trade are explained at the outset. A manufacturer or merchant sending goods abroad is called a *shipper*, and he (or his *forwarding agent*) generally makes an ordinary contract of carriage by sea (or *contract of affreightment*) with a *shipowner* (the carrier) or with an agent for the latter, a *loading broker*. Many, if not all, of the terms of the contract will be embodied in a document known as a *bill of lading*. The shipper may, however, make an alternative kind of contract with the shipowner known as a *charter-party*, and this may take one of several forms. Usually a bill of lading is required for certain commercial purposes notwithstanding the existence of a charter-party.

It is sometimes suggested that at common law a shipowner is always liable for loss of goods (subject to the recognised exceptions, *e.g.*, act of God) whether he is a common carrier or not, but the better view appears to be that his liability varies with the circumstances. Since it is the invariable practice for a special contract to be made limiting liability, the question is not of great importance. Liability may be varied to any extent, except where the contract is subject to the Carriage of Goods by Sea Act, 1924.

(a) Charter-party

(1) Types of Charter-party

A charter-party is used where a merchant hires a ship for the carriage of goods on a particular voyage (a *voyage charter*), or during a particular period (a *time charter*), for a sum of money called *freight*. By the terms of such a charter-party the charterer only contracts for the use of the ship; possession remains with the owner, and navigation is carried on by his servants. Sometimes, however, there is an absolute letting of the whole ship (a *charter by demise*), which then leaves the possession of the owner to come under the absolute control of the charterer, and be navigated by his servants. Charters by demise are not of great importance today, and are not further considered here.

(2) *Terms of Charter-party*

The usual terms of a voyage charter consist of an undertaking by the shipowner that the ship, being seaworthy and furnished with necessaries, shall be ready by a certain day to receive the cargo, shall sail when loaded, and deliver the cargo at the port of destination. A further clause is usually inserted exonerating the shipowner from any liability in respect of loss which may arise by the act of God, the Queen's enemies, arrest and restraint of princes, rulers and people, fire, barratry of the master or crew, gales, stranding, and other dangers of navigation. The charterer, on his part, undertakes to load and unload the ship within a specified number of days, called *lay* days, and if he delays the ship longer, to pay *demurrage*; he also undertakes to pay freight as agreed.

In every charter-party the following undertakings on the part of the shipowner are implied by law:

(i) That the owner undertakes to make the ship seaworthy.

The warranty of seaworthiness applies only at the commencement of the voyage: there is no implied condition or warranty that the ship will continue seaworthy during the whole of the voyage, although, if the voyage is divided into several distinct parts, the ship must be seaworthy at the commencement of each part (*The Vortigern* [1899] P. 140).

(ii) That the ship shall be ready to commence the voyage and load the cargo and proceed on the voyage with reasonable dispatch.

If the delay is such as goes to the root of the contract, and thereby the charterer loses all benefit under the contract, he may refuse to perform his part of the contract altogether (*Freeman* v. *Taylor* (1831) 8 Bing. 124); otherwise the charterer merely has a right of action for damages against the shipowner (*Hong Kong Fir Shipping Co., Ltd.* v. *Kawasaki Kisen Kaisha, Ltd.*, *ante*, p. 24).

If the delay is caused by supervening circumstances over which the shipowner has no control, and is such that the whole commercial object of the venture is frustrated, the rights and obligations of both parties to the contract are destroyed. The Law Reform (Frustrated Contracts) Act, 1943, does not apply to a voyage charter-party (see Chap. I, § 12 (c)).

(iii) That the ship shall not deviate except for good cause or as provided for in the contract.

The circumstances under which deviation is excusable are substantially the same as those under which a deviation is permitted in a contract of marine insurance (see Chap. VI, § 4 (k)).

If the breach goes to the root of the contract the shipowner cannot rely on any of the exceptions contained in the charter-party. His position then becomes that of an ordinary common carrier, and in order to escape liability for loss or damage to the goods, he must show that such loss or damage was caused by the act of God, Queen's enemies, or inherent vice of the goods, *and* that it was bound to have occurred even if the undertaking complained of had not been broken. This is so in the case of a deviation whether the loss or damage occurred before, during, or after the deviation (*Joseph Thorley, Ltd.* v. *Orchis S.S. Co., Ltd.* [1907] 1 K.B. 660).

(3) *Form of Charter-party*

The following is a form of voyage charter-party:

LONDON   , 19

IT IS THIS DAY MUTUALLY AGREED BETWEEN
of the good Ship or Vessel called the
of the measurement of   Tons, or thereabouts,

now at   , and   Merchants,

That the said Ship, being tight, staunch and strong, and every way fitted for the Voyage, shall with all convenient speed, sail and proceed to
or so near thereunto as she may safely get, and there load from the Factors of the said Affreighters a full and complete Cargo of

to be brought to, and taken from alongside, free of risk and expense to the Ship, not exceeding what she can reasonably stow and carry over and above her Tackle, Apparel, Provisions and Furniture, and being so loaded, shall therewith proceed to

or so near thereunto as she may safely get, and there deliver the same on being paid freight as follows:

in full of all Port Charges and Pilotage. (The Act of God, the Queen's Enemies, Restraint of Princes and Rulers, Fire and all and every other Dangers and Accidents of the Seas, Rivers and Navigation, of whatever nature and kind soever during the said voyage always excepted.) Charterer's liability under this charter-party to cease on the cargo being loaded, the master and owners having a lien on the cargo for all freight and demurrage.
The Freight to be paid on unloading and right delivery of the Cargo.
The necessary cash for ship's ordinary disbursements to be advanced by Shippers at port of loading on usual terms.

days to be allowed the said Merchants (if the Ship is not sooner dispatched) for loading and discharging.
The Ship to address to Charterer's Agents at port of discharge, paying

commission.

And   days on Demurrage over and above the said lay days at
Pounds per day.

Penalty for non-performance of this Agreement, estimated amount of Freight.
The Brokerage at   per cent., by the Ship, on the amount of Freight,
Primage, and Demurrage, is due on signment of this Charter-party and payable
to

Witness to the Signature of

Witness to the Signature of

> The Vessel to be reported at Custom House in the port of
> by

A charter-party does not require a stamp.

(4) *Duties of Parties*

It is the owner's duty to bring the ship to the port agreed upon from
which the voyage is to start, and the charterer's duty, upon notification, to bring his goods to that port, and deliver them to the servants
of the shipowner alongside the ship (*Grant* v. *Coverdale* (1884) 9 App.
Cas. 470). The words 'as near thereunto as she can safely get,' enable
the shipowner to call upon the consignee to take delivery, if for some
cause the ship cannot actually get to the port of delivery within a
reasonable time; the shipowner must bring the ship to the port of
delivery with dispatch, and be ready as soon as reasonably possible to
discharge the cargo in the usual manner (*Nelson* v. *Dahl* (1879) 12
Ch. D. 568).

(5) *Demurrage*

Demurrage is a sum fixed by the parties by way of liquidated
damages, which the charterers become liable to pay if they detain the
ship by failure to load or unload within the specified *lay days*. Lay
days are usually either 'working days,' 'running days,' or 'weather
working days.' 'Working days' are those on which work is usually
done at the port, *i.e.*, every day excluding Sundays and holidays, no
regard being had to bad weather. 'Running days' mean every day,
Sundays and holidays included. 'Weather working days' are those on
which work is not stopped through bad weather.

When the charter-party specifies that the ship is to be taken to
certain docks or wharves for the purpose of loading or discharging,
the lay days commence from the time when she arrives there. But
when no dock or wharf is mentioned, the lay days commence to run
from the time when the ship arrives in such a part of the port as is
customary for ships to lie at, either while loading or unloading, or
waiting for a berth.

As soon as the lay days have commenced to run, the charterer is
under an absolute obligation to complete the loading or unloading

within the time named, otherwise he will be bound to pay demurrage at the agreed rate, unless the delay is caused by the fault of the ship-owner or by some executive act of the lawful port authorities. He is, however, entitled to extend the loading (or unloading) over the whole of the lay days, and is under no obligation to accelerate loading to suit the owner's convenience (*Margaronis Navigation Agency, Ltd.* v. *Peabody & Co., Ltd.* [1964] 2 All E.R. 296).

Where the charter-party simply provides for demurrage at a certain rate, but does not name any particular number of days as lay days, demurrage will be payable after a reasonable time for loading or un-loading has elapsed, having due regard to the existing circumstances at the port at that time (*Hick* v. *Raymond* [1893] A.C. 22). In such a case, therefore, if loading or unloading was delayed by reason of a strike of stevedores, that fact would be taken into consideration in determining what was a reasonable time; whereas, if lay days had been provided for in the charter-party, a strike would not of itself relieve the charterer from completing the operation within the specified time.

(6) *Cesser Clause and Lien Clause*

The clause which provides that the charterer's liability under the charter-party shall cease on the cargo being loaded is known as the 'cesser clause', and puts an end to the charterer's liability upon the shipowner acquiring a lien upon the goods for the freight and de-murrage due to him. But where the lien clause does not cover the whole amount due to the shipowner by way of freight or demurrage, the cesser clause only relieves the charterer to the extent that the ship-owner has a lien (*Hansen* v. *Harrold* [1894] 1 Q.B. 612); and where by the charter-party it is agreed that bills of lading shall be given in a certain form, even if such bills are given, the cesser clause will not protect the charterer if no lien is given by the bills of lading (*Jennesen* v. *Secretary of State for India* [1916] 2 K.B. 702).

(b) Bill of Lading

Where cargo is sent in a general ship, all or most of the terms of the contract of affreightment are generally embodied in a bill of lading which operates as:

 (i) a receipt for the goods shipped;

 (ii) a document of title, enabling the consignee to obtain delivery of the goods; and

(iii) evidence of the contract of affreightment.

It does not strictly constitute the contract itself, since the contract was made prior to the bill of lading having been signed (*Sewell* v. *Burdick* (1884) 10 App. Cas. 74). Where a shipper contracts with a shipowner by way of charter-party, so that a bill of lading is not wanted as evidence of the contract of affreightment, it is nevertheless the general practice for a bill or bills to be drawn up to serve as receipts and documents of title in the usual manner.

(1) *Form of Bill of Lading*

The following is the form of a bill of lading:

SHIPPED in good Order and well-conditioned by   , in and upon the good Steam Ship called the   , whereof is Master for this present Voyage, and now riding at anchor in
                              and bound for

being marked and numbered as in the margin and are to be delivered in the like good Order and well-conditioned at the aforesaid Port of
(The Act of God, the Queen's Enemies, Fire, Machinery, Boilers, Steam, and all and every other Dangers and Accidents of the Seas, Rivers and Steam Navigation of whatever nature and kind soever excepted) unto
or to his Assigns. Freight for the said Goods
with primage and average accustomed. IN WITNESS whereof the Master or Purser of the said Ship hath affirmed to   Bills of Lading, all of this tenor and date, one of which Bills being accomplished the others to stand void.
    Dated in London,   19   ;
Weight and contents unknown.

A bill of lading does not require a stamp.

(2) *Rights and Liabilities of Parties*

By s. 1 of the Bills of Lading Act, 1855:

'every consignee of goods named in a bill of lading, and every indorsee of a bill of lading, to whom the property in the goods therein mentioned shall pass upon or by reason of such consignment or indorsement, shall have transferred to and vested in him all rights of suit, and be subject to the same liabilities, in respect of such goods, as if the contract contained in the bill of lading had been made with himself.'

This does not mean that every consignment or indorsement will transfer the property to the consignee or indorsee. In order to ascertain whether or not the property passes, the intention of the parties must be considered, as in the case of an ordinary sale of goods.

A bill of lading is not a negotiable instrument in the strict sense of that term, as the transferee can get no better title under the document than the transferor had. There are cases where, as against the true owner, the transferee of a bill of lading gets a better title than his transferor; but these cases arise, not by virtue of the instrument itself, but by reason of the provisions of the Factors Act, 1889, and the Sale of Goods Act, 1893 (see *Cahn* v. *Pockett's Bristol Channel Steam Packet Co., Ltd., ante,* p. 131).

Where bills of lading are drawn in a set, and different parts handed to different persons, the first transferee for value is entitled to the goods (*Barber* v. *Meyerstein* (1870) L.R. 4 H.L. 317); but if the master acting *bona fide* delivers goods to the first person presenting one of the bills forming the set, he will not be liable if it should subsequently transpire that that person was not the first transferee (*Glyn Mills & Co.* v. *East and West India Dock Co.* (1882) 7 App. Cas. 591).

Under s. 2 of the Bills of Lading Act, 1855, there is a right of stoppage *in transitu* and a lien for freight. But where a consignee of goods is lawfully in possession of the bill of lading, the transfer by him of the bill of lading by way of sale to a person who takes the document in good faith and for valuable consideration defeats the consignor's rights of lien or stoppage *in transitu*; and if the transfer is by way of pledge, the consignor can only reclaim the goods upon payment of the amount of the advance (Sale of Goods Act, 1893, s. 47; see Chap. III, § 1 (d)).

By s. 3 of the Act, the bill is made conclusive evidence as against the master or other person signing it that the goods have been shipped, unless the holder has had actual notice that the goods had not been put on board, or the party signing shows that the misrepresentation was wholly caused by the fraud of the shipper, the holder, or some other person under whom the holder claims. But the master, by signing, does not bind the shipowner to deliver the amount specified, nor is the shipowner thereby estopped from showing that the goods were not put on board, since the master has no authority to sign bills of lading unless the goods have been received on board; only the party signing is bound. The onus is then on the shipowner to show that in fact the goods were not shipped.

Where a 'clean' bill of lading is given, *i.e.*, where there is a declaration that the goods are shipped 'in good order and condition,' the master and the shipowner are bound thereby, since there is an admission that the goods or packages were externally in good condition at the time of shipment. The master is not under obligation to open packages to ascertain or verify quantity, condition, etc. The shipowner would therefore only be responsible for defects which could have been apparent on reasonable examination, and should the goods be found to be damaged upon unloading, the onus is on the shipowner to show that such damage was due to some other cause such as might arise from an excepted risk.

(3) *Mate's Receipt*

It is usual, when shipping from lighters, for an acknowledgment of goods shipped to be first given on what is known as the 'mate's receipt,' which is afterwards handed back in exchange for the actual bill of lading signed by the master of the ship. The master is not, however, bound to retain the bill of lading pending production of the mate's receipt, if the goods have been loaded, so long as he is not aware of any interests in the goods other than those of the person shipping them (*Hathesing* v. *Laing* (1873) L.R. 17 Eq. 92).

The shipowner is entitled to pass the bill of lading to a person in possession of the mate's receipt, if he is not aware of any other claim (*Evan* v. *Nichol* (1842) 3 M. & G. 614); but if the mate's receipt is in the hands of one party, and the bill of lading is in the hands of another party, the property must be handed over to the person in possession of the bill of lading (*Baumwoll* v. *Furness* [1893] A.C. 8).

A mate's receipt is only evidence that the goods have been put on board and that they belong to the party named therein; and the mere transference or indorsement of a mate's receipt does not pass the property in the goods, unless the shipowner or his agent has notice that the property has been so dealt with.

(4) *Carriage of Goods by Sea Act, 1924*

The Carriage of Goods by Sea Act, 1924, was passed to give statutory force, as far as this country is concerned, to the International Convention for the unification of certain rules relating to bills of lading.

The rules contained in the Act apply to the carriage of goods, other than live animals or deck cargo so stated, by sea *from* any port in Great Britain or Northern Ireland under a bill of lading. Generally speaking, a shipowner may not seek to decrease his liabilities under the Act.

In any contract for the carriage of goods by sea to which the Act applies:

(i) An *absolute* undertaking by the carrier to provide a seaworthy ship is not implied, but the carrier is bound, before and at the beginning of the voyage, to *exercise due diligence* to:

(*a*) make the ship seaworthy;
(*b*) properly man, equip and supply the ship;
(*c*) make the holds, etc., fit and safe for the reception, carriage and preservation of the goods.

(ii) The carrier must properly and carefully load, handle, stow, carry, keep, care for and discharge the goods carried.

(iii) Upon receipt of the goods into his charge, the carrier or the master or the agent of the carrier must, on demand of the shipper, issue to the latter a bill of lading stating that it is subject to the rules laid down by the Act, and showing:

(*a*) the leading marks necessary for identification of the goods as the same are furnished in writing by the shipper before the loading of such goods starts, provided such marks are stamped or otherwise shown clearly upon the goods if uncovered, or on the cases or coverings in which such

goods are contained, in such manner as should ordinarily remain
legible until the end of the voyage;

(b) either the number of packages or pieces or the quantity or weight, as
the case may be, as furnished in writing by the shipper;

(c) the apparent order and condition of the goods.

The carrier is not bound to include particular marks, number,
quantity or weight if he has reasonable grounds for suspecting
that the information supplied to him does not accurately represent the goods actually received or if he has had no reasonable
means of checking them.

(iv) Upon the actual loading of the goods, there must be issued to
the shipper, if he so demands, a 'shipped' bill of lading which
will contain, *inter alia*, the name of the ship, the date of shipment, and a statement that the goods have been put on board.

(v) Notice of loss or damage must be given to the carrier or his
agent before or at the time of the removal of the goods into the
custody of the consignee, or, if the damage is not apparent, then
within three days. Any action in respect of such loss or damage
must be brought *within one year* after delivery, or the date
delivery should have taken place.

(vi) Neither the carrier nor the ship shall be responsible for loss or
damage resulting from:

(a) act, neglect or default of the master, mariner, pilot or the servant of the
carrier in the navigation or in the management of the ship;

(b) fire, unless caused by the actual fault or privity of the carrier;

(c) perils, dangers or accidents of the sea or other navigable waters;

(d) act of God;

(e) act of war;

(f) act of public enemies;

(g) arrest or restraint of princes, rulers or people, or seizure under legal
process;

(h) quarantine restrictions;

(i) act or omission of the shipper or owner of the goods, his agent or
representative;

(j) strikes or lock-outs or stoppage or restraint of labour from whatever
cause, whether partial or general;

(k) riots and civil commotions;

(l) saving or attempting to save life or property at sea;

(m)wastage in bulk or weight or any other loss or damage arising from
inherent defect, quality or vice of the goods;

(n) insufficiency of packing;

(o) insufficiency or inadequacy of marks;

(p) latent defects, not discoverable by due diligence;

(q) any other cause arising without the actual fault or privity of the carrier
or the fault or neglect of his agents or servants.

(vii) Any deviation in saving or attempting to save life *or property* at
sea, or any reasonable deviation shall not be deemed to be an
infringement of the rules or of the contract of carriage, and the

carrier shall not be liable for loss or damage resulting therefrom.

(viii) The limit of liability in any case of loss is £100 per package or unit or the equivalent in other currency, unless the value has been declared and inserted in the bill of lading.

No exception to the rule of privity of contract is made in the case of the carriage of goods by sea, so that this limitation of liability cannot be relied on by a person who is not a party to the contract, *e.g.*, stevedores employed by shipowners who damage goods while unloading them (*Midland Silicones, Ltd.* v. *Scruttons, Ltd., ante,* p. 58).

(ix) Goods of an inflammable, explosive or dangerous character may be destroyed or rendered innocuous by the carrier without incurring liability, if the goods have been shipped without disclosure of their nature. Such goods may be disposed of in this way where their nature has been disclosed, if they become a danger to the ship or cargo.

The rules under the Act are not applicable to charter-parties, unless expressly incorporated therein.

It will be noted that the list of 'excepted risks' is considerably enlarged, and the warranty of seaworthiness is reduced to an obligation by the shipowner to exercise due diligence to make the ship seaworthy. The result is to make the shipowner liable only for negligence in respect of any of the matters specified, though once unseaworthiness is shown the burden of proving due diligence is cast on the shipowner.

(c) Freight

A shipowner, whether he carries by charter-party or by bill of lading, is entitled to a reward for his services, and this will take the form of freight, as specified in the contract. Freight is not generally payable until the contract has been completed and the goods delivered, unless non-delivery is caused by the default of the consignee.

(1) *Advance Freight*

It is sometimes a term of the contract that the freight shall be paid before the completion of the voyage. This is called *advance freight,* and is due at the time of starting, unless otherwise agreed. If it has not been paid, it can be recovered by the shipowner, even though the ship is lost, provided that the ship was lost through an excepted peril (*Byrne* v. *Schiller* (1871) L.R. 6 Ex. 319). If, however, goods are destroyed before the commencement of the voyage, no freight could have been earned by the ship in respect of such goods, and advance freight is not recoverable thereon.

(2) *Lump Sum Freight*

Lump sum freight is the amount agreed to be paid by a charterer irrespective of the quantity of goods actually shipped, and whether or not he loads a full cargo.

(3) *Dead Freight*

Where the charterer fails to load a full and complete cargo, and a lump sum is not payable, the shipowner may suffer loss in not being able to secure the shipment of other goods. The charterer is liable in damages for this loss, such damages being called *dead freight*.

(4) *Back Freight*

If the cargo owner does not take delivery within a reasonable time after the ship's arrival at the port of discharge, or send instructions as to the disposal of the cargo, the master has power to deal with the goods in the interest of the cargo owner at the latter's expense. He can either land the goods or convey them to some other port convenient to the cargo owner. If he so conveys them, he is entitled to charge for carriage to that port, such a charge being called *back freight*.

(5) *Pro Rata Freight*

Where the contract has not been completed, and goods have been delivered at a port short of the destination in such a manner as to show an acceptance of a new contract in place of the old, *e.g.*, a voluntary acceptance of the goods at another port, there is an implied obligation to pay a proportionate freight for that part of the voyage which has been accomplished; this is known as *pro rata freight*.

(6) *Shipowner's Lien*

A shipowner has a lien for freight and charges due to him upon the goods which he carries. The lien may extend to goods which are warehoused, so long as notice is given at the time the goods are so dealt with. The lien for freight or for general average contributions is a possessory lien, but that for expenses incurred in protecting the goods is a maritime lien (see Chap. V, § 8).

There is no lien at common law for dead freight, but frequently such a lien is given by express contract between the parties.

(d) Merchant Shipping Act, 1894

By s. 502 of the Merchant Shipping Act, 1894, an owner of a British sea-going ship, a charterer, any other person interested in or in possession of such a ship and any manager or operator of such a ship, shall not be liable to make good any loss or damage happening, without his actual fault or privity:

(1) where any goods, merchandise or other things whatsoever taken in or put on board his ship are lost or damaged by reason of fire on board the ship;

(2) where any gold, silver, diamonds, watches, jewels or precious stones taken in or put on board the ship are lost or damaged by reason of any robbery, embezzlement, making away with or secreting thereof, the true nature and value of which have not at the time of shipment been declared to the owner or master of the ship in the bills of lading or otherwise by writing.

Section 503 of the Act, as amended by the Merchant Shipping (Liability of Shipowners and Others) Act, 1958, limits the liability of such a person in respect of loss of life, personal injury and damage to property where, without his actual fault or privity, there is caused:

(1) loss of life or personal injury to any person being carried in the ship;

(2) damage or loss to any goods, merchandise or other things on board the ship;

(3) loss of life or personal injury to any person not carried in the ship, or loss or damage to any property, or infringement of any right through the act or omission of any person (whether on board ship or not) in the navigation or management of the ship or through any other act or omission of any person on board the ship;

to 3,100 gold francs for each ton of the ship's tonnage (minimum 300 tons) in respect of loss of life or personal injury, and to 1,000 gold francs per ton in respect of damage to or loss of goods.*

(e) Salvage

Salvage is the reward given to those who save a vessel, apparel and cargo, or that which had formed part of them, from shipwreck. (The term is sometimes also used to describe the property salved.) The right to payment for salvage may arise, but does not necessarily do so, out of express contract (*The Five Steel Barges* (1890) 15 P.D. 142). The owners of a ship responsible for a collision are not entitled to any reward for the performance of salvage services, but if another vessel in the same ownership as the ship responsible renders such services, salvage remuneration can be claimed (*The Kafiristan* [1938] A.C. 136).

To recover salvage, where not undertaken under special contract, it is necessary for the salvor to show:

(1) that he rendered voluntary service;

(2) that such services involved skill and danger, and that enterprise was shown in the performance thereof;

(3) that benefit resulted from such services;

(4) that the vessel saved was in a position of danger.

Normally, a person under a duty to perform services is not entitled to a reward for salvage. Thus, a master who successfully brings his ship to port during a storm cannot claim salvage, as he is merely performing the duties for which he was engaged.

* By the Merchant Shipping (Limitation of Liability) (Sterling Equivalents) Order, 1958, £73 8s. 10$\frac{5}{32}$d. and £23 13s. 9$\frac{27}{32}$d. have been specified as the respective sterling equivalents of 3,100 and 1,000 gold francs.

There is always a presumption when salvage services are rendered voluntarily that nothing will be paid unless some property is saved as a result of the operations of the salvors. This presumption normally applies also when the salvage operations are performed under contract.

§ 4. *Carriage by Air*

(a) Carriage by Air Act, 1932

At common law persons who hold themselves out as willing to carry goods in aircraft are common carriers. The Carriage by Air Act, 1932, which was designed to give effect as part of English law to an International Convention of 1929, provided special rules for the 'international' carriage of persons, luggage or goods by aircraft for reward, and the Carriage by Air (Non-international Carriage) (United Kingdom) Order, 1952, applied many of these special rules to carriage which is not 'international' within the meaning of the Convention. The practical consequence is that the common law is entirely superseded and all air carriage in or from the United Kingdom is subject to one of two substantially similar sets of rules based on the Convention.

These rules provide, *inter alia*, for the limitation of the carrier's liability. In order to avail himself of these provisions, the carrier must have issued a passenger or luggage ticket, or, in the case of goods, an 'air consignment note,' setting out the particulars specified in the Convention.

Liability attaches to the carrier in the event of the death or bodily injury of a passenger, caused by an accident on board the aircraft or in the course of embarking or disembarking, and also damage due to delay, unless the carrier can prove that he and his agents have taken all necessary measures to avoid the damage or that it was impossible to take such measures. The liability in respect of passengers is limited to 125,000 gold francs for each passenger. A higher sum may be agreed upon between the carrier and the passenger by special contract. Any provision attempting to fix a lower scale is null and void. If the injury is due to the wilful misconduct of the carrier, he is not entitled to the protection of this limitation.

Similar provisions are made with regard to the destruction of, damage to, or loss of registered luggage or goods, the limitation of liability being a sum of 250 francs per kilo, unless the consignor has made, at the time of handing the package over to the carrier, a special declaration of value and paid an increased charge if required to do so.

If the passenger retains charge of any luggage, the carrier's liability is limited to 5,000 francs per person.

(d) Carriage by Air Act, 1961

The International Convention of 1929 was modified by a further

Convention in 1955, the most important effects of which are to increase the carrier's liability in respect of passengers to a maximum of 250,000 francs for each passenger, and to extend the limitation of liability to servants and agents of the carrier. The Carriage by Air Act, 1961, was enacted to incorporate these amendments into English law, and contains the amended version of the original Convention. The Act came into force by Order in Council, on 1st June 1967 and on that date the Carriage by Air Act, 1932, was repealed.

A further amendment to the Convention is provided for by the Carriage by Air (Supplementary Provisions) Act, 1962, which came into effect in 1964. This Act clarifies the position where the carriage is to be performed by successive carriers. In such a case both the carrier who entered into the contract of carriage (the 'contracting carrier') and the carrier who is actually performing the carriage during which any loss or accident takes place (the 'actual carrier') are protected by the limitation of liability in the Convention, and the plaintiff may sue either of them, but may only recover in total the amount prescribed by the Convention.

The provisions of the 1961 and 1962 Acts have been extended by Order in Council to 'non-international' carriage. The maximum limit of liability for carriers on such flights is increased to 875,000 francs for each passenger.

(c) Licensing of Air Carriers

Apart from the British Overseas Airways Corporation and British European Airways, which are governed by the Air Corporations Acts, 1949–1962, no person may operate any flight for reward or in connection with any trade or business in respect of any flight in any part of the world by an aircraft registered in the United Kingdom, or any flight beginning and ending in the United Kingdom by an aircraft registered in any other country, unless he has obtained a licence to do so from the Air Transport Licensing Board (Civil Aviation (Licensing) Act, 1960, s. 1).

The Civil Aviation Act, 1949, makes provision for liability of owners of aircraft (with prescribed limitations of amount) for damage caused to persons or property on land or water by aircraft while in flight, taking off or landing, whether the owner of the aircraft was negligent or not. Third party insurance is compulsory.

CHAPTER VIII

PARTNERSHIP

The law of partnership is substantially contained in the Partnership Act, 1890, and in the Limited Partnerships Act, 1907. The former Act codified the existing law, and the latter introduced the principle of limited liability in partnerships.

§ 1. *The Partnership Contract*

(a) Definition of Partnership

Partnership is defined by s. 1 (1) of the Partnership Act, 1890, as 'the relation which subsists between persons carrying on a business in common with a view of profit.' The relation between members of a *body corporate* is not a partnership (s. 1 (2)).

By s. 45 'business' includes every trade, occupation, or profession, so that, for example, a firm of solicitors, architects or accountants carries on 'business' within the meaning of the Act. The hope of profit qualifies the meaning of 'occupation' and makes it plain that a social club is not a partnership. Further, the statutory definition must be read in conjunction with s. 2 which lays down certain rules for determining whether a partnership does or does not exist. These rules are:

(1) Joint or part ownership of property does not of itself create a partnership, whether or not the owners share any profits made by the use of the property. Such relationships are distinguished from partnership by the fact that there is no presumption of agency in dealing with the property. In such cases a partnership can only exist by express contract, from which the additional factor of agency will arise.

(2) The sharing of gross returns, *e.g.*, from property held under joint tenancy, does not of itself create a partnership.

(3) The receipt by a person of a share of the profits of a business is *prima facie* evidence that he is a partner in the business, but the receipt of such a share, or of a payment contingent on or varying with the profits of a business, does not of itself make him a partner in the business; and in particular:

(*a*) The receipt by a person of a debt or other liquidated amount by instalments or otherwise out of the accruing profits of a business does not of itself make him a partner in the business or liable as such.

(*b*) A contract for the remuneration of a servant or agent of a person engaged in a business by a share of the profits of the business, does not of itself make the servant or agent a partner in the business or liable as such.

(c) A person being the widow or child of a deceased partner, and receiving by way of annuity a portion of the profits made in the business in which the deceased person was a partner, is not by reason only of such receipt a partner in the business or liable as such.

(d) The advance of money by way of loan to a person engaged or about to engage in any business on a contract with that person that the lender shall receive a rate of interest varying with the profits, or shall receive a share of the profits arising from carrying on the business, does not of itself make the lender a partner with the person or persons carrying on the business, or liable as such; provided that the contract is in writing, and signed by or on behalf of all the parties thereto.

(e) A person receiving by way of annuity or otherwise a portion of the profits of a business, in consideration of the sale by him of the goodwill of the business, is not by reason only of such receipt a partner in the business, or liable as such.

In order that parties sharing in profits shall be liable as partners, it is necessary that the business should have been carried on on their behalf, or that they should have exercised some of the rights of partners; as, for instance, the right to demand an account, to direct how the business shall be carried on, or to state when it shall be wound up.

Where a person lends money in consideration of a rate of interest varying with the profits, or where a person takes a proportion of the profits in consideration of the sale of goodwill, he is deferred to the other creditors of the business in case of the bankruptcy or insolvency of the person or persons to whom the money is lent or who purchases such goodwill (s. 3). Such a person is thus to be treated for this purpose as a partner of the borrower or purchaser of goodwill, even though no partnership, in fact, exists between them.

An agreement between parties that they shall not be regarded as partners will not prevent them being liable as such. The facts in each case must be carefully examined, and the rights of the parties will depend upon the *real* nature of their agreement (*Walker* v. *Hirsch* (1884) 27 Ch. D. 460).

In *Cox* v. *Hickman* (1860) 8 H.L.C. 268, a trader carried on his business under the supervision of his creditors, who were to be gradually paid off out of the profits arising from the business.

Held: No partnership existed between the trader and the creditors.

In *Syers* v. *Syers* (1875) 1 App. Cas. 174, in consideration of £250 lent by B, A undertook to execute a deed of co-partnership for a one-eighth share of the profits of a music hall and tavern.

Held: This was an ordinary partnership, and not a loan contract; though as between the parties B was not liable for losses.

In *Ex parte Tennant* (1877) 6 Ch. D. 303, A, becoming an underwriting member of Lloyd's, agreed in writing with B, his father, that in consideration of B making the necessary deposit, and giving the necessary guarantee, he would engage a particular underwriting agent and pay to B one-half of the net profits.

Held: No partnership existed between A and B, the relationship being that of debtor and creditor.

An agreement to share losses as well as profits is perhaps the strongest evidence of a partnership, but even this is not conclusive.

In *Walker* v. *Hirsch, supra,* H and B entered into an agreement with W, whereby for the part taken by him in the business W was to receive a fixed salary of £180, and in addition a one-eighth share of net profits, and bear a one-eighth share of the losses as shown by the books when balanced; and W was to advance £1,500 to the business. The agreement was to be determined by four months' notice on either side. W had previously been a clerk, and continued to perform similar duties after the execution of the agreement, and did not sign the name of the firm on bills. H and B, being dissatisfied, gave W notice to determine the agreement, and excluded him from the place of business. W applied to the court for the winding-up of the partnership. The application was refused on the grounds that W was merely in the position of a servant, and that no partnership existed.

(b) Illegal Partnerships

S. 434, Companies Act, 1948 has now been amended by s. 120, Companies Act, 1967 so that the following kinds of partnership may be unlimited in number:

(*a*) of solicitors;

(*b*) of accountants, each of whom is qualified as auditor of a company or authorised by the Board of Trade to be so appointed (ss. 161 (1) (*a* and *b*);

(*c*) of members of a recognised stock exchange;

(*d*) of patent agents, each of whom is registered under the Patents Act, 1949;

(*e*) of surveyors, auctioneers, valuers, estate agents, land agents or estate managers provided that not less than three-quarters of the members are members of one or more of the following bodies:

(1) The Royal Institution of Chartered Surveyors

(2) The Chartered Land Agents' Society

(3) The Chartered Auctioneers' and Estate Agents' Institute

(4) The Incorporated Society of Valuers and Auctioneers

S. 429, Companies Act, 1948, whereby the maximum number of persons who could carry on a banking business was limited to ten, has been amended by s. 119, Companies Act, 1967, so that the maximum number is now increased to twenty.

Other kinds of partnership are limited to twenty persons (s. 434, Companies Act, 1948).

Certain types of partnership are rendered illegal by statute, *e.g.,* under the Solicitors Act, 1957, it is illegal for a solicitor to enter into a partnership agreement, *as a solicitor*, with an unqualified person.

Partnerships may also be illegal at common law if they are formed for an unlawful purpose, *e.g.,* a partnership entered into for the commission of a crime (see Chap. I, § 9 (b)). Illegality is never presumed, but must always be proved by those who assert its existence.

Persons associated together in an illegal partnership are incapable of exercising their rights against third parties, though in most cases third parties can exercise their rights against them, *i.e.*, an illegal partnership can be sued, but is incapable of suing. The parties themselves, as a general rule, will be unable to enforce any rights against each other as partners. By s. 34, a lawfully constituted partnership is in every case dissolved by the happening of any event which makes it unlawful for the business of the firm to be carried on, or for the members of the firm to carry it on in partnership. (The operation of this section where there are 'alien' partners is considered below.)

(c) Capacity to Enter into Partnership Agreement

A person can become a partner if he has the capacity to enter into contracts generally (see Chap. I, § 7).

(1) *Persons of Unsound Mind*

A person of unsound mind is capable of entering into a partnership contract during a period of sanity. If, after the partnership has commenced, he asserts that at the time the contract was entered into he was insane, he cannot escape from the liability attaching to a partner, unless he proves that he actually was insane at the time, and that the party with whom he entered into the contract knew of his insanity. Otherwise he is both capable of binding the firm as a partner, and liable to be bound by his co-partners.

Insanity is a ground for application to the court to dissolve the partnership (see *post*, § 4 (a) (4)); but it is not necessarily a ground for dissolution if a limited partner becomes insane (Limited Partnerships Act, 1907, s. 6 (2)).

(2) *Infants*

A partnership contract is one of the so-called 'continuous' contracts which is binding upon an infant unless and until he repudiates it, which he must do during infancy or within a reasonable time of coming of age. If he repudiates the contract after coming of age, he will be released from any liability in respect of partnership debts incurred during his minority, but he will remain liable for all debts contracted after his majority (*Goode* v. *Harrison* (1821) 5 B. & Ald. 159). On repudiation he can only recover his share of the partnership fund as then ascertained (*Hamilton* v. *Vaughan-Sherrin, &c., Co.* [1894] 3 Ch. 589), unless he can show that he has never received any benefit under the contract, in which case he can recover all sums invested in the partnership, including any premium paid. The infant, however, cannot claim to be credited with profits and not be debited with losses, and he is bound by the partnership accounts as between himself and his co-partners.

An infant cannot be made bankrupt in respect of any debts contracted by the firm of which he is a partner; the remedy of creditors is only against the adult members of the firm. The adult partners, however, have a right to exercise their equitable lien upon the partnership assets, and to see that these are applied in payment of the partnership debts.

(3) *Aliens*

There is nothing to prevent the existence of a partnership between a British subject and the subject of a foreign country; but if war should be declared between the two countries in which the partners respectively reside, the partnership is immediately dissolved.

The term 'alien enemy' includes a person of any nationality who resides and trades voluntarily in the enemy country (*Porter* v. *Freudenberg* [1915] 1 K.B. 857). Thus, if one partner of a firm resides in this country and the other resides and trades in a foreign country (even though the latter is an Englishman), the outbreak of war between England and the foreign country would automatically dissolve the partnership (*R.* v. *Kupfer* [1915] 2 K.B. 321). On the other hand, the mere fact that a partner in a firm is the subject of a country with whom England is at war will not dissolve the partnership, provided that at the time the alien is resident and trading in this country.

(d) Form of Partnership Agreement

A contract of partnership may arise from express agreement between the parties, whether oral or in writing, or be implied from the circumstances. The most usual practice is to execute a formal deed of partnership which sets out the conditions of the partnership, and the terms upon which it is to be conducted. This puts on record the intention of the parties to create a partnership, and prevents a merely verbal arrangement being subsequently repudiated, and enables provision to be made for such modification of the general law of partnership affecting the relations of the parties as they may desire to introduce into the agreement, particularly in regard to the position arising on the death or retirement of a partner. This can be achieved equally effectively by an unsealed written agreement.

(e) The Firm Name

A partnership has no corporate existence apart from the members composing it (although this is legally the case in Scotland), and the law goes no further than to recognise the members of a partnership collectively as a 'firm,' and the name under which their business is carried on as the 'firm name' (s. 4).

Under the Rules of the Supreme Court, however, actions may be taken by or against partners in the name of the firm of which they are members. This procedure also applies to those cases where a firm brings an action against one of its own members, and to actions between firms having one or more members in common.

When a firm is carried on under a name which does not consist of the true surnames of all the partners, with no addition thereto (other than Christian names or initials) it must be registered under the Registration of Business Names Act, 1916. When a corporation is a partner, the firm name must contain the corporate name if registration is to be avoided.

Registration must also be effected when a partner has changed his name, except (i) where the former name was changed or disused before the partner attained the age of eighteen years or at least twenty years ago (Companies Act, 1947, s. 116 (4)), or (ii) where the former name was that of a female partner before her marriage. If a female married partner carries on business in her maiden name, registration is required (*Seymour* v. *Chernikeef* [1946] K.B. 434).

The Registrar must be furnished with the following information:

(1) The business name.

(2) The general nature of the business.

(3) The principal place of business.

(4) The present Christian name and surname, any former Christian name or surname, the nationality, the usual residence and the other business occupation (if any) of each of the individuals who are partners, and the corporate name and registered or principal office of every corporation which is a partner.

(5) The date of commencement of business.

Particulars of any change in the constitution of the firm must also be registered.

Failure to register a firm required to be registered under the Act within fourteen days of the commencement of business or to register any change within fourteen days of the change renders every partner liable to a fine of £50. The firm cannot enforce by action or other legal proceeding any contract into which it has entered during the period of default, although such contracts are enforceable against the firm by the other parties thereto. The court may, however, grant relief to the firm in default if failure to register was accidental, or due to inadvertence or some other sufficient cause, or in any case where it is just and equitable that relief should be granted.

Every firm required to be registered must also disclose in legible characters the full names and any former names of the partners on all trade catalogues, trade circulars, show-cards and business letters, on or in which the business name appears and sent to any person in any part of the British Commonwealth. If any partner is not of British nationality, his nationality must also be given.

§ 2. *Liability of Partners to Third Parties*

(a) Power of Partner to Bind Firm

Every partner is an agent of the firm and of his other partners for the purpose of the business of the partnership; and the acts of every partner who does any act for carrying on in the usual way business of the kind carried on by the firm of which he is a member bind the firm and his partners, unless the partner so acting has in fact no authority to act for the firm in the particular matter, and the person with whom he is dealing either knows that he has no authority, or does not know or believe him to be a partner (s. 5).

The effect of notice of a partner's lack of authority is restated in s. 8, which provides that if it has been agreed between the partners that any restriction shall be placed on the power of any one or more of them to bind the firm, no act done in contravention of the agreement is binding on the firm with respect to persons having notice of the agreement.

The implied authority of a partner only extends to what is necessary for the usual conduct of the partnership business. This has been held to include:

(1) Selling any goods of the firm.
(2) Purchasing goods on behalf of the firm, if they are of a kind necessary for or usually employed in the business.
(3) Receiving payment of debts due to the firm and giving receipts.
(4) Engaging servants for the partnership business, and probably in discharging them if the other partners raise no objection.

And if it is a trading partnership a partner may also bind the firm in the following matters:

(5) Drawing, accepting or indorsing bills and other negotiable instruments in the name of the firm.
(6) Borrowing money on the credit of the firm.
(7) Pledging goods or personal chattels belonging to the firm.
(8) Making an equitable mortgage by deposit of deeds or otherwise of real property belonging to the firm.
(9) Employing a solicitor to defend an action against the firm for goods supplied or to bring an action in the firm name.

Professional, agricultural, and mining partnerships have been held to be non-trading partnerships, as also have partnerships carried on by commission agents and cinema proprietors. A banking partnership is a trading partnership.

A partner has no implied authority to bind the firm by the execution of a deed (*Harrison* v. *Jackson* (1797) 7 T.R. 207), or by a submission to arbitration (*Stead* v. *Salt* (1825) 3 Bing. 101), or by giving a guarantee unless this is usual in the particular firm or in a particular trade (*Brettel* v. *Williams* (1849) 4 Ex. 623). Neither has a partner implied authority to accept shares in satisfaction of a debt due to the firm, even though such shares are fully paid (*Niemann* v. *Niemann* (1889) 43 Ch. D. 198).

Authority to execute a deed must itself be given under seal; and the fact that the partnership agreement is in the form of a deed is not of itself sufficient (*Marchant* v. *Morton Down & Co.* [1901] 2 K.B. 829); but if one partner executes a deed in the presence of the other partners in their name and with their consent, this will be binding upon them (*Ball* v. *Dunsterville* (1791) 2 R.R. 394).

The following matters are dealt with specifically by the Act:

(1) *Pledging the Firm's Credit.* Where one partner pledges the credit of the firm for a purpose apparently not connected with the firm's ordinary course of business, the firm is not bound, unless the partner was in fact specially authorised by the other partners; but this does not affect any personal liability incurred by an individual partner (s. 7).

(2) *Admissions and Representations.* An admission or representation made by a partner concerning the partnership affairs, and in the ordinary course of business, is evidence against the firm (s. 15). This section has, however, no application to a representation made by a partner as to the extent of his own authority to bind the firm (*Ex parte Agace* (1792) 2 Cox 312).

(3) *Notice to a Partner.* Notice to any partner who habitually acts in the partnership business of any matter relating to partnership affairs operates as notice to the firm, except in the case of a fraud on the firm committed by or with the consent of that partner (s. 16). It is doubtful whether notice would be deemed to have been received by the firm where it was given to a person before he became a partner in the firm.

The firm may, of course, authorise some person other than a partner to act for it, and, by s. 6, an act or instrument relating to the business of the firm and done or executed in the firm name, or in any other manner showing an intention to bind the firm, by any person thereto authorised, whether a partner or not, is binding on the firm and all the partners. This section does not, however, affect any general rule of law relating to the execution of deeds or negotiable instruments.

A firm is not presumed to be the agent of a partner and, therefore, payment to the firm of a debt due to a partner does not discharge the debt without proof that the firm had power to receive payment (*Powell* v. *Brodhurst* [1901] 2 Ch. 160).

(b) Debts and Contracts

Every partner in a firm is liable *jointly with the other partners* for all debts and obligations of the firm incurred while he is a partner; and after his death his estate is also *severally* liable in a due course of administration for such debts and obligations so far as they remain unsatisfied, subject to the prior payment of his separate debts (s. 9).

The term 'joint' in this connection means that in respect of debts and obligations arising from contract, the plaintiff can only bring one action and not several separate actions against the members of the firm since there is only one contract. He is not bound to join all members of the firm in the action, but if he does not do so, he loses his rights against those whom he has omitted. The court may, however, at the instance of the defendant, order the omitted members of the firm to be added as co-defendants if they are within the jurisdiction. The defendant also has a right to claim that the other joint debtors, if within the jurisdiction, shall be joined as co-defendants.

The fact that the liability is joint does not affect the *extent* of each partner's liability; each partner is individually liable, subject to the restricted liability of a limited partner, for the whole amount due by the firm, and it is only the nature of the liability and the nature of the remedy which are in question.

Although judgment against one partner, even though it remains unsatisfied, is a bar to further action on the same cause, there will sometimes be another distinct cause upon which a further action may be taken against another partner. Thus, where a cheque or bill has been given in payment of a partnership liability, judgment obtained against one partner on the instrument is no bar to an action against the other partners on the original contract, for there are two rights of action in such a case, one on the contract, and one on the instrument (*Wegg-Prosser* v. *Evans* [1895] 1 Q.B. 108).

Partners differ from ordinary joint debtors in the following respects:

(1) The estate of a deceased partner is severally liable for the debts of the firm; whereas the estate of an ordinary joint debtor does not become severally liable. This means that a judgment recovered against members of a firm, but not satisfied, does not prevent the bringing of an action against the estate of a partner who had died before judgment and who had not been joined in the original action, nor does a judgment against the estate of a deceased partner prevent an action being brought against the surviving partners.

(2) Since each partner is an agent for the others in all matters relating to the firm's transactions, part payment or acknowledgment by

one partner in respect of a joint debt will prevent that debt from becoming statute-barred, or will revive it as against the others. This is not so with ordinary joint debtors, since in this case there is no question of agency.

(c) Torts

Where, by any wrongful act or omission of any partner acting in the ordinary course of the business of the firm, or with the authority of his co-partners, loss or injury is caused to any person not being a partner in the firm, or any penalty is incurred, the firm is liable therefor to the same extent as the partner so acting or omitting to act (s. 10).

In the following cases s. 11 specifically provides that the firm is liable to make good the loss:

(1) Where one partner acting within the scope of his apparent authority receives the money or property of a third person and misapplies it; and

(2) Where a firm in the course of its business receives money or property of a third person, and the money or property so received is misapplied by one or more of the partners while it is in the custody of the firm.

Every partner is liable jointly with his co-partners, and also severally, for everything for which the firm, while he is a partner therein, becomes liable under either s. 10 or s. 11 (s. 12).

The meaning of joint and several liability as affecting torts is that if the plaintiff recovers judgment against one partner, this is not a bar to an action against another partner; but the plaintiff cannot recover in total more than the amount of the damages awarded by the judgment first given (Law Reform (Married Women and Tortfeasors) Act, 1935, s. 6).

Where one partner both receives and misapplies the money or property of a third person, he must, for the firm to be liable, receive it whilst acting within the scope of his apparent authority. Thus, if a partner in a firm of solicitors receives money from a client to be invested in a specific security, and misappropriates it, the remaining partners are responsible for the loss, since to invest money in specified investments is within the ordinary scope of a solicitor's business (*Blair* v. *Bromley* (1847) 2 Ph. 354); but this would not be the case if the money had been given to the defaulting partner with a mere direction to invest it at his discretion (*Harman* v. *Johnson* (1853) 2 E. & B. 61).

The firm, however, is always liable to make good a loss where it has become answerable for the money or property of a third person, and this has been misappropriated by one or more of the partners whilst in the custody of the firm (*Blair* v. *Bromley, supra*).

(d) Trust Money improperly Employed in Partnership

If a partner, being a trustee, improperly employs trust property in the business or on the account of the partnership, no other partner is liable for the trust property to the persons beneficially interested therein; but this does not affect any liability incurred by any partner by reason of his having notice of a breach of trust, and does not prevent trust money from being followed and recovered from the firm if still in its possession or under its control (s. 13).

(e) Persons Liable by Holding Out

By s. 14:

(1) Every one who by words spoken or written or by conduct represents himself, or who knowingly suffers himself to be represented, as a partner in a particular firm, is liable as a partner to any one who has on the faith of any such representation given credit to the firm, whether the representation has or has not been made or communicated to the person so giving credit by or with the knowledge of the apparent partner making the representation or suffering it to be made.

(2) Provided that where after a partner's death the partnership business is continued in the old firm name, the continued use of that name or of the deceased partner's name as part thereof shall not of itself make his executors or administrators or his estate or effects liable for any partnership debts contracted after his death.

Thus, a person who is not a partner may incur liability for the debts of the firm by holding himself out as being a partner. Holding out may take place by words written or spoken, or by conduct, e.g., a man may state in writing or say that he is a partner, or may stand by and hear someone else say it without offering any repudiation, and be so doing he will be liable for any credit given by third parties upon the strength of his actions. It is not necessary for the credit to have been given by the person to whom the representation was made; it is sufficient that credit was given on the facts represented by the apparent partner and communicated by others to the creditor. The person giving credit to the firm must have been aware of the holding out, and must have been induced thereby to give credit.

(f) Incoming and Outgoing Partners

(1) Liability for Debts Contracted Before Becoming a Partner

When a person is admitted into an existing partnership, he will immediately assume the liability of a partner. He does not, however, thereby become liable to the creditors of the firm for anything done before he became a partner (s. 17 (1)); but he would be liable in respect of new debts arising out of a continuing contract made by the firm before he became a partner.

An incoming partner may become liable for antecedent debts by an agreement to that effect with creditors, either by deed, or for valuable consideration, or by novation.

(2) *Liability for Debts Incurred Before Retirement*

Where a partner in a firm retires from the partnership, he will still be liable for debts and obligations incurred before his retirement (s. 17 (2)). But he may be discharged from any existing liabilities by an agreement to that effect between himself and the members of the firm as newly constituted and the creditors. This agreement may be express or may be inferred as a fact from the course of dealing between the creditors and the firm as newly constituted (s. 17 (3)).

Such an agreement is known as a *contract of novation* (see Chap. I, § 11 (d)). By the terms of the agreement the creditor agrees to release the old debtor, and accept in his place the liability of the new debtor. A new agreement between the partners themselves, without the consent of the creditor, will be of no effect, as the creditor would be a stranger to such an agreement, and could neither acquire nor lose rights thereunder.

(3) *Notice of Retirement*

A retiring partner will also continue to be liable for the debts of the firm, even if contracted after his retirement, unless proper notice is given of the dissolution of the partnership. By s. 36 it is provided that:

(i) Where a person deals with a firm after a change in its constitution, he is entitled to treat all apparent members of the old firm as still being members of the firm until he has notice of the change.

(ii) An advertisement in the *London Gazette* shall be notice as to persons who had had no dealings with the firm before the date of the dissolution or change so advertised.

(iii) The estate of a partner who dies, or who becomes bankrupt, or of a partner who, not having been known to the person dealing with the firm to be a partner, retires from the firm, is not liable for partnership debts contracted after the date of the death, bankruptcy, or retirement respectively.

Although notice in the *Gazette* is sufficient so far as persons who have had no dealings with the firm prior to the date of dissolution are concerned, it is necessary to give specific notice to persons who have had prior dealings with the firm in order to avoid further liability to them.

But, even where no notice is given, a former partner is not liable to a person who did not know him to be a partner.

In *Tower Cabinet Co., Ltd.* v. *Ingram* [1949] 2 K.B. 397, the continuing proprietor of a business ordered goods from suppliers on notepaper bearing the name of a partner who had recently retired. The suppliers had not previously had dealings with the firm, but the retirement had not been advertised in the *Gazette*. It was held that as the retiring partner had not authorised the use of the old notepaper, he had not held himself out as a partner within the meaning of s. 14, and as the suppliers had no knowledge, beyond that furnished by the notepaper, that the retiring partner had ever been a partner, they could not hold him liable under s. 36.

This would apply particularly on the retirement of a 'dormant' partner, *i.e.*, one who took no active part in the business (*Heath* v. *Sansom* (1832) 38 R.R. 237), though notice would be necessary if disclosure had been made under the Registration of Business Names Act, 1916.

(4) *Continuing Guarantees*

A continuing guarantee given either to a firm, or to a third person in respect of the transactions of a firm is, in the absence of agreement to the contrary, revoked as to future transactions by any change in the constitution of the firm to which, or of the firm in respect of the transactions of which, the guarantee or obligation was given (s. 18). Such a guarantee is not revoked by a change in the constitution of the firm by whom it is given. (And see Chap. V, § 4 (c).)

§ 3. *Relation of Partners to One Another*

(a) Variation of Terms of Partnership

As between themselves, partners can enter into any agreement they choose, and to this extent may render many provisions of the Act inapplicable; but they cannot by agreement *inter se* affect the rights of third parties, unless those third parties actually contract to be bound by such agreement.

The terms of the agreement into which partners enter may, with the consent of all the partners, be varied at any time, and such consent may be express or inferred from a course of dealing (s. 19).

It is possible, therefore, by a course of dealing, to vary a written contract or deed, and if this is done without dissent by any of the partners, such course of dealing becomes binding upon all parties. These variations frequently take place in respect of such matters as capital, interest on capital, drawings and salaries; and where a particular method is prescribed by the partnership agreement for valuation of partnership property for the purpose of the accounts, but a different method is consistently adopted with the consent of the partners, the accounts so taken are binding upon them, and upon

their personal representatives or assignees (*Coventry* v. *Barclay* (1864)
33 Beav. 1).

(b) Partnership Property

All property and rights and interests in property originally brought
into the partnership stock or acquired, whether by purchase or otherwise, on account of the firm or for the purposes and in the course of
the partnership business, are partnership property, and must be held
and applied by the partners exclusively for the purpose of the partnership and in accordance with the partnership agreement (s. 20 (1)).

Where co-owners of an estate or interest in any land, not being
itself partnership property, are partners as to profits made by the use
of that land and purchase other land out of the profits to be used in
like manner, the land so purchased belongs to them, in the absence of
an agreement to the contrary, not as partners, but as co-owners for
the same respective estates and interests as are held by them in the
land first mentioned at the date of the purchase (s. 20 (3)).

Property, as distinct from money, brought into the partnership and
credited to the capital account of the partner bringing it in, is partnership property, and if on dissolution it realises more than its book
value, the profit thereon is divisible as profits of the business (*Robinson*
v. *Ashton* (1875) L.R. 20 Eq. 25).

Property bought with partnership money is deemed to have been
bought on account of the firm, unless a contrary intention appears
(s. 21). There is evidence of a contrary intention if property is purchased with the firm's money by one partner, and his account is
debited with the cost, so that the property will not belong to the
partnership, but to the partner charged therewith (*Smith* v. *Smith*
(1800) 5 Ves. 189).

Where land has become partnership property, it shall, unless the
contrary intention appears, be treated as between the partners (including the representatives of a deceased partner) as personal and not
real estate (s. 22). The partners are therefore deemed, for the purpose
of the law of property, to have a beneficial interest, not in the land
itself, but in the proceeds of sale thereof.

The property of the partnership may be taken in execution on a
judgment against the firm, but not on a judgment against a separate
partner. A judgment creditor of a partner may, however, obtain an
order charging that partner's interest in the partnership property and
profits with payment of the amount of the judgment debt and interest
thereon, and the appointment of a receiver of that partner's share of
profits (whether already declared or accruing), and of any other
money which may be coming to him in respect of the partnership. In
the event of such an order being made, the other partner or partners

will be at liberty at any time to redeem the interest charged, or in the case of a sale being directed, to purchase the same (s. 23). The charging of a partner's share is also ground for dissolution at the option of the other partners (s. 33 (2)), except where the judgment debtor is a limited partner (Limited Partnerships Act, 1907, s. 6).

(c) Rules as to Rights and Duties of Partners

In the absence of any agreement to the contrary, the following rules as to the interests, rights, and duties of partners in relation to the partnership will apply (s. 24):

(1) All the partners are entitled to share equally in the capital and profits of the business, and must contribute equally towards the losses, whether of capital or otherwise, sustained by the firm.

(2) The firm must indemnify every partner in respect of payments made and personal liabilities incurred by him:

   (a) in the ordinary and proper conduct of the business of the firm; or

   (b) in or about anything necessarily done for the preservation of the business or property of the firm.

(3) A partner making, for the purpose of the partnership, any actual payment or advance beyond the amount of capital which he has agreed to subscribe, is entitled to interest at the rate of five per cent. per annum from the date of the payment or advance.

(4) A partner is not entitled, before the ascertainment of profits, to interest on the capital subscribed by him.

(5) Every partner may take part in the management of the partnership business.

(6) No partner shall be entitled to remuneration for acting in the partnership business.

(7) No person may be introduced as a partner without the consent of all existing partners.

(8) Any difference arising as to ordinary matters connected with the partnership business may be decided by a majority of the partners, but no change may be made in the nature of the partnership business without the consent of all existing partners.

(9) The partnership books are to be kept at the place of business of the partnership (or the principal place, if there is more than one), and every partner may, when he thinks fit, have access to and inspect and copy any of them. A partner may have the books inspected and copies taken by an agent, provided that the agent undertakes not to use the information obtained for any other

purpose, and is not a person to whom the other partners can reasonably object (*Bevan* v. *Webb* [1901] 2 Ch. 59). A limited partner is given a statutory right to inspect the partnership books through the medium of an agent (Limited Partnerships Act, 1907, s. 6).

(d) Expulsion of a Partner

Unless the power to do so has been conferred by express agreement between the partners, no majority of the partners can expel any partner (s. 25). Even where the partnership agreement provides that a majority of partners may expel a partner, the power must be exercised in good faith, and the court will always prevent such a power being exercised harshly or inequitably.

(e) Express Assignments

Although a partner cannot introduce another partner into the business, in substitution for himself, without the consent of all the other partners, there is nothing to prevent him mortgaging or assigning his share to a third party, who would then acquire a right to payment of what, upon taking the accounts of the partnership, might be due to that partner.

An assignment by any partner of his share in the partnership, either absolute or by way of mortgage or redeemable charge, does not, as against the other partners, entitle the assignee, during the continuance of the partnership, to interfere in the management or administration of the partnership business or affairs, or to require any accounts of the partnership transactions, or to inspect the partnership books, but entitles the assignee only to receive the share of profits to which the assigning partner would otherwise be entitled, and the assignee must accept the account of profits agreed to by the partners (s. 31 (1)).

In case of a dissolution of the partnership, whether as respects all the partners or as respects the assigning partner, the assignee is entitled to receive the share of the partnership assets to which the assigning partner is entitled as between himself and the other partners, and, for the purpose of ascertaining that share, to an account as from the date of the dissolution (s. 31 (2)).

The assignee is bound by any *bona fide* agreement entered into subsequently by the partners, even an agreement to charge salaries in respect of services rendered by the partners to the firm (*Re Garwood's Trusts* [1903] 1 Ch. 236).

(f) Partnership at Will

In the ordinary course a partnership is entered into for a fixed term, and can only be dissolved before the expiration of that term by agreement, or the fulfilment of certain conditions; but where a partnership has not been entered into for a fixed term, it is a partnership at will, and a partner may retire from it at any time by giving notice of his intention so to do to all the other partners (s. 26).

But even when no fixed term has been agreed upon, the partnership will not be a partnership at will if there is some agreement to the contrary. Thus, where a partnership for no fixed term was to be dissolved 'by mutual arrangement only,' it was held that one partner could not give notice to dissolve, the assent of the other partners being necessary (*Moss* v. *Elphick* [1910] 1 K.B. 846).

Where a partnership entered into for a fixed term is continued after the term has expired, without any express new agreement, it becomes a partnership at will, and the rights and duties of the partners remain the same as they were at the expiration of the term, so far as this is consistent with the incidents of a partnership at will.

A continuance of the business by the partners or such of them as habitually acted therein during the term, without any settlement or liquidation of the partnership affairs, is presumed to be a continuance of the partnership (s. 27).

(g) Specific Duties of Partners

(1) *To Act in Good Faith*

The primary duty of a person who has entered into the contract of partnership is to perform his part of the contract. Whatever he may have agreed to at the time of entering into partnership is binding upon him, so far as the other partners are concerned, whether the matter concerned is to their advantage or otherwise.

A partnership contract is one that falls into the class known as contracts *uberrimae fidei* (see Chap. I, § 8 (b)), and every member of the firm must show the utmost good faith to every other member. Thus, a partner must not, at the expense of his co-partners, obtain any secret profit or other advantage; he must do his best for the firm business, and must render to his partners their proper share of all benefits which he may have been able to obtain in respect of partnership transactions.

The court will never order specific performance of an agreement to enter into partnership, as it would be impossible to enforce the good faith necessary to such a contract. Damages only could be obtained in the event of the breach of such an agreement.

(2) *To Render Accounts and Information*

Partners are bound to render true accounts and full information of all things affecting the partnership to any partner or his legal representatives (s. 28).

(3) *To Account for Private Profits*

Every partner must account to the firm for any benefit derived by him without the consent of the other partners from any transaction concerning the partnership, or from any use by him of the partnership property, name, or business connection (s. 29 (1)).

The section applies also to transactions undertaken after a partnership has been dissolved by the death of a partner, and before the affairs thereof have been completely wound up either by any surviving partner or by the representatives of the deceased partner (s. 29 (2)).

(4) *Not to Compete with the Firm*

If a partner, without the consent of the other partners, carries on any business of the same nature as, and competing with, that of the firm, he must account for and pay over to the firm all profits made by him in that business (s. 30).

Where a competing business is carried on with the consent of the other partners, it must be carried on strictly in accordance with the terms of the consent given, so that if any limitations are imposed they must be complied with. The section does not apply to businesses carried on which are not of a nature competitive with the actual partnership business; in any such case the person carrying on the business is personally entitled to the profit he makes (*Aas* v. *Benham* [1891] 2 Ch. 244; *Dean* v. *MacDowell* (1877) 8 Ch. D. 345). A partner may, therefore, be a member of another firm engaged in the same trade so long as there is no question of competition between the two firms (*Trimble* v. *Goldberg* [1906] A.C. 494).

§ 4. *Dissolution of Partnership*

(a) Grounds for Dissolution of Partnership

A partnership is only binding upon the members of a firm for the actual period for which it has been agreed that it shall continue, though it frequently goes on for a longer period by reason of a renewal for a further period, or by its continuance as a partnership at will.

A partnership can be dissolved at any time by mutual agreement. The Act provides for dissolution in the following circumstances:

(1) *Effluxion of Time, Termination of Adventure, or Notice*

Subject to any agreement between the partners, a partnership is dissolved:

(i) if entered into for a fixed term, by the expiration of that term;

(ii) if entered into for a single adventure or undertaking, by the termination of that adventure or undertaking;

(iii) if entered into for an undefined time, by any partner giving notice to the other or others of his intention to dissolve the partnership.

In the last case the partnership is dissolved as from the date mentioned in the notice as the date of dissolution, or, if no date is so mentioned, as from the date of the communication of the notice (s. 32).

(2) *Death or Bankruptcy*

Subject to any agreement between the partners, every partnership is dissolved as regards all the partners by the death or bankruptcy of any partner (s. 33 (1)).

A partnership may, at the option of the other partners, be dissolved if any partner suffers his share of the partnership property to be charged under the Act for his separate debt (s. 33 (2)).

Mere insolvency is not of itself a ground for dissolution, unless the partnership agreement so provides; but if a partner (other than a limited partner) allows his interest in the partnership to be charged as a result of his insolvency, the partnership may be dissolved at the option of the other partners.

(3) *Illegality*

A partnership is in every case dissolved by the happening of any event which makes it unlawful for the business of the firm to be carried on, or for the members of the firm to carry it on in partnership (s. 34).

The question of illegal partnerships has already been considered (*ante*, § 1 (b)).

(4) *Decree of the Court*

On application by a partner, the court may decree a dissolution of the partnership in any of the following cases (s. 35):

(i) Where the court is satisfied, after considering medical evidence, that a partner is incapable, by reason of mental disorder, of managing and administering his property and affairs (Mental Health Act, 1959, ss. 101, 103, replacing s. 35 (*a*) of the Partnership Act, 1890). Application may be made on behalf of the partner so incapacitated, or by a creditor, as well as by any other partner.

(ii) When a partner, other than the partner suing, becomes in any other way permanently incapable of performing his part of the partnership contract.

(iii) When a partner, other than the partner suing, has been guilty of such conduct as, in the opinion of the court, regard being had to the nature of the business, is calculated prejudicially to affect the carrying on of the business.

(iv) When a partner, other than the partner suing, wilfully or persistently commits a breach of the partnership agreement or otherwise so conducts himself in matters relating to the partnership business that it is not reasonably practicable for the other partner or partners to carry on the business in partnership with him.

(v) When the business of the partnership can only be carried on at a loss.

(vi) Whenever in any case circumstances have arisen which, in the opinion of the court, render it just and equitable that the partnership be dissolved.

The last ground gives the court a wide discretion to decree a dissolution in circumstances which do not fall within any of the specific grounds laid down by the section, e.g., where the business cannot be carried on because of deadlock between the partners, or where one partner is excluded from the business by the other partners.

(b) Notification of Dissolution

It has already been pointed out that a retiring partner should give notice of retirement (*ante*, § 2 (f) (3)). On the dissolution of a partnership or retirement of a partner any partner may publicly notify the same, and may require the other partner or partners to concur for that purpose in all necessary or proper acts, if any, which cannot be done without his or their concurrence (s. 37).

(c) Agreement as to Substituted Partner

An agreement that a partner shall have power to nominate another person as a partner of the firm is binding upon the other partners, but merely optional upon the nominee (*Byrne* v. *Reid* [1902] 2 Ch. 735). Where the admission of the nominee is to take place on the death or retirement of the partner by whom he was nominated and the nominee does not choose to enter the firm, it will be dissolved in the ordinary way.

(d) Continuation of Authority of Partners

After the dissolution of a partnership, the authority of each partner to bind the firm, and the other rights and obligations of the partners, continue notwithstanding the dissolution so far as may be necessary to wind up the affairs of the partnership, and to complete transactions begun but unfinished at the time of the dissolution, but not otherwise.

Provided that the firm is in no case bound by the acts of a partner who has become bankrupt; but this proviso does not affect the liability of any person who has, after the bankruptcy, represented himself or knowingly suffered himself to be represented as a partner of the bankrupt (s. 38).

Where judgment has been obtained against a debtor and one of the partners retires from the creditor firm, the remaining partners may issue a bankruptcy notice without special leave (*Re Hill* (1921) 125 L.T. 736).

(e) Partnership Lien

On the dissolution of a partnership every partner is entitled, as against the other partners in the firm, and all persons claiming through them in respect of their interest as partners, to have the property of the partnership applied in payment of the debts and liabilities of the firm, and to have the surplus assets after such payment applied in payment of what may be due to the partners respectively after deducting what may be due from them as partners to the firm; and for that purpose any partner or his representatives may on the termination of the partnership apply to the court to wind up the business and affairs of the firm (s. 39).

This equitable lien conferred upon partners will not extend to property mortgaged or pledged by a person apparently entitled so to dispose of it, unless the pledgee had notice of absence of authority for the purpose.

(f) Appointment of Receiver of Partnership Property

The Act does not confer any actual right to the appointment of a receiver, but such an appointment may be obtained by application to the court when dissolution has taken place or is contemplated, and sufficient grounds for such an appointment can be shown to exist.

The following would constitute grounds for such an appointment:

(1) When a partner has so misconducted himself that the property of the firm is in danger of being lost.

(2) When a partner desires to enforce his equitable lien on the partnership property and have the assets of the firm applied in accordance with the provisions of the Act.

(3) When all partners are dead and an action is pending between their personal representatives.

The court is usually unwilling to appoint a receiver when dissolution is not contemplated, but an appointment may be obtained on the following grounds:

(i) To receive a certain sum of money and apply it to a specific purpose when there is reason to fear that if it were received by the partners it would be misapplied.

(ii) To protect the property of the firm during a dispute between the partners.

(g) Return of Premium

Very frequently an existing firm takes in an additional partner, and charges him a premium for the right which he acquires to share in the profits of an established business. This premium is really a payment for that portion of the goodwill in which he obtains an interest.

Where one partner has paid a premium to another on entering into a partnership for a fixed term, and the partnership is dissolved before the expiration of that term otherwise than by the death of a partner, the court may order the repayment of the premium, or of such part thereof as it thinks just, having regard to the terms of the partnership contract and to the length of time during which the partnership has continued; unless:

(1) the dissolution is, in the judgment of the court, wholly or chiefly due to the misconduct of the partner who paid the premium, or

(2) the partnership has been dissolved by an agreement containing no provision for a return of any part of the premium (s. 40).

If the partnership agreement itself provides for a return of premium upon dissolution, this must of course be complied with; otherwise the only remedy is by application to the court, who will in a proper case order a return of a portion bearing the same ratio to the whole premium as the unexpired term of the partnership bears to the whole term, according to the agreement (*Attwood* v. *Maude* (1868) L.R. 3 Ch. 369).

(h) Rights of a Defrauded Partner

Where a partnership contract is rescinded on the ground of the fraud or misrepresentation of one of the parties thereto, the party entitled to rescind is, without prejudice to any other right, entitled:

(1) to a lien on, or right of retention of, the surplus of the partnership assets, after satisfying the partnership liabilities, for any sum of money paid by him for the purchase of a share in the partnership and for any capital contributed by him, and is

(2) to stand in the place of the creditors of the firm for any payments made by him in respect of the partnership liabilities, and

(3) to be indemnified by the person guilty of the fraud or making the representation against all the debts and liabilities of the firm (s. 41).

(i) Right of Retiring Partner to Share in Profits after Dissolution

Where any member of a firm has died or otherwise ceased to be a partner, and the surviving or continuing partners carry on the business of the firm with its capital or assets without any final settlement of accounts as between the firm and the outgoing partner or his

estate, then, in the absence of any agreement to the contrary, the outgoing partner or his estate is entitled at the option of himself or his
representatives to:

(1) such share of the profits made since the dissolution as the court
    may find to be attributable to the use of his share of the partner-
    ship assets, or

(2) to interest at the rate of five per cent. per annum on the amount
    of his share of the partnership assets (s. 42 (1)).

Where the partnership agreement has given an option to the surviving or continuing partners to purchase the interest of a deceased or
outgoing partner, and the option is duly exercised, the estate of the
deceased partner, or the outgoing partner or his estate, as the case
may be, is not entitled to any further or other share of the profits; but
if any partner assuming to act in exercise of the option does not in all
material respects comply with the terms thereof, he is liable to account
in the manner set out above (s. 42 (2)).

If there is any provision in the partnership agreement as to the
mode of settlement with a retiring partner or the estate of a deceased
partner it must be complied with, and the rights of the outgoing
partner will only exist in accordance with such agreement; this is
particularly emphasised by s. 42 (2).

It is not infrequent to find that the provisions as to sharing profits
in the event of the death of a partner are different from those applicable when the partner retires.

In *McLeod* v. *Dowling* (1927) 43 T.L.R. 655, a partner had sent by post notice
of his retirement, but he died during the night and prior to the receipt of the
notice by his co-partners. It was held that the partners' interests were to be determined in accordance with the agreement operative in the event of death, the
notice having no effect until receipt by the other partners.

If an account of profits is ordered, the court can make an allowance
to the continuing partner for carrying on the business (*Manley* v.
Sartori [1927] 1 Ch. 157).

(j) Goodwill

A partner, upon retiring, is entitled to the value of his share of the
goodwill, unless the partnership agreement vests it in the continuing
or surviving partners; and it is usually provided by the agreement how
the value of such share is to be fixed and paid.

Goodwill has been defined as the value attaching to the reputation
of a business, and to the likelihood that custom will continue to be
attracted in the future as in the past, notwithstanding any change in
the proprietorship. Goodwill may originate, broadly speaking, in one
of three ways, or a combination of them:

(1) by means of the reputation of the article produced, as apart from the personality of the proprietors;

(2) by reason of the possession by the business of special advantages in the shape of local or partial monopoly, patents, trade marks, situation of premises, etc.;

(3) by the personal reputation and influence of the proprietors.

Upon an absolute dissolution, every partner has a right to have the goodwill sold for the benefit of all the partners, but a partner must not make use of it for his own exclusive gain, or do anything detrimental to its value before it is sold (*Turner* v. *Major* (1862) 3 Giff. 442).

Should the goodwill not be sold upon dissolution, every partner can carry on business in competition with the others, and even use the firm name, so long as his act does not expose the other partners to liability, *e.g.*, by holding them out as his partners (*Burchell* v. *Wilde* [1900] 1 Ch. 551).

The value of the goodwill, if not previously standing in the partnership books, is divisible amongst the partners as they share profits and losses.

The rights of a purchaser of goodwill are:

(1) The right to represent himself as continuing or succeeding to the business of the vendor.

(2) The exclusive right to use the name of the firm in respect of which the goodwill is acquired.

(3) The sole right to solicit the old customers.

As against this the purchaser, though entitled to carry on the business as successor of the vendor, must not do so in such a manner as to suggest that the vendor is a partner in the business, and liable for the debts incurred (*Townsend* v. *Jarman* [1900] 2 Ch. 698).

The vendor of the goodwill may carry on a similar business in competition with the purchaser (subject to any clause in restraint of trade embodied in the contract of sale), but he must not trade in the old firm name or represent himself as continuing that business (*Churton* v. *Douglas* (1859) Johns. 174), nor may he solicit his old customers (*Trego* v. *Hunt* [1896] A.C. 7).

Where the partnership agreement provides that, on the death of a partner, his share of the property and assets shall be taken over by the surviving partners, the executor of the deceased partner can be restrained by injunction from canvassing the customers of the firm (*Boorne* v. *Wicker* [1927] 1 Ch. 667). But a partner who has been expelled from the firm under powers contained in the partnership agreement may compete with his former firm and solicit the customers thereof, subject to any term in restraint of trade in the agreement (*Dawson* v. *Beeson* (1882) 22 Ch. 504).

(k) Amount due to Outgoing Partner is a Debt

Subject to any agreement between the partners, the amount due from surviving or continuing partners to an outgoing partner or the representatives of a deceased partner in respect of the outgoing or deceased partner's share is a debt accruing at the date of the dissolution or death (s. 43). Thus, time begins to run from that date for the purpose of the Limitation Act, 1939.

(l) Rules for Distribution of Assets after Dissolution

In settling accounts between the partners after a dissolution of partnership, the following rules shall, subject to any agreement, be observed:

(1) Losses, including losses and deficiencies of capital, shall be paid first out of profits, next out of capital, and lastly, if necessary, by the partners individually in the proportion in which they were entitled to share profits.

(2) The assets of the firm, including the sums, if any, contributed by the partners to make up losses or deficiencies of capital, shall be applied in the following manner and order:

   (i) in paying the debts and liabilities of the firm to persons who are not partners therein;

   (ii) in paying to each partner rateably what is due from the firm to him for advances as distinguished from capital;

   (iii) in paying to each partner rateably what is due from the firm to him in respect of capital;

   (iv) the ultimate residue, if any, shall be divided among the partners in the proportion in which profits are divisible (s. 44).

Although the partnership agreement can provide an alternative method of distribution as between the partners, it cannot take away the rights of third parties to be paid in due order of priority.

Where, upon dissolution, one of the partners has a deficiency of capital, after a realisation of the assets, and he is unable to bring in such deficiency, this will not be treated as an ordinary trade loss (which would be borne between the partners as they share profits and losses), but must be regarded as a debt due to the remaining partners individually, and not as a debt due to the firm. The deficiency must, therefore, be borne by the solvent partners in proportion to their respective capitals in the business (*Garner* v. *Murray* [1904] 1 Ch. 57).

Money advanced to a firm by a partner is in part lent by the partner to himself, and cannot therefore be recovered by a common law action for money lent: the accounts required by s. 44 (2) must be taken (*Green* v. *Hertzog* [1954] 1 W.L.R. 1309).

§ 5. *Limited Partnerships*

(a) Limited Partnerships Act, 1907

Under the Limited Partnerships Act, 1907, it is possible for some members of a firm to obtain limited liability by the registration of the firm under the Act.

Limited partnerships have never been very common because, simultaneously with the passing of the Act, the legislature created the private limited company, so that it became possible for an association of persons, with a minimum number of two, to secure limited liability for all its members under the Companies Acts. In a limited partnership this advantage is only obtainable by some, as at least one partner of such a firm must be a general partner with unlimited liability.

(b) Essentials of a Limited Partnership

A limited partnership may not consist, in the case of a partnership carrying on the business of banking, of more than ten persons, and, in the case of any other partnership, of more than twenty persons, and must consist of one or more persons called *general* partners, who are liable for all debts and obligations of the firm, and one or more persons called *limited* partners, who, at the time of entering into the partnership, contribute thereto a sum or sums as capital or property valued at a stated amount, and who are not liable for the debts or obligations of the firm beyond the amount so contributed (s. 4 (2)).

The limited partner must contribute his capital at the time of entering into the partnership; it cannot be left to be called upon as and when required.

A limited partner may not during the continuance of the partnership, either directly or indirectly, draw out or receive back any part of his contribution, and if he does so he is liable for the debts and obligations of the firm up to the amount so drawn out or received back (s. 4 (3)).

Thus, if a limited partner desires to dispose of his interest in the firm, he has no alternative but to assign his share, with the consent of the general partners, to some other person.

(c) Registration

Every limited partnership must be registered as such with the Registrar of Companies, and in default thereof it will be deemed to be a general partnership, and every limited partner will be deemed to be a general partner (s. 5).

The registration of a limited partnership is effected by sending to the Registrar of Companies a statement signed by the partners containing the following particulars:

(1) The firm name.

(2) The general nature of the business.

(3) The principal place of business.

(4) The full name of each of the partners.

(5) The term, if any, for which the partnership is entered into, and the date of its commencement.

(6) A statement that the partnership is limited, and the description of every limited partner as such.

(7) The sum contributed by each limited partner, and whether paid in cash or how otherwise (s. 8).

If during the continuance of a limited partnership any change is made or occurs in any of these particulars, a statement, signed by the firm, specifying the nature of the change must be sent to the Registrar within seven days (s. 9).

The limited partner must himself see that the partnership is registered, as otherwise he will be deemed to be a general partner; but the duty of registering any change in the partnership rests with the general partners, who are liable to a fine not exceeding £1 for each day during which a default continues.

Notice of any arrangement or transaction under which any person will cease to be a general partner in any firm, and will become a limited partner in that firm, or under which the share of a limited partner in a firm will be assigned to any person, must be advertised forthwith in the *London Gazette*, and until notice of the arrangement or transaction is so advertised, the arrangement or transaction is for the purposes of the Act deemed to be of no effect (s. 10).

The amount registered as the capital contributed by a limited partner is subject to stamp duty at the rate of ten shillings per cent. If the capital of a limited partner is increased the same rate of duty is payable on the increase.

The Registrar of Companies is required to keep a register and index of all limited partnerships, and of all statements filed thereby, and such records are open to the inspection of any person on payment of the usual search fees. Certified copies of any documents may be obtained on payment of the usual fees.

(d) Modifications of General Partnership Law

The provisions of the Partnership Act, 1890, and the rules of equity and common law applicable to partnerships also apply to limited partnerships in so far as they are not inconsistent with the

Limited Partnerships Act, 1907 (s. 7). The general law has been modified in the following ways (s. 6):

(1) A limited partner may not take part in the management of the partnership business, and has no power to bind the firm. A limited partner may, however, by himself or his agent at any time inspect the books of the firm and examine into the state and prospects of the partnership business, and may advise with the partners thereon.

   If a limited partner takes part in the management of the partnership business, he is liable for all debts and obligations of the firm incurred while he so takes part in the management as though he were a general partner.

(2) A limited partnership is not dissolved by the death or bankruptcy of a limited partner, and the insanity of a limited partner is not a ground for dissolution of the partnership by the court unless that partner's share cannot be otherwise ascertained and realised.

(3) In the event of the dissolution of a limited partnership, its affairs are wound up by the general partners unless the court otherwise orders.

(4) Subject to any agreement expressed or implied between the partners:
   (i) any difference arising as to ordinary matters connected with the partnership business may be decided by a majority of the general partners;
   (ii) a limited partner may, with the consent of the general partners, assign his share in the partnership, and upon such an assignment the assignee becomes a limited partner with all the rights of the assignor;
   (iii) the other partners are not entitled to dissolve the partnership by reason of any limited partner suffering his share to be charged for his separate debt;
   (iv) a person may be introduced as a partner without the consent of the existing limited partners;
   (v) a limited partner is not entitled to dissolve the partnership by notice.

(e) Dissolution

The death or bankruptcy of a limited partner does not, in the absence of agreement, dissolve the partnership. If the limited partner becomes insane, the partnership is only dissolved if his share cannot be otherwise ascertained.

The business will be wound up by the general partners unless the court otherwise directs. It may, however, be wound up in bankruptcy, and on all the general partners being adjudicated bankrupt, the assets of the limited partnership vest in the trustee in bankruptcy (Bankruptcy Act, 1914, s. 127).

CHAPTER IX

ARBITRATION

§ 1. *Arbitrations Generally*

(a) Definitions

Arbitration consists of the reference of a dispute to one or more independent persons for settlement, instead of to a court of law.

There can be no arbitration out of court without an agreement between the parties to refer the decision of differences to one or more arbitrators. If the arbitration is to be under the Arbitration Act, 1950, the agreement must be in writing: an oral submission would give rise to an arbitration at common law to which the Arbitration Act would have no application. Under certain Acts of Parliament specified notices and proceedings are made equivalent to an arbitration agreement; and the court has power in certain circumstances to refer a matter to arbitration without the consent of the parties.

The meaning of 'reference' is, strictly, the proceedings during the arbitration; but the term is also used to denote the agreement to submit differences to arbitration. The word 'submission' is sometimes used to mean the agreement to submit to arbitration.

The *arbitrator* is the person to whose decision the matters in dispute are referred. His decision is called the *award*.

An *umpire* is a person appointed, when the reference is to more than one arbitrator, to give a decision if the arbitrators cannot agree. His decision is called the *umpirage*.

(b) Advantages and Disadvantages of Arbitration

The principal advantages of arbitration, as compared with litigation in a court of law, are:

(1) the avoidance of publicity, since arbitrations are conducted privately;

(2) the simplicity of procedure;

(3) the avoidance, to a certain extent, of the delays, uncertainty and expense involved in appeals, as the award, assuming it to be valid, is final;

(4) the saving of time;

(5) the saving of expense;

(6) possible technical knowledge of the arbitrator, who may be appointed because of his special knowledge of the business concerned.

The principal disadvantages of arbitration are:

(1) the arbitrator may be incompetent or biased;

(2) injustice may result from the informality of the procedure.

The parties to arbitration proceedings are free to choose any person they please as arbitrator, and the choice of a suitable arbitrator often causes difficulty. If a man of business is chosen, he may not be well versed in the law; or, if a lawyer is chosen, he may not have the special knowledge and experience which ought to be brought to bear on the dispute. If appointed by one of the parties, he is liable to be biased in favour of that party; while if two arbitrators are appointed, each is liable to consider himself the advocate of the party who appointed him. To obviate these disadvantages, the practice of naming an independent person to appoint the arbitrator, e.g., the President of the Institute of Chartered Accountants, is frequently adopted.

An unsuitable choice of arbitrator may give rise to two serious consequences. If he is an incompetent person he may make a bad award, which will render all the proceedings void; and, on the other hand, if he is competent but biased, although he may give no cause for complaint in the conduct of the proceedings, he may make an award which is not in accord with the facts and the true legal rights of the parties, and such award will be final and binding, unless it can be shown to be bad in law.

Another point which, although advantageous from one aspect, may yet operate disadvantageously, is that the procedure on a reference is not so strictly defined as that which applies in a court of law, this being a matter which the arbitrator may control, within certain limits, at his discretion.

(c) References which are not Arbitrations

The essence of an arbitration is that there must be differences either existing or prospective between the parties, which the parties agree, or which the court orders, shall be finally and conclusively settled by the judicial decision of the arbitrator.

If a third party has to decide the amount to be paid for certain property on his own judgment or experience without hearing evidence or arguments on either side, this is not an arbitration but a *valuation.*

In *Re Carus-Wilson and Greene* (1886) 18 Q.B.D. 7, a contract for the sale of an estate provided that the timber should be taken at a valuation, each party to appoint his own valuer, and that such valuers should, in case of difference, appoint an umpire. It was held that the court had no power to set aside the umpire's decision, as he was a valuer, and not an arbitrator.

The position of an architect or engineer who has to give certificates for the payment of the price of work done under a contract is a doubtful one. The earlier cases regarded him as a valuer only; later cases have treated him as, in some respects, an arbitrator.

In *Chambers* v. *Goldthorpe* [1901] 1 K.B. 624, a building contract provided for payments on account of the price of works during their progress, and for the payment of the balance after their completion, upon certificates of the architect; and the final certificate was to be conclusive evidence of the works having been duly completed, upon which the contractor was entitled to receive payment of the final balance. The Court of Appeal held that the architect occupied the position of an arbitrator, on the ground that he had to settle matters in respect of which, though there was no actual dispute, there would probably be a dispute unless they were so settled.

The essential differences between an arbitration and a valuation are:

(1) The provisions of the Arbitration Act, 1950, relating to arbitrations have no application to valuations.

(2) An arbitration is a proceeding of a quasi-judicial nature; a valuation is not.

(3) An arbitrator, being in a semi-judicial position, is not liable to an action for negligence by the parties; a valuer is liable to the party appointing him according to the terms of the contract whereby he undertakes the valuation.

(4) An award can be enforced by leave of the court, in the same manner as a judgment or order of the court; a valuation simply fixes a term of a contract, leaving the parties to their remedies on the contract.

(d) Who may Refer to Arbitration

Any person, whether an individual or a corporation, who can enter into a contract can submit to arbitration. A person who cannot contract cannot be bound by an arbitration agreement. Thus, an infant, although he may submit to arbitration, may avoid the award, unless it is in respect of a contract binding on him (*Slade* v. *Metrodent, Ltd.* [1953] 2 Q.B. 112).

Persons having no beneficial interest in the subject-matter of the reference may submit to arbitration, *e.g.*, executors, trustees, a trustee in bankruptcy; but the submission will amount to an admission of assets and involve personal liability, unless otherwise stipulated.

An agent duly authorised may bind his principal by submission to arbitration; and an implied authority may arise from the nature of the agency. If the submission is to be by deed, the agent must be appointed by deed. But the fact that the arbitration agreement must be in writing to come within the Arbitration Act, 1950, does not mean that the agent must be authorised in writing. The agent should submit in the principal's name, otherwise he will be personally bound.

One partner cannot submit to arbitration so as to bind the others without their assent; but the partner submitting will be personally bound by the award, and the other partners may become bound by implication, as, for instance, if they appear before the arbitrator without objecting (*Thomas* v. *Atherton* (1878) 10 Ch. D. 185). The fact that one partner has authorised the other, upon a dissolution, to collect the firm debts and to take legal proceedings in their joint names to recover them does not authorise the acting partner to bind the retiring partner by the reference to arbitration of an action brought under the power conferred (*Hatton* v. *Royle* (1858) 27 L.J. Ex. 486).

(e) Subject-Matter of the Reference

All matters that might be settled by action between the parties in a court of law may be referred to arbitration, with the following exceptions:

(1) Purely criminal matters, since the party concerned, if guilty, should be punished, and that only the courts can do. If, however, the party injured by a criminal offence has also a civil remedy, the civil claim may be referred to arbitration; but if a criminal prosecution has been commenced, the consent of the court is required to refer the civil claim to arbitration.

(2) Matters affecting status, such as a suit for dissolution of marriage, or proceedings in bankruptcy.

§ 2. *Methods of Referring to Arbitration*

A reference to arbitration may be made in any of the following ways:

(a) Under certain Acts of Parliament;

(b) By order of the court;

(c) By voluntary submission of the parties either orally at common law or in writing under the Arbitration Act, 1950.

(a) References under Acts of Parliament

Provision is made by various Acts of Parliament for the reference to arbitration of certain matters. In some instances, arbitration is compulsory, but in others it is optional. The former include matters concerning agricultural holdings, housing, public utilities, street works and tramways. Provisions for arbitration at the option of the parties or of one of them exist in relation to disputes in connection with rent restriction, public health, friendly societies, industrial and provident societies and building societies. In particular, the Companies Act, 1948, s. 287, makes provision for the valuation by arbitration of a company's shares held by a member dissenting from a scheme of reconstruction.

The provisions of the Arbitration Act, 1950, (with certain exceptions) apply to every arbitration under any other Act of Parliament, except in so far as the Arbitration Act is inconsistent with that other Act or with any rules of procedure authorised or recognised thereby (Arbitration Act, 1950, s. 31).

(b) References by Order of the Court

Under s. 15 of the Administration of Justice Act, 1956, and the Rules of the Supreme Court, the court may refer to an official or special referee for inquiry or report any question arising in any cause or matter, other than a criminal proceeding by the Crown. The report of the referee may be adopted wholly or partially by the court or a judge, and if so adopted may be enforced as a judgment or order to the same effect. Such a reference may be made even against the wishes of the parties.

In the following cases the court may order the whole cause or matter, or any question or issue of fact arising therein, to be tried before a special referee or arbitrator respectively agreed on by the parties, or before an official referee or officer of the court:

(1) if all the parties interested who are not under disability consent; or

(2) if the cause or matter requires any prolonged examination of documents or any scientific or local investigation which cannot in the opinion of the court or a judge conveniently be made before a jury or conducted by the court through its other ordinary officers; or

(3) if the question in dispute consists wholly or in part of matters of accounts.

In these cases of reference for trial, judgment is entered in accordance with the decision of the referee or arbitrator.

Under the County Courts Act, 1959, a county court judge has similar powers to refer a matter to the registrar or a referee for inquiry and report, but he may only refer a matter for trial with the consent of the parties to the action.

(c) References by Voluntary Submission of the Parties

A valid submission to arbitration by consent of the parties can be made orally at common law. The provisions of the Arbitration Act, 1950, have no application to such a submission. An oral submission of this kind has the following disadvantages:

(1) There may be a conflict of evidence as to the terms of the arbitration agreement.

(2) If one party commences legal proceedings in lieu of going to arbitration, the court has no power to stay those proceedings.

(3) If one party refuses to proceed with the arbitration, the only course of the other party is to sue for breach of the contract to refer.

(4) There is no means of enforcing the award of the arbitrator except by action in the courts.

(5) All the terms of the submission must be agreed, as the Arbitration Act has no application.

(6) If the subject-matter of the dispute is a contract for which evidence in writing is required under s. 4 of the Statute of Frauds, 1677, or s. 40 of the Law of Property Act, 1925, no action can be taken to enforce an award based on an oral submission.

A voluntary submission *in writing* is governed by the provisions of the Arbitration Act, 1950.

§ 3. *Arbitration Act, 1950*

(a) The Arbitration Agreement

For the purposes of the Act, an arbitration agreement is a written agreement to submit present or future differences to arbitration, whether an arbitrator is named therein or not (s. 32).

The submission may be by writing under hand only, by deed, or by bond, signed either by the party or by his duly authorised agent. If the award would have to be carried out by the execution of a deed, the submission should itself be by deed. A party who has not signed may be bound if the agreement to refer, having been signed by one party, is confirmed by the subsequent conduct of the party who has not signed.

In *Baker* v. *Yorkshire Fire and Life Assurance Co.* [1892] 1 Q.B. 144, a fire insurance policy contained a clause that any differences under it should be referred to arbitration. The assured sued the insurance company and by so doing affirmed the policy as his contract, and thereby constituted the arbitration clause a submission, although he had not signed the policy; and the court stayed proceedings under the Arbitration Act, 1889.

Where the articles of a company contain a clause providing that all disputes between the company and any member shall be referred to arbitration, a member is bound by the clause, as he is deemed to have signed and sealed the articles under what is now s. 20 of the Companies Act, 1948 (*Hickman* v. *Kent or Romney Marsh Sheep Breeders' Association* [1915] 1 Ch. 881).

The parties may agree to refer to arbitration a dispute which has actually arisen or some difference that may conceivably arise in the future in relation to some contract into which they have entered.

Agreements to refer future disputes to arbitration are frequently found in deeds of partnership, insurance policies, leases and contracts for the sale of goods.

The terms of an arbitration agreement may, with the agreement of the parties, be altered at any time before the arbitrator has given his decision. The alterations must be in writing, and if the submission is by deed, any alteration of its terms must be similarly executed. The submission cannot be altered so as to include a dispute about which an action has already been commenced by one of the parties against the other. Any alteration must be made at the instance of the parties: the arbitrator has no authority to effect an amendment.

(b) Effect of Death or Bankruptcy

An arbitration agreement is not discharged by the death of any party thereto, either as respects the deceased or any other party, but is in such an event enforceable by or against the personal representatives of the deceased; nor is the authority of an arbitrator revoked by the death of any party by whom he was appointed (s. 2).

If a party to a contract containing an arbitration clause becomes bankrupt, the clause is enforceable by or against the trustee in bankruptcy if he adopts the contract (s. 3 (1)). If, on the other hand, an arbitration agreement made by a bankrupt before the commencement of his bankruptcy does not relate to a contract adopted by the trustee, but relates to a matter requiring to be determined in the bankruptcy proceedings, a different rule applies. In that event, any other party to the agreement or, with the consent of the committee of inspection, the trustee in bankruptcy may apply to the court having jurisdiction in the bankruptcy proceedings for an order directing that the matter in question shall be referred to arbitration in accordance with the agreement, and that court may, if it is of opinion that, having regard to all the circumstances of the case, the matter ought to be determined by arbitration, make an order accordingly (s. 3 (2)).

(c) Ouster of Jurisdiction of Court

An agreement which purports to oust the jurisdiction of the court is *prima facie* void, since it is presumed to be contrary to public policy (see Chap. I, § 9 (b)). An agreement to refer to arbitration does not as a rule oust the jurisdiction of the court, because it is still open to the parties to take legal proceedings instead of going to arbitration, though it may well be in such a case that the court will exercise its power under s. 4 to stay the proceedings.

If, however, the parties agree not to require the arbitrator to state a special case for the opinion of the court (see (h), *infra*), this will constitute an ouster of the court's power to order a case to be stated, and such a clause will be void (*Czarnikow* v. *Roth, Schmidt & Co.*

[1922] 2 K.B. 478); and a clause by which the parties agree not to make the arbitrator a witness in any proceedings arising out of the arbitration is similarly void (*E. Rotheray & Sons, Ltd.* v. *Carlo Bedarida & Co.* [1961] 1 Lloyd's Rep. 220).

Where the agreement provides that a reference to arbitration shall be a condition precedent to the right to sue, or that no cause of action shall arise until the dispute has been referred to arbitration, no action can successfully be brought until a reference to arbitration has taken place, because, by the terms of the agreement itself, no cause of action exists until then (*Scott* v. *Avery* (1856) 5 H.L.C. 811). A '*Scott* v. *Avery* clause,' as such agreements are commonly known, is perfectly valid, as it does not oust the jurisdiction of the court, but merely suspends the right of action until the condition precedent is fulfilled. Moreover, by s. 25 (4), where it is provided that an award under an arbitration agreement shall be a condition precedent to the bringing of an action with respect to any matter to which the agreement applies, the court, if it orders that the agreement shall cease to have effect as regards any particular dispute, may further order that the provision making an award a condition precedent to the bringing of an action shall also cease to have effect as regards that dispute. In this way a cause of action may arise in spite of the provisions of the agreement. (For the circumstances in which the court may make such an order, see (d), *infra*.)

(d) Stay of Proceedings

Specific performance will not be granted in respect of an agreement to refer to arbitration; but if arbitration has been agreed upon, and notwithstanding this an action is brought by one of the parties, the court *may*, under certain conditions, stay the proceedings on the application of the other party, which will have the effect of compelling the parties to go to arbitration if they wish to have their dispute settled.

The conditions which must be satisfied are:

(1) the applicant must not have delivered any pleadings or taken any other step in the proceedings, other than entering an appearance;

(2) the court must be satisfied that there is no sufficient reason why the matter should not be referred in accordance with the agreement; and

(3) the applicant must be, at the time when the proceedings were commenced, and still remain, ready and willing to do all things necessary for the proper conduct of the arbitration (s. 4 (1)).

A 'step in the proceedings' is any formal act done by a party to an action instituted in a court of law which recognises that action as proceeding and is material to it. It must be in the form of an application to the court and not in the form of an application from one party to the other (*Ives and Barker* v. *Willans* [1894] 2 Ch. 478). The entering of an appearance by the defendant, which indicates his intention to defend the action, is not a 'step in the proceedings' for this purpose. The following, *inter alia*, are 'steps in the proceedings':

(i) Taking out a summons for an extension of time in which to deliver a defence.
(ii) Applying to the master for security for costs.
(iii) Obtaining an order for the delivery of interrogatories.
(iv) Attending at chambers on a hearing of a summons for directions, without objection.
(v) Obtaining an order for particulars and agreeing to an order for discovery.
(vi) Opposing a summons for leave to sign final judgment.

The following are not 'steps in the proceedings':

(i) A demand made to the plaintiff for a statement of claim.
(ii) Obtaining from the plaintiff to the action an extension of time for delivery of defence.
(iii) Filing affidavits in answer to a motion for the appointment of a receiver.
(iv) Taking out a summons to have the proceedings transferred from one list to another.

The making of an order staying legal proceedings is obligatory on the court in the case of arbitration agreements with subjects of foreign states with which the United Kingdom Government has signed a protocol in that behalf, the object being to ensure that arbitration agreements are honoured internationally. Even in such cases, however, proceedings will not be stayed if the applicant has taken any 'step' in the proceedings, or if the agreement or arbitration has become inoperative, or if there is no dispute in regard to the matter agreed to be referred (s. 4 (2)).

In all other cases, if the conditions of s. 4 (1) are satisfied, it is within the discretion of the court whether or not it will stay proceedings, and the burden of proof is upon the party opposing the stay to satisfy the court that there is good reason for proceeding with the action instead of granting the stay.

In particular, the court may refuse to stay proceedings where it has power under s. 24 (1) and (2) to order that an arbitration agreement shall cease to have effect, or to give leave to revoke the authority of an arbitrator or umpire, on the grounds that the arbitrator is or may not be impartial, or that the dispute involves the question whether one of the parties has been guilty of fraud (s. 24 (3)).

The court will also usually refuse a stay if the only question to be decided is a question of law, which the arbitrator would have to deal with by stating a case for the court under s. 21 (*Bristol Corporation* v. *John Aird & Co., Ltd.* [1913] A.C. 241); or if the whole dispute cannot be dealt with by arbitration.

In *Taunton-Collins* v. *Cromie* [1964] 2 All E.R. 332, the plaintiff entered into contracts with an architect and a firm of building contractors for the building of a house. The building contract, to which the architect was not a party, contained an arbitration clause. The house had certain defects, and the plaintiff sued the architect who, in his defence, blamed the contractors. The plaintiff therefore joined the contractors as co-defendants. The contractors claimed that in so far as it affected them the dispute should be referred to arbitration, and applied for a stay of proceedings.

Held: It was undesirable that there should be separate proceedings before two different tribunals, which might reach inconsistent findings. The whole matter should be dealt with in one proceeding, and accordingly, in the exercise of its discretion, the court would refuse to stay the action against the contractors

If a dispute between parties in connection with a contract containing an arbitration clause is whether the contract has ever been entered into at all, or if it is contended that the contract is void *ab initio*, for example, on account of illegality or mistake, the matter cannot be referred to arbitration and so no stay of proceedings will be ordered, because the arbitration clause will fall if the contract falls. But if the parties do not dispute that they have entered into a binding contract, but the question is whether there has been a breach by one side or the other, or whether circumstances have arisen excusing further performance of the contract, the court can quite properly exercise its discretion to stay proceedings (*Heyman* v. *Darwins, Ltd.* [1942] A.C. 356). Similarly, if there is a deviation from the terms of the contract by one party, this will not put an end to the arbitration clause nor disentitle the court to grant a stay of proceedings upon the application of that party (*Woolf* v. *Collis Removal Service* [1948] 1 K.B. 11).

The court will not normally refuse a stay if the agreement contains a '*Scott* v. *Avery* clause,' unless the circumstances justify the setting aside of the clause under s. 25 (4) (*supra*), nor if the agreement provides for the submission of disputes to a foreign court, unless the dispute can be more appropriately tried by an English court (*The Fehmarn* [1958] 1 All E.R. 333).

(e) Arbitration Clause and Third Parties

If the benefit of a contract is assignable, as it will be if it is not of a personal nature, the arbitration clause will follow the assignment of the contract and be enforceable by and against the assignee (*Shayler* v. *Woolf* [1946] Ch. 320).

If, although an assignment has taken place, arbitration proceedings are instituted between the original parties, the arbitrator must take account of the legal position created by the assignment, and if he gives an award in favour of the assignor it will be bad, because it is no longer the assignor who is entitled to the benefit of the contract (*Cottage Club Estates* v. *Woodside Estates Co.* [1928] 2 K.B. 463).

(f) Arbitrators and Umpires

(1) *Appointment of Arbitrator*

The arbitrator will be appointed in accordance with the provisions of the arbitration agreement. If no other mode of reference is provided, the reference will be to a single arbitrator (s. 6). Where the reference is to a single arbitrator and all the parties do not, after differences have arisen, concur in the appointment of an arbitrator, or if the appointed arbitrator refuses to act, or is incapable of acting, or dies, and the parties do not supply the vacancy, any party may serve upon the others written notice to appoint an arbitrator, and, if the appointment is not made within seven clear days after service of the notice, the court may appoint (s. 10).

If the reference is to two arbitrators, the two arbitrators must appoint an umpire immediately after they are themselves appointed (s. 8 (1)). This provision is made to ensure that there will be no deadlock in the event of disagreement between the arbitrators.

Where an arbitration agreement provides that the reference shall be to three arbitrators, one to be appointed by each party and the third by the two arbitrators appointed by the parties, the agreement has effect as if it provided for the appointment of an umpire, and not for the appointment of a third arbitrator by the two arbitrators appointed by the parties (s. 9 (1)). Where the appointment of three arbitrators is made in any other way, they will all three act as arbitrators, and the award of any two will be binding (s. 9 (2)). The distinction between a third arbitrator and an umpire is that a third arbitrator is one of three arbitrators who must all act together and whose duties commence immediately, whereas an umpire does not act with the arbitrators, but enters upon the reference only when they have disagreed.

If, on a reference to two arbitrators, one to be appointed by each party, one of the appointed arbitrators refuses to act or is incapable of acting, or dies, the party who appointed him may appoint a new arbitrator in his place (s. 7 (*a*)). If that party does not so appoint, and the arbitration agreement does not show that it was intended that the vacancy should not be supplied, the court may appoint (s. 10).

If, on such a reference, one party fails to appoint for seven clear days after the other party, having appointed his arbitrator, has served notice on the first party to make the appointment, the party who has appointed an arbitrator may appoint him to act as sole arbitrator, and his award is binding on both parties as if he had been appointed by consent (s. 7 (*b*)). In such a case, it is essential that the party shall actually appoint the arbitrator as sole arbitrator, as the arbitrator has no authority to proceed alone with the arbitration unless he has been so appointed (*Drummond* v. *Hamer* [1942] 1 K.B. 352). An appointment under s. 7 may be set aside by the court.

(2) *Appointment of Umpire*

An umpire will be appointed where s. 8 (1) or s. 9 (1) applies, or where the arbitration agreement provides for the appointment of an umpire. The usual method of appointment of the umpire is by writing signed by both arbitrators in the presence of each other, but a parol appointment will not be invalid where no other mode is prescribed.

If the parties or the arbitrators, being at liberty to appoint an umpire, fail to do so, or if an appointed umpire refuses to act, or is incapable of acting, or dies, and the submission does not show that it was intended that the vacancy should not be supplied, and the parties or arbitrators do not supply the vacancy, the court may appoint (s. 10).

If the arbitrators have delivered to any party to the reference, or to the umpire, a notice in writing stating that they cannot agree, the umpire may forthwith enter on the reference in lieu of the arbitrators, if no contrary intention is shown in the arbitration agreement (s. 8 (2)). At any time after the appointment of an umpire, however appointed, the court may, on the application of any party to the reference and notwithstanding anything to the contrary in the arbitration agreement, order that the umpire shall enter upon the reference in lieu of the arbitrators and as if he were a sole arbitrator (s. 8 (3)).

(3) *Duration of Arbitrator's Authority*

The authority of the arbitrator commences from the time when the agreement to refer is entered into, unless the agreement states when the reference is to begin, and is terminated by the making of the award, or the expiration of the time limited for the making of the award, or by the revocation of his authority.

By s. 1 the authority of an arbitrator appointed under an arbitration agreement is irrevocable except by leave of the court, unless a contrary intention is expressed in the agreement. This provision, while preventing the termination of a reference to arbitration by one party against the will of the other, does not presumably prevent a revocation by mutual agreement.

The court may remove the arbitrator, or give leave to revoke his authority, in the following cases:

(i) If the arbitrator is not, or may not be, impartial, either party may, if the arbitrator was named or designated in the agreement and a dispute has arisen, apply to the court for leave to revoke the authority of the arbitrator, or for an injunction to restrain the other party or the arbitrator from proceeding with the arbitration; and it is not a ground for refusing the application that the party so applying knew or ought to have known that the arbitrator, by reason of his relation towards any other party to the agreement or of his connection with the subject referred, might not be capable of impartiality (s. 24 (1)).

(ii) The court has power to order that an arbitration agreement shall cease to have effect, and that the authority of the arbitrator shall be revoked, so far as may be necessary to enable a question whether a party to the agreement has been guilty of fraud to be determined by the court (s. 24 (2)).

(iii) The court may remove an arbitrator who has misconducted himself or the proceedings (s. 23 (1)).

(iv) The court may, on the application of any party to the reference. remove an arbitrator who fails to use all reasonable dispatch in entering on and proceeding with the reference, and an arbitrator who is removed on this ground is not entitled to receive any remuneration for his services (s. 13 (3)).

Where an arbitrator who has not entered on the reference is removed by the court, the court may, on the application of any party to the arbitration agreement, appoint a person to act as arbitrator in place of the person so removed (s. 25 (1)). Where the authority of an arbitrator is revoked by leave of the court, or an arbitrator who has entered on the reference is removed by the court, the court may, on the application of any party to the arbitration agreement, either appoint a person to act as sole arbitrator in place of the person removed or order that the arbitration agreement shall cease to have effect with respect to the dispute referred (s. 25 (2)).

These provisions apply also to an umpire.

(4) *Powers of Arbitrator and Umpire*

Unless a contrary intention is expressed in the arbitration agreement, the arbitrator or umpire has power:

(i) subject to any legal objection, to examine the parties to the reference on oath or affirmation, and to require them to produce before him all documents within their possession or power which may be required or called for, and to do all other things which during the proceedings on the reference he may require (s. 12 (1));

(ii) to examine witnesses on oath or affirmation (s. 12 (2));

(iii) to administer oaths to and take the affirmations of parties and witnesses (s. 12 (3));

(iv) to make an interim award (s. 14);

(v) to order specific performance of any contract other than a contract relating to land or any interest in land, in accordance with the same powers as those possessed by the court (s. 15);

(vi) to correct any clerical error in any award (s. 17).

(g) Proceedings on the Reference

The reference must be conducted in accordance with the terms of the arbitration agreement, but subject thereto the rules set out below will apply.

(1) *Proceedings before an Arbitrator*

The arbitrator fixes a time and place for the hearing, and gives notice thereof to the parties. If a party applies for an extension of time, on the ground that he cannot be ready with his witnesses by the date fixed, the arbitrator should grant an extension if reasonable, and refusal to do so might be a ground for setting aside the award.

If one of the parties refuses to attend at the time and place fixed by the arbitrator for the hearing, the arbitrator should serve him or his solicitors with a written notice clearly indicating that, unless he appears on the date fixed by the notice, the arbitrator will proceed with the arbitration *ex parte*. If he proceeds in the absence of one of the parties without having given such notice, the award may be set aside if that party can show a reasonable excuse for not attending (*Gladwin* v. *Chilcote* (1841) 9 Dowl. 550).

The conduct of the proceedings is in the discretion of the arbitrator, but it is desirable as far as possible that the practice of the court should be followed during the hearing. Although the arbitration proceedings are private, the arbitrator should not exclude interested persons without sufficient reason, but the court is disinclined to interfere at the instance of an aggrieved party, as the matter is regarded as one for the discretion of the arbitrator (*Tillam* v. *Copp* (1847) 5 C.B. 211).

The arbitrator must follow the rules of law and equity in arriving at his decision, but the fact that a decision is arrived at by the arbitrator contrary to the true legal rights of the parties will not invalidate the award unless the mistake of law actually appears upon the face of the award itself.

Any party to a submission may compel the attendance of witnesses and the production of documents by them by means of a subpoena (s. 12 (4)). The arbitrator cannot himself call witnesses without the consent of the parties (*Re Enoch and Zaretsky* [1910] 1 K.B. 327).

Although as a general rule an arbitrator, like a judge, should decide the issue solely in the light of the evidence tendered, yet, where he has been appointed because of his special knowledge or experience, he is entitled to apply that knowledge or experience to the question at issue without receiving expert evidence (*Mediterranean and Eastern Export Co., Ltd.* v. *Fortress Fabrics* (*Manchester*), *Ltd.* [1948] 2 All E.R. 186). On the other hand it would be quite improper for an arbitrator, in coming to his decision, to take account of knowledge of the particular dispute which he had obtained in some other capacity than that of arbitrator, as when a registrar of a county court, acting as arbitrator in a dispute between parties as to whether a partnership existed, used his knowledge of previous bankruptcy proceedings in that court to assist him in deciding the issue (*Owen* v. *Nicholl* [1948] 1 All E.R. 707).

The court has the same power to make interlocutory orders for discovery of documents and interrogatories, and for a number of other purposes, in an arbitration as it has in relation to an action in court (s. 12 (6)). This power of the court is without prejudice to any similar power which the arbitrator may have by the terms of the arbitration agreement, under the Arbitration Act, or otherwise.

If any party considers that he has cause for complaint in the conduct of the proceedings, such as where the arbitrator acts *ex parte* un-justifiably, he should at once protest and apply to the court for his removal. Pending the court order, the party could then continue to conduct his case before the arbitrator without prejudice to his rights. If he withdrew from the proceedings, and the court declined to interfere upon his application, he would be placed at a disadvantage.

When the arbitrator has heard all the evidence which the parties are prepared to offer, and has ascertained that neither party proposes to produce further evidence, he should give distinct notice to the parties that the proceedings are at an end, and that he is prepared to make his award. He may, however, at any time before making the award, permit or require the production of further evidence.

(2) *Proceedings before an Umpire*

The umpire has the same powers and duties as the arbitrators.

Unless he has sat with the arbitrators all through the case and has made his own notes of the proceedings, the umpire must re-hear the matter, and must examine such witnesses as the parties may produce, even though the arbitrators have already examined them (*Re Salkeld and Slater* (1840) 10 L.J. Q.B. 22). He must not take the evidence from notes of the arbitrators unless the parties consent to his doing so (*Re Firth and Howlett* (1850) 19 L.J. Q.B. 169). In commercial arbitrations, however, it is the recognised practice that, unless the parties express a desire or intention to attend or to be represented, the arbitrators themselves can submit the evidence to the umpire and act as advocates (*Bourgeois* v. *Weddell & Co.* [1924] 1 K.B. 539).

The umpire must decide between the parties to the reference, and not between the arbitrators. He must decide on all matters in dispute and not merely those upon which the arbitrators have failed to come to an agreement (*Tollit* v. *Saunders* (1821) 9 Price 612), unless the submission gives him power to decide on particular points on which the arbitrators differ.

(h) Special Case

An arbitrator or umpire may, and shall if so directed by the court, at any stage of the proceedings in a reference, state in the form of a special case for the opinion of the court any question of law arising in the course of the reference before he reaches a decision himself (a 'consultative case'), or he may give his award or any part thereof in the form of a special case (s. 21 (1)). In doing this he should state the facts as he has found them, leaving the court to settle the points of law involved. Either party may, at any time before the award is made, apply to the court to order the arbitrator to state a case; and, if the arbitrator is requested to state a case, refusal to do so, or refusal to delay his award until an application can be made to the court, may amount to misconduct, unless the arbitrator's findings upon a question of fact render immaterial the question raised on the point of law (*Buerger & Co.* v. *Barnett* (1919) 35 T.L.R. 260). Where the arbitrator has refused to state a case, he should adjourn the hearing pending an application to the court for an order directing him to do so, unless it is evident that the request to state a case was actuated by a desire to delay the proceedings (*Re Palmer and Hosken* [1898] 1 Q.B. 131).

A special case with respect to an interim award or with respect to a question of law arising in the course of the reference may be stated, or may be directed by the court to be stated, notwithstanding that proceedings under the reference are still pending (s. 21 (2)).

No appeal lies from the decision of the court on a special case, without the leave of the court or of the Court of Appeal (s. 21 (3)).

An award in the form of a special case is not strictly final, for the question of law is left to be determined by the court, and it has an unfettered power to remit of its own volition if justice cannot otherwise be done, whether or not there is an application by one of the parties to the reference for this purpose (*Universal Cargo Carriers Corporation* v. *Citati* [1957] 3 All E.R. 234).

(i) The Award

(1) *Time for Making Award*

Unless the submission otherwise provides, there is no time limit within which an award must be made (s. 13 (1)). The arbitrator cannot be compelled to make an award unless he has contracted to do so, but the court may remove him unless he uses all reasonable dispatch in making his award, and in such case he forfeits his remuneration (s. 13 (3)). If, however, an award has been remitted by the court for the reconsideration of the arbitrator, he must make the award within three months of the date of the order unless the order otherwise directs (s. 22 (2)), or unless the court extends the time (s. 13 (2)).

If a time limit is provided for in the arbitration agreement, the arbitrator cannot himself extend or shorten the time; this can only be done by the parties themselves, or by the court under s. 13 (2).

When the award is ready, the arbitrator must give notice to the parties and hand it to any party applying for it on payment of the arbitrator's charges. A copy will be handed to any other party on application.

(2) *Effect of Award*

Unless a contrary intention is expressed in the arbitration agreement, the award will be final and binding on the parties and the persons claiming under them (s. 16). There is no appeal from it, the only remedy being by application to have it set aside or referred back, in circumstances which would justify the application (see (l) and (m), *infra*).

(3) *Interest*

A sum directed to be paid by an award shall, unless the award otherwise directs, carry interest as from the date of the award at the same rate as a judgment debt (s. 20). An arbitrator has the same power as the court to order interest to be paid for the whole or any part of the period between the date when the cause of action arose and the date of the award (*Chandris* v. *Isbrandtsen-Moller Co., Inc.* [1951] 1 K.B. 240).

(4) *Requisites of Valid Award*

To be valid an award must be final, certain, consistent and possible, and must decide all matters submitted and not go beyond the matters submitted.

(i) *Award must be final*

The award may be set aside if the arbitrator makes a conditional award, or fails to give directions necessary for carrying out the award, or leaves something to be afterwards determined either by himself or some other person. The arbitrator may, however, make an interim award, unless the agreement expresses a contrary intention (s. 14). An interim award is an order or decision of the arbitrator or umpire pending the final determination of the whole case by him, *e.g.*, an order that an instalment under a contract be paid pending determination of the full amount due (*Fidelitas Shipping Co., Ltd.* v. *V/O Exportchleb* [1965] 2 All E.R. 4).

The arbitrator may direct in his award the doing of a ministerial act by some other person, such as the measurement of land, the arbitrator having decided what amount is to be paid per acre (*Thorp* v. *Cole* (1836) I M, & W. 531).

(ii) *Award must be certain*

The award must show clearly what has to be done and who is to do it. The court will always try to hold that the award is certain, and any uncertainty must appear on the face of the award. Thus, a direction that an administrator shall pay to the next-of-kin their distributive shares, without saying what these are, is sufficiently certain, since this is determined by the degree of relationship, which is not in dispute (*Perry* v. *Mitchell* (1844) 12 M. & W. 792). An award that one of two persons shall do a certain act, without stating which is to do it, is bad (*Lawrence* v. *Hodgson* (1826) 1 Y. & J. 16); but an award that one person shall do one of two things is good, if either is capable of being performed (*Lee* v. *Elkins* (1702) 12 Mod. 585).

It is an implied term of an arbitration agreement that an award for the payment of money, as opposed to a mere declaratory award, shall be for a sum certain so that it is capable of being enforced in the same manner as a judgment under s. 26; and an award may be remitted by the court so that it may be amended and put into a form in which it will be so enforceable (*Margulies Bros.* v. *Dafnis Thomaides & Co.* [1958] 1 All E.R. 777).

The following awards have been held to be certain:

(a) An award directing that a nuisance on a defendant's soil shall be removed, without saying by whom; the court presumes that the owner of the soil is intended.

(b) An order to pay a specified sum within a certain time of the date of the award, the award bearing no date; the time runs from delivery of the award.

(c) An award directing A to pay a sum of money but mentioning no date for payment; it must be paid within a reasonable time.

The following are void for uncertainty:

(a) An award that payment for land should be made at a rate varying according as it lay on one side or other of a line which was not clearly defined.

(b) An award that the defendant should deliver up certain specified goods, and several books, without naming the books.

(c) An award that a party shall put up certain fixtures, without defining their value or description.

(d) An award finding that a sum of money is due to the defendant from A, B and C, some or one of them, and directing the sum to be paid by them, some or one of them.

(iii) *Award must be possible and consistent*

The award must be capable of performance at the time of the award, though subsequent impossibility will not invalidate it. The award must also be consistent with the findings of the arbitrator as stated therein (*Ames* v. *Milward* (1818) 8 Taunt. 637).

(iv) *Arbitrator must decide on all matters submitted*

Failure to decide on all matters submitted is a ground for setting aside the whole award. It is not always necessary that each matter should be stated in detail; in some cases silence may amount to a decision.

(v) *Arbitrator must not exceed jurisdiction*

The award may be set aside where the arbitrator has decided on matters not submitted to him, or has exceeded certain specified powers of giving directions, or has given directions affecting strangers, or has directed acts to be done affecting the property of strangers.

In these cases, if the excess can be separated from the rest of the award, that which is bad may be set aside and the rest upheld. If the excess cannot be separated the whole award is bad.

The following are instances of excess of jurisdiction:

(*a*) Where an arbitrator had to decide whether a buyer had the right to reject goods as inferior in quality, and the arbitrator awarded that the buyer should take them with an allowance.

(*b*) Where the arbitrator had to decide as to the boundaries of certain land, and he decided as to title.

(*c*) Where he decides as to persons who are not parties to the submission, *e.g.*, by directing the transfer of an apprentice or articled clerk who is not a party to the proceedings.

(j) Costs of the Arbitration

Unless a contrary intention is expressed in the arbitration agreement, the costs of the reference and award shall be in the discretion of the arbitrator, who may direct to and by whom and in what manner those costs or any part thereof shall be paid, and may tax or settle the amount of the costs to be so paid or any part thereof, and may award costs to be paid as between solicitor and client (s. 18 (1)). Unless the award otherwise directs, any costs awarded are taxable in the High Court (s. 18 (2)).

A provision in an arbitration agreement to the effect that a party thereto shall in any event pay his own costs is void, except where such a provision relates to a dispute which has already arisen before the making of the arbitration agreement; and the agreement takes effect as if no such provision had been included therein (s. 18 (3)).

If no provision is made by an award with respect to costs, any party may within fourteen days of the publication of the award, or such further time as the court may direct, apply to the arbitrator for an order directing by and to whom such costs shall be paid, and thereupon the arbitrator shall, after hearing any party who may desire to be heard, amend his award by adding thereto such directions as he may think proper with respect to the payment of the costs (s. 18 (4)).

If the arbitrator has a discretion as to costs, it must be exercised judicially, and in the absence of special circumstances a successful party should receive his costs. If the award states reasons for the order as to costs, from which the court can see that the discretion has not been exercised judicially, the order can be set aside (*Lloyd del Pacifico* v. *Board of Trade* (1930) 46 T.L.R. 476). Where an arbitrator does not give costs to the successful party, he ought to set out the reasons for his action if he makes his award in the form of a special case, in order to assist the court in reviewing the award (*Smeaton Hanscomb & Co., Ltd.* v. *Sassoon I. Setty, Son & Co. (No.2)* [1953] 2 All E.R. 1588); but otherwise he need not do so (*Perry* v. *Stopher* [1959] 1 W.L.R. 415).

An arbitrator does not exercise his discretion judicially where he takes into consideration a preliminary friendly talk between the parties and the refusal by one of them of an offer made without prejudice (*Stotesbury* v. *Turner* [1943] K.B. 370), or where he orders each party to pay his own costs on the ground that no serious attempt had been made by either to settle the dispute (*Lewis* v. *Haverfordwest R.D.C.* [1953] 2 All E.R. 1599).

(k) Remuneration of Arbitrator or Umpire

Where the appointment of the arbitrator or umpire does not express a contrary intention, he may himself fix the amount of his remuneration. If the arbitrator or umpire refuses to deliver his award except on payment of the fees demanded by him, any party who has not entered into a written agreement with the arbitrator or umpire fixing his fee may apply to the court to have the fee taxed; and the court may order that the arbitrator shall deliver the award to the applicant on payment into court of the fee demanded, and further that the fee demanded shall be taxed by the taxing officer, and that out of the money paid into court there shall be paid out to the arbitrator or umpire by way of fee such sum as may be found reasonable on taxation, and that the balance of the money, if any, shall be paid out to the applicant (s. 19).

Apart from the operation of this section, the arbitrator or umpire has a lien on the arbitration agreement and the award for the amount of his charges, but the lien does not extend to documents handed to the arbitrator in the course of the reference.

An arbitrator may bring an action to recover the amount of his remuneration against any party who has agreed, expressly or impliedly, to pay it, and it appears that there is an implied promise by the parties to a submission to pay the remuneration of a lay arbitrator. It is probable that this implication extends also to a legal arbitrator.

(l) Setting Aside the Award

The court has powers under the Arbitration Act and by virtue of its inherent jurisdiction to set aside an award in certain cases.

(1) *Improper Conduct of the Reference*

Where an arbitrator has misconducted himself or the proceedings, or an arbitration or an award has been improperly procured, the court may set the award aside (s. 23 (2)). 'Misconduct' within the meaning of this section may be either *actual*, as when the arbitrator accepts a bribe or hospitality corruptly offered by one of the parties; or *technical*, as by hearing evidence in the absence of one of the parties.

In *Czarnikow* v. *Roth, Schmidt & Co., ante, p.* 308, an award was set aside on the ground that the arbitrator had been guilty of misconduct in not allowing a case to be stated on a point of law, the arbitrator relying upon a clause incorporated in the submission that no party was to require any such case to be stated. The arbitrator should have allowed the validity of the clause to be determined by the court.

The court may set aside an award on the grounds of misconduct if the proper procedure has not been followed in the arbitration proceedings, where there has been a breach of the agreed procedure, or where otherwise there has been a violation of the rules of natural justice. Thus, it has been held to be misconduct if the arbitrator causes the parties to appear before him separately, and hears the evidence of each party in the absence of the other (*Ramsden & Co.* v. *Jacobs* [1922] 1 K.B. 640). Moreover, in relation to a point of procedure, the court may imply a term in the contract, if there is nothing in the express or necessarily implied terms of the contract to prevent its inclusion, as by importing a custom or trade practice. The custom or practice must be reasonable, however, and not one which tends to produce an unjust result (*London Export Corporation, Ltd.* v. *Jubilee Coffee Roasting Co., Ltd.* [1958] 2 All E.R. 411).

If it is considered that there has been misconduct on the part of the arbitrator, and no steps are taken for the award to be set aside on that ground, the aggrieved party will be precluded from pleading such misconduct if an action is brought against him for enforcement of the award.

The section only applies in relation to misconduct by the arbitrator who has made the award sought to be set aside. Thus, where the arbitrator's award is superseded by the award of an umpire or board of appeal (when this is provided for in the agreement), the misconduct of the arbitrator will not be a ground for setting aside the award of the umpire or board of appeal (*Giacomo Costa Fu Andrea* v. *British Italian Trading Co., Ltd.* [1962] 2 All E.R. 53).

Where an application is made to set aside an award, the court may order that any money made payable by the award shall be brought into court or otherwise secured pending the determination of the application (s. 23 (3)).

(2) Mistake in Fact or Law

The court has an inherent power to set aside an award which involves an error in fact or law, and such an error may also constitute 'misconduct' under s. 23 (2).

The mistake must appear on the face of the award, or of some document forming part of it; otherwise, if the arbitrator has acted within his authority, the award will hold good. For the award to be set aside, either the mistake must be admitted by the arbitrator who himself applies for relief (*Dinn* v. *Blake* (1875) 44 L.J.C.P. 276), or the mistake must be clear beyond reasonable doubt (*Re Hall and Hinds* (1841) 2 M. & G. 847), and it must be material to the decision (*Buerger & Co.* v. *Barnett, ante*, p. 317).

A mistake in law appearing upon the face of the award will lead to the award being set aside, even if the arbitrator has been misled by the opinion of the court to which he has stated a consultative case on a point of law (*British Westinghouse Electric, &c., Co.* v. *Underground Electric Railway* [1912] A.C. 673).

Where a specific question of law has been submitted to an arbitrator for his decision, and he has decided it wrongly, that alone is not a sufficient ground for setting aside the award (*Government of Kelantan* v. *Duff Development Co., Ltd.* [1923] A.C. 395); but where the determination of a point of law (which has not been specifically referred) becomes necessary in the decision of the matters which have been referred and the arbitrator makes a mistake apparent on the face of his award, the award can be set aside (*F. R. Absalom, Ltd.* v. *Great Western (London) Garden Village Society, Ltd.* [1933] A.C. 592).

Where the arbitrator expressly incorporates some or all of the terms of a contract in his award, these terms can be read as part of the award for the purpose of determining whether an error of law appears on the face of the award; but a general reference to the contract following a finding of fact, *e.g.*, 'and therefore the contract is void,' will not enable the court to look at the contract for an error of law: only the award itself can be inspected (*Giacomo Costa Fu Andrea* v. *British Italian Trading Co., Ltd., supra*).

(3) Invalidity of Award

The court has an inherent power to set aside an award which does not satisfy all the formal requisites of a valid award (see (i) (4), *supra*).

(m) Referring back the Award

Even though an award is not set aside, it may, on application, be remitted by the court for reconsideration by the arbitrator (s. 22 (1)). The object of this is to enable the arbitrator to correct an error which would make the award bad, without entirely setting it aside. In the case of a final award, as opposed to an award in the form of a special case, because the parties agree on an arbitrator and are bound to accept his award for good or ill, the court's discretion to remit as an alternative to the setting aside of the award will not be readily exercised; and the Court of Appeal has intimated that the exercise of discretion should be strictly confined to specific grounds (*Universal Cargo Carriers Corporation* v. *Citati, ante,* p. 317).

The main grounds for remitting an award are as follows:

(1) An award may be referred back on any of the grounds which would justify the court in setting aside an award, although, if the ground is misconduct of the arbitrator, the award will not be remitted to the same arbitrator unless it is technical misconduct only.

(2) An award may also be referred back when the arbitrator has admittedly made some mistake and desires the award to be remitted in order that he may correct it, or where there is some accidental omission, such as the failure by the arbitrator to give directions as to the payment of costs (*Re Becker, Shillan & Co. and Barry Bros.* [1921] 1 K. B. 391).

(3) A further ground for referring back an award is the discovery of fresh evidence, but the court will not make an order remitting an award on these grounds unless the evidence is such that a tribunal of fact could properly give it some weight, and the party desiring to adduce it could not, by the exercise of any reasonable diligence, have procurred it before the first trial (*Dower & Co.* v. *Corrie MacColl & Son, Ltd.* (1925) 22 L1. L. Rep. 256).

When the award is referred back, all the original powers of the arbitrator revive, and the original award becomes void, unless it has only been remitted for amendment on a specific point.

(n) Enforcing the Award

An award on an arbitration agreement may, by leave of the court, be enforced in the same manner as a judgment or order to the same effect, and where leave is so given, judgment may be entered in terms of the award (s. 26). In this way the award is turned into a final judgment, and can be enforced by execution or any other way allowed in the case of a judgment, and not merely by an action on the award, as would otherwise be the case.

(o) Time Limit for Arbitrations and Enforcing Awards

The Limitation Act, 1939, and subsequent enactments relating to the limitation of actions apply to arbitrations as they apply to actions in the High Court. This is so even where the agreement contains a term to the effect that no cause of action shall accrue until an award is made under the agreement. Time begins to run from the date on which the claimant first acquired a right of action or a right to have the dispute submitted to arbitration.

In some cases the contract prescribes a time limit within which arbitration must be commenced. In such cases the court, if it is of opinion that in the circumstances of the case undue hardship would otherwise be caused, may extend the time for such period as it thinks proper, notwithstanding that the time fixed has expired (s. 27).

Where an award is set aside or an arbitration clause is nullified by the court, the court may order that the period between the commencement of the arbitration and the date of the order of the court shall be excluded in computing the running of time (Limitation Act, 1939, s. 27 (5)).

When an award is made and judgment is entered in the terms of the award, the original cause of action merges in the judgment, and the right of action on the judgment will not be barred until the expiration of twelve years. If judgment is not entered in terms of the award, an action to enforce the award will be barred after six years from the making of the award, or, if the award is in pursuance of an arbitration agreement under seal, after twelve years.

(p) Enforcement of Foreign Awards

Part II of the Arbitration Act, 1950, makes an award obtained in an arbitration conducted in a foreign country enforceable in England if certain conditions are satisfied.

The arbitration agreement must be one to which the League of Nations Protocol of 1923 (set out in the First Schedule to the Act) applies, and must be between persons who are subject to the jurisdiction of such States as are declared by Order in Council to be parties to the Convention set out in the Second Schedule to the Act, the award being made in one of the territories to which the Convention applies (s. 35).

The award must have:

(1) been made in pursuance of an agreement for arbitration which was valid under the law by which it was governed;

(2) been made by the tribunal provided for in the agreement or constituted in a manner agreed upon by the parties;

(3) been made in conformity with the law governing the arbitration procedure;

(4) become final in the country in which it was made;

(5) been in respect of a matter which may lawfully be referred to arbitration under the law of England;

and the enforcement thereof must not be contrary to the public policy or the law of England (s. 37 (1)).

If these conditions are satisfied, the foreign award is enforceable in England either by action or by obtaining leave to enforce it as a judgment under s. 26 (s. 36).

Such an award will not, however, be enforceable if the court dealing with the case is satisfied that:

  (i) the award has been annulled in the country in which it was made; or

 (ii) the party against whom it is sought to enforce the award was not given notice of the arbitration proceedings in sufficient time to enable him to present his case, or was under some legal incapacity and was not properly represented; or

(iii) the award does not deal with all the questions referred or contains decisions on matters beyond the scope of the agreement for arbitration (s. 37 (2)).

An award is not deemed to be final, and is not therefore enforceable, if any proceedings for the purpose of contesting the validity of the award are pending in the country in which it was made (s. 39).

INDEX

327

Arbitration (*continued*)
costs of, 320
court, references by order of, 306
death of a party to, effect of, 308
definition of, 302
disadvantages of, 302
matters which may not be referred, 305
methods of referring to, 305
mistake in fact or law, 323
oral submission, disadvantages of, 306
ouster of jurisdiction of court, 52, 308
proceedings, 315
reference,
  by order of court, 306
  by voluntary submission of parties, 306
  improper conduct of, 322
  meaning of, 302
  proceedings on, 315
  subject-matter of, 305
  under Acts of Parliament, 305
  which are not arbitrations, 303
'*Scott* v. *Avery* clause,' 309
special case, 317
stay of proceedings, 309
'step in the proceedings,' definition of, 309
submission, meaning of, 302
third parties and arbitration clause, 311
time limit for, 324
umpire,
  appointment of, 313
  definition of, 302
  powers of, 314
  proceedings before, 316
  remuneration of, 321
valuation, compared with, 304
who may refer to, 304

Arrangements with Creditors, 14

Assignment,
contracts, of, 59
copyright, of, 16
equitable, 60
leases, of, 61
legal, 61
moneylenders' debts, of, 62
partnership, share in, of, 288
policies of insurance, of, 62, 239, 242, 248

Auction Sales, 112, 139

Auctioneers, 18, 111

Average,
clause, effect of, 241
general, 250
particular, 251

Bailments,
care, standard of, required of bailee, 204
classification of, 203
definition of, 203
duties of bailee, 204
for reward, 203
gratuitous, 203
involuntary bailee, 205
liability of bailor, 206
right of bailee to dispose of goods, 206
subject to special contract, 205

Bank Notes, 201

Banker,
authority of, to pay cheques, when revoked, 195
collecting, protection of, 197
disclosure of information by, 194
letters of credit, 142
lien of, 231
misrepresentations by, 44
paying, protection of, 195
references by, 44
relationship of, and customer, 193

Barratry,
meaning of, 248

Bills of Exchange,
acceptance for honour, 179
acceptance of, 176
acceptance *supra* protest, 179
acceptor, definition of, 165
acceptor, obligations of, 171
accommodation, 169, 188
accommodation party, 169
agent, signature by, 173
allonge, 181
alteration of, 189
bearer, 174, 180
cancellation of, 188
capacity to contract by, 168
case of need, 179
cheques, 190
circuity of action, 182
conditional acceptance, 178
conditional indorsement, 182
conflict of laws, 86
consideration for, 16, 168
damages, measure of, 187
date of, 165
days of grace, 184
definition of, 163
delivery of, 176
discharge of, 187
discharge of surety, 189
dishonour of, 184
documents which are not bills, 163, 164
domiciling of, 179, 200
drawee, definition of, 165